China Bibliography

China Bibliography

A Research Guide to Reference Works about China Past and Present

Harriet T. Zurndorfer

University of Hawai'i Press

HONOLULU

First published by E.J. Brill, 1995
© Koninklijke Brill NV, Leiden, The Netherlands

Paperback edition
© 1999 University of Hawai'i Press

Printed in the United States of America

99 00 01 02 03   5 4 3 2 1

Library of Congress Cataloging-in-Publication Data

Zurndorfer, Harriet T.
China bibliography : a research guide to reference works about China
past and present / Harriet T. Zurndorfer.
    p.   cm.
Originally published: Leiden ; New York : E. J. Brill, 1995.
Includes bibliographical references and index.
ISBN 0–8248–2212–9 (paper : alk. paper)
   1. China—Bibliography.   2. Reference books—Bibliography.
I. Title.
Z3016.Z87   1999
[DS706]
016.951—dc21   99–12374
                                                 CIP

Printed by Edwards Brothers Inc.

In Honor of Two Remarkable Teachers of Chinese Civilization:

Wolfram Eberhard (1909-1989)

Edward Hetzel Schafer (1913-1991)

TABLE OF CONTENTS

Preface and Acknowledgements XIII

I Introduction 1
   The Use of this Guide 1
   A Brief History of Chinese Studies and Sinology 4
   Classification Systems and the Chinese Library 45
   A Note on the Library of Congress Classification System ... 54

II Bibliographies 56
   Introduction 56
     Western Language Bibliographies 56
     Chinese Language Bibliographies` 57

References 60
  General and Specialized Bibliographies in Western
  Languages 61
    General Bibliographies 61
      Cumulative 61
      Annual 62
    Specialized Bibliographies 66
      Composite Bibliographies 66
      Guides to History—General 67
      Guides to History—Specific by period 67
      Some Important References for the 19th and
        20th Centuries 70
      Classics, Philosophy, and Religion 72
      Language 75
    Literature 76
      Science and Technology 78
      Miscellaneous 79
      "State of the Field" Bibliographies 81

References 83
  General and Specialized Bibliographies in Chinese and
  Japanese 84
    General Bibliographies 84
      Cumulative 84
      Annual 85
      Kung-chü-shu 86

Specialized Bibliographies 88
  Chinese History—General and Specific by period 88
  'Periodical' Bibliographies on Chinese History 95
  Chinese Literature 96
  Language 98
  Miscellaneous 98
    Classics 98
    Philosophy and Religion 98
    Law 99
    Art 100
    Social Sciences.. 100

III Journals and Newspapers 101
  Introduction 101
    Western Language Journals 101
    Western Language Newspapers 104
    Chinese Journals 106
    Chinese Newspapers 112

References 115
  Western Language Journals: Premodern China 116
  Western Language Journals: Modern China 118
  A Partial Listing of Important Current Chinese Journals   120
  A Partial Listing of Important Chinese Newspapers Past
    and Present 125
  A Partial Listing of Important Japanese Journals for
    Sinology 128
  Union Catalogues of Chinese Journals and Newspapers... 131
  Indexes to Chinese Journals—General and Specialized ... 134

IV Biography in China: Past and Present 137
  Introduction 137
    Chinese Names and their Alternatives 141

References 144
  Guides to Alternative Names 145
  Comprehensive Biographical Dictionaries 147
  Biographical Dictionaries Specific by Period 149
    Western Languages 149
    Chinese 152
  Biographical Dictionaries—Topical 162
  Other Biographical Aids 167

V China's Geography: Historical and Modern Sources 170
   Introduction 170
   Basic Units of Territorial Administration: Past and
      Present 172
   Chinese Historical Geographies and their Modern
      Guides 175
   Historical and Modern Atlases 176

References 180
   Historical Atlases 181
   Modern Atlases 183
   Geographical Dictionaries 185

   Local Gazetteers 187
      Introduction 187
      Principal Subject Headings in Local Gazetteers 191

References 196
   Catalogues of Local Gazetteers 197
   Local Gazetteer Reprint Series 198
   Other Aids for the Study of Local Gazetteers 199

VI Dictionaries 201
   Introduction 201
   How to Use and Find Chinese Dictionaries 205

References 208
   Modern Chinese Dictionaries 209
      Chinese-Chinese 209
      Chinese-Foreign Language 211
   Classical Chinese Dictionaries 214
      Chinese-Chinese 214
      Chinese-Foreign Language 216
   Specialist Dictionaries for Modern Chinese 220
      Linguistic Dictionaries 220
      Proverbs and Sayings 221
   Dictionaries for Politics, Economics, Law, and Agricul-
      ture 224
   Science and Technology 228
   Dialects 229
   Specialist Dictionaries for Aspects of Premodern and
      Modern China 232
      Literary Dictionaries 232

Religion (including mythology) and Philosophy 235
Administrative Terminology 238
History 240
Japanese Names 241

VII Encyclopedias, Yearbooks, and Statistical References ... 243
Introduction 243

References 251
Early Western Language Works of an Encyclopedic Nature
on China 252
Current Western Language Encyclopedias and 'Year-
books' 253
Chinese Encyclopedias and 'Yearbooks' 256
Encyclopedias 256
Ch'ing 256
Contemporary 257
Yearbooks 259
Further Sources for Statistics of China 262
Late Imperial and Republican China 262
PRC 264

VIII *Ts'ung-shu* and Miscellaneous Collectanea 266
Introduction 266
Traditional and Modern *Ts'ung-shu* 268
Documentary Collections, Archives, and Buddhist/
Taoist Collectanea 271

References 279
Indexes to the Contents of *Ts'ung-shu* 280
Guides to the Collected Works of Individual Authors 282
Important Collections of Published Archival Docu-
ments 284
Catalogues of Rare Books and Guides to Editions 287

IX Indexes and Concordances 289
Introduction 289
How to Use the Harvard-Yenching Index System 292
Information on the ICS Concordance Series 293

Reference 295
Guides to Indexes 296

X   The Chinese Calendar 297
     Introduction 297
     Structure of the Traditional Chinese Calendar 298
     Converting Chinese and Western Time 304

References 308
     Chronologies 309
     Concordances 310

XI   Translations 313
     Introduction 313

References 315
     Guide to Translations 316
     Chinese Literature 316
     Scientific Publications 317
     Current Affairs in the PRC 318
     Official Documents 320

Appendices 323
     Ch'iu's Classification System for the East Asian Library
     Table of Main Classes 324
     Works in the Harvard Yenching Index Series and Centre-
     Franco-chinois d'Études sinologiques 327
     The Twenty-four Festivals and their Concordances with
     the Seasons 336

Index of Persons 337
Index of Titles 346
Subject Index 370

PREFACE AND ACKNOWLEDGEMENTS

The recent steady output of new reference publications about China, including dictionaries, bibliographies, atlases, indexes, etc., from East Asia, which constitutes, according to some experts, an "explosion" may leave one in doubt on how to approach, and eventually digest, these new riches. At the same time, one may also wonder how these new works should be used in conjunction with the 'classical tools' of sinology, e.g. the Harvard-Yenching indexes or *Tz'u-hai*. The purpose of this volume then is twofold: to summarize, in an accessible way, current scientific publications on China from all disciplines; and to put these new sources, such as yearbooks and statistical records, into the context of what past scholarship has achieved. This book is not meant as a comprehensive bibliography, nor an overview of 'all things Chinese', but rather a systematic guide to the most obvious sources, topics, and problems of China study. Unfortunately, lack of time and space prohibited any thorough investigation of two important regions outside the Chinese mainland, i.e. Hong Kong and Taiwan. The seemingly awesome number of economic, social, political, and cultural changes that all these regions are experiencing defied the limited parameters of this present work.

This volume has several origins. Like many academic books, it derives from a series of lectures prepared for a university course, in this case 'Chinese Bibliography', which I have been teaching for some ten years now at Leiden University's Sinologisch Instituut. Although I had always planned to publish the "handouts" I gave to my students in a one volume handbook, my determination to carry through with this project was all the more intensified after I took part in the Nordic Foundation sponsored 'Scandinavian Summer Course on Research Methods in Chinese Study', held in Oslo, Norway during June 1990. At that meeting a group of European and American scholars, including Poul Andersen, Michel Cartier, Albert Dien, Patricia Ebrey, Søren Egerod, Christoph Harbsmeier, Michael Loewe, Susan Naquin, Edwin Pulleyblank, Leon Vandermeersch, Pierre-Étienne Will, and myself prepared a series of workshops on our academic specialities for some fifty students from the four Scandinavian countries. For all the participants, including the teachers, students, and organizers (Harald Bøckman, Leif Littrup, and Donald Wagner), it was a common conclusion that some kind of handbook be made available that would systematically review the fundamental sources and methodology of sinological study, and also inform the user about new publications. Because my own teaching in Leiden also included a certain amount of instruction on contemporary China, I decided that a manual covering premodern, modern, and contemporary China might be most practical.

Several persons and institutions in the Netherlands have been most generous with their time and interest in helping me to execute this project. Mrs. Ank Merens typed and re-typed many versions of the original class stencils from which this book originated; Ms. Pauline Millington-Ward read and commented upon various sections for their grammar and composition; and Mr. H.W. Chan patiently, and diligently, supplied the characters for several drafts. The Foundation for the Advancement of Chinese Studies at Leiden University (Stichting ter Bevordering van de Studie Chinees aan de Rijksuniversiteit te Leiden) contributed a grant toward production costs of the final draft. I am also grateful to Brill's Oriental Editor, Dr. Fokke Dijkema who helped oversee this project in its later stages. The 'anonymous reader', who read this manuscript thoroughly and gave much insightful advice, must also be acknowledged. Of course, I alone am responsible for the errors in fact or judgment. Finally, I should also like to thank the Netherlands Institute for Advanced Study in the Humanities and Social Sciences where I held a research fellowship during the 1993-94 academic year. The Institute provided comfortable and hospitable facilities that contributed most favorably to this book's completion.

Harriet T. Zurndorfer
Autumn, 1994

CHAPTER ONE

INTRODUCTION

The Use of this Guide

This work assumes that the user is already familiar with the outlines of both premodern and modern Chinese history, and has, to a certain degree, some knowledge about Chinese literature. With that basis, s/he, hopefully, will find a systematic way to approach the overwhelming number of publications related to China, in Chinese, and other languages. This volume also presumes that the user will take advantage of the information presented here in this chapter on the organization of a Chinese library. Familiarity with library classification schema will allow one to find works that might not be listed in even the most up-to-date bibliographical guides. For this purpose, an historical essay is offered in this chapter to introduce the two principal modern classification systems, i.e. the Harvard-Yenching and the Library of Congress cataloging orders. Although library automation systems, found now in many major East Asian collections, are responsible for cataloguing current publications, there is still a need to know conventional library classification schema. Current automation control systems do not cover retrospective publications. The vast majority of American and European East Asian library holdings remain outside automated control, and therefore it is necessary to consult 'manual catalogues'. Familiarity with their historical background seems essential for further understanding.

The remaining chapters in this book concentrate on one subject, introduced by an historical essay and followed by a list of references. In some instances, e.g. the chapter on China's geography, this pattern is not followed so closely. That chapter contains several subdivisions, including a separate section for the study of local gazetteers. In general, the listings of reference works are arranged according to topic, and thereafter listed either by order of importance, or sub-divided further, according to chronological sequence. General reference works precede specific ones.

The reader may ask how does this volume incorporate other 'handbooks' and bibliographical guides. Every effort has been made to avoid duplicating the information already presented in Endymion Wilkinson's excellent manual, *The History of Imperial China—A Research Guide* (Cambridge, Mass., 1973), and its recent addendum, *Updating Wilkinson: An Annotated Bibliography of Reference Works on Imperial China Published since 1973* (New York, 1991) by James H. Cole. Reference to info in Wilkinson/Cole is given where necessary, when new works have superseded those in their presentations. But the Wilkinson/Cole volumes were limited to the study of Chinese history, and this present work endeavors to review publications that might also help in the investigation of Chinese literature, linguistics, and not least, PRC economic and political policies. It also attempts to "update" information in Andrew Nathan's useful *Modern China, 1840-1972: An Introduction to Sources and Research Aids* (Ann Arbor, 1973). Lastly, this book also tries to encourage the user to consult a number of bibliographical works that may seem "outdated", but still offer a comprehensive listing of materials for particular subjects. These include Teng and Biggerstaff, *An Annotated Bibliography of Selected Reference Works* (Cambridge, Mass., 1971; third revised edition) for premodern historical and literary sources; Fairbank and Liu, *Modern China: A Bibliographical Guide to Chinese Works 1898-1937* (Cambridge, Mass., reprinted 1961) for major topics on the late Ch'ing and early Republic; and Berton and Wu, *Contemporary China: A Research Guide* (Stanford, 1967) for all aspects of the earliest stages of the PRC's evolution.

There are a number of matters that *China Bibliography: A Research Guide to Reference Works about China Past and Present* does not cover. While there are some references to Buddhist and Taoist materials, those research works pertaining to archaeological, law, Manchu, or missionary subjects are limited. In certain instances these topics may be mentioned in passing, but the reader is well advised to turn to more specialized references after finding the most basic works on these subjects that are listed here. Two broad based subjects are entirely disregarded: the main genres of historical writing (annalistic and dynastic), covered expertly by Wilkinson; and the Classics, also examined in part by Wilkinson, and even more thoroughly in the recent important publication, edited by Michael Loewe, *Early Chinese Texts: A Bibliographical Guide* (Berkeley, 1993). Also, information concerning on-going or completed Ph.D. dissertations is not given. For this subject, one should refer to the excellent publications of Frank Shulman.

It is hoped that the reader/user of this guide will come to comprehend not only how to find reference works but also how to determine how one work supersedes another. For example, in learning about the use of bibliographies, s/he may find that the perusal of general Western language bibliographies should be completed first before the examination of specialized bibliographies in either Western languages or Chinese. Or, with regard to the matter of translations, the reader/user has at disposal a chapter on dictionaries, which is further subdivided according specialized topics. Thus, for someone seeking to translate imperial official ranks and titles, s/he would turn to the dictionary section on 'administrative terminology', and not Chapter XI on translations in general. In sum, this guide should direct the user where s/he can determine a particular reference, or guide her/him to where s/he may find an even more specialized bibliographic source.

Most users of this guide will probably not be able to read Japanese, but as some Japanese source materials are essential, and may actually be utilized with reasonable competence in modern Chinese, they are mentioned where applicable. The titles and information concerning the most common Japanese learned journals used for the study of China are given. In general, the reader should keep in mind that Japanese sinology still plays an important role in China study, and where certain works are relevant I have mentioned them.

Chinese works are cited in Wade-Giles transcription, since the Chinese library from where these references are drawn continues to employ it, as do a great number of other Chinese libraries as well. In many instances the reader will find that the title of a particular work follows the romanization conventions employed by Chinese libraries so that the spelling of a particular word may not be same as that found in dictionaries, e.g. the general modifier *te* 的 is consistently spelled *ti* by libraries. Thus, the Chinese references listed in this volume will following that spelling. *Pinyin* transcription is applied only to place-names of PRC source publications, to distinguish them from those works published in Republican China, and present-day Taiwan.

In general, the names of publishers are not supplied, unless there are several editions available, and it is necessary to distinguish one from another, either by title or author/editor, or in some cases, when it is unclear from the general title of a publication which particular work is under investigation. Also every at-

tempt has been made to list all authors/editors of particular
works and I apologize in advance, when these efforts were not successful. I have also endeavoured to determine where reprints exist
for particular works. As veterans of China study are well aware, the
proliferation of "pirate editions" in Taiwan may cause uncertainty
about the status of a specific edition, and I have tried to make
clear which works may be original, reprinted, or a revision.

This present volume tries to cope with the fundamental differences in the approaches to the study of China: the more traditional sinological method that lays emphasis on the reading of
texts as the prerequisite for understanding China, versus, that
based on 'discipline', whereby one applies knowledge of China
within a 'discipline' such as history or geography. In most institutions of higher learning, "Chinese studies" consists of language
training in modern Chinese and one or more disciplines. This
book tries to address the problems of following either or both of
these practices by providing relevant bibliographical information.
To put these different approaches into an historical context,
there follows a brief introduction to the history of sinology and
Chinese studies, which may help inform the reader what significance the differences have held for the development of learning
about China. Admittedly, this history gives most attention to
sinological study developments in Europe and America where
most of the readers of this volume originate. But the evolution of
sinological study in Japan and China is also considered, and special regard paid to those debates and controversies affecting
sinological study in East Asia.

Finally, it is remarked that nowadays Chinese studies like many
other fields of scholarship is divided into specialities, and even
further broken down according to chronology. The historian specializing on the 20th century cultural renaissance may not know
much about the cultural renaissance occurring during the Sung
dynasty, but here in this volume, an attempt is made to help guide
her/him to where materials about this premodern development
might be found.

A Brief History of Chinese Studies and Sinology

The origin of the modern academic subject of Chinese studies, or
sinology as it is still known in Europe, may be traced to the examination which Chinese scholars made of their own civilization.

Throughout the imperial period, i.e. since the Han dynasty, the study of the Classics (*ching* 經) and Dynastic Histories formed the basis of education in China, and as students and scholars reviewed their cultural heritage, they read and annotated upon the Confucian canon. In the process, they formulated an unwritten "program" for traditional classical studies: textual analysis, phonology, and the authentication and compilation of texts. The products of these studies included what we would, in modern terms, consider reference works: dictionaries, encyclopedias, and bibliographies, etc..[1]

The high point of this scholarship was reached in the 18th century when the 'school of empirical scholarship' (*k'ao-cheng hsüeh* 考證學) or the school of Han learning became the dominating intellectual trend. 'Han hsüeh' scholars had a certain goal: they wanted to purge those texts which had distorted what they considered the true meaning of the Classics; they sought to clarify the archaic language and the philosophical biases of Neo-Confucian metaphysics that had obscured the reading of the Classics. Not all scholars of that era subscribed to this form of learning, but 'Classical studies', as embodied in the writing of commentaries and exegetical works, continued to flourish in the 19th century, and even in the Republican era, traditional forms of learning were taught in Chinese universities. Nevertheless, no matter how particularly "Chinese" the academic subject of 'Classical studies' in China was to remain, the sinological heritage since the 19th century was also influenced by the examination of its riches in other academic communities, including those in Japan, the United States, and Europe. The cumulative history of how Chinese studies and sinology developed in the last 200 years is yet to be formulated, and what follows is a brief outline of some of its highlights.

As is well known, the Jesuits had a monopoly on the study of China in Europe until the beginning of the 19th century, but

---

[1] For a brilliant introduction to the history of 'precise scholarship', see Benjamin Elman, *From Philosophy to Philology: Intellectual and Social Aspects of Change in Late Imperial China* (Cambridge, Mass., 1984). By the 18th century Chinese scholars had made a crucial division between "great learning" (*ta-hsüeh* 大學), the study of canonical texts leading to the elaboration of a moral philosophy, and "minor learning" (*hsiao-hsüeh* 小學). *Hsiao-hsüeh* included ancillary branches of scholarship that could elucidate the canonical texts, such as philology, and those which permitted the implementation of moral philosophy deduced from the canons, for instance, statecraft, and by extension, astronomy and hydraulics. A general introduction to the history of sinology is José Frèches, *La sinologie* (Paris, 1975).

there were some efforts in various European countries to examine more closely the nature of the Chinese language, outside Church circles. Some of these instances are discussed below. Nevertheless, sinology, meaning the examination of Chinese texts, did not become an acceptable subject for academic study in universities until circa 1860, except in France. Among the nations of Asia (in the broadest sense), China was the last to be studied seriously in Europe. Assyriology and egyptology were popular because of their connections to the biblical record, and indology was affiliated with Indo-European linguistics.[2] According to the late Edward Schafer, a possible reason for the circumscribed interest in the study of China was its irrelevance for the broader comprehension of the principles of philology, as practised in Europe at that time.[3]

The earliest information about China in Europe was entirely dependent on the reports of visitors there. The first publication about China to gain a wide readership was Gonzalez de Mendoza's *Historia de las cosas mas notables, ritos y costumbres del Gran Reyno de la China* (Rome, 1585), which was based in large part on an account by Friar Martin de Rada, who visited Fukien in 1575.[4] With the Jesuits gaining entrance into China, led by Matteo Ricci, an entire new phase in the development of Chinese studies began. The Jesuit monographic works included not only general descriptions,[5] but also specialized studies on many aspects of Chi-

---

[2] An important work for understanding the relationship between modern linguistics and interest in non-Western civilizations is Garland Cannon, *The Life and Mind of Oriental Jones: Sir William Jones, the Father of Modern Linguistics* (Cambridge, 1990). See also the collection of essays by Hans Aarsleff, *From Locke to Saussure* (London, 1982).

[3] Edward H. Schafer, *What and How is Sinology?* (Boulder, Colo., 1982), reproduced in *T'ang Studies* 8-9 (1990-91):23-44. It is interesting to note that it was this appreciation for philology that became one of the hallmarks of French sinology.

[4] Mendoza's work includes an examination of China's geography, religious condition, and political and social order. For an excellent study of similar literature, see C.R. Boxer, "Some Aspects of Western Historical Writing on the Far East, 1500-1800," in W.G. Beasley and E.G. Pulleyblank, eds., *Historians of China and Japan* (London, 1961), pp.307-321.

[5] The most important of these works is Nicolas Trigault, *De christiana expeditione apud Sinas suscepta a Societate Jesu, ex. P. Matth. Riccii ejusdem Societatis commentariis libri V* (Augsburg, 1505; 10 editions in six languages between 1605 and 1626); part of this work has been translated into English by Louis J. Gallagher, *China in the Sixteenth Century: The Journals of Matteo Ricci, 1583-1610* (New York, 1953); Trigault's volume should be compared with Alvarez Semedo, *Relazione della Grande Monarchia della China* (Rome, 1643; 11 editions in five languages between 1643 and 1678).

nese civilization. Works on Chinese geography,[6] early Chinese history,[7] botany and medicine,[8] appeared along with the first complete translation of the *Four Books* into Latin.[9] Even the Ming-Ch'ing transition received extensive coverage: Martino Martini's account of the Manchu conquest went through twenty-eight editions in eight languages between 1654 and 1666.[10] The Jesuits may also be credited with "inventing Confucius". They not only created the name 'Confucius', but they also propagated a certain view of 'Confucianism'; their genuinely positive image of both the man and the ideology was a constant topic of discussion in the literary salons of 18th century Europe.[11]

It was not just the Jesuits' interest in Chinese ways of thinking that attracted the attention of others outside their Order, their investigation of the Chinese language also stimulated further study.[12] The first large-scale publication on the Chinese language was by an Englishman, John Webb (1611-1672). The second (posthumous) 1678 edition of his work *The Antiquity of China, or an Historical Essay, Endeavouring a Probability That the Language of the Em-*

---

[6] Martino Martini, *Novus Atlas Sinensis* (Amsterdam, 1655). This work consists of 17 maps, based in part on Martini's use of contemporary Chinese local histories (*ti-fang-chih* 地方志) and 171 pages of text describing the geographical location, the history of administration, climate, soil, famous mountains, main cities, places of historical interest, social life, religion, customs, etc. of various regions.

[7] Martino Martini, *Sinicae historiae decas prima* (Munich, 1658), which was based in part on compilations like Chu Hsi's *T'ung-chien kang mu* 通鑑綱目.

[8] Michael Boym, *Flora Sinensis* (Vienna, 1656); Michael Boym, *Clavis medica ad Chinarum doctrinam de pulsibus* (published by Andreas Cleyer in his *Specimen medicinae Sinicae* [Frankfurt, 1682]).

[9] Prospero Intorcetta (et.al.), *Confucius Sinarum Philosophus sive Scientia Sincia Latine exposita* (Paris, 1687).

[10] Martino Martini, *De bello Tartarico historia* (Antwerp, 1654).

[11] See Paul Rule, *K'ung-tzu or Confucius? The Jesuit Interpretation of Confucianism* (Sydney, 1986). Preface. Also relevant is Lionel M. Jensen, "The Invention of 'Confucius' and His Chinese Other," *Positions*, 1.2 (1993):414-449.

[12] Matteo Ricci's preoccupation with the Chinese language had a considerable intellectual impact in Europe. See Jonathan Spence, *The Memory Palace of Matteo Ricci* (London, 1984). Compare Howard Goodman and Anthony Grafton, "Ricci, the Chinese, and The Toolkits of Textualists," *Asia Major* 3rd series, 3.2 (1990):95-148. An interesting "explanation" of the Chinese language may be found in Athanasius Kircher's (1602-1680) *Oediupus aegyptiacus* (1652), in which the author claimed that the Chinese received their language from wise Egyptian priests. This interest in the link between China and ancient Egypt continued into the 18th century. See Joseph de Guignes, *Mémoire dans lequel on prouve, que les chinois sont une colonie égyptienne* (Paris, 1759). For a modern study of this development, see Martin Bernal, *Black Athena: The Afroasiatic Roots of Classical Civilization, Volume I* (London, 1987).

*pire of China is the Primitive Language Spoken Through the Whole World
Before the Confusion of Babel* argued that Chinese was the original
language of mankind before the building of the tower of Babel.[13]
The Dutch mathematician and linguist Isaac Golius (1596-1667)
also examined the Chinese language. Golius' interest in chronology led him to investigate the "Catayan" system of twelve cycles or
duodecimal cycles from a Persian work of the 15th century. After
meeting, in Leiden, Martino Martini, who was on a homeward
journey to Italy, Golius discovered that Catay referred to China.
With the aid of a dictionary[14] and Martini's advice, he was able to
publish the cycle of twelve in Chinese characters. This was the first
instance of Chinese characters printed (from wood) in Europe.[15]

The history of Western sinology began yet another chapter with
the posthumous appearance of the Dominican missionary Francisco Varo's (1627-1687) *Arte de la lengua mandarina* (1703). This
was a pioneering grammar; it introduced the Chinese language
entirely on the basis of transliterations, without characters. *Arte...*
was plagiarized by Étienne Fourmont (1683-1745) whose knowledge of Arabic, Syriac, Coptic, and Hebrew had earned him mem-
bership in the Académie des Inscriptions et Belles-Lettres in Paris.
Fourmont had taken an interest in Chinese when he was asked in
1716 by the Regent Phillippe d'Orléans to continue the work of
Arcade Huang (also known as Arcadius Hoang) (d. 1716), a Chinese brought to France under Jesuit patronage to study for the
priesthood, but who later gave up all religious interests. Eventually he began to work on a dictionary of his language.[16] By the
time Huang was resident in France, there was a considerable collection of Chinese books in the Bibliothèque du Roi, most of
which had reached there as gifts, either from the K'ang-hsi Emperor or from the French Jesuits. Fourmont began to collect materials for such a dictionary, and in the process, also composed

---

[13] See John Bold, "John Webb: Composite Capitals and the Chinese Language," *Oxford Art Journal* 4 (1981):9-17; and Ch'en Shou-yi, "John Webb: A For-
gotten Page in the Early History of Sinology in Europe," *Chinese Social and Political
Science Review* 19 (1935):295-330. For a survey of the doxography of the Chinese
language during the 17th century, see David Mungello, *Curious Land: Jesuit Accommodation and the Origins of Sinology* (Wiesbaden, 1985).

[14] Probably the Chinese-Dutch-Latin dictionary compiled in 1628 by the Protestant missionary Justius Heurnius, resident on Java.

[15] See J.J.L. Duyvendak, "Early Chinese Studies in Holland," *T'oung Pao*, 32
(1936):293-344.

[16] On Huang, see Danielle Elisséeff, *Moi, Arcade, interprète chinois du Roi-Soleil*
(Paris, 1985).

the *Linguae Sinarum mandarinicae hieroglyphicae grammatica duplex* (1742), based on Varo's work.

The mediocrity of Fourmont's publication was in strong contrast to another grammar to which he had access, but did not utilize, the *Notitia linguae sinicae* by the French Jesuit Joseph Henri-Marie de Prémare (1666-1736), written around 1700, but first published in 1831.[17] This latter work was a comprehensive textbook for the study of the Chinese language and its literature. Prémare was the first Western scholar to write about the distinction between the classical language (*wen-yen* 文言) and spoken or vernacular language (*pai-hua* 白話). By vernacular Chinese, Prémare meant the speech as written in Yüan dramas, or in the dialogues of popular novels.[18] Nowadays, Westerners tend to apply the term "classical Chinese" to mean both these kinds of Chinese. This usage of the expression is often imitated by modern Chinese scholars, who include poetry of the eighth century and fiction of the 18th century in the term *ku-tien wen-hsüeh* 古典文學, which is the Chinese equivalent of 'classical literature'.

But it should be understood that the term 'classical' as applied to Chinese studies can have two meanings. As a result of the ninth century Confucianist revival, it became the practice among Chinese men of letters in the late T'ang and Sung to write in "an archaic, obsolete style of Chinese modelled on the writings of the ancients," while the language of speech was used as a written medium for works of a popular nature: fiction, drama, lyric poetry, Zen dialogues.[19] In sum, Chinese literature is written in two different languages, the original classical, and the colloquial, also

---

[17] Printed in Malacca in 1831. There is a manuscript edition kept in the Bibliothèque nationale [MSS orient. Chinois 9259]. See Knud Lundbaeck, *Joseph de Prémare (1666-1736), s.j.: Chinese Philology and Figurism* (Aarhus, 1991). Prémare was the author of two other manuals, *La pronunciation chinoise* and *L'orthographe des noms chinois écrits en caractères d'Europe*.

[18] Prémare also made the first translation in 1735 of *Chao-shih-ku-erh* 趙氏孤兒 [The Little Orphan of the House of Chao], a Yüan drama which eventually became a "big hit" all over Europe in the 18th century. From French, it was translated into English, German, and Dutch. See Ch'en Shou-yi, "The Chinese Orphan: A Yüan Play: Its Influence on European Drama of the Eighteenth Century," *T'ien-hsia Monthly* 3 (1936):89-115, and Liu Wu-chi, "The Original Orphan of China," *Comparative Literature* 5 (1953):193-212.

[19] For further explanation on the two different kinds of Chinese, see David Hawkes, "Chinese: Classical, Modern, and Humane," in John Minford and Siu-kit Wong, eds., *David Hawkes: Classical, Modern, and Humane: Essays on Chinese Literature* (Hong Kong, 1989), pp.3-23.

known as vernacular, or old *pai-hua*. The serious student of Chinese literature needs to know both.

To be sure, Prémare's great contribution was no isolated achievement for it was the 18th century when the greatest of the French Jesuit works on China were issued. One might consider Jean Baptist du Halde's *Description géographique, historique, chronologique, politique, et physique de l'Empire de la Chine* (Paris, 1735) the '*summa*' of all the Jesuits' 'lettres édifantes', voyages, canonical literature translations, and scientific study of China's geography, history, linguistics, and philosophy.[20] This cumulative work did have considerable influence on 18th century Europe—one must immediately think of its role in the debates between the Enlightenment thinkers, Montesquieu and Boulanger (both anti-China) versus Voltaire, Quesnay, Rousselot de Surgy (known for pro-China attitudes and their approval of its 'enlightened despotism')[21]—but, the fact remains whatever their achievements to communicate about China, the Jesuits were missionaries, and they devoted the bulk of their time to presenting Christianity to the Chinese.

By the second half of the 18th century, it must have been increasingly apparent, that in Europe, sinophilia was on the wane, and in China, frustration among the Jesuit missionaries was on the rise. As the modern scholar Paul Rule writes, "they [i.e. the Jesuits] had crossed the world to preach gospel, and instead found themselves producing playthings for the amusement of the Emperor and his court."[22] About the same time, the requirements of an ever-expanding French trading empire which included southern China, prompted greater interest in the production of a layman's dictionary for use in commercial transactions.

---

[20] *Lettres édifantes et curieuses écrites des missions étrangères par quelques missionnaires de la Compagnie de Jésus*, vols. 1 (Paris, 1702) to 34 (Paris, 1776) form a rich collection of Jesuit reporting on China for the 18th century. See the recent unpublished Ph.D. dissertation on this collection by Li Jian-jun, "Lettres édifantes et curieuses de Chine: de l'édification à la Propaganda" (Harvard University, 1990).

[21] As Arthur Wright postulated in his classic article "The Study of Chinese Civilization," *Journal of the History of Ideas*, 21 (1960):233-55, the image that the Jesuits cast took a long time to fade. That image was of order, stability, symmetry, and 'rationality' in strong contrast to the divided, uneasy, strife-ridden world of the West.

[22] From Paul Rule, *K'ung-tzu*, p.184. Here Rule notes the account of Pierre Jartoux in which he laments the fact that despite 13 years in the mission, he had done no real missionary work, and had been 'a mere workman' for the Emperor, producing clocks, mapping the Great Wall, and teaching mathematics to one of the Emperor's sons.

As Henri Cordier in his study of sinology in France during the Revolution and the First Empire has noted, the compilation of a dictionary was the most important thread linking 18th and 19th century Chinese studies.[23] Although the Jesuit Joseph Amiot (1718-1793) had directed the publication of the *Dictionnaire mandchou-française* and another work *Dictionnaire polyglotte sanskrit-tibétain-mandchou-mongol-chinois*, these works were really impractical and not easily available. In England, which at this point was also set on expanding its commercial interests in China, efforts to go beyond, what the modern scholar Tim Barrett characterizes 'East Indian Company Sinology', had minimal results. Preparation for the Macartney Embassy launched in 1792 included the search for suitable interpreters for which none could be found; members of the Embassy depended on whatever Jesuit authored materials were available.[24]

In France, the person who was most instrumental in promoting the printing of a Chinese dictionary at this time was, interestingly, not a 'China expert', but a specialist on the languages of Western Asia (Persian, Chaldean, and classical Arabic). Baron Antoine Isaac Silvestre de Sacy (1758-1838), considered by several modern scholars to be the first modern institutional European Orientalist,[25] pushed the dictionary project. In a report presented in 1808 to the Instituut National, a post-Revolutionary institution that governed academic standards in the sciences and arts, de Sacy indicated how helpful a knowledge of Manchu was for the study of Chinese, and urged that existing translations of Manchu books in the Bibliothèque imperiale (the forerunner of today's Bibliothèque nationale) be used to help in the compilation of a dictionary. He recommended that the French Government undertake responsibility for this project.[26]

---

[23] Henri Cordier, "Les Études chinoises sous la Révolution et l'Empire," *T'oung Pao* 19 (1918-19):62.

[24] T.H. Barrett, *Singular Listlessness: A Short History of Chinese Books and British Scholars* (London, 1989), pp.53-58. See also the discussion in Susan Reed Stifler, "The Language Students of the East India Company's Canton Factory," *Journal of the North China Royal Asiatic Society*, 69 (1938):46-83, and in particular, 51-56.

[25] There are accounts about de Sacy in Raymond Schwab, *The Oriental Renaissance: Europe's Rediscovery of India and the East 1680-1880* (English translation; New York, 1984), and Edward Said, *Orientalism* (New York, 1978).

[26] See *Rapports à l'Empereur sur le progrès des sciences, des lettres et des arts depuis 1789: Section IV Histoire et littérature ancienne,* "Langues et littératures orientales" [reproduced, Paris, 1989], pp.101-106. It was well known among linguists of de Sacy's stature that Manchu was an excellent basis for learning Chinese. Manchu is

A Chinese-French/Latin dictionary finally appeared in 1813. This work, comprising a study of more than 14,000 characters, was printed by the Imperial publisher and compiled by a man known as de Guignes Fils (1749-1845).[27] As Consul in Canton, he was the last Frenchman to reside in China until after the Opium War. Upon his return from Asia in 1804 he was named Chief of the Interpreters in the Ministry of Foreign Affairs, and after the publication of his memoirs, *Voyages à Pekin, Manille et l'Ile de France dans l'intervale des années 1784-1801*, in 1808, Napoleon charged him with compiling a comprehensive dictionary of the Chinese language. Shortly after its publication, it was discovered that this dictionary was nothing more than a copy of an older work composed by the Franciscan friar, Basilio Brollo de Glemona (1648-1704), the *Han-tzu hsi-i* 漢字西譯. While de Guignes Fils had altered the original slightly, by arranging the characters according to the order of the 214 radicals (as opposed to Basilio's tone-based order), it was generally agreed that the Napoleonic edition was nothing more than a "typographical curiosity" and hardly advanced the study of the Chinese language at all.

The dictionary received strong criticism from the first person to be appointed a professor of Chinese in a European institution of higher learning, Jean-Pierre Abel-Rémusat (1788-1832). Abel-Rémusat, as a medical student, became enchanted by China and the Chinese language after seeing an illustrated Chinese botanical study. He taught himself the fundamentals of Chinese by using Fourmont's work, and studying Manchu in the grammars and dictionaries composed by the Jesuits, and from them, learned to translate Chinese.[28] Abel-Rémusat became a protege of de Sacy. The two had first become acquainted after de Sacy had read two of Abel-Rémusat's publications, "l'Étude des langues étrangères chez les Chinois" which appeared in the *Magasin encyclopédique*, and *Essai sur la langue et la littérature chinoise*.[29] De Sacy recognized

---

ralement written in an alphabetic script and has a rich concise morphology for nouns and verbs, plus a consistent sentence structure.

[27] De Guignes Fils was the son of Joseph de Guignes (1721-1800) author of a study on the origins of Chinese [see footnote #12], and Professor of Syriac at the Collège Royale (former name of the Collège de France).

[28] Abel-Rémusat's doctoral thesis dealt with the Chinese art of diagnosing diseases from inspection of the tongue. He defended it in 1813.

[29] Abel-Rémusat knew about the *Notitia Linguae Sinicae* from Fourmont's work, found a copy of it in the Bibliothèque du Roi, and copied it. In the preface to his 1822 publication, *Élements de la grammaire chinoise ou principes généraux du kou-wen ou style antique et du kouan-hou, c'est-à-dire, de la language commune géné-*

Abel-Rémusat's genius and proposed his nomination to the Collège de France as the first professor of Chinese, known in French as the chair "de langues et littératures chinoises et tartares-mandchoues", which he held from 1814 until his death.

By the time Abel-Rémusat came to occupy this chair, the study of Chinese in France (and later, elsewhere in Europe) was beginning to take the form it was to hold for the next 150 years. The study of the spoken language was taught in the l'École des langues orientales vivantes, an institution created in 1795 for the purpose of training those who would work in commerce and trade, both in and outside of France. The instruction of Chinese in that institution began after 1843, and was led often by men with a long stint in the diplomatic services. Similar institutions, like the 'Seminar für orientalische Sprachen' in Berlin founded in 1887, were established as European nations expanded their trade interests in China. In contrast, the study of the classical language and Chinese culture was confined to elitist institutions like the Collège de France, or in other countries, to universities.[30]

Abel-Rémusat and his successors set high standards of scholarship which was to become the hallmark of the French school of sinology, known by its preference for philology and translation. The intellectual interests and publishing achievements of Abel-Rémusat and his successors extended far beyond the learning of Chinese according to the Confucian canon. While the Jesuits in the 17th and 18th centuries had denigrated the study of Chinese religion, especially matters related to Buddhism or Taoism, the holders of the chair in Chinese at the Collège de France, in particular Abel-Rémusat's pupil, and later successor, Stanislas Julien (1797-1873) did much to advance understanding about the variation of Chinese religious beliefs. Translations of the *Fo-kuo-chi* 佛國記, *San-tsang fa-shih chuan* 三藏法師傳 (biography of Hsüan-tsang), and the *Tao-te-ching* are only some of the important titles that these scholars made.[31]

---

ralement usitée dans l'empire chinois, which was the first usable grammar written in Europe, he acknowledges his debt to Prémare.

[30] The Collège de France was not a university teaching institution. It was served by a group of men, chosen solely for their learning, who were obliged only to give two public lectures per week. They had no students, and were not involved in examinations for degrees. Those who wished to study Chinese did on their own initiative, and with permission of the Professor. The Collège de France traces its origins back to the Collège Royale, founded in 1589 by François Premier.

[31] For a general history of Buddhism in 19th century Europe, see Philip C. Almond, *The British Discovery of Buddhism* (Cambridge, 1988). Buddhism was not

However, it would take some time, until the image of China as an essentially Confucian society would be dismissed. The necessity for sinologists to acquaint themselves with the Classics and with the enormous scholarly literature which they inspired, as well as the Jesuit conception of Confucianism that had well penetrated learned Europe, may explain the widespread academic interest in that ideology. Furthermore, it was common in 19th century European society to classify the 'cultures of the East' as timeless, and thus, the study of the Chinese Classics, which were thought the key to the fundamental principles of Chinese civilization, fulfilled the basic requirements of this supposition.[32] Both Abel-Rémusat and Julien taught the rudiments of translating Confucian texts, but they had wide-ranging intellectual interests with regard to China, and their pioneer work on Buddhism and Taoism was to provide a firm foundation for further study of Chinese religion by Julien's successors at the Collège de France, including Édouard Chavannes (1865-1918), Henri Maspero (1883-1945), and Paul Demiéville (1894-1979). Chavannes, it should be remarked upon, was the first Western sinologist to see Chinese history as a series of "époques" in which each era had distinctive characteristics.

While France may have regularized the principles for good sinological study, other European countries were slow to follow. The chairs of Chinese at Oxford, Cambridge, and London were held by a series of former missionaries and diplomats. In Germany, the first professorship for Chinese was not appointed until as late as 1909 in Hamburg. In the Netherlands where overseas trade and colonial interests in Southeast Asia dominated public policy, a chair at Leiden University, first instituted in 1876, was strongly tied to government interests.[33] The problem in these

---

Abel-Rémusat's only interest; the first article he published after he became professor was a study of jade; it appeared in the *Journal des Savants* in 1818. For a complete listing of his publications, and that of other notable sinologists in the 19th and 20th centuries, one should turn to Shinsho Hanayama, *Bibliography on Buddhism* (Tokyo, 1961).

[32] With reference to this idea, one thinks immediately of the quick and widespread acceptance of James Legge's translations of the *Classics*, which appeared in F. Max Müller's collection, *Sacred Books of the East*, published between the 1870s and the 1890s. See Lauren F. Pfister, "Some New Dimensions in the Study of the Works of James Legge (1815-1897): Part I," *Sino-Western Cultural Relations* 12 (1990):29-50.

[33] See my article "Sociology, Social Science, and Sinology in the Netherlands before World War II: with Special Reference to the Work of Frederik van Heek." *Revue européenne des sciences sociales* 27 (1989):19-32.

countries was not that the study of Chinese was considered unworthy—one only has to reflect upon the esteem held by contemporary anthropologists, historians, and sociologists for the Dutch scholar J.J.M de Groot (1854-1921)—it was that the learning of Chinese in the 19th century remained more of an 'exotic ornament' than a firm 'academic tradition'.[34]

In sum, until the end of the 19th century Western educators made a strong distinction between 'research-orientated' academic studies and the teaching of spoken Chinese for practical purposes. Those wishing to study the written 'classical' language were probably motivated by a dose of unworldly scholarly curiosity.[35] Nevertheless, much scholarship that emerged from that era, and perhaps even later into this century, fell into what may be considered the 'commentarial tradition', the approach to Chinese civilization through critical annotated translation. While this methodology of learning about a civilization by translating a number of 'standard texts' has its merits (it is impossible to understand China without being able to read Chinese), it may also result in what the eminent sinologist Étienne Balazs (1905-1963) once described as the 'stamp collectors' mentality', i.e. the tendency for scholars to preoccupy themselves with marginal or curious aspects of Chinese tradition. In an article published in 1960, he wrote "that sinology at the time had become nothing more than 'philological hair-splitting', a repository of private curiosities, preoccupied with external forms and unique events."[36]

One of the problems with the preference for the 'commentarial tradition' was that it inhibited the study of China within a broader context utilizing social science methodology or making comparisons with other humanistic traditions. Even as late as the 1960s, it was not possible to study the modern anthropology of China in the Netherlands. At that time, to become in Holland an anthropologist specialized in China, one first had to complete a

---

[34] See comments by Herbert Franke, "In Search of China: Some General Remarks on the History of European Sinology." Unpublished paper delivered at the International Conference on the History of European Sinology, Taipei, April 1992.

[35] This situation is not meant as a point of criticism. One only has to mention the fine sinological works by such men as Édouard Biot (1803-1850), a railway engineer, or Arthur Waley (1889-1966), a print cataloguer at the British Museum, or Robert H. van Gulik (1910-1967), a Dutch diplomat.

[36] See E. Balazs, "The Birth of Capitalism in China," *Journal of the Economic and Social History of the Orient*, 3 (1960), p.196.

study of Chinese, of classical Chinese mainly, and then gain permission to take up the sociology of China as a "sideline".[37]

The 'commentarial tradition' was also the favoured method for the study of China in Japan. For centuries Japanese scholars known as *kangakusha* 漢学者 examined the Confucian canon through the same methodology of textual criticism (*kôshôgaku* 考証学) and general philological (as well as ethical) training as their Chinese counterparts had done. After the Meiji Restoration, when modern Western style universities were established, the curriculum remained committed to the 'commentarial tradition'. Even nowadays it is usual at Tokyo University for a *sensei* 先生 (professor) to lead a group of younger colleagues and students in a typical seminar known as a *kenkyûkai* 研究会 or *dokushokai* 読書会 in the punctuation and translation of a Chinese text. Nevertheless, the 19th century educational reforms in Japanese education did bring certain changes to the study of China, which in the long term were to affect sinology in China itself during the modern era.

Modern Japanese sinology has evolved out of three distinct influences. The first, as mentioned above, is the tradition of Tokugawa studies of the Chinese Classics. The second contributing factor was the experience of field work and studies conducted under the influence, if not the aegis of Japanese colonialism and imperialism.[38] The third influence was Western, including the impact of Leopold Ranke, and then later, Marx and the sociology of Max Weber.[39] In 1887, Leopold Ranke's former student Dr. Ludwig

---

[37] P.E. de Josselin de Jonge, "Introduction," in *idem.*, ed., *Structural Anthropology in the Netherlands* (Dordrecht, 1983), p.3.

[38] The most famous of the Japanese government sponsored research organizations was the Mantetsu Chôsabu (South Manchurian Railway Company, Research Bureau). Others included the Tôa Kenkyûjo (East Asian Institute), and the Tôa Keizai Chôsakyoku (Research Bureau of East Asian Economics). For further information, see John Young, *The Research Activity of the South Manchurian Railway Company, 1907-1945* (New York, 1966), especially pp. 3-34. Many of the publications of these institutions are referred to in John Fairbank, M. Banno, and S. Yamamoto, *Japanese Studies of Modern China: A Bibliographic Guide to Historical and Social Science Research on the 19th and 20th Centuries* (Cambridge, Mass, 1955; second edition, 1975 [updated]). For a stimulating discussion of early 20th century Japanese influence on Chinese education, see Sophia Lee, "The Foreign Ministry's Cultural Agenda for China: The Boxer Indemnity," in Peter Duus, Ramon H. Myers, and Mark R. Peattie, *The Japanese Informal Empire in China, 1895-1937* (Princeton, 1987), pp.272-306.

[39] The impact of Marxian-inspired Japanese historiography on China is discussed at a later point in this survey. For a comprehensive listing of the most im-

Reiss (1861-1928) went to Tokyo Imperial University where he was hired to teach history and historical methods. Ranke has been known for his famous characterization of the Chinese as "die Völkern des ewigen Stillstandes",[40] and Reiss became the inspiration for Shiratori Kurakichi 白鳥庫吉 (1865-1942), the principal founder of a specialized form of study, tôyôshigaku 東洋史学, literally Oriental historiography. Convinced of the superiority and universality of Western civilization, Shiratori made his life's work to undermine and destroy Chinese influence in Japan.[41] In 1910 he began a series of public debates with the leading rival scholar of China, Naitô Konan 内藤湖南 (1866-1934).

Before Naitô became a professor at Kyoto University, he had lived in China as a journalist and observed the failure of China's self-strengthening policy. Fearing Western imperialist advances in Asia, Naitô wrote about the future of Japan's links with China.[42] By arguing that the period of the middle T'ang and early Sung saw the transformation of Chinese economic, social, political, and cultural life into a 'modern' stage, Naitô's views were in variance with those of Tokyo-based scholars.[43] He defended the mature

portant 20th century Japanese sinologists, with short characterizations of their areas of specialization, see John Timothy Wixted, compiler, Japanese Scholars of China: A Bibliographical Handbook (Lewiston, N.Y., 1992).

[40] The full quote: "Zuweilen sind wohl die von uralter Zeit vererbten Zustände eines oder des anderen orientalischen Volkes als Grundlage von Allem betrachtet worden. Unmöglich aber kann man von den Völern eines ewigen Stillstands augehen, um die innere Bewegung der Weltgeschichte zu begreifen." from Leopold von Ranke, Weltgeschichte (Leipzig, 1881), vol. I, p.vi. Ranke was not the first European to comment on the "changelessness" of non-European peoples. Already in 1774, Herder argued that non-European civilizations were static, and irrelevant to any study of the historical process. John Stuart Mill, writing in 1838, referred to "Chinese stationariness". See Arthur Wright, "The Study of Chinese Civilization," p.241, footnote #12.

[41] Stefan Tanaka, Japan's Orient: Rendering Pasts into History (Berkeley, 1993) provides excellent analysis of Shiratori's impact. Shiratori was highly influenced by Naka Michiyo 那珂通世 (1851-1908), who coined the term tôyôshi 東洋史 (East Asian history) in 1894 when he proposed that the middle school curriculum separate world history into Occidental and Oriental history, a suggestion accepted by the Ministry of Education two years later.

[42] Naitô's life and work have been analyzed in a superb monograph by Joshua Fogel. See his Politics and Sinology: The Case of Naitô Konan (Cambridge, Mass., 1984).

[43] Naitô's influence on the study of Chinese history is still evident. As Fogel notes, ibid., p.xv, two major textbooks, i.e. that of Fairbank, Reischauer, and Craig, East Asia: Tradition and Transformation [(Boston, 1978); revised under the title China: Tradition and Transformation (Boston, 1989)] and Gernet, A History of Chinese Civilisation [(Cambridge, 1982); originally in French, Le monde chinois (Paris, 1972)] employ Naitô's periodization to Chinese history. Further details of

and enduring qualities of Chinese culture and predicted that younger nations like Japan would, in some distant future, conform to the pattern of change followed earlier by China. In contrast to Shiratori and his followers who sought to destroy the sinocentric notion of the universality of Chinese civilization, Naitô and his adherents, who came to be known as *Shinagaku* 支那学 (or the Kyoto school), sought to inspire a renaissance of Chinese civilization by working out a cultural synthesis which would combine the best elements of both Eastern and Western cultures.

Naitô and other pre-war Japanese sinologists consciously lacked a coherent characterization of Chinese civilization, but they became deeply involved in the study of its parts, and saw China as a culture, a way of life, and *not* as an independent state—at least not the unstable, nation-state of Republican China. Accordingly, the key to understanding China was its culture, for it was this phenomenon which held Chinese loyalties, not its feeble government. What intellectual justification was given for this Japanese attitude may be ascribed to adherence to a rigid form of historical positivism (*jisshôshugi* 実証主義 or *kôshô shigaku* 考証史学). Many early 20th century Japanese sinologists subscribed to the premise that facts were determined through rigorous textual criticism, not through theory and interpretation. By the 1920s the result of this academic formulation was clear: publications were either compilations, such as massive, detailed encyclopedias, or translations from dynastic histories, or limited studies of such topics as Manchu-Mongol history or T'ang poetry. In Japan, reverence for the 'commentarial tradition' was manifested in these minute exegetical studies of isolated terms or institutions.

Naitô's ideas were also to become an important source of inspiration for a whole generation of Chinese Classical scholars. Several eminent Chinese academics knew Naitô personally and shared with him a strong disdain for the early 20th century "literary revolution" and the intellectual activities of the "May Fourth crowd". Some of the most important of these professors included Lo Chen-yü 羅振玉 (1866-1940), the father of Chinese archaeology, and his protege Wang Kuo-wei 王國維 (1877-1927), considered by some modern writers to be China's greatest 20th century

---

the Naitô hypothesis can be found in Hisayuki Miyakawa, "An Outline of the Naitô Hypothesis and Its Effects on Japanese Studies of China," *Far Eastern Quarterly*, 14.4 (1955):533-52.

classical scholar.[44] Lo had first become acquainted with the Anyang (Honan) finds of bones and tortoise shells through the pioneer collectors Liu O 劉鶚 (1857-1909), and Wang I-jung 王懿榮 (1845-1900).[45] Lo and Wang had led the way in their decipherment and analysis; they demonstrated that information could be deduced from them which confirmed many statements in ancient texts that had come to be neglected as completely untrustworthy if not actually forged. Wang Kuo-wei also showed that the list of Yin kings as given in the Bamboo Books was generally accurate. It should also be noted that 19th century studies of bronze inscriptions by a number of Chinese scholars had laid a certain basis for the later work done on the bones and shells.[46]

Mention should also be made of the fact that both Lo and Wang were active in publicizing about the important finds of literature, manuscripts, wooden strips, and Buddhist works of art in northwest Kansu in 1894.[47] The discovery of the monastic library at Tun-huang also "revealed a whole new genre of 'popular' literature deriving from the world of the 'semi-literate' which underlay the highly cultivated and sophisticated milieu of the literti."[48] It was this aspect of the Tun-huang treasures that most attracted Chinese scholars since these literary discoveries coincided with the contemporary interest in old colloquial literature provoked by the movement to write in the spoken language.

Both Lo Chen-yü and Wang Kuo-wei had found in contemporary Japanese scholarship, as professed by Naitô and his followers,

---

[44] The starting point for any investigation on the life of Wang should be the excellent study by Joey Bonner, *Wang Kuo-wei: An Intellectual Biography* (Cambridge, Mass., 1986).

[45] For biographies of Liu and Wang, see Arthur Hummel, *Eminent Chinese of the Ch'ing Period* (Washington, D.C., 1943-44), pp. 516-518, and pp.826-828, respectively.

[46] Among the more important of these contributions were those by Wu Ta-ch'eng 吳大澂 (1835-1902) and Sun I-jang 孫詒讓 (1848-1902). Both these scholars deciphering of bronze and stone inscriptions led to the development of etymology and to the correct reading of oracle bone inscriptions. Their work was based, in turn, on the pioneer studies of Juan Yüan 阮元 (1764-1845) and Wu Jung-kuang 吳榮光 (1773-1843). Until their achievements in this field became known, bronze inscriptions had only been assembled in imperial palaces.

[47] The Chinese local authorities did not report the findings until the visit of Sir Aurel Stein (1862-1943) thirteen years later. For a brief account in English of the Tun-huang finds and, in particular, the Stein Collection in the British Museum, see L.Giles, *Six Centuries of Tunhuang* (London, 1944). On the life of Stein, see Jeanette Mirsky, *Sir Aurel Stein: Archaeological Explorer* (Chicago, 1977).

[48] Denis Twitchett, *Land Tenure and the Social Order in T'ang and Sung China* (London, 1962).

a sympathetic forum for their ideas and work. Both men may be considered members of that first generation of Chinese intellectuals who witnessed and, more significantly, participated in the intellectual transformation of China through Japanese influence. The period most crucial to this development was 1898 through 1907, characterized by some modern scholars as the 'Golden Decade'.[49] While it is well known that a number of Chinese reformers who took part in the failed 'Hundred Days of Reform' in 1898 fled to Japan and developed close intellectual contacts there, e.g. K'ang Yu-wei 康有為 (1858-1927) and Liang Ch'i-ch'ao 梁啓超 (1873-1929), what is less well-known is the extent to which other scholars like Lo and Wang absorbed Japanese influences, and utilized them in the scholarly study of China.

Following the lead of Liang Ch'i-ch'ao, Chinese in Japan translated hundreds of Japanese works, many of which were originally in Western languages. The most common category of translation was textbooks (including lectures and class notes of Japanese teaching in both China and Japan) and encyclopedias.[50] For example, German historical methodology reached China via the work of Tsuboi Kumazô 坪井九馬三 (1858-1936) whose textbook *Shigaku Kenkyû* 史学研究法 (Methods for the Study of History), written after his stay in Germany, was translated into Chinese in 1902. The model for what a new comprehensive history of China might look like was Naka Michiyo's *Shina tsûshi* 支那通史 (Comprehensive History of China; Tokyo, 1888-90).[51] For the first time, Chinese in-

---

[49] The American scholar Douglas Reynolds points out that Japan served both as an alternative channel of information concerning the non-Chinese world, and a point of reference for the important reforms that this period witnessed. For Reynolds, the reforms themselves constitute a "quiet" revolution, and hence the title of his book, *China, 1898-1912: The Xinzheng Revolution and Japan* (Cambridge, Mass., 1993).

[50] As Reynolds, *ibid.*, pp.117-121, points out, surviving copies or even bibliographies of what was produced in the period 1896-1912 are rare, if not non-existent. The interest in encyclopedias may be considered a response to the "sudden, urgently felt need for comprehensive knowledge beyond China's traditional categories of learning." [p.118]. Compare Huang Fu-ch'ing and Katherine P.K. Whitaker (translator), *Chinese Students in Japan in the Late Ch'ing Period* (Tokyo, 1982), pp.132-145 on translation activities at this time.

[51] For further information on this phase of Chinese-Japanese contact, see Yü Tan-ch'u 俞旦初, "Erh-shih shih-chi ch'u-nien Chung-kuo ti hsin-shih-hsüeh ssu-ch'ao ch'u-k'ao 二十世紀初年中國的新史學思潮初考," *Shih-hsüeh-shih yen-chiu* 史學史研究 3(1982):54-66; Chou Yü-t'ung 周予同, "Wu-shih-nien lai Chung-kuo chih hsin-shih-hsüeh 五十年來中國之新史學," *Hsüeh-lin* 學林 4 (February, 1941):1-36.

tellectuals witnessed how their country's history could be written without the dynastic prototype.

Lo and Naitô had first met in 1899 in Shanghai where the Chinese scholar had established a language school the year before, the Tung-wen hsüeh-she 東文學社 (Eastern Culture Society) that emphasized the study of the Japanese language. Another of Lo's Japanese contacts, the eminent scholar Fujita Toyohachi 藤田豊八 (1869-1929), a graduate of Tokyo Imperial University in Chinese classical studies, became the first teacher at the Tung-wen hsüeh-she.[52] The effect of Lo linking himself to contemporary Japanese intellectuals was profound: throughout his life, Lo believed in the closeness of China and Japan, and their distance from European culture.[53] Wang, although acquainted with 19th century European philosophy, also relinquished Western studies, and devoted himself to the study of ancient China and the Classics, on the basis of a study of Ch'ing dynasty *k'ao-cheng* methods. Wang Kuo-wei's importance from the point of view of sinological methodology is that he brought the techniques of the Ch'ing dynasty *k'ao-cheng* masters Ku Yen-wu 顧炎武 (1613-1682), Tai Chen 戴震 (1724-1777), and others to bear on the Classics in a 20th century context of new archaeological evidence. Wang Kuo-wei also published on the history of Chinese drama, works which have never been wholly superseded.[54] In the aftermath of the 1911 Revolution both Lo and Wang came at Naitô's invitation to Kyoto where they lived for seven years and published much of their work.

---

[52] One of Fujita's many accomplishments was to help Lo edit *Chiao-yü shih-chieh* 教育世界 (Education World), China's first modern journal of education launched in 1901. See Reynolds, *ibid.*, pp.135-137.

[53] Unfortunately, Lo Chen-yü is still lacking a good biography. The negative image that continues to haunt his reputation, long after his death, probably relates to his outright collaboration with the Manchuko regime in the 1930s. However, whatever his wartime activities, his involvement in the evolution of Chinese studies should be examined carefully. Lo may also be credited with saving from a Peking paper pulp merchant, documents and archives that had once belonged to the Ch'ing dynasty's Grand Council. He paid twice the price for which they had been sold, selected some of the most valuable documents, recompiled, and published them under the title, *Shih-liao ts'ung-k'an ch'u pien* 史料叢刊初編 (First Collection of Historical Materials). The remaining items went to the documentary collections in the Academia Sinica and Peking University. See A. K'ai-ming Ch'iu, "Chinese Historical Documents of the Ch'ing Dynasty, 1644-1911," *Pacific Historical Review*, 1 (1932):324-336.

[54] The most influential of his many publications on popular literature was his study, *Sung Yüan hsi-ch'ü k'ao* 宋元戲曲考 [originally titled, and sometimes called, *Sung Yüan hsi-ch'ü shih* 宋元戲曲史], a study of Sung and Yüan drama.

It should be noted that although both Lo Chen-yü and Wang Kuo-wei continued to write commentary upon the Tun-huang finds during the 1920s, Japanese scholars were already gaining a monopoly on the study of land documents. When the first printed collections of Tun-huang fragments were published in China, and when other pieces transcribed by Japanese visiting scholars in the Bibliothèque nationale and the British Museum came to their attention, these scholars were quick to seize upon their importance. Following his country's own long tradition of specialized knowledge of legal history centring upon the T'ang dynasty (when Japan borrowed institutions wholesale from China), the scholar Niida Noboru 仁井田陞 (1904-1966) began to analyze these documents. The result of his work was summed up in one of the great works of Japanese sinology, his monograph *Tô Sô hôritsu bunsho no kenkyû* 唐宋法律文書の研究 (Legal Documents of the T'ang and Sung Periods), published in 1937. Niida's legal studies paralleled another group of contemporary Japanese economic historians, Tamai Zehaku 玉井是博, Hamaguchi Shigekuni 濱口重国, and Suzuki Shun 鈴木俊 who all worked on Tun-huang documents to evaluate their importance for social history.[55]

Interestingly, one of the first victims of China's scholarly excursions in sinological re-orientation, inspired, at least in part, by Japanese scholars, was Confucius. Through their acquaintance with Japanese interpretations of Chinese civilization, some of the greatest conservators of China's ancient literary traditions found new ways of reading China's past. For example, Chang Ping-lin 章炳麟 (1869-1936), a Peking University professor, did much to demystify Confucius. At the beginning of this century, Chang had earned a reputation as a rabid anti-Manchu radical, but after the 1911 Revolution became a staunch conservator of China's literary tradition. Like Naitô, with whom he too had contact, Chang believed that the May Fourth Movement was founded on ignorance of China's history and culture. Chang argued that Ch'ing textual scholarship demonstrated Confucius was only an historian among other historians, and a classical philosopher among several classical philosophers such as Mo-tzu or Chuang-tzu.[56] Chang's distin-

---

[55] Twitchett, *Land Tenure and the Social Order*, p.22.

[56] On Chang Ping-lin, see Shimada Kenji, *Pioneer of the Chinese Revolution: Zhang Binglin and Confucianism*, trans. by Joshua Fogel (Stanford, 1990); and Charlotte Furth, "The Sage as Rebel: The Inner World of Chang Ping-lin," in Furth, ed., *The Limits of Change: Essays on Conservatives in Republican China* (Cambridge, Mass., 1976), pp.113-150.

guished pupils included Lu Hsün 魯迅 (1881-1936), who would become the foremost spokesman of the literary revolution, and Ku Chieh-kang 顧頡剛 (1893-1980), leader of China's "back to the people" folk literary movement.

Although Chang and Ku had their differences, Ku too turned his back on Confucius. But unlike his teacher who came to this view through 'Han hsüeh' studies, Ku drew upon his experience as a fervent theatre-goer. His interest in drama led him to probe its history and, eventually, he began, methodically, to accumulate material to compare divergent versions of plays as performed by different companies. His interest spread to the familiar folk-tales of his youth and to folk music.[57] From his research, he concluded that much of the material of the Classics was developed from oral tradition, and a substantial portion of his work was finding evidence for his theory that themes in drama or traditional novels reflect the classical stories of the emperors Yao, Shun, Yü, and their legendary predecessors. When Hu Shih 胡適 (1891-1962) came to teach at Peking University in 1917, Ku found a sympathetic ear, and with him formed a cluster of students and other teachers who were to publish on the classical texts and the criticism thereof.[58]

Despite their innovative approaches to the study of Chinese culture, these scholars in their work and interests, in at least one way followed an age-old pattern by which knowledge was transmitted, i.e. that of the master-disciple relation. In effect, many of these academics were acting upon the 18th century k'ao-cheng legacy. To date there has not yet appeared a general intellectual history of this transmission process,[59] but one can trace the intellectual lineage of many individuals. For example, Chang Ping-lin was a disci-

---

[57] On Ku's activities, see Hung Chang-tai, *Going to the People: Chinese Intellectuals and Folk Literature, 1918-1937* (Cambridge, Mass., 1985); Ursula Richter, *Zweifel am Altertum: Gu Jiegang und die Diskussion über Chinas alte Geschichte als Konsequenz der 'Neuen Kulturbewegung' ca.1915-1923* (Stuttgart, 1992); Laurence A. Schneider, *Ku Chieh-kang and China's New History: Nationalism and the Quest for Alternative Traditions* (Berkeley, 1971), and Wang Fan-sen 王汎森, *Ku-shih-pien yün-tung ti hsing-ch'i I-ko ssu-hsiang-shih ti fen-hsi* 古史辨運動的興起 一個思想史的分析(Taipei, 1987).

[58] The results of these discussions were published yearly in the compilation *Ku shih pien* 古史辨 (1926-41). The preface to this work was translated by Arthur Hummel as, *The Autobiography of a Chinese Historian Being the Preface to a Symposium on Ancient Chinese History* (Leiden, 1931).

[59] An important contribution that explores the relationship between evidential research and late 19th century reformers is a recent book by Benjamin Elman, *Classicism, Politics, and Kinship: The Ch'ang-chou School of New Text Confucianism in Late Imperial China* (Berkeley, 1990).

ple of Yü Yüeh 俞樾 (1821-1906), who in turn was a follower of the
k'ao-cheng (father and son) scholars Wang Nien-sun 王念孫 (1744-
1832) and Wang Yin-chih 王引之 (1766-1834), both closely associated with Tai Chen's views on phonology and etymology.[60] Like
his teacher, Chang was a brilliant student of philology; he put his
talents to work when he devised the first national phonetic alphabetic script with the aim to eradicate illiteracy.[61] Chang's idoliza-
tion of Tai Chen's work *Meng-tzu tzu-i shu-cheng* 孟子字義疏證 (Exegesis of the Meanings of Terms in the *Mencius*), later made famous by Hu Shih's book on Tai Chen, also demonstrates Chang's
links to 18th century empirical studies. Thus Chang, as Yü Yüeh's
disciple and Lu Hsün's teacher, exemplifies how the revolutionary
spirit of the 20th century had roots deep in Classical writings and
was passed along to leaders of China's 'literary revolution'.

Hu Shih too may be seen in this way. While it is true that Hu
played a great role in the literary reform movement, one of whose
major aims was to make acceptable the use of the spoken language for published works, he was also a vigorous defender of the
Ch'ing Classical scholarship—he wrote that the methods of Classical scholarship were analogous to those of contemporary European science.[62] Hu's attitudes toward the reading of literature
were also important in the long term for the study of China's
greatest literary works. He outlined an approach to the writing of
the history of popular literature which he produced in the preface to a new edition of the *Dream of the Red Chamber.*

---

[60] Yü Yüeh's life is described by Tu Lien-chê in Arthur Hummel, ed., *Eminent Chinese of the Ch'ing Period* (Taipei, 1975 reprint), pp.944-45. Yü's fame as a teacher spread to Japan, and in his lifetime, he acquired a number of eminent Japanese pupils.

[61] Shimada, *Pioneer of the Chinese Revolution*, p.14.

[62] *Hu Shih wen-ts'un* 胡適文存, vol.2, p. 539 (Taipei, 1953). No doubt Hu's ideas of 'scientific scholarship' would seem dubious to us: by counting the number of proofs supplied by various Ch'ing *k'ao-cheng* scholars arguing the authenticity or spuriousness of sections of the Classics, he would then point to this as evidence of an indigenous 'scientific' strain in Chinese scholarship. In this way, Hu was following many of the ideas that Liang Ch'i-ch'ao had laid out in his book *Ch'ing-tai hsüeh-shu kai-lun* 清代學術概論 [later published in English as *Intellectual Trends in the Ch'ing Period*, translated and introduced by Immanuel C.Y. Hsü (Cambridge, Mass., 1959)]. For example, Liang considered that works like Chang Ping-lin's *Hsiao-hsüeh wen-ta* 小學問答 (Questions and answers in linguistics), or his own *Kuo-wen yü-yüan chieh* 國文語原解 (Explanation of the etymology of our national language) were 'scientific' linguistic studies. For biographical information on Hu, see Chou Min-chih, *Hu Shih and Intellectual Choice in Modern China* (Ann Arbor, 1984); Jerome Grieder, *Hu Shih and the Chinese Renaissance: Liberalism in the Chinese Revolution (1917-1937)* (Cambridge, Mass., 1970).

It is impossible in such a brief survey to do justice to the many thousands of Chinese sinologists who taught and worked in the decades of the 20s and 30s and altered the study of China. Suffice it to say that this era may be considered a time of rapid change and innovation that spurred higher education from gentry academies focused on Classical studies toward modern broad-based public and private universities offering a variety of disciplines ranging from Chinese literature or history to modern contemporary sociology.[63] Nevertheless, even in this changing atmosphere, a number of academic conventions persisted. For one thing, contemporary scholars of whatever persuasion saw themselves as proponents of a "school", and thus their new work, was 'continuing an older tradition'.

Liang Ch'i-ch'ao, Hu Shih, and Ku Chieh-k'ang may be considered members of the 'I-ku p'ai' 疑古派 (a school suspecting the authenticity of ancient China). They traced their ideas back to Ts'ui Shu 崔述 (1740-1816) whose work *Shih-chi t'an-yüan* 史記探源 (Source tracing of the *Shih chi*) challenged the authority of Ssu-ma Ch'ien; Ts'ui demonstrated many paragraphs in that work were inserted or forged.[64] Ts'ui and his successors (including K'ang Yu-wei) charged that the Han dynasty scholar Liu Hsiang 劉向 (79-8 B.C.) and his son Liu Hsin 劉歆 (d. A.D.23) had forged many Classics to suit the political purposes of Wang Mang.[65]

---

[63] The starting point for understanding this transformation is the brilliant study by Yeh Wen-hsin, *The Alienated Academy: Culture and Politics in Republican China, 1919-1937* (Cambridge, Mass., 1990). Also useful are Georges-Marie Schmutz, *La sociologie de la Chine: Matériaux pour une histoire 1748-1989* (Berne, 1993), and, E-tu Zen Sun, "The Growth of the Academic Community 1912-1949," in John Fairbank, ed., *The Cambridge History of China* vol.XIII (Cambridge, 1986), pp.361-420.

[64] Around 1920, Ku began the process of editing and punctuating Ts'ui's writings, the final product appearing in 1936, under the title *Ts'ui Tung-pi i-shu* 崔東壁遺書 (Collected works of Ts'ui Shu). Ku was assisted by a number of eminent contemporaries, including William Hung (Hung Yeh 洪業 1893-1987), chief editor of the Harvard-Yenching Sinological Index Series [discussed below in the text]. The fact that Hung chose to make a separate index of Ts'ui's collected works has led Joshua Fogel to write, "Considering all the truly seminal works in Chinese culture that still have no indexes, this index for Ts'ui's works stands out remarkably." Quoted from his essay, "On the 'Rediscovery' of the Chinese Past: Ts'ui Shu and Related Cases," in Fogel and William Rowe, eds., *Perspectives on a Changing China* (Boulder, Colorado, 1979), p.296, footnote 4. Interestingly, in his introduction to the *Ts'ui Tung-pi...*, Ku makes no mention that Ts'ui's works had already been published 32 years earlier in Japan.

[65] Ts'ui's challenge is part of the Old versus New Text Debate which rekindled in the 18th century, when a number of scholars examining the Classics com-

Another 'school' which became popular in the early part of this century was the 'K'ao-ku p'ai' 考古派 (archaeological school) which propagated that only those "facts" of early Chinese history which were supported by archaeological evidence were "real facts". Among the most important scholars of this persuasion (beside Lo Chen-yü and Wang Kuo-wei) were members of the Academia Sinica's Institute of History and Philology. In 1928 the then newly founded Institute sent the first organized expedition to the Anyang site and the archaeologists Li Chi 李濟 (1896-1979) and Tung Tso-pin 董作賓 (1895-1963) made important advances. Their excavations of the late Shang capital at Anyang between 1928 and 1937 became a training center for a whole generation of Chinese archaeologists.[66] Both "schools" gained great popularity, and many scholars published on topics related to the recent finds. Publications concerning the dating of a work or the compilation of particular books became common, and research on minute or peculiar subjects were fashionable.

The Academia Sinica was established by Ts'ai Yüan-p'ei 蔡元培 (1867-1940) in Nanking, and rapidly achieved the reputation of being the leading educational institution in China at that time.[67] Formerly the head of Peking University, Ts'ai had been educated in Leipzig where he studied philosophy, literature, psychology, and ethnology for three years. Ts'ai not only introduced Western ethnology and anthropology to China, but also created the Ethnology Institute as part of the Academia Sinica's Institute of Social Research.[68] The Academia's Language Section (*yü-yen tsu* 語言組),

---

piled from T'ang and Sung sources, alleged the Old Texts were a fabrication. See Elman, *Classicism, Politics, and Kinship*, pp.xxv-xxx.

[66] Much information on the entire development of archaeological study in China may be found in Gregory Eliyu Guldin, *The Saga of Anthropology in China: From Malinowski to Moscow to Mao* (Armonk, N.Y., 1994). For an earlier summary of the progress made in this subject, see L.C. Goodrich, "Archaeology in China: The First Decades," *Journal of Asian Studies*, 17 (1957):5-15. Goodrich brings up to date what Chinese, European, and American scholars had achieved in the decades from 1920, and also discusses the organization of archaeology in the PRC until 1957.

[67] On Ts'ai's life, see William J. Duiker, *Ts'ai Yüan-p'ei: Educator of Modern China* (University Park, 1977).

[68] Although Ts'ai may be considered the person who was most responsible for ethnology's introduction to China, he did not do much field work himself. However, he was instrumental in sending colleagues to research China's minorities, including the Miao, Li, She, Yao, and Yunnan Province's Lolo (with the support of the White Russian Sergei M. Shirokogoroff, a foreigner who was to have great influence on Chinese anthropology. An expert on the Tungus and the Manchus,

under the leadership of Chao Yuen-ren 趙元任, and other important scholars like Li Fang-kuei 李方桂, and Fu Ssu-nien 傅斯年 was
another key division of this institution; it pioneered the field of
Chinese linguistics, combining Western linguistic theory and
methodology with traditional Chinese language study.

About the same time, contemporary social and economic conditions spurred a number of thinkers toward Marxism and there
developed from the 20s onward, keen interest in the materialistic
interpretation of Chinese history according to Marx and Hegel.
Chinese intellectuals had first become acquainted with Marxist
historical theory as early as the 1910s through a mixed selection
of primary and secondary sources in Japanese, but their established grasp of historical materialism came only in the 1930s. Until then few authors distinguished the materialist conception from
other socio-economic approaches to history. The landmark
Marxist work that changed Chinese historical attitudes was Kuo
Mo-jo's 郭沫若 (1892-1978)   Chung-kuo ku-tai she-hui yen-chiu
中國古代社會研究 (Research in ancient Chinese society), published
in 1932. Kuo's portrayal of late Yin-early Chou society (circa
B.C.1000) as a slave society was very provocative, and following his
example, other writers tried to re-write Chinese history in a way
that wiped out the traditional approach of treatment, dynasty by
dynasty.[69]

Before publication of this work, Kuo has distinguished himself
as a short-story writer, poet, and essayist, and had spent much
time in Japan as a student (1914-1924) and as a political exile,
from 1928 onward. During his stay there, he made an extensive
study of bone and metal inscriptions as a fundamental and scholarly approach to the understanding of the nature of ancient society. Kuo's 1932 work launched a major controversy over slavery in
China, and the view he presented dominated historical interpretation in the PRC, at least until the 1980s.[70]

Shirokogoroff issued comprehensive studies of the peoples he studied, including
physical and linguistic materials along with ethnographic.) See Guldin, *The Saga
of Anthropology*, p.44ff.

[69] Although Japanese writers on China had already abandoned the dynastic
model some 30 years before, Chinese scholars were not comfortable without this
conceptualization until much later.

[70] On the early phase of Kuo's career, see David Roy, *Kuo Mo-jo: The Early
Years* (Cambridge, Mass., 1971). Kuo's work in the context of Marxism is dis-
cussed in Arif Dirlik, *Revolution and History: Origins of Marxist Historiography in
China, 1919-1937* (Berkeley, 1978), p.98.

Besides Kuo, a number of important writers emerged in the 1930s, which even today scholars look back and characterize as a 'golden age'. Among the most prominent were Ch'üan Han-sheng 全漢昇, and Yang Lien-sheng 楊聯陞, both writing on economic and social history. Also, another social historian, T'ao Hsi-sheng 陶希聖, who professed that China's historical experience had been conditioned by the operation of commercial capital, attracted attention. It was commercial capital, according to T'ao, that had been the dynamic element of the Chinese economy since the Warring States period, long before Western intrusion in China.[71] Specific dynastic studies became favored foci of interest. The work done by late Teng Kuang-ming 鄧廣銘 on the Sung, or Wu Han 吳晗, Wang Ch'ung-wu 王崇武, and Li Kuang-ming 黎光明 on the Ming became "classics" for all interested in the development of these periods. In Chinese philosophy, Feng Yu-lan 馮友蘭 became a highly respected authority;[72] Feng Yüan-chün 馮沅君 and Ch'ien Nan-yang 錢南揚 followed up the pioneering work of Wang Kuo-wei on the study of the Chinese theatre.

In the social sciences, foreign ideas heavily penetrated Chinese university departments. At Yenching University, a Christian mission institution, where half of the faculty were foreigners and where most of the Chinese teachers replicated the thinking and approach of their Western teachers, Western social scientific thinking set the mode of learning.[73] The well-known anthropologist Fei Hsiao-t'ung 費孝通 (b.1910), in his introduction to his classic study *Earthbound China*, written with Chang Chih-i 張之毅 (b.1911), recalled how studies at Yenching and Tsing Hua Universities were unashamedly American in focus: "We learned from books about Chicago gangs and Russian immigrants in America, but we knew very little or nothing about the Chinese gentry in the town and the peasants in the village, because they were not in the books."[74] Fei's teacher Wu Wen-tsao 吳文藻 (1902-1985) and his

[71] On T'ao, see Arif Dirlik, "T'ao Hsi-sheng: The Social Limits of Change," in Furth, *Limits*, pp.305-331.

[72] On Feng Yu-lan, see Michel Masson, *Philosophy and Tradition: The Interpretation of China's Philosophical Past: Fung Yu-lan (1939-49)* (Taipei, 1985).

[73] See Wong Siulun, *Sociology and Socialism in Contemporary China* (London, 1979), p.16 makes the point that much sociology was a missionary sociology. For further discussion, see A. King and Wang Tse-sang, "The Development and Death of Chinese Academic Sociology: A Chapter in the Sociology of Sociology," *Modern Asian Studies* 12 (1978):37-58.

[74] From Fei Hsiao-t'ung and Chang Chih-i, *Earthbound China: A Study of Rural Economy in Yunnan* (Chicago, 1945), p.viii. Fei's life is the subject of some inter-

friend and classmate P'an Kuang-tan 潘光旦 (1899-1967) who both
had studied anthropology and sociology with Franz Boas at Columbia University in New York were to have a great impact on a
whole generation of pre-1949 students of the social sciences. Contacts made abroad also gave rise to invitations to foreigners to
come lecture in China. In 1935 the well-known British advocate of
functionalism Archibald Reginald Radcliffe-Brown came to
Yenching University briefly as a visiting scholar. He advocated in-
tensive studies of Chinese villages for one to two years' duration.[75]

Chinese intellectuals of the 1930s no longer had to disguise
their innovations in the rhetoric of past scholarship, nor make
constant reference to nationalism and revolution. This was a time
when several Chinese universities witnessed the development of
distinguished history and literary schools. In her stimulating study
of Republican period institutions of higher learning, the modern
scholar Yeh Wen-hsin posits that there was "a certain hierarchy of
quality and prestige that divided national from regional and regional from purely provincial institutions."[76] Peking University,
the former Ch'ing imperial academy, became a bastion of philological scholarship. Missionary colleges competed with state sponsored universities in order to attract prestigious faculty members.
When Yenching University won over such important scholars as
Ku Chieh-kang and Jung Keng 容庚, an expert on early Chinese
bronzes, and calligraphy, who succeeded another brilliant Chinese sinologist, Ch'en Yüan 陳垣 as director of the Harvard-
Yenching Institute (see below), to the faculty, its status as a school
of higher learning changed.[77] Among the most eminent Chinese
scholars who either attended or taught at Yenching, one can mention Ch'ien Mu 錢穆, Chou Tso-jen 周作人, Wen I-to 聞一多, Chang
Erh-t'ien 張爾田, Fang Chao-ying 房兆楹, Cheng Te-k'un 鄭德坤,
Ch'ü T'ung-tsu 瞿同祖, Liu Tzu-chien 劉子建 (James T.C. Liu), and

---

esting biographical studies. See David Arkush, *Fei Xiaotong and Sociology in Revolutionary China* (Cambridge, Mass., 1981). Compare essays in James P. McGough,
ed., *Fei Hsiao-t'ung: The Dilemma of a Chinese Intellectual* (White Plains, N.Y., 1979).

[75] The outcome of this pronouncement may be seen in the classic studies of
Fei Hsiao-t'ung, *Peasant Life in China* (London, 1939) or Chen Ta, *Emigrant Communities in South China* (London, 1939). For further elaboration on the brillance
of these early studies and others, see Schmutz, *La sociologie de la Chine,* especially
Chapters IX and X.

[76] Yeh, *Alienated Academy,* p.4.

[77] On the history of Yenching University, see Philip West, *Yenching University
and Sino-Western Relations, 1916-1952* (Cambridge, Mass., 1976).

Yü Ying-shih 余英時. Another major change that occurred in the 1930s concerns the written work of these great scholars, which came more and more to be published in academic and specialized periodicals instead of the more general political or intellectual journals.[78]

Finally, one should add that a certain achievement in Chinese sinology of the 1930s concerned the production of indexes, and other reference works, such as dictionaries, chronological tables, maps, charts, and library catalogues, for academic research. And among the most significant of these references was the Harvard-Yenching Sinological Index Series (HYSIS), under the directorship of William Hung.[79] As a young lecturer at Harvard in 1932, Hung proposed to his superiors that the newly established Harvard-Yenching Institute (created in 1928 as a joint project of Harvard University in Cambridge, Massachusetts and Yenching University in Peking, where Hung also held a professorship), finance a series to compile systematic indices to all the Chinese Classics and make them accessible to modern scholars.[80] The result was an extremely useful tool.[81] One might argue that even though nowadays much of the indexing of Chinese texts has been relegated to computer technology, the HYSIS remains a highly valuable asset: it is not just a set of indices, but also, in many instances, authorative texts, meticulously edited and punctuated, with all variant readings listed.[82] Another classic reference tool that first emerged in this period was S.Y. Teng and Knight Biggerstaff's *An Annotated Bibliography of Selected Chinese Reference Works*, first published in Peking in 1936 as a monograph in the *Yenching Journal of Chinese Studies*, and then reissued in 1950 by

---

[78] Some titles of the many journals reflecting this development include: *Yü-kung* 禹貢 (Chinese Historical Geography); *Shih-huo* 食貨 (Journal of Economic History); or *Kuo-hsüeh chi-k'an* 國學季刊 (Journal of Sinological Studies).

[79] For Hung's life history, see his autobiographical account, as told to Susan Egan, *A Latterday Confucian: Reminiscences of William Hung (1893-1980)* (Cambridge, Mass., 1987).

[80] The story of the creation of the Harvard-Yenching relationship is outlined in West, *ibid.*, pp.187-194. West stresses the religious element in the tie. Yenching University was supported by the Christian Life Fellowship whose members dominated the trusteeship, even into the 1960s. See also, Egan, *Latterday Confucian*, pp.111-117, for a somewhat more personal account of its creation.

[81] For a complete list of the titles, see the Appendix of this work.

[82] As Egan reminds the readership in her book, p.143: "Many of the prefaces are major pieces of research that give a modern evaluation of the nature of the work and discuss the history of its transmission and the merits of the various editions."

Harvard University Press. Although it has its shortcomings, it remains a useful reference tool.[83]

Harvard University's involvement here is an important reminder that the United States too became an academic community for the study of China. Until the 1930s, American scholarship on China was a limited affair—there was no major China or Japan center in any American university, in contrast to European institutions of higher learning at this time.[84] And where some teaching on China was done, it was usually conducted by a European who resided in America. The Germans Paul Carus and Bernard Laufer, both at the University of Chicago, Frederic Hirth at Columbia University, the Englishman John Fryer at Berkeley are obvious examples of this trend. And not least, one has to mention the eminent French sinologist Paul Pelliot (1878-1945), who lectured at Harvard 1928-29, but declined the offer to become the director of the newly established Harvard-Yenching Institute at Harvard.

The man who did accept this post, however, was another eminent European scholar, the naturalized French citizen, Serge Elisséeff (1899-1972), originally born in Russia, and trained as a Japanologist. He was the first Westerner to graduate from Tokyo Imperial University, where he was also educated in Classical Chinese studies. At Harvard, Elisséeff helped to establish the first department of Far Eastern Languages of its kind in the United States, expanded the Harvard-Yenching Library (under the leadership of the late Alfred Kai-ming Ch'iu), now one of the greatest East Asian collections in the world, and aided in the foundation in 1936 of the *Harvard Journal of Asiatic Studies*, still America's leading sinological journal. He remained director until 1957.[85] Not surprisingly, Elisséeff as a teacher stressed the 'sinological approach'

---

[83] This work has gone through three editions, 1950, 1969, and lastly, 1971. See the excellent critique of the third edition by Sören Edgren in *Acta Orientalia*, 34 (1972):213-219.

[84] For a survey of early American sinology, see Laurence G. Thompson, "American Sinology, 1830-1920: A Bibliographical Survey," *Tsing-hua Journal of Chinese Studies* (new series) 2.2 (1961):244-285. Thompson maintains that what American sinology did exist was heavily dominated by the missionary enterprise, and what was written about China, originated out of "spare time research". For further information on the lack of Chinese studies in America at this time, see Robert A. McCaughey, *International Studies and Academic Enterprise* (New York, 1984), especially, pp.82-83.

[85] He was succeeded by Edwin O. Reischauer, an eminent American Japanologist, who had once been a student of Elisséeff's. Reischauer's first major

to China, i.e. heavy emphasis on the techniques of philology and
the use of classical Chinese.[86]

Harvard also pioneered another kind of Chinese studies, i.e.
the study of 'China within a discipline'. For this achievement, one
must look at the life history of the most eminent American China
scholar of this century, John King Fairbank (1907-1991). However,
to gain some idea of what the study of China at Harvard was like
before Fairbank "changed things", one might refer to the comments of the late Theodore White, Fairbank's first student and
lifelong friend. According to White, Harvard's approach to the
study of Chinese civilization before Fairbank came along was a
"form of comic opera": in order to study Chinese, one first had to
qualify in French, on the grounds that Oriental Studies was a
branch of French culture.[87]

All joking aside, it was still the case directly before World War II
that a "Paris-based type of sinology" continued to dominate learning about China, even outside France.[88] At that time, French
sinology was ruled by a "trinity": Paul Pelliot, Henry Maspero, and
Marcel Granet (1884-1940). Pelliot established himself as a certain kind of scholar which to this day evokes the expression
"Pelliotism", referring to his footnotes, in the aggregate, for any
work he authored, comprised many more words than the text. His
reputation lay in a sound knowledge of bibliographical problems
and a display of an incredible breath of reading in primary and
secondary sources. His knowledge of Chinese, and many other
languages, especially those of Central Asia, enabled him to write
in detail about a myriad of complex problems, and to correct the

---

book, *Ennin's Diary: The Record of a Pilgrimage to China in Search of the Law* (completed as a Ph.D. thesis in 1939, and published in 1955), remains a testimony of
what good sinological scholarship a committed student of Japanese was expected
to demonstrate.

[86] According to William Hung (see Egan, *A Latterday Confucian*, p.202),
Elisséef was something of a (benign) dictator. "Steeped in old-world etiquette",
he would send his secretary around in the summer to see that faculty members
did not take their jackets off.

[87] Quoted in Paul Evans, *John Fairbank and the American Understanding of Modern China* (New York, 1988), p.58.

[88] Perhaps, the outstanding exception to this generalization is Max Weber,
the German sociologist who applied the 'Protestant Ethic' analogy to China to try
to understand the development of capitalism (and its non-existence) in China.
"Paris-based type of sinology" also dominated the pages of Europe's leading
sinological journal, *T'oung Pao*, founded in 1890, a joint Dutch-French publication.

errors of others in the many, many lengthy reviews and articles that he published.

Maspero was an historian of China with a masterful grasp over all aspects of its ancient civilization; he saw linguistic history, textual criticism, art, mythology, epigraphy, and the history of science all contributing factors to Chinese development. Maspero's expertise extended over a variety of disciplines: archaeology, philosophy, Taoism, Buddhism, popular religion, and economic history, for all of which he was able to synthesize into brilliant exposes on Chinese civilization.[89]

Granet, perhaps less well-known that the other two scholars, was an expert of Chinese religion. He applied Durkheimian sociology in the analysis of ancient Chinese society, and focused upon the family and ritual as central to its development. His methodology employed textual and linguistic documentation of the texts, about which he postulated the "ancient popular religion lying behind the official religion for which the texts officially speak."[90] What also made his work unique was his use of the ethnographic element (he spent time both in China and Indo-China): the observation of 'modern folkways' in the reconstruction of ancient beliefs. True to the Paris tradition, all of these sinological giants put heavy emphasis on translation in their teaching and their research.

To return to Fairbank's role in the development of a different type of approach to the study of China, one must also take into consideration the activities of others who also saw deficiencies in American education on China in the pre-World War II era. Doubts about the wider prospects of sinological methodology were shared by leading educational administrators. Already in 1928 Mortimer Graves of the American Council of Learned Societies (ACLS) organized the first 'Committee on the Promotion of Chinese Studies', chaired by Arthur W. Hummel of the Library of Congress, the leading depository in the United States for Chinese

---

[89] For a tribute to Maspero's achievements in each of these fields, see the series of essays written in his honour, *Hommage à Henri Maspero 1883-1945* (Paris, 1984). Maspero's *La Chine antique*, first published in 1927, with a posthumous second edition issued in 1955, remains so readable that an English translation of this second edition was published as recently as 1979.

[90] Quoted in Maurice Freedman, "Introductory Essay," in Marcel Granet, *The Religion of the Chinese People* (New York, 1975) [translation of *La Religion des Chinois* (Paris, 1922)], p.14.

(and Japanese) books.[91] In 1937, Graves wrote: "As I see it, we have in the study of China, Japan, India, the USSR, and the Arabic world to create a new (American) attitude, and probably new techniques; we cannot borrow either from academic learning of the 19th century...For in dealing with these newer civilizations we are not dealing with dead ones, but on the contrary with civilizations that are very much alive...we have to *participate*, and that means to know what the Orientals are doing and try to do it with them."[92]

Fairbank's own education on China gave him plenty of experience "to participate" in what was going on in China. His graduate education as an Oxford Rhodes scholar sent him to China in the early 30s where he combined language study with doctoral thesis research on 19th century Chinese foreign relations. With his degree completed, Fairbank returned to Harvard in 1936 as an instructor in the history department which he then described as "western-oriented and parochial". What Fairbank envisioned was a curriculum where the study of modern and contemporary China was considered a serious topic.[93]

America's entry into the Pacific War speeded up revisions of American educational curricula that Graves and others like Fairbank were proposing. The transition from sinological philological and literary study to a broader-based "area study" was a direct result of the tremendous changes that World War II stimulated. 'Area Studies,' as they developed from that time involved holistic approaches to the cultures of major world civilizations, with the systematic employment of one or more standard academic disciplines.[94] Generally speaking, 'area studies' committed a student to engage in learning a foreign language, say Chinese or Arabic, while focusing on the history, anthropology, or sociology, i.e. through the methodology of a specific discipline, of the region where the language was spoken.

---

[91] On Hummel's life and achievements, see his obituary (with a list of his publications), in the *Journal of Asian Studies*, 35.2 (1976):265-276. On the history of the Library of Congress' Chinese collection, the largest compilation of its kind in the Western world, see Shu Chao-hu, *The Development of the Chinese Collection in the Library of Congress* (Boulder, Colo., 1979).

[92] From Evans, *John Fairbank...*, p.59. Fairbank's own personal recollections about his life and work may be read in his fascinating autobiography, *Chinabound: A Fifty-Year Memoir* (New York, 1982).

[93] Evans, *ibid.*, p.57.

[94] For a general evaluation of the success/failure of these programs, see Robert A. McCaughey, "The Current State of International Studies in American Universities," *Journal of Higher Education*, 51 (1980):381-399.

In the case of Fairbank and Harvard, what this meant was a total new program for the study of China. Although sinology and the study of Far Eastern languages continued to be part of the Harvard curriculum, Fairbank added 'Modern China' studies, the investigation of contemporary politics and institutions, economic history, and the social life of Asia. From 1946 to 1949, Fairbank directed the 'Regional Studies Program on China and Peripheral Areas,' which offered an M.A. degree, requiring two years of language instruction, a detailed research project, and seminar work in the social sciences. Fairbank invited guest lecturers such as Talcott Parsons to teach on social relations, and Edward Mason on economic matters.[95] The results were overwhelming: by 1965, 220 graduates had passed through the program among whom were some of the most prominent figures in the China studies field, including Benjamin Schwartz, Joseph Levenson, and Rhoads Murphey.[96] At the same time Fairbank continued to teach his well-known Ch'ing documents course, from which an important compilation first appeared in published form in 1952.[97] This course was designed to instruct beginning graduate students in the most rapid way to gain mastery over archival materials. No one could accuse Fairbank of neglecting the importance of learning classical Chinese for the study of China; what he achieved, unlike his more sinological tradition oriented colleagues, was an effective means to combine language study with history. As he noted: "for historians the problem is to use the language rather than be used by it."[98]

By the 1960s not everyone at Harvard was satisfied that Fairbank had succeeded in removing the exclusivity of Chinese studies from the Harvard-Yenching Institute and the Department of Far Eastern languages. Even though the majority of graduates and Ph.D. candidates at Harvard chose as their 'discipline' history, a subject considered well within the boundaries of sinological schol-

---

[95] For an interesting account of these early seminars, see reports by Robert Scalipino, David Nivison, and Marius Jansen in Paul A. Cohen and Merle Goldman, comps., *Fairbank Remembered* (Cambridge, Mass., 1992), pp.71-79.

[96] From Evans, *John Fairbank...*, pp.192-193. The M.A. degree was preparation for a Ph.D. degree that was to be awarded in a discipline, such as history or economics.

[97] That compilation was entitled *Ch'ing Documents: An Introductory Syllabus* (Cambridge, Mass., 1952; third revised edition, 1970).

[98] Evans, *John Fairbank...*, pp.61-62. Later, under the auspices of the National Defense Education Act, students were encouraged to get 'on the spot' language training in Taiwan at American sponsored training centers.

arship, voices of discontent were sounded. This disapproval was not only heard at Harvard, but within other universities where the acceptance and popularity of 'area studies' had grown over the post-War decades.[99] In response, the prestigious Association for Asian Studies (originally founded in 1941 as the Far Eastern Association but later renamed in recognition for its scholastic interests in South and Southeast Asia) in 1964 sponsored a symposium 'On Chinese Studies and the Disciplines', organized by the anthropologist G.W. Skinner, in which a number of leading China scholars, including Joseph Levenson, Mary Wright, Maurice Freedman, Frederick Mote, Rhoads Murphey, and Benjamin Schwartz all exchanged views.[100]

Looking back at the issues as they were discussed in this period may lead one to postulate that there was a real dichotomy between the modern China experts and the sinological 'diehard' specialists (many of whom were located in departments of Oriental languages).[101] This is somewhat of an exaggeration, and what is curious, is that a penetrating, critical, evaluation of Fairbank and his followers did not originate out of this dualistic opposition. What did emerge, however, was strong lamentation about the state of contemporary Chinese studies in the United States.

According to John Lindbeck's survey of this speciality, published in 1971, there was too little understanding of post-1949

---

[99] For specific attacks on Fairbank, see Evans, *ibid.*, pp.202-206. By that time, Columbia University, the University of Michigan, Stanford, the University of Washington, and the University of California at Berkeley, had developed into major China centers offering area studies programs.

[100] The written versions of the presented papers were published in the *Journal of Asian Studies*, 23 (1964):505-538. Compare further comments by Denis Twitchett, "Comments on the 'Chinese studies and the Disciplines' Symposium: A Lone Cheer for Sinology," *Journal of Asian Studies*, 24 (1964):109-112.

[101] On the other hand, the study of Chinese literature, and in particular, modern literature did find itself in a dichotomy. See comments in *Modern China* 19.1 (1993):3-101, an entire issue devoted to understanding the progress of the study of modern Chinese literature in the United States, with some reference to Europe. The first eminent work on the study of communist fiction that was written in the Western world was C.T. Hsia's *A History of Modern Chinese Fiction* (New Haven, 1971). For a contemporary view of Chinese communist literature, written in the 1960s, see the collection of articles published in *The China Quarterly* 13 (1963), which was based on a conference on that theme held in August, 1962 at Ditchley Park, England. For understanding many of the issues involved in studying premodern Chinese literature in the post-war decades, refer to the collection of interesting essays, William Nienhauser et. al., *The Indiana Companion to Traditional Chinese Literature* (Bloomington, 1986).

China. Lindbeck reproached the American scholarly community for:

> the superficial and abstract quality of much research. Less than full interpretive use is made of available data. Virtually no American scholars who are not of Chinese origin are bilingual; not more than two or three can write a scholarly article in Chinese for a Chinese publication...[102]

Lindbeck's regrets may also be measured in financial terms. He calculated that between 1959, the year in which the ACLS and the Social Science Research Council set up the Joint Committee on Contemporary China, and 1970 more than some $41 million had been spent for the promotion of China area studies in American institutions of higher education, and more than half of it for contemporary China studies.[103] The money was allocated to make up for the lack of scholarly analysis of the post-1949 China that characterized the 1950s (despite Fairbank's efforts). Even later work of the 1960s seemed inadequate. Then scholarship focused upon Chinese totalitarianism, the mechanics of political control over China's economy and society, and the purposes to which these mechanisms were put.[104]

The transition from this period of what may be seen as a time, when a high level of generality passed for most analysis on China to one of greater discretion, was rapid. In contrast to this earlier work, the research of the 1970s was directed toward the concept of *disaggregation*: the effort to obtain a better understanding of the whole through a greater appreciation of its parts. 'Case studies' (of socio-economic policy, on specific cities and provinces, some on individual leaders, others on specific periods in contemporary Chinese history, and still others on particular sections of society and their relationship to the State) were common, and as the Cultural Revolution unfolded, scholars tried to discover some of the informal mechanisms by which decisions were made by China's political leadership.[105]

---

[102] John M. Lindbeck, *Understanding China: An Assessment of American Scholarly Resources* (New York, 1971), p.97.

[103] *Ibid.*, p.79. This amount does not include the funds spent by public and private institutions of higher education to support contemporary China studies.

[104] See Harry Harding, "The Evolution of American Scholarship on Contemporary China," in David Shambaugh, ed., *American Studies of Contemporary China* (Armonk, N.Y., 1993), pp.14-40.

[105] *Ibid.* Works which trace the evolution of the totalitarian paradigm of the 1950s to a 'modernization-convergence-pluralism' approach in the 1970s, include

Contemporary Chinese studies achieved a certain respectability by the 1970s, and it was about this time that Fairbank himself retired from his productive teaching career, only to devote even more time to publishing and writing. His work was one of the central foci of interest in a revealing book authored by the Fairbank-trained scholar Paul Cohen. *Discovering History in China*, published in 1984, is an "insider's discussion" of all the leading conceptual approaches to the study of China that had informed American scholarship in the post-War decades. In Cohen's opinion, "the supreme problem for American students of Chinese history" had been 'ethnocentric distortion'. Cohen reviews how Fairbank, and others, had educated streams of students in at least one of three paradigms, depending on the time of writing: 'impact-response', 'tradition-modernity', both popular in the 1950s and early 1960s, and 'imperialism', particularly fashionable during the time of America's involvement in the Vietnam War.[106] Cohen concludes his work by tracing the efforts of an increasing number of American scholars to move beyond Western-centric paradigms toward what he calls a "China-centered approach", whereby the reconstruction of the Chinese past is conceived on the basis of how the Chinese themselves experienced and wrote about it.

Cohen's stimulating work coincides with broader critiques that have been made about the motivation of scholars studying the cultures of the non-Western world.[107] Among the most censorious is

---

Andrew Walder, *Communist Neo-Traditionalism: Work and Authority in Chinese Industry* (Berkeley, 1986); Vivienne Shue, *The Reach of the State* (Stanford, 1988); and Victor Nee and David Stark, "Toward an Institutional Analysis of State Socialism," in Nee and Stark, eds., *Remaking the Economic Institutions of Socialism: China and Eastern Europe* (Stanford, 1989), pp.1-31. There have been other typologies made to characterize American research on China. See Tai-chün Kuo and Ramon H. Myers, *Understanding Communist China: Communist China Studies in the United States and the Republic of China 1949-1978* (Stanford, 1986).

[106] The problem with the 'impact-response' framework lies in its assumption that 'China responded to the West's impact', and that much that had happened in China would not have happened without the West making an impact [note the title of Fairbank's 1954 work, *China's Response to the West*]. Cohen's criticism of the tradition-modernity paradigm concerns the simplistic division between the 'ideal types',i.e. 'tradition' (the old days) and 'modernity' (an assumption based on a universal historical process). For this approach, Cohen is particularly critical of Fairbank's student, Joseph Levenson who later came to write a number of very influential books on the role of Confucianism in Chinese intellectual life. Cohen questions the usefulness of assigning Western-Chinese conflicts under the rubric 'imperialism' given the multi-faceted varied character of all the events and trends occurring in the late 19th and early 20th centuries. Cohen does not see 'imperialism' as a useful analytical tool.

[107] Cohen's work was not the only critique among China scholars either. See

that by Edward Said, a professor of comparative literature at Columbia University. He argued in his book *Orientalism* (1978) that the study of the cultures of the Middle East and Asia by Western scholars was motivated by a desire to enforce the political, economic, and cultural dominance of the West. What he calls 'Orientalism' was a mode of discourse, "an enormously systematic discipline through which Western culture was able to create an image of the Orient for its own purposes".[108] Not everyone would agree with Said's somewhat polemical view and, as Benjamin Schwartz noted in a lecture "Area Studies as a Critical Discipline" before the Association for Asian Studies in 1980, the motivation of this approach "was to bring the experience of the entire human race to bear on our common concerns."[109]

It is difficult to challenge this incentive from either a moral or political perspective, and if a cursory glance at any list of books about China published in the United States during the last 40 years or so is any indication, then the approach was indeed successful. What Fairbank and other great teachers in major American China centers did in the 50 years following World War II was nothing short of making a revolution out of the concept 'Chinese studies'; it is now certainly a major subject of academic interest in the United States.[110]

Ramon H. Myers and Thomas A. Metzger, "Sinological Shadows: The State of Modern China Studies in the United States," *Australian Journal of Chinese Affairs* (1980), 4:1-34.

[108] Both Said and Cohen were members of a Leiden University symposium on Orientalism, held in April 1992 under the auspices of the University's Center for Non-Western Studies. At that meeting no dissenting voice over Said was expressed, but that does not mean that Said's definition of Orientalism is standard. Others have criticized the concept 'Orientalism' but in another context. For example, the late Albert Hourani referred to Orientalism as "the elaboration of techniques for identifying, editing, and interpreting written texts, and the transmission of them from one generation to another, by a chain...of teachers and students." From his book, *Islam in European Thought* (Cambridge, 1992), p.1. Here, 'Orientalism' is viewed as a problem for education. There is another expression of Orientalism that needs further study, especially as more researchers visit China to make social scientific studies. The determined search for some 'authentic' China, by definition different from the official portrayal, risks the imposition by the foreign observer of his/her own wishes on the "evidence" collected, and the very process of data gathering. For further comments about problems of sinology and Chinese studies in instruction, see my article, "JESHO and East Asia: Some Remarks on the Evolution of a Field of Study," *Journal of the Economic and Social History of the Orient*, 36 (1993):183-191.

[109] Quoted from Benjamin I. Schwartz, "Presidential Address: Area Studies as a Critical Discipline," *Journal of Asian Studies*, 40 (1980), p.25.

[110] In contrast, the study of China in European countries since the War has

Finally, something must be said about post-War developments in Japanese sinology. As the structure of the pre-War academic world was destroyed with all governmental and semi-governmental research institutions except universities dissolved, Japanese sinologists again looked toward new ways of viewing China. This re-evaluation was also tainted by a certain sense of guilt arising from the knowledge that pre-War sinologists had supported Japanese military aggression, and displayed a deep contempt for China and its people. The reappraisal of scholarly analysis of Chinese civilization developed out of the chaotic social and economic conditions of the immediate post-War years. On the one hand, the dynamism of the young PRC government helped rekindle the appreciation of Marxist theories, once fashionable in Japan during the 20s and 30s in many disciplines (but not Chinese studies), now into some sinological circles. On the other hand, the concept of "modernization" (*kindaikaron* 近代化論), popularized through the writings in Japanese by the then U.S. Ambassador Edwin Reischauer (on leave from his duties at Harvard), and other American academics, cast post-Meiji Japan's success with political modernization in a strong contrast with China's "failure" to come to terms with the 20th century.[111]

In broadest terms, the Japanese Marxist view, which came to be known as the 'Tokyo school',[112] posited that the origins of Chinese feudal society could be traced to the late T'ang-early Sung period, when the older, aristocratic dominated society and

---

not experienced the same dynamic thrust (Compare Balazs' comment cited earlier in the text, and the reference in footnote #36). As Fairbank himself remarked during a trip to Europe in 1972, whatever "remaining remnants of the great sinological tradition" or "flashes of research brilliance" evident, there was still too much of the "almost feudal" structure of the system which placed the control of research in so few hands. Discussed in Evans, *John Fairbank...*, p.306. Unfortunately, Fairbank's observations still hold true, even nowadays, for many European academic communities where China study is offered.

[111] The role of the 'modernization' concept in post-War Japan is still open to debate as Sheldon Garon points out in a recent article, "Rethinking Modernization and Modernity in Japanese History: A Focus on State-Society Relations," *Journal of Asian Studies*, 53.2 (1994):346-366.

[112] The expression 'Tokyo school' now refers to those scholars often based at Tokyo University who subscribed to a Marxist vision of history in the post-War era, but there is a definite intellectual genealogy between the earlier 'Tokyo school' of Shiratori Kurakichi and his protege Tsuda Sôkichi 津田左右吉 (1853-1961) and later pro-Marxist historians. See Tanaka, *Japan's Orient*, pp.234-237. For a Chinese view of post-War Japanese studies of Chinese history, see Kao Ming-shih 高明士, *Chan-hou Jih-pen ti Chung-kuo shih yen-chiu* 戰後日本的中國史研究 (Taipei, 1982).

economy broke down. A 'feudal society' developed slowly, reaching a major transition stage in the late Ming and early Ch'ing. A key factor in this Marxist conception was the changing status relationship between landlord and tenants. 'Tokyo' scholars claimed that the weakness of central rule in the late T'ang and Five Dynasties period, when local military and civilian officials seized much land for themselves to form large estates, led to severe legal restrictions upon the personal liberty of tenant farmers in the 10th and 11th centuries. Landless peasants, impoverished tenants, and "half-freed" slaves tilled these estates under conditions of hereditary bondage to the land and in servitude to their masters.[113]

Thus for Japanese Marxist historians, the period from about A.D. 1000 saw the transition of Chinese society from the stage of 'slavery' to that of 'feudalism' or 'medieval serfdom'. Moreover, they saw these estates as the whole foundation of the official class. Sutô Yoshiyuki 周藤吉之 (1907-1981) in a study of the connections between high office and land-holding showed clearly that the great estate was most highly developed in precisely those regions, i.e. the modern provinces of Kiangsu, Anhui, Chekiang, and later Fukien, from which came the vast majority of chin-shih 進士 candidates and high officials.[114]

The 'Tokyo' Marxists and others shunned Naitô Konan's periodization, and in particular, attacked Naitô's idea that China became "modern" in the Sung, for if China had indeed become "modern" way back in the Sung and continued through to this century, then the events of the 19th and 20th centuries had no special significance. Not everyone in the Japanese scholarly world agreed with the attack on Naitô, but it would take some time before other theoretical approaches gained an audience. In the meantime, Naitô's intellectual heir at Kyoto University, Miyazaki Ichisada 宮崎市定 (1901–), and others like Saeki Tomi 佐伯富 (1910–) defended Naitô's position by expanding upon his theory.[115] They argued that changes in land tenure in the Sung were accompanied by, and stimulated by other developments,

---

[113] This view was elaborated most thoroughly by Niida Noboru in his *Chûgoku hôseishi kenkyû: dorei nôdo hô kazoku sonaraku hô* 中国法制史研究：奴隷農奴法・家族村落法 (Tokyo, 1962).

[114] Sutô, *Chûgoku tochi seidoshi kenkyû* 中国土地制度史研究 (Tokyo, 1954).

[115] Miyazaki's most notable work is *Ajia shi kenkyû* アジア史研究 (Kyoto, 1957; 4 volumes), which is a collection of 64 reprinted articles, written between his graduation from Kyoto University in 1923 and 1956. These articles deal in the main with Chinese history, despite the title.

such as the spread of the market into the countryside and the increasing commercialization of agricultural production. Miyazaki's 1952 critique of Sutô's and Niida's interpretation of Sung tenancy set the tone for several decades of debate between 'Tokyo' and 'Kyoto' scholars.[116] Throughout the 50s and 60s the opposing claims of these schools were documented in countless learned journal articles with the result that the regional approach whereby scholars analyzed local evidence from a particular place and then projected conclusions as symptomatic for the entire empire became a standard practice.[117]

In more recent years the disputes of these schools have been resolved through even more detailed studies of regions, but restricted to particular time era. Many Japanese scholars have concentrated on developing another important concept, i.e. *kyôdôtai* 共同体 ("community"), as a device to explain the social cohesion, or "communitarian bonds" between literati-aristocrats and peasant-commoners. Tanigawa Michio 谷川道雄, a Kyoto-based scholar, has pioneered efforts to trace Chinese social structure from the Han through the early T'ang, a critical time for the development of 'slavery', and argued that *kyôdôtai* factor worked against "those elements of social life which seemed to transcend class distinctions."[118] Ironically, Tanigawa's work draws upon Naitô's identification of local society as the highest level of any meaning for understanding the mechanics of how China operated in historical times.

This discussion was not meant to be a comprehensive review of all the many individual contributions in the history of sinology, or Chinese studies during the last two centuries. Its purpose was rather to trace a number of general characteristics and themes—and also some obvious limitations—in an attempt to set the scene for what bibliographical scholarship on China has emerged in this century, and to a certain extent, before.

In some respects it is possible to see the 19th century as a formative period. For one thing, there is a great deal of 'continu-

---

[116] Miyazaki's critique appeared in his article, "Sôdai igo no tochi shoyû keitai" 宋代以後の土地所有形体 *Tôyôshi kenkyû* 東洋史研究, 12.2 (1952):97-130.

[117] This scholarship is well-analyzed by Joseph P. McDermott, "Charting Blank Spaces and Disputed Regions: The Problem of Sung Land Tenure," *Journal of Asian Studies*, 44.1 (1984):13-41.

[118] Tanigawa Michio, *Medieval Chinese Society and the 'Local Community'*, trans. by Joshua Fogel (Berkeley, 1985).

ity' both within and connected to the various sinological academic approaches in Europe, Japan, China, and the United States over the last two centuries. The 'commentarial tradition' with its stress on translation and exegesis was the conventional mode to approach learning about China, and to a certain extent, this technique continues to dominate classrooms in many European universities today. Continuity can also be applied with regard to the Jesuit 17th century publications on every aspect of Chinese civilization from philosophy to geography that formed a firm basis from which academic study would later follow.

Yet, Jesuit writings on China also contributed a certain misrepresentation, which we are also still rectifying nowadays, concerning the importance of Confucianism to the development of Chinese civilization. It is to the great credit of the first French professors of Chinese that they took such a positive interest in promoting the importance of Buddhism, Taoism, and local religion, as well as vernacular literature, outside the Confucian 'mainstream', as central to understanding China. Unfortunately, in many other 19th century European academic communities diplomatic, commercial, and colonial interests dictated how China was to be studied. There, a conventional curriculum subscribed to a 'changeless China' perpetuated a program based on the study of the Classics, and eventually, religion, philosophy, and literature, all well within the 'central tradition' of Confucianism. Another factor of consistency which bounds almost all European institutions of higher learning, even in France until quite recently, is that students had little to no chance to learn to speak Chinese.

Although a thorough understanding of Japan's intellectual role in the development of sinological study in China has yet to be achieved (one suspects that emotional factors are still very much relevant), it is clear that early 20th century Chinese scholars, especially those involved in newly found archaeological and material resources, were inspired by contact between the two countries. Changes in the approach to Chinese history seems to have been a crucial catalyst in the passage of sinology to its modern form in China. As the Japanese incorporated concepts of Western historiography into their own educational program, Chinese students and scholars absorbed these new techniques in learning and writing about their past. Historical studies were transformed from simply an examination of chronicles and epigraphy into a sophisticated, analytical science, based on specialised insight and creative interpretation. Chinese studies in China became 'exclusive',

as evidenced by the great number of learned journals and research institutes that appear from the 20s and 30s onward.

Chinese studies in the quarter century following 1945 rapidly
changed. In the West, Europe's dominant stance in this field lost
its footing as America maximized upon its world leadership position. While Fairbank as an individual, and Harvard University as
an institution, played pivotal roles in this transformation, one
must also reckon that this one scholar and this one university
were only part of a larger enterprise that defied earlier perim-
eters. Japan's experience with China, prior, during, and after the
War was a crucial element in the making of that undertaking. The
Japanese language skills that many of Fairbank's graduate students possessed, an inheritance from their days at wartime army
language training, allowed them access to all the published Japanese secondary materials on China, and not least, the bibliographical riches of Japanese libraries and helpful bibliographical
tools (indexes, dictionaries, maps, etc.). Although Japanese post-
War scholars became caught in intense ideological disputes, their
controversies spurred further research and their efforts are an explanation for the in-depth nature of their close analyses of Chinese local society during the imperial era.

By the end of the 1950s what lagged behind historical and literary studies of China in the United States was an examination of
contemporary China. However, this "gap" was filled quickly and
professionally within a short space of time, and no doubt due to
changing political circumstances within East Asia itself. Within
some 20 years the importance of contemporary China studies
both within the academic community and outside it became a
fact.

Finally, a word should be said scholarship on China in present-
day East Asia. Both the Republic of China and the People's Republic of China since 1949 have contributed greatly toward this
academic enterprise. Although in certain periods, such as that of
the Cultural Revolution, publications were not as forthcoming,
the fact remains that during most of the last 50 years, there has
been a scientific and systematic effort to preserve, catalogue, classify, and make available for the general public in both regimes the
rich sinological treasures that at one time were available only to a
very select audience. The efforts of scholars from both these regions provide the great bulk of the references listed in this guide,
and therefore stand testimony to their valuable contributions.

Classification Systems and the Chinese Library

The classification system of libraries containing works in Chinese vary considerably. The librarians of Chinese collections must reconcile the kinds of Chinese written materials and the traditions of Chinese bibliography with the needs and habits of the modern student/researcher. Given the fact that the printed book in China has a history of more than two thousand years, the problem of establishing a classification system for imperial collections arose rather early on in Chinese history.[119]

The oldest known classification system originated in the Early Han dynasty when efforts were made to rebuild the imperial library. The infamous book burning by Ch'in Shih Huang-ti had destroyed the archival treasures of China's antiquity, and the early Han emperors initiated a systematic collection of books throughout the empire. The first library catalogue of the imperial collection was introduced by the Han scholar Liu Hsiang, and completed by his son Liu Hsin. Liu Hsin's *ch'i-lüeh* 七略 (seven epitomes) was composed of seven main classes:

(1) General Summary
(2) Classics
(3) Philosophy
(4) Poetry
(5) Military Science
(6) Science and Occultism
(7) Medicine

The 'General Summary' outlined the information in the other six divisions, which contained thirty-eight subdivisions. Under 'Philosophy' various leading philosophers, Taoists, Astrologists, Legalists, Logicians, Mohists, Diplomatists, Syncretists, Agriculturalists, and Novelists, as well as Confucianists were included. Under the heading 'Medicine', the subjects of 'Sexology' and 'Longevity' were listed. The universality of these selections is an indication of the state of scholarship during the time of the *ch'i-lüeh*'s composition. The original catalogue by the Lius had been lost but it is generally assumed that when Pan Ku 班固 (A.D. 32-92) compiled the *Han-shu* 漢書, he incorporated the booklist of the Lius and their book classification scheme in the *I-wen-chih* 藝文志 (Essay on

---

[119] A valuable introduction to this subject may be found in Tsuen-hsuin Tsien, "A History of Bibliographic Classification in China," *The Library Quarterly*, 22.4 (1952):307-324.

Literature), chapter 30 of the *Han-shu*. Pan Ku followed Liu Hsin's system, except he preceded each main division with a general summary, instead of putting the whole summary at the beginning of the complete work. Pan Ku's work was the first dynastic history, and the first history to include a record of bibliography, and in this way, a precedent was established for all dynastic histories.

The *ch'i-lüeh* schema remained the standard classification until Hsün Hsü 荀勖 (231-289), curator of the Chin imperial library, of the Chin dynasty compiled the *Chin Chung-ching* 晉中經 (Important Books of the Chin Inner Palace), in which he used four main divisions, according to the first cyclical numbers: *chia* 甲 (classics, lexicography, philology), *i* 乙 (philosophy, military science, mathematics and division); *ping* 丙 (history, anecdotes, state documents, and miscellaneous writings; *ting* 丁 (poetry, eulogies). Each of these main divisions was then sub-divided. The original *Chin Chung-ching* also got lost, but by the Sui dynasty, preference for a four-fold classification system was apparent. The book catalogue of the Sui Dynasty, the *Sui-shu ching-chi chih* 隋書經籍志 (which is extant) divides works into four classes: *ching* 經 (classics); *shih* 史 (history); *tzu* 子 (philosophers); and *chi* 集 (belles lettres). This format, which was known as *ssu-pu* 四部 (four departments) or *ssu-k'u* 四庫 (four treasuries, i.e. of the imperial library), endured during the following dynastic periods, was incorporated into the bibliographical sections of five dynastic histories,[120] and formed the basis of the greatest bibliographical project ever committed in Chinese history, the collection and classification of all books extant in the empire, for preservation in the *Ssu-k'u ch'üan-shu* 四庫全書 (The Treasures of the Imperial Library) (hereafter, SKCS) during the reign of Emperor Ch'ien-lung (1736-1796), completed in 1782.

The project began with a famous edict in 1772 in which the Emperor declared his interest in preserving literature and asked that a search be made for works of real value that might supplement the then existing collection in the Imperial Library.[121] One

---

[120] The dynastic histories referred to here were the new and old histories of the T'ang, the Sung, the Ming, and the draft history of the Ch'ing, the exception being those histories of the barbarian states. In the essays, the main divisions were arranged in the order of *ching-shih-tzu-chi*.

[121] See the superb study of the Four Treasuries project by R.Kent Guy, *The Emperor's Four Treasuries: Scholars and the State in the Late Ch'ien-lung Era* (Cambridge, Mass., 1987).

should, however, not underestimate the complexity of the Emperor's motives here. No doubt 'sponsorship of learning', 'self-glorification', and the desire to outdo his grandfather's, the K'ang-hsi Emperor, impressive achievement, the 10,000 *chüan* 卷 encyclopedia, *Ku-chin t'u-shu chi-ch'eng* 古今圖書集成 (Grand Encyclopedia of Ancient and Modern Knowledge) were all germane here. In any event, the result of his proclamation was the retrieval of 385 works from the *Yung-le ta-tien* 永樂大典, a compilation of books incorporated into the early Ming imperial library in 1407, the reprinting by moveable type of some 140 rare works, the creation of seven imperial libraries (including libraries in Chekiang and Kiangsu provinces which had contributed the largest number of books to the project, and one in the Hanlin Academy) in each of which were deposited hand-written copies of 3461 works deemed most important, the compilation of a bibliography containing 10,254 titles with description and notes far more detailed than anything seen before, and finally, the destruction of 2320 works, which made it the greatest disaster in the history of Chinese letters. Very soon after the project began, it became clear that the Emperor utilized the enterprise to censor works critical of the Manchus, and official Neo-Confucian ideology.[122]

The scale of the SKCS undertaking demanded a huge work force and adequate space. The project was coordinated in Peking, from where booklists were sent out to the provinces. Local officials either induced or intimidated private collectors into loaning their books for copying. The books were then collected and assembled in the Hanlin Academy within the Forbidden City where they were collated and emended. During the enterprise's ten-year period a total of 360 Hanlin scholars and other scholar-officials critically read and edited, while 3,826 expert scholar-officials transcribed the manuscript in uniform format. Eventually a special bureau within the imperial palace grounds, the Wen-yüan-ko 文淵閣 was built to house and manage the project.

At least four of the seven copies were destroyed during the 19th

---

[122] According to a contemporary Korean emissary Pak Chi-won, who visited China in 1780, the SKCS project was another form of scholarly persecution. He stated that "instead of burying the scholars alive as the Ch'in dynasty did, the [Ch'ing] court buries them in labors of collation; and instead of burning the books as the Ch'in did, it scatters them in the Bureau of Assembled Pearls [a court publishing office]." from Min Ku-ti, *National Polity and Local Power: The Transformation of Late Imperial China* (ed. by Philip Kuhn and Timothy Brook) (Cambridge, Mass., 1989), p.14.

century. The copy in the Summer Palace was destroyed in 1861 during the British incursion there, while those in the lower Yangtze region were lost as a result of devastation there during the Taiping Rebellion. One manuscript may be found in the National Library (Beijing), another in the National Palace Museum Library (Taipei), and possibly a third in the Wen-su-ko 文溯閣, the old Manchu Imperial Library in present day Shenyang. In 1984, the National Palace Museum in Taipei reproduced a uniform printing in photo-facsimile of the entire SKCS using its Wen-yüan-ko set. A number of East Asian libraries in the United States and Europe have acquired sets.

The bibliography to the SKCS compiled under the directorship of Chi Yün 紀昀 (1724-1805), the *Ssu-k'u ch'üan-shu tsung-mu* 四庫全書總目 (Annotated Catalogue of the Complete Collection of the Four Treasuries), dated 1782, is still the most important and useful annotated bibliography of traditional Chinese books. It includes the 3461 works incorporated in the SKCS and the 6793 less important works which existed at the time. Extensive descriptions are given for each work, including publishing details and critical notes.

The four bibliographical divisions of the SKCS were sub-divided further, to total 44 categories of works. The four-fold divisions reflected the preoccupations and priorities of the Confucian scholar, whose primary concern was classical and historical studies, and their relevance to politics and society. Thus, publications relating to science and technology came to be classified under philosophy. While the books classified under 'history' were sub-divided according to form, those works under 'philosophy' were listed according to subject. The 44 subdivisions were as follows:

Classics: (1) Changes; (2) Documents; (3) Poetry; (4) Rituals; (5) Spring and Autumn Annals; (6) Filial Piety; (7) Commentaries on the Classics; (8) The Four Books; (9) Music; (10) Dictionaries.

History: (1) Dynastic Histories; (2) Annals; (3) Topical Records; (4) Unofficial Histories; (5) Miscellaneous Histories; (6) Official Documents (Edicts, Petitions, etc.); (7) Biographies; (8) Historical Excerpts; (9) Contemporary Records; (10) Chronography, Books on the Seasons, etc.; (11) Geography; (12) Official Registers; (13) Institutions; (14) Bibliographies and Epigraphy; (15) Historical Criticism.

Philosophy: (1) Writers on Confucianism; (2) Military Strategy; (3) Legalists; (4) Agriculturalists; (5) Writers on Medicine; (6) Astronomy and Mathematics; (7) Calculating Arts; (8) Arts; (9)

Repertories of Science; (10) Miscellaneous Writers; (11) Encyclopedias; (12) Essays and Tales; (13) Buddhism; (14) Taoism.

Literature: (1) Elegies of Ch'u; (2) Individual Collections; (3)
General Anthologies; (4) Literary Criticism; (5) Songs and
Drama.

For each of the four main categories, first were listed the *chu-lu*
著錄, those works copied into the SKCS, and then following, the
ts'un-mu 存目, those works not included in the SKCS, but still wor-
thy of having a place in the bibliography. The latter notices tend
to be shorter than the former. Each of the notices consists of the
following information: the title of the book and number of *chüan*,
the source of the book (the imperial library, the *Yung-le ta-tien* re-
covery project, provincial officials or private collectors). The dynasty and author began the critique which includes a brief life-his-
tory of the author on his first appearance in the bibliography, a
review of the authority of the book, its value, and perhaps, why it
was considered worthwhile to be included.

Chi Yün and his colleagues must have considered their own
complete catalogue, consisting of 200 *chüan* (modern Taipei version counting ten volumes) too cumbersome for everyday use, because at the same time they produced an abridged version, i.e. the
Ssu-k'u ch'üan-shu chien-ming mu-lu 四庫全書簡明目錄 (Simplified Annotated Catalogue of the Imperial Library), also completed in
1782, but in twenty *chüan* (modern edition being two volumes).[123]
The seven original sets of the SKCS, at the time of the compilation, were bound up in distinctive coloring: green for Classics, red
for history, blue for philosophy, grey for literature, and yellow for
the catalogue.

Although there were no further radical developments in bibliographical classification during the 19th century, a number of
scholars busied themselves with the improvement of cataloguing.
Scholars followed the great model and manual for starting a library, the *Shu-mu ta-wen* 書目答問 (Answers to Inquiries on Chinese Bibliography) written in 1875 by Chang Chih-tung 張之洞
(1837-1909) and Miao Ch'üan-sun 繆荃孫 (1844-1919), founder of
the Kiangsu Sinological Library at Nanking, and one-time Director of the Imperial Library in Peking.

---

[123] It should be noted that the *Ssu-k'u ch'üan-shu chien-ming mu-lu* contains
only very brief versions of the annotations of only the 3461 works copied into the
SKCS. For indices relevant to this volume and other books connected to the
SKCS, see Chapter VIII '*Ts'ung-shu* and Miscellaneous Collectanea'.

At the beginning of this century when modern books in both Chinese and Western languages, in great numbers, were introduced, attempts were made to create additional categories alongside the four-fold system to accommodate the new subjects, or to adopt Western classification schemes, in particular the Dewey Decimal System, to traditional material, first instituted in 1907 in the Library of the North China Branch of the Royal Asiatic Society in Shanghai.

But the modern system that gained the most widespread favor both inside and outside of China (and which is still used in many PRC libraries) is the one devised by Alfred K'ai-ming Ch'iu (1898-1973), one time Custodian of the Chinese and Japanese collection at Harvard University Library.[124] The scheme had its beginnings in 1926 and was developed from cataloguing the collection of Yenching University in Peking and the Chinese-Japanese Collection of Harvard University, and came to be known as the Harvard-Yenching system. Ch'iu attempted to compromise between the cataloguing divisions Chang Chih-tung and Miao Ch'üan-sun had advocated and certain aspects of the modern systems introduced into China by then. In its final form, it was published with the text in both Chinese and English, by the American Council of Learned Societies in 1929, entitled *A Classification Scheme for Chinese and Japanese Books* (xxiv + 361 pp.)

The main divisions are based upon the four-fold scheme of Hsün Hsü (of the Chin dynasty, see infra), plus additional divisions for books on new topics. With the exception of the Classics division which uses three Arabic digits, the other divisions use four. The main classes are:

100-999	Chinese Classics
1000-1999	Philosophy and Religion
2000-3999	Historical Sciences
4000-4999	Social Sciences
5000-5999	Language and Literature
6000-6999	Fine and Recreative Arts
7000-7999	Natural Sciences
8000-8999	Agriculture and Technology
9000-9999	Generalia and Bibliography

The final result of the classification system also included Japa-

---

[124] See his delightful discussion on how he devised his cataloguing system, in A. K'ai-ming Ch'iu, "Reminiscences of a Librarian," *Harvard Journal of Asiatic Studies*, 25 (1964-65):7-115.

nese and Korean works.[125] The system was widely adopted by many East Asian library collections in America and Europe. It is not unusual in these institutions, as well as in the libraries of Taiwan and the PRC,[126] to separate Chinese works from those in European languages, and the reader/user of these libraries will invariably confront two completely different systems of classification.

Nowadays, libraries outside of China wanting to build up their collections to include PRC publications may be confronted with huge gaps in their holdings. From late 1949 to the late 1970s, it was not possible to purchase books directly from the PRC. "Local publications" were issued in limited print runs, and even when cleared for export, they often were difficult to obtain. Moreover, many publications had a *nei-pu* 內部 (internal classification), which made them totally unavailable. It should be understood that *nei-pu* is a generic term used for publications not meant for public distribution, but not all *nei-pu* publications are 'secret' or 'classified' in the Western security sense. Many scholarly publications, translations, and even reference works fall under the *nei-pu* classification.[127]

Since the 1980s, East Asian libraries all over the world have engaged in automatizing their collections. The two most common processing systems are the Research Librairies Information Network (RLIN) and the Online Computer Library Center (OCLC). In these databases books published in the 1980s account for 53 percent and 55 percent respectively of the RLIN Chinese, Japanese, and Korean languages (CJK) materials and OCLC (CJK) totals.[128] These two systems cover only current publications; they do

---

[125] Further divisions within these main listings may be found in the Appendix of this volume.

[126] For an excellent overview of the development of major library collections in the PRC since 1949, see Huang Jungui, "Bibliographic Control in the People's Republic of China" (trans. by Charles Aylmer), *Bulletin of the European Association of Sinological Librarians* 4(1990):1-15.

[127] For a bibliography of these internally distributed works, see Li P'ao-kuang 李泡光, *Ch'üan-kuo nei-pu fa-hsing t'u-shu tsung-mu (1949-1986)* 全國內部發行圖書總目 (Beijing, 1988). This bibliography covers 17,754 first editions and 547 revised editions, arranged according to subject, with information about the author, year, and place of publication, followed by an index. For a review of this publication, see Flemming Christiansen, "The *Neibu* Bibliography: A Review Article," *CCP Research Newsletter* 4 (1989):13-19.

[128] From Eugene W. Wu, "Library Resources for Contemporary China Studies," in David Shambaugh, ed., *American Studies of Contemporary China* (Armonk, N.Y., 1993), pp.264-280. Statistics may be found on p.274.

not extend to retrospective publications. In other words, the vast majority of East Asian libraries in America and Europe remain outside automated control, and their users must consult manual catalogues.[129] Thus, knowledge of libary classification schema is essential for gaining access to research materials. Many Western-language publications are now available on "CD-ROMs" (Compact Disk-Read-Only-Memory), especially reference works and indexes. But to find these works, one still must check a library catalogue, which will classify its contents according to the Harvard-Yenching or Library of Congress schema.

Finally, a word should be said about libraries in China. Until this century, there were no public libraries in China. The imperial libraries were depositories for the use of the imperial family, high officials, and noted scholars. Presumably, the three libraries built specially in Chiangnan to house SKCS editions were open to the scholar-officialdom in that region, but it was probably more common for private individuals to visit the libraries of well-known *shu-yüan* 書院 (academies) and those of private families, of which the most famous was the T'ien-i ko 天一閣 (Pavilion of Everything Limited under Heaven), located in Ningpo.[130]

In 18th century Hangchow, which was a favorite place of book collectors and scholar-printers, there grew an "interlibrary loan group" of seven libraries that lent books for private copy.[131] Another example of a private collection that became "public" was that of Chou Yung-nien 周永年 (1730-1791) whose personal library, the Chieh-shu yüan 藉書園 (Lending Library) attracted scholars from all over the empire. In the preface to the catalogue of this collection, Chou wrote an essay "Ju-tsang shuo" 儒藏說 (A Plea for Confucian Libraries) in which he argued for the establishment of public libraries on the basis of those collections in Taoist and Buddhist institutions. Like the *Tao-tsang* 道藏 and the *Shih-tsang* 釋藏 there should be, according to Chou, a Confucian

---

[129] Automation seems to be moving along far more rapidly in East Asia than elsewhere. For example, the National Library of China in Beijing has allowed the operators of OCLC to catalogue its 130,000 title collection of books published during the Republican Period (1911-49) into its database. For information on automated indexes, see Chapter IX 'Indexes and Concordances'.

[130] For information about this famous library, see Ulrich Stackmann, *Die Geschichte der Chinesischen Bibliothek Tian Yi Ge vom 16.Jahrhundert bis in die Gegenwart* (Stuttgart, 1990).

[131] Nancy Lee Swann, "Seven Intimate Library Owners," *Harvard Journal of Asiatic Studies*, 1 (1936):363-390; and Benjamin Elman, *From Philosophy to Philology*, pp.143-150.

catalogue printed for easy access to the scholarly community. In the main, however, the 500 some private collections that were in existence during the Ch'ing were not libraries in the modern sense of the term; they were really, as their Chinese name indicates, *ts'ang-shu-lou* 藏書樓 (store houses of books).[132]

Over half these libraries were located within the provinces of Chekiang and Kiangsu.[133] Many of these collections were destroyed in the havoc of the Taiping Rebellion, but four were to remain particularly famous, and two of these four were to form the basis of some the greatest public collections in the world. They were:

T'ieh-ch'in t'ung-chien lou 鐵琴銅劍樓

Hai-yüan ko 海源閣

Pa ch'ien chüan lou 八千卷樓

This collection became the foundation of the National Central Sinological Library in Nanking during the Republican period, which later became the National Central Library in Taiwan.

Pi Sung lou 百百宋樓

In 1907 this collection was sold to Japan's Iwasaki Yanosuke 岩崎弥之助 (1851-1908); it forms the basis of the present-day Seikadô Bunko 静嘉堂文庫 in Tokyo, one of the greatest Chinese libraries in the world. The original owner of this collection was Lu Hsin-yüan 陸心源 (1834-1894), a well-known Chinese diplomat and bibliophile.[134]

---

[132] For a compact 'who's who' of book-collecting and printing in imperial times (about 3400 individuals), one should turn to Liang Chan 梁戰 and Kuo Ch'ün-i 郭羣一, eds., *Li-tai ts'ang-shu-chia tz'u-tien* 歷代藏書家辭典 (Xi'an, 1991). Arranged according to number of strokes for an individual's surname, each entry generally includes the person's dates, place of origin, other names, and major activities.

[133] Although the most famous bookshops were located in Peking, in the Liu-li-ch'ang 琉璃廠 district, still nowadays a center for book purchase. There was also a "standard" guide for book collectors, *Ts'ang-shu chi-yao* (Bookman's Manual) by the Ch'ing scholar Sun Ts'ung-t'ien. This work has been translated by Achilles Fang, "Bookman's Manual," *Harvard Journal of Asiatic Studies*, 14 (1951):215-260. Compare Achilles Fang's other relevant translation, "Bookman's Decalogue," *Harvard Journal of Asiatic Studies*, 13 (1950):132-173. For a list and translation of terms used in the printing and binding of Chinese books, see "Appendix II" in Chih-ber Kwei, *Bibliographical and Administrative Problems Arising from the Incorporation of Chinese Books in American Libraries* (Peiping, 1931), pp.128-136.

[134] Iwasaki Yanosuke was one of the few Meiji entrepreneurs from a samurai background who had successfully adjusted to the new age. With his elder brother Yatarô 弥太郎 (1835-1885), he had founded Mitsubishi, one of Japan's important *zaibatsu* (financial clique) combines. The Lu collection comprised 4000 individual titles in some 50,000 volumes. Its Sung editions amounted to 127 titles, a

Despite the prolific destruction of private collections of libraries and academies during the last 50 years of Ch'ing rule, one factor did save some valuable works. Chinese book collectors, in particular those with wealth and status, enjoyed reprinting the best works of their collections. Also, many library owners had the habit of compiling catalogues, some of which are listed in Teng and Biggerstaff, *An Annotated Bibliography*..., under the section 'Annotated Catalogues of Rare Editions'. Thus, even in spite of the many disasters of the 19th century, private libraries in China would remain an important social institution, attracting reverence and prestige for their owners. It would take the catastrophes of the Sino-Japanese War and the Boxer Rebellion before leading educators advocated a system of public libraries and museums.[135]

A Note on the Library of Congress Classification System

Many major libraries in the United States, while maintaining the Harvard-Yenching classification system for their East Asian collections, will also utilize the Library of Congress (LC) classification system for Western language books about China, and in some instances, for East Asian language books as well. In this case, a Chinese or Japanese book may have two call numbers. In broadest outlines, the LC system contains the following divisions:

A   General Works
B   Philosophy, Religion
C-G   History, Geography. Anthropology
H-L   Social Sciences. Political Science. Education
M-N   Music. Fine Arts
P   Language. Literature
Q   Science
R-V   Medicine. Agriculture. Technology
Z   Bibliography and Library Science

---

total surpassed only by the National Libraries in Beijing and Taipei. The Seikadô Bunko became the main data base for the encyclopedic dictionary *Daikanwa jiten* 大漢和辞典, compiled by Morohashi Tetsuji 諸橋轍次, [see Chapter VI 'Dictionaries'], the Seikadô's chief librarian, though part-time, for 35 years until his retirement in 1958. For further information, see Yu-ying Brown, "The Origins and Characteristics of Chinese Collections in Japan," *Journal of Oriental Studies*, 31.1 (1983):19-31. This article gives much background info on leading sinological libraries in Japan.

[135] See Roger Pélissier, *Les Bibliothèques en Chine première moitié du xx siècle* (Paris, 1971) for an excellent analysis of all aspects of Chinese library development in China until 1949.

There are further subdivisions within this system, so that a classification number may contain two letters from the alphabet. Many books about Chinese history begin with DS..., while those concerning Chinese literature start with PL.... By using this system over time, one should acquire passive knowledge of which call numbers denote a particular subject.

The Library of Congress catalogues its East Asian materials into the RLIN database and makes available a tape to OCLC for the latter's use.

CHAPTER TWO

BIBLIOGRAPHIES

INTRODUCTION

Western Language Bibliographies

By definition, a bibliography is a systematic study of books/journal articles relating to a particular subject. In the field of Chinese studies, there are a large number of bibliographies covering many different subjects, history, literature, linguistics, art, music, women, violence, etc. to name but a few of the subjects that have published bibliographies.

It is possible to divide existing bibliographies on China, into two basic groups: (1) 'general' and (2) 'specialized' bibliographies. In the first category, belong both cumulative and annual bibliographies. Cumulative bibliographies include references to works that cover all publications concerning China over a long period of time. For example, Henri Cordier's *Bibliotheca sinica* is a classified bibliography of books and articles, in European languages, about China from the late 16th century to about 1924. Annual bibliographies give classified listings of books or journal articles on every aspect of Chinese civilization, that have been published in a *given year*.

'Specialized bibliographies' list publications either according to subject, or (occasionally), according to time period. There are specific bibliographies for subjects as particular as the 1911 Revolution, to subjects as broad as Chinese society from 1644 to 1970. Even those specialized bibliographies that seem out of date, because they may be as old as 10 years, can be useful, since they give classified information for what was important up until that time. A student can expand his own bibliography of a given subject by building upon these bibliographies with up-dated information. From time to time, various newsletters or journals, such the *Journal of Asian Studies*, publish "State of the Field" essays that conclude with an extended bibliography of the most current references.

To use a bibliography properly, it is important to understand the difference between a primary and a secondary source. A primary source refers to information (written or not) which has *not* yet been utilized by a modern scholar for research purposes. The information may not have even been compiled for scholarly purposes. Examples of primary sources for the study of China include: autobiographies, diplomatic papers and archives, personal writings, poetry and novels, newspaper reports, bureaucratic papers such as "memorials", interviews, and translations of Chinese literary works. An example of a primary source for European observations of China is Marco Polo's description of China, published as *The Description of the World*. A secondary source, which also may or may not be in Chinese, focuses upon the work of others who have examined the primary sources. A book like Raymond Dawson's *The Chinese Chameleon*, which discusses European conceptions of Chinese civilization, is a secondary source for the study of Marco Polo and his observations on China.

Generally speaking, students should acquaint themselves with the principal secondary sources of a particular subject before embarking upon a major study of the primary material. In certain cases, the distinction between primary and secondary sources may seem blurred. A traditional Chinese historian who quoted whole documents verbatim will have composed a primary source, but later traditional historians who wrote about that first historian and his work will have written a secondary study. One reliable way to familiarize oneself with the difference between primary and secondary studies is to examine the bibliographies in modern studies of traditional subjects. In books published by Princeton University Press, for example, authors are asked to divide their references into primary and secondary sources.

Chinese Language Bibliographies

While bibliographies have existed in Chinese history at least since the Han dynasty (Pan Ku's *I-wen-chih* essay in the *Han-shu* may be considered a bibliography), it was only in the 18th century that annotated bibliographies and descriptive catalogues became quite common. Large-scale publishing and book collecting, encouraged by the spread of printing, gave access to scholars to more works than ever before in Chinese history. Scholars who engaged in *k'ao-cheng* scholarship produced numerous bibliographic guides as well as manuals on how to make a bibliography. For example, Chu I-tsun's 朱彝尊 (1629-1709) *Ching-i k'ao* 經義考 [Critique of Classical studies] was a descriptive bibliography of all commentar-

ies and other studies of the Classics written from the beginning of
the Han dynasty to 1700. Chang Hsüeh-ch'eng 章學誠 (1738-1801)
compiled in 1799 the *Chiao-ch'ou t'ung-i* 校讎通義 [General principles of bibliography] in which he discussed how to analyze, catalogue, and compare texts in order to determine authenticity, authorship, and completeness.[1] These are only a few of the countless number of such works produced at this time.[2]

Although a comprehensive study of Chinese bibliography in the
19th century and later has yet to be written, the beginning student
of sinology may receive some idea how its history developed by examining the titles and their author/compilers in the works listed
under 'Bibliographies', in Teng and Biggerstaff, *An Annotated Bibliography of Selected Chinese Reference Works.* Another useful indicator
about the history of Chinese bibliography is Yao Ming-ta's 姚名達
Chung-kuo mu-lu-hsüeh nien-piao 中國目錄學年表 (Changsha, 1940),
which is a chronological listing of Chinese bibliographies, with
reference to their historical context, from earliest times until
1936. Yao (1905-1942) had been a promising historian who had
published in 1938, the first truly comprehensive history of Chinese bibliography, entitled *Chung-kuo mu-lu-hsüeh shih* 中國目錄學史
(Shanghai, 1936; reprinted, 1957).[3]

It would be a mistake to conclude that in the Republican period
scholars ceased to employ the modes of empirical scholarship that
their 18th century predecessors had devised. Even Lu Hsün in-
dulged in *chi-i* 集遺 (collecting the lost), *chiao-k'an* 校刊 (proofread-
ing), and philology, the three major scholarly contributions of
Ch'ing learning. Academic classical scholarship continued
through the 1920s and 1930s, and formed an important part China's educational curriculum.[4] In the last 15 years or so, scholars in
the PRC have also begun to make general and specialized bibliographies of their intellectual heritage, and one may see from the

---

[1] See David Nivison, *The Life and Thought of Chang Hsüeh-ch'eng* (Stanford,
1966), especially 'Books on Books', pp.56-81.
[2] For a fuller explanation, see Elman, *From Philosophy to Philology.* Compare
Liang Ch'i-ch'ao, *Intellectual Trends in the Ch'ing Period.*
[3] The earliest published bibliography of Chinese bibliographies was the *Shu-
mu chü-yao* 書目舉要, compiled by Chou Chen-liang 周貞亮 and Li Chih-ting
李之鼎(Nan-ch'eng, 1920). For further information on the history of bibliographies of Chinese bibliographies, see Sören Edgren, "A Bibliography of Bibliographies of Chinese Bibliographies," in Joakim Enwall, ed., *Outstretched Leaves on his
Bamboo Staff: Studies in Honour of Göran Malmquist on his 70th Birthday* (Stockholm,
1994), pp.63-69.
[4] Yeh Wen-hsin, *The Alienated Academy.*

list of titles in this section, that these works include publications from as far back as the turn of the century.

Another kind of Chinese bibliographical reference may be seen in those works entitled *kung-chü-shu* 工具書 (reference works on reference works). These publications guide the user to specific bibliographies of reference works. James Cole's publication *Updating Wilkinson...*, pp.16-19, gives an annotated listing of some more recent outstanding examples of *kung-chü-shu* (usually found under the Harvard-Yenching classification number 9550). Another source for finding Chinese bibliographies are those publications containing *tz'u-tien* 辭典 in the title. These works may not always be dictionaries in the form of a lexicon (despite the title!) but reference guides for specific subjects. These "connoisseur's" dictionaries contain not only elaborate discussions on the etymology and historical background of particular terms and expressions, but also extensive references to primary and secondary documentation, and in that way may also be considered a form of bibliographical reference.

REFERENCES—BIBLIOGRAPHIES

General and Specialized Bibliographies in Western Languages
General Bibliographies 61
    Cumulative 61
    Annual 62

Specialized Bibliographies
    Composite Bibliographies 66
    Guides to History—General 67
    Guides to History—Specific by Period 67
    Some Important References for the 19th and 20th Cen-
        turies 70
    Classics, Philosophy, and Religion 72
    Language 75
    Literature 76
    Science and Technology 78
    Miscellaneous 79
    "State of the Field" Bibliographies 81

GENERAL BIBLIOGRAPHIES

Cumulative

Tsien Tsuen-hsuin, comp., *China: An Annotated Bibliography of Bibliographies* (Boston, 1978).

To date, the most comprehensive and complete listing of bibliographies about China; includes 2500 bibliographies, mainly in English, Chinese, and Japanese, with some in French, German, Russian, and other European languages; consists of separate works, bibliographies in periodicals and serials, bibliographic essays, surveys of literature on specific periods or fields, and comprehensive listings of bibliographies in monographs, published up to the end of 1977 with a few forthcoming in 1978.

Cordier, Henri, *Bibliotheca sinica: dictionnaire bibliographique des ouvrages relatifs à l'empire chinoise* [(second ed., rev. Paris, 1904-1908), 4 volumes; supplement, 1922-24, 1 vol.; reprints: Peiping, 1938; Taipei, 1966. 5 vols.].

A classified bibliography of 70,000 books, reprints, and articles in European languages from the late 16th century to about 1924. Most comprehensive and indispensable for Western students on all subjects relating to China. *Author Index to the Bibliotheca sinica of Henri Cordier* (New York, 1953) includes an English translation of the detailed table of contents; unfortunately this particular index is somewhat unreliable in parts.

Yüan Tung-li, *China in Western Literature: A Continuation of Cordier's Bibliotheca Sinica* (New Haven, 1958).

Covers 18,000 monographs in English, French, German, and Portuguese, from 1921 to 1957; classified under 21 subject headings and 7 geographical divisions. Periodical literature not included. Comprehensive coverage of Western writings on China published during the period. Appended is a list of serial publications on China. Contains author index.

Lust, John with Werner Eichhorn, *Index sinicus: A Catalogue of Articles Relating to China in Periodicals and Other Collective Publications, 1920-1955* (Cambridge, 1964).

Includes 19,734 articles, reviews, and obituary notices in Western languages, published in periodicals, memorial volumes, symposia and proceedings of congresses and conferences between 1920 and 1955. A continuation of Cordier's *Bibliotheca sinica* and a supplement to Yüan's *China in Western Literature*, upon which the classification is substantially based. Author and subject indices.

Unlike Yüan Tung-li's work, this bibliography also includes Russian entries.

Lust, John, *Western Books on China Published up to 1850 in the Library of the School of Oriental and African Studies, University of London: A Descriptive Catalogue* (London, 1987).

This is a very useful catalogue of Western language publications (including translations) arranged according to broad categories, e.g. geography, travels, history, economic affairs, etc.. There are two major indices, one for titles and the other for names. There is also a separate index of Chinese titles (characters only). This volume is an invaluable source for following publishing trends on China in Europe from medieval missions to great explorations.

Cumulative Bibliography of Asian Studies, 1941-70 (Boston, 1969-70). 14 volumes. Author bibliography, 1941-65, 4 v.; suppl., 1966-70, 3 v.; Subject bibliography, 1941-65, 4 v.; suppl., 1966-70, 3 vols.

Accumulated from the *Bibliography of Asian Studies* and its predecessors, it includes over 100,000 entries both by authors and by subjects in the volume for 1941-65. Supplemental volumes include almost 70,000 entries by authors and over 61,000 by subjects. Author bibliography is alphabetical by author or main entry, with multiple entries for joint authors. Subject bibliography is arranged by countries or geographical areas, which are further divided alphabetically by subjects. The most comprehensive bibliography of all publications on Asia in Western languages with more entries on China than on other countries.

Annual

Bibliography of Asian Studies (Ann Arbor, Mich., 1956... ≥).

Formerly known as *Bulletin of Far Eastern Bibliography*, edited by E.H. Pritchard, 1936-40 (mimeographed); continued in *Far*

Eastern Quarterly, 1941-46; issued as a separate volume, *Far Eastern Bibliography*, 1947-55 and as *Bibliography of Asian Studies* since 1956. Comprehensive listing of books and articles in Western languages concerning the countries of East, Southeast, and South Asia. Entries are collected from national and special bibliographies, in addition to some 700 periodicals devoted to Asian studies, and over 1500 other periodicals of a more general nature. Classification varies from issue to issue. Unfortunately, this is now issued some five to seven years after the year in review. Thus, coverage up to the second half of the 1980s is only now available.

Tôyôshi Kenkyû Bunken Ruimoku 東洋史研究文献類目 ("Annual bibliography of Oriental studies") (Kyoto, 1934...). Until 1964, entitled *Tôyôgaku Bunken Ruimoku* 東洋学研究文献類目.

Each issue includes three parts: (1) bibliography for works concerning *tôyôshi* (the history of East Asia which is here defined as Chinese, Islamic, Indian, and Central Asian but not Japanese!) in the Japanese, Chinese, and Korean languages; (2) a bibliography for publications in Western languages (including those in Russian); (3) author index, subdivided according to (a) Japanese authors—arranged in *kana* order; (b) Chinese authors—arranged by number of strokes in author's surname, followed by multi-authored/edited works; (c) Korean authors; (d) Western language authors—arranged alphabetically; (e) Russian authors. Entries are classified by broad subject, and further subdivided into more specialized subjects. Includes both books and journal articles. Noted for international coverage. What makes this such a valuable reference is that it also includes book reviewers, whose names are also listed in the author index.

Revue bibliographique de Sinologie (Paris, 1957-68; Paris, 1983... ≥).

This bibliography is more than a yearly listing of books and articles in Chinese, Japanese, and to a certain extent Western language publications. It also includes, per entry, a critical review, usually written in French, about the particular book or article. Listings include works about history, literature, linguistics, art and archaeology, religion, philosophy, and the history of science. However, major Western works are barely covered, and for some subjects, this bibliography is highly selective. One should not expect to find all that was published in a given year on a particular subject, e.g. landholding during the Sung dynasty. The value of this series is that it "introduces" the beginning student to the names of well-known scholars and publications in East Asia.

Bibliography of Chinese Studies (Hamburg, since 1983).
Annual bibliography which lists publications according to the selections found in the monthly bibliography of the Hamburg based journal, *China aktuell.* The listing includes selected articles in Chinese, English, and German arranged in broad categories. Includes info on Taiwan and Hong Kong, and has a separate author index. Although there are some references to history, the major emphasis in this publication is on contemporary affairs. Useful for keeping up with current trends in China's internal and financial affairs.

Current Contents of Foreign Periodicals in Chinese Studies—Wai-wen ch'i-k'an Han-hsüeh lun-p'ing hui-mu 外文期刊漢學論評彙目 (Taipei, 1984-)
Quarterly publication that lists articles in Western language and Chinese/Japanese journals. Includes book reviews. Arranged alphabetically by journal title.

Books and Articles on Oriental Subjects, Published in Japan (Tokyo, since 1954).
This annual publication which usually appears about one year after the cover date is a listing of all Japanese publications in fields including: history, philology, literature, philosophy, religion, art, archaeology, social sciences, and comprehends all the geographical regions of Asia and Africa. The entries, each of which has an English translation, are divided into two sections, books and articles. The works are listed in alphabetical order of the authors' names. There is a separate alphabetically ordered author index at the end of the volume. In later issues, the section on China is sub-divided into premodern history (until 1900), modern history, literature and philology, philosophy, thought, and religion, art and archaeology, and miscellaneous.

Current Contents of Academic Journals in Japan: The Humanities and Social Sciences (Tokyo, since 1974).

This work lists publications of Japanese journals and periodicals of a given year in English in an annual series. Although the coverage is international, one can see at a quick glance in sections such as 'History of Asia and Others' or 'Literature, Linguistics, Philology' what Japanese scholars have published in which journals about Chinese subjects. Divided according to subject, and listings in alphabetical order of author's name (with characters). Contains author index, and alphabetical list of journals (with characters).

Composite Bibliographies

Although all five of these bibliographies are 'out-dated', they still remain basic introductions to the field of Chinese studies. For a beginning student in sinology or modern Chinese studies, these selections give a broad overview of relevant scholarship for those topics.

Hucker, Charles O., *China: A Critical Bibliography* (Tucson, 1962).
     A well-selected, graded, and annotated list of 2,285 books and articles on traditional and modern China with a brief introduction to each of the seven sections; contains English materials since 1940, plus some in French and German.

Chang Chung-shu, *Premodern China: A Bibliographical Introduction* (Ann Arbor, 1974).
     In 3 parts: part I is an introduction to the field of sinology; part II lists major reference works in Western languages; part III is a bibliography arranged by topics and historical periods. Updates Hucker, but not so well annotated and organized. Author index.

Nathan, Andrew J., *Modern China, 1840-1972: An Introduction to Sources and Research Aids* (Ann Arbor, 1973).
     An introduction to research aids, library collections, and the major types of primary sources for the study of modern and contemporary China. Author and title indices.

Fairbank, John and K.C. Liu, *Modern China: A Bibliographical Guide to Chinese Works 1898-1937* (Cambridge, Mass., 1950; reprinted 1961).
     Although not comprehensive, it is still a valuable introduction to the major topics of the late Ch'ing and early Republic. Includes references to foreign affairs, economic data, social problems, intellectual, and literary history.

Berton, Peter and Eugene Wu, *Contemporary China: A Research Guide* (Stanford, 1967).
     An annotated analysis of primary and secondary sources in Chi-

nese, Japanese, and Western languages on the PRC. Gives much information on bibliographical sources, textbooks, and all primary sources. There are separate subject, author, and title indices.

Guides to History—General

Wilkinson, Endymion P., *The History of Imperial China: A Research Guide* (Cambridge, Mass., 1973).
A well-selected and critically annotated bibliographical guide of about 900 titles in Chinese, Japanese, and Western languages, covering general references, primary sources, and standard secondary works on traditional Chinese history. Author, title and subject indices. This has been "updated" by James Cole, *Updating Wilkinson: An Annotated Bibliography of Reference Works on Imperial China Published since 1973* (New York, 1991). Invaluable.

Leslie, Donald D., Colin Mackerras and Wang Gungwu, *Essays on the Sources for Chinese History* (Canberra, 1973).
Contains 26 bibliographical surveys of sources for the study of Chinese histories, universal histories, local gazetteers, unofficial regional records, genealogical registers, legal sources, archives on modern China, Chinese newspapers, sources on the KMT and the PRC, and sources on overseas Chinese, each with detailed footnotes and a select bibliography. With a glossary-index.

Guides to History—Specific by Period

The Cambridge History of China (Cambridge, 1978-).
This work is published in a series of volumes, starting from the Ch'in-Han period to the PRC, and edited by two leading China-scholars, Denis Twitchett and the late John Fairbank. To date, the following volumes have appeared;
vol. 1 : *The Ch'in and Han Empires* (1986)
       3 : *Sui and T'ang* (1979)
       7 : *Ming* Part I (1988)
       6 : *Alien Regimes and Border States, 710-1368* (1994)
      10 : *Late Ch'ing, 1800-1911*, Part 1 (1978)

11 : *Late Ch'ing, 1800-1911,* Part 2 (1980)
12 : *Republican China, 1912-1949,* Part 1 (1983)
13 : *Republican China, 1912-1949,* Part 2 (1986)
14 : *The People's Republic 1949-1979,* Part 1 *The Emergence of Revolutionary China, 1949-1965* (1987) For a broad overview of primary sources on the PRC, see the essay by Michael Oksenberg, "Politics Takes Command: An Essay on the Study of Post-1949 China", pp. 543-590.
15 : *The People's Republic 1949-1979,* Part 2 *Revolutions within the Chinese Revolution, 1966-1982* (1991)

Each of these volumes consists of a series of essays, written by different authors, on specific subjects, e.g., a reign period or an important event like the Taiping Rebellion. What makes the *Cambridge History* ... so valuable is that each volume (except Vol. 3 to date) contains a bibliographic essay discussing the most relevant primary and secondary literature. Each volume also contains detailed indices (with characters). Indispensable!

Loewe, Michael, ed., *Early Chinese Texts: A Bibliographical Guide* (Berkeley, 1993).
Gives descriptive notices on 64 literary works written or compiled before the end of the Han dynasty. Each of the entries, authored by different leading scholars, summarizes the contents, presents conclusions regarding authorship, authenticity, dating and textual history, and indicates outstanding problems that await solution, together with lists of commentaries, editions and translations. Invaluable.

Frankel, Hans H.C., *Catalogue of Translations from the Chinese Dynastic Histories for the Period 220-960* (Berkeley, 1957).
Covers 16 of the 24 standard dynastic histories from the Three Kingdoms to the Five Dynasties, arranged by period, with subject index and index of translations. More than a guide to translations, this work is also a bibliography to this period.

Hervouet, Yves, *Bibliographie des travaux en langues occidentales sur les Song parus de 1946 à 1965* (Bordeaux, 1969).
Annotated bibliography of about 500 books and articles in Western languages on the history of the Sung, with an appen-

dix of 100 Russian works published between 1945 and 1967; supplemented by Michael McGrath in *Sung Studies Newsletter* no. 3 (1971), 38-49; no. 13 (1977), 132-135; no. 15 (1979), 54-78; no. 19 (1987), 98-126; no.23 (1993), 167-172; and by, Robert Foster no. 22 (1990-92), 125-146; and Françoise Aubin and Thomas H. Hahn, "A Bibliography of European Non-English Works on Sung, Liao, Chin, Hsi-hsia, and Yüan", no. 21 (1989), 115-148. [Note: *Sung Studies Newsletter* was renamed *Bulletin of Sung and Yüan Studies*; and more recently, has been known as *Journal of Sung Yuan Studies*]

Hasegawa Yoshio, "Trends in Postwar Japanese Studies in Sung History: A Bibliographical Introduction." *Acta Asiatica* 50 (1986): 95-120.
  As the title suggests, a useful summary of major trends in Japanese about Sung history. Introduces the most important scholars and debates between them.

Hervouet, Yves and E. Balazs, *A Sung Bibliography* (Hong Kong, 1980).
  Brief synopses of primary sources with lists of editions and critical comments. Entries vary in depth. In English and French. Excellent indices.

Bol, Peter, *Research Tools for the Study of Sung History* (Binghampton, N.Y., 1990).
  This is a guide to bibliographies, indices and other research aids concerning all aspects of Sung history.

Kuhn, Dieter and Helga Stahl, *Annotated Bibliography to the Shike shiliao xinbian [New Edition of Historical Materials Carved on Stone]* (Heidelberg, 1991).
  A comprehensive annotated listing of stone inscriptions of various types (including land deeds) from the Sung, Liao, and Chin dynasties. Arranged alphabetically by title. Has author index.

Mori Masao, "A Survey of Ming Historical Studies in Japan: Past and Present." *Ming Studies* 27 (1989):67-83.

Franke, Wolfgang, *Introduction to the Sources of Ming History* (Kuala Lumpur, 1969).
  Lists more than 800 annotated titles of Ming materials, ar-

ranged under 9 sections, each preceded by an introduction. With title and author indices. A revised version of *Preliminary notes on the important Chinese literary sources for the history of the Ming dynasty (1368-1644)*, first published in 1948, with addenda and corrections in 1950.

Rowe, William, "Approaches to Modern Chinese Social History," in Oliver Zunz, ed., *Reliving the Past: The Worlds of Social History* (Chapel Hill, 1985), pp.236-96.
A very useful essay that introduces many of the issues that Chinese social historians write about. Contains an extensive bibliography.

Zurndorfer, Harriet, "A Guide to the 'New' Chinese History: Recent Publications concerning Chinese Social and Economic Development before 1800", *International Review of Social History* 33 (1988):148-201.
Summarizes publications between 1970 and 1987 on Chinese history from Sung to 1800. Includes a 16-page bibliography of Western language books and journal articles.

Some Important References for the 19th and 20th Centuries

Teng Ssu-yü, *Historiography of the Taiping Rebellion* (Cambridge, Mass., 1962).
Annotates Chinese, Japanese, Western-language, and Russian sources, as covered in Teng's *New Light on the History of the Taiping Rebellion* (Cambridge, Mass., 1950).

Teng Ssu-yü, *Protest and Crime in China: A Bibliography of Secret Associations, Popular Uprisings, Peasant Rebellions* (New York, 1981).
Contains entries on 4,000 articles, books, reviews, dissertations, local gazetteers, unpublished papers, and rare editions in Chinese, Japanese, English, French, German, Russian, Dutch, and Korean in collections in the U.S.A., PRC, Taiwan, Hong Kong, Japan, and Europe—cf. bibliographical notes in Harriet Zurndorfer, "Violence and Political Protest in Ming and Qing China—Review and Commentary on Recent Research," *International Review of Social History*, 28.3 (1983):304-319.

Hsieh, Winston, *Chinese Historiography on the Revolution of 1911: A Critical Survey and a Selected Bibliography* (Stanford, 1975).
> Provides a selective list of 368 entries, including books, collected works, pamphlets, and periodicals, published up to 1972, arranged alphabetically by author. Most of the works cited are available at the Hoover Institution or accessible outside of China.

Chan, Ming K., *Historiography of the Chinese Labour Movement, 1895-1949: A Critical Survey and Bibliography of Selected Source Materials at the Hoover Institution* (Stanford, 1981).

Feuerwerker, Albert and S. Cheng, *Chinese Communist Studies of Modern Chinese History* (Cambridge, Mass., 1961).

Chow Tse-tung, *Research Guide to the May 4th Movement: Intellectual Revolution in Modern China, 1915-1924* (Cambridge, Mass., 1963).
> A partially annotated list of 1,479 books, periodicals, and articles, organized into 3 parts: periodicals and newspapers, Chinese and Japanese books and articles, and Western-language materials. Index of periodical titles and glossary.

Skinner, G.W., *Modern Chinese Society 1644-1970: An Analytical Bibliography* (Stanford, 1973) volume I.
> This is the first of three volumes that lists according to Skinner's 'local systems' approach materials in English, Chinese, and Japanese respectively. There is an author, title, and subject index. Difficult to use, but one of the most important sources for local history.

Bauer, Wolfgang and Shen-chang Hwang, *German Impact on Modern Chinese Intellectual History* (Wiesbaden, 1982).
> An extensive bibliography of both Western (not only German) and Chinese language materials concerning intellectual exchange between China and the West. Includes material on philosophy, science, religion, literature, the arts, economy, education, and politics. Contains an index of German personal names and subjects. Indispensable for the study of Hegel and Marxism in China.

Alan Lawrence, *Mao Zedong: A Bibliography* (New York, 1991).
   This annotated bibliography of Western language works on
   Mao and his principal writings supersedes previous publications. This work is divided into 14 sections, including six
   separate sections for works according to the leader's life: early
   life to 1921, 1921 to 1935, 1935 to 1949, 1949 to 1959, 1960 to
   1969, 1970 to 1976. There are separate sections for "Mao the
   Poet" and "Historiography".

Classics, Philosophy and Religion

De Bary, Wm. Theodore and Amslie T. Embree (eds.), *A Guide to
Oriental Classics* (New York, 1964; revised eds. 1970, 1989).
   Includes bibliographies of important translations of Chinese
   Classics and great Chinese novels and poetry, and of secondary
   works, as well as a list of topics for discussion. Most of the bib-
   liographical entries include a brief but cogent evaluation.

Chan Wing-tsit, *An Outline and an Annotated Bibliography of Chinese
Philosophy* (New Haven, 1959; rev. ed. 1969).
   Arranged chronologically into the ancient, middle, modern,
   and contemporary periods, listing references in European languages on various philosophers and topics. Graded into essential, supplementary, or optional reading. Translations of Chinese texts are listed under names of translators in the outline,
   but under titles or names of authors in the bibliography. Well
   selected and organized as a syllabus.

Chan Wing-tsit and Charles Wei-hsun Fu, *Guide to Chinese Philosophy* (Boston, 1978).
   Supersedes 1969 work and includes studies divided according
   to subjects, including human nature, ethics, philosophy of religion, philosophical psychology, epistemology, metaphysics,
   philosophy of language, logic, social philosophy, philosophy of
   science.

Totok, Wilhelm, "Die Philosophie der Chinesen," in *Handbuch der
Geschichte der Philosophy*, Bd. 1 (Frankfort, 1964), pp. 50-67.
   Includes items which supplement Chan, especially those other
   than in English.

Kwee Swan-liat, "Chinese filosofie", *China Informatie* 2:2 (1968):8-15.

A survey of Western-language publications on Chinese philosophy. Also covers works on Taoism, Confucianism, Legalism, Mohism, Buddhism, Logic, etc.

Thompson, Lawrence G., *Chinese Religion in Western Languages: A Comprehensive and Classified Bibliography of Publications in English, French, and German through 1980* [(Tucson, 1985); updated as *Chinese Religion: Publications in Western Languages 1981-1990* (Ann Arbor, 1993)].

A systematic bibliography of studies on Chinese religion in Western languages, with an author index. This bibliography is divided into Buddhist and non-Buddhist literature. Both editions should also be used in consultation with *Publications on Religions in China, 1981-1989*, compiled by Alvin P. Cohen (Amherst, Mass., 1991).

Yu, David C., *Guide to Chinese Religion* (Boston, 1985).

This bibliography includes publications until 1977. Coverage extends to Confucianism and state religion. The majority of citations concern publications in English, but some literature in French and German is also given. Unlike Thompson's bibliography, the annotations are more extensive. Contains author and subject indices, updated as *Religion in Postwar China* (Westport, Conn., 1994).

Reynolds, Frank E. with John Holt and John Strong, *Guide to Buddhist Religion* (Boston, 1981).

Although this extremely useful annotated bibliography is not restricted to China, it provides much information on relevant Western language materials. Gives both general and specialized references to a wide variety of materials on the historical development of Buddhism, religious thought and texts, popular beliefs and literature, the arts, practices (including ritual), as well as social and economic aspects, and mythology. Has separate sections for dictionaries, bibliographies, and encyclopedias. Also contains author/title index and subject index. Indispensable for the beginning student.

Conze, Edward, *Buddhist Scriptures: A Bibliography* (New York, 1982; revised edition by Lewis Lancaster).

Yoo, Y., *Buddhism: A Subject Index to Periodical Articles in English, 1728-1921* (London, 1973).

Hôbôgirin: dictionnaire encyclopédique du bouddhisme d'après les sources chinoises et japonaises... (Tokyo, since 1929).

Pas, Julian F., *A Select Bibliography on Taoism* (Stonybrook, N.Y., 1988).
    An excellent annotated and catalogued list of works pertaining to all aspects of Taoism, including local cults.

Walf, Knut, *Westliche Taoismus-Bibliographie (WTB): Western Bibliography of Taoism* (Essen, 1986; rev. ed. 1989).
    Divided into five sections (translations of the *Tao-te-ching*; translations of *Chuang-tzu*; translations of other Taoist texts; secondary literature; bibliographies), this compact work is suitable for the very beginning student seeking info on historical translations, and the history of the study of Taoism in English, German, and French.

Boltz, Judith M., *A Survey of Taoist Literature: Tenth to Seventeenth Centuries* (Berkeley, 1987).
    A comprehensive and scholarly introduction to all aspects of the development of the Taoist Canon, including ritual, hagiography, and exegesis. Indispensable for the scholar of religion.

Seidel, Anna, "Chronicle of Taoist Studies in the West 1950-1990," *Cahiers d'Extrême-Asie* 5 (1989-90):223-347.
    Provides an excellent overview of the development of Taoist studies in the last 40 years, including a 40 page annotated bibliography, with recent indices and concordances, as well.

Israeli, Raphael, *Islam in China: A Critical Bibliography* (Westport, 1994).
    Annotates Sino-Islamic works in Western languages, from earliest times until 1992, with a separate appendix for specialized journals. Contains separate author, title, and subjext indexes.

Language

Lucas, A. *Linguistique chinoise: bibliographie, 1975-1982* (Paris, 1985).

A systematic bibliography in French. Discusses research published in Chinese, Japanese, and Western languages for the period 1975-1982. Contains an author index.

Yang, Paul Fu-mien, *Chinese Lexicology and Lexicography: A Selected and Classified Bibliography* (Hong Kong, 1985).

Discusses dictionaries as well as book reviews of them. Contains information up to and including 1982.

Yang, Paul Fu-mien, *Chinese Linguistics: A Selected and Classified Bibliography* (Hong Kong, 1974).

Discusses linguistics in general and earlier bibliographies. Systematically organized with articles and books in Chinese, Japanese, and Western languages according to subject. The Chinese and Japanese titles are given in characters. Relevant up to 1973 and indexed according to authors only.

Yang, Paul Fu-mien, *Chinese Dialectology: A Selected and Classified Bibliography* (Hong Kong, 1981).

Includes bibliographical studies of Chinese dialects up to 1979. Indicates all dictionaries of Chinese dialects.

Yang, Winston L.Y. and Teresa S. Yang (comp.), *Bibliography of the Chinese Language* (New York, 1966).

The first comprehensive bibliographical guide to the Chinese language. Lists under broad subject headings over 2,000 sources, including books, articles, theses, dissertations, and reference and teaching materials.

Chao Yuen-ren and others, *Linguistics in East Asia and South East Asia* (The Hague and Paris, 1967).

Literature

Nienhauser, William H., Jr. and others, eds., *The Indiana Companion to Traditional Chinese Literature* (Bloomington, 1986).

> Like the *Oxford Companion to English Literature*, on which it was modeled, it features the most generally useful information: in Part I, essays on Confucian and Buddhist literature, drama, fiction, literary criticism, poetry, popular literature, prose, rhetoric, and Taoist and women's literatures; and in Part II, name and title identifications and subject discussions. An indispensable literary tool.

Yang, Winston L.Y., Peter Li, and Nathan K. Mao, *Modern Chinese Fiction: A Guide to its Study and Appreciation, Essays, and Bibliographies* (Boston, 1981).

Idem., *Classical Chinese Fiction: A Guide to its Study and Appreciation, Essays, and Bibliographies* (Boston, 1982).

> These two bibliographies include: general discussion of important literary genres, annotated bibliographies divided according to genres, important authors, as well as secondary studies and lists of translations. There is an author index.

A Selective Guide to Chinese Literature, 1900-1949 (Leiden, 1988-1990) 4 parts. Dolezélova-Velingerova, Milena, ed. vol I: *The Novel,* 1988; Slupski, Zbigniew, ed. vol II: *The Short Story,* 1988; Haft, Lloyd, ed. vol. III: *The Poem,* 1988; Eberstein, Bernd, ed. vol. IV: *The Drama,* 1990.

> Descriptive bibliography of the most important Chinese works of the four genres for this century until 1949, by an international group of scholars. In each volume, there is an extensive bibliographic introduction in essay form of the genre, and then an individual discussion per author, arranged alphabetically according to pinyin transcription. There are two indices, one for names of authors with cross-references for pseudonyms and alternative names, and the other by names of publishers, journals, and titles of literary series.

Hightower, James Robert, *Topics in Chinese Literature: Outlines and Bibliographies* (Cambridge, Mass.,1953).

> Probably still the best general reference work on the genres and topics in Chinese literature. Includes well-selected biblio-

graphies of Chinese, Japanese, and Western language sources on major topics of Chinese literature.

Feifel, Eugen, *Bibliographie zur Geschichte der chinesischen Literatur* (Hildesheim, 1992)
> Divided into two parts. The first part lists printed studies according to form, e.g. anthology, bibliography, biography, etc.. Second part is a bibliography of authors and themes, with cross-references. Includes sections on Buddhism and Taoism.

Li Tien-yi, *The History of Chinese Literature: A Selected Bibliography* (New Haven, 1969; rev. ed.).
> A selected and classified bibliography of books in Chinese, English, French, German, and Japanese. Arranged under: (1) bibliographies (2) indices and concordances (3) glossaries (4) anthologies and sources (5) general works (6) poetry (7) fiction (8) drama (9) prose (10) literary theory and criticism (11) biographical dictionaries and monographs (12) histories, philosophical works, etc. Arranged alphabetically by author in each section without annotations.

Idema, Wilt and Lloyd Haft, *Chinese letterkunde: Inleiding, historisch overzicht en bibliografieën* (Utrecht, 1985).
> A well-known Dutch-language "guide" for second-year sinology students.

Gibbs, Donald A. and Li Yun-chen, *A Bibliography of Studies and Translations of Modern Chinese Literature, 1918-1942* (Cambridge, Mass., 1975).
> A bibliography of studies and translations (into Western languages) of Chinese works, published between 1918 and 1942. Arranged according to Wade-Giles transcription of author's name (or, the name by s/he was best known). Gives Chinese characters.

Nienhauser, William, *Bibliography of Selected Western Works on T'ang Dynasty Literature* (Taipei, 1988).
> A very complete list of Western language secondary studies on this one dynasty, including information on Buddhist and Taoist literature.

Lopez, Manuel D., *Chinese Drama: An Annotated Bibliography of Commentary, Criticism, and Plays in English Translation* (Methuchen, N.J., 1992).

> With its sprawling index, this is the most up-to-date reference work on Chinese drama in English now available.

E. Yee, "Ming Drama: A Selected and Annotated Bibliography." *Ming Studies* 28 (1989):46-64.

> Gives information on some 56 references concerning Ming drama published between 1981 and 1987. Includes characters of authors and titles mentioned.

Berry, Margaret, *The Chinese Classic Novels: An Annotated Bibliography of Chiefly English-language Studies* (New York, 1988).

> Helpful guide to the six great Chinese novels, including translations and secondary studies. Contains author/title index.

Tsai, Meishi, *Contemporary Chinese Novels and Short Stories, 1949-1974: An Annotated Bibliography* (Cambridge, Mass., 1979).

> Annotated bibliography of works by authors from the PRC who were active in the period 1949-1974. Some biographical information, and a list of translations in Western languages, where possible. Arranged according to the Wade-Giles transcription of the name of the author. Gives Chinese characters.

Louie, Kam and Louise Edwards, *Bibliography of English Translations and Critiques of Contemporary Chinese Fiction (1945-1992)* (Taipei, 1993).

Science and Technology

Needham, Joseph, *Science and Civilisation in China* (Cambridge, 1954-to date, 15 vols., projected to include 7 more volumes).

> Each volume contains a comprehensive list of books and journal articles in Chinese, Japanese, and Western languages. The Chinese and Japanese list, including some Korean and Vietnamese items, is further divided into works before or after 1800 with translation of the titles and date of their compilation or publication. Vol. IV, part 3 includes an interim list of editions of Chinese texts used.

Neu, S., "Ninety-sixth Critical Bibliography of the History of Science and its Cultural Influences, to January, 1971. Section Hs. 35.2: the Far East to ca. 1600," *Isis* 62.5 (1971): 69-72.

Sivin, Nathan, "Science and Medicine in Imperial China—The State of the Field," *Journal of Asian Studies* 47 (1988): 41-90.
   Contains an extensive list and discussions of publications from both the PRC and Taiwan on the history of science and medicine.

Miscellaneous

Cheng, Lucie, et al., *Women in China: Bibliography of Available English Materials* (Berkeley, 1984).
   Contains citations to 4107 items, arranged by subject. Includes pre-1911 coverage. Has author index and "index of Chinese women as subjects".

Wei, Karen T., *Women in China: A Selected and Annotated Bibliography* (Westport, 1984).
   Includes pre-1911 coverage. Limited to Western-language items, arranged by subject. Has author and title indices.

Johnson, Marshall, *Research on Women in Taiwan* (Taipei, 1992).

Hartwell, Robert M., *A Guide to Sources of Chinese Economic History, A.D. 618-1368* (Chicago, 1964).
   Index to memorials, essays, and other occasional writings on economic topics included in 155 collected works of the T'ang, Sung and Yüan.

Lieberman, Frederic, *Chinese Music: An Annotated Bibliography*, (New York, 1979).
   Not systematic, but certainly an extensive and well-annotated bibliography about all aspects of Chinese music. Author and journal title indices. Also has an extensive subject index.

Vanderstappen, H.A., *The T.L. Yuan Bibliography of Western Writings on Chinese Art and Archaeology* (London, 1975).
   Relevant for the period 1920-1965 and includes Chinese influences on Tibet, Mongolia, Korea, and Japan.

80 CHAPTER TWO — REFERENCES

Hovell, Lin-cheung, *An Annotated Bibliography of Chinese Painting: Catalogues and Related Texts* (Ann Arbor, 1973).
A companion to J.C. Ferguson's *Li-tai chu-lu hua mu* 歷代著錄畫目, a review of each of the 108 titles used by him in this work, as well as 22 other texts, not cited by Ferguson.

Cahill, James, *An Index of Early Chinese Painters and Paintings: T'ang, Sung, and Yüan* (Berkeley, 1980).
Catalogue of all existing paintings from these era (except wall paintings). Arranged according to period, and then painter. For anonymous works, arrangement according to subject. For each painter, there is a biography (with characters supplied), a full list of his known paintings, and a list of secondary works about him and or his genre. At the end, there is an extensive bibliography of Chinese, Japanese, and Western sources, and a list of reproductions.

Nevadonsky, J. and Alice Li, *The Chinese in Southeast Asia: A Selected and Annotated Bibliography of Publications in Western Languages, 1960-1970* (1970).

Vogel, Hans Ulrich, comp., "Bibliography of Works on Salt History Published in China between 1980 and 1989", in *Commission Internationale d'Histoire du Sel (CIHS)* (Innsbruck, 1992).

Parker, Franklin and Betty Parker: *Education in the People's Republic of China, Past and Present—An Annotated Bibliography* (New York, 1986).

Zürcher, Erik, Nicolas Standaert s.j., and Adrianus Dudink, *Bibliography of the Jesuit Mission in China ca. 1580-ca.1680* (Leiden, 1991).
An indispensable guide to the vast secondary literature in Western languages on this subject.

Wang, James C.F., *The Cultural Revolution in China: An Annotated Bibliography* (New York, 1976).

Ma, Lawrence J.C., *Cities and City Planning in the People's Republic of China: An Annotated Bibliography* (Washington, D.C., 1980).

Goehlert, Robert, *Urbanism in China: A Selected Bibliography* (Monticello, Ill., 1988).

Yuan, Florence C., *A Selected Bibliography on Urbanization in China* (Washington, D.C., 1991).

Schmidt, Marlis, *Economic Reforms in the People's Republic of China since 1979: A Bibliography of Articles and Publications in English-language Magazines and Newspapers* (West Cornwall, Ct., 1987).

Jacobs, J. Bruce et. al., *Taiwan: A Comprehensive Bibliography of English Language Publications* (Bundoora, 1984).

Lee, Wei-chin, *Taiwan* (Oxford, 1990).

"State of the Field" Bibliographies

These are essays that have appeared in the *Journal of Asian Studies* (hereafter JAS), and include extensive bibliographies to bring the reader up to date on that particular subject.

Frederic Wakeman, Jr., "Rebellion and Revolution: The Study of Popular Movements in Chinese History," JAS 36.2 (1977):291-327.

K.C. Chang, "Chinese Archaeology since 1949," JAS 36.4 (1977): 623-646.

Hsu Cho-yin, "Early Chinese History: The State of the Field," JAS 38.3 (1979):453-475.

Peter Golas, "Rural China in the Song, " JAS 39.2 (1980):291-325.

Dwight Perkins, "Research on the Economy of the People's Republic of China: A Survey of the Field," JAS 42.2 (1983):345-372.

Jerome Silbergeld, "Chinese Painting Studies in the West," JAS 46.4 (1987):849-897.

Nathan Sivin [See under *Science and Technology*].

William Lavely, James Lee, and Wang Feng, "Chinese Demography: The State of the Field," JAS 49.4 (1990):807-834.

Evelyn Rawski, "Research Themes in Ming-Qing Socioeconomic History," JAS 50.1 (1991):84-111.

Robert E. Hegel, "Traditional Chinese Fiction: The State of the Field," JAS 53.2 (1994):394-426.

References – Bibliographies

General and Specialized Bibliographies in Chinese and Japanese
 General Bibliographies 84
  Cumulative 84
  Annual 85
 Kung-chü-shu 86
 Specialized Bibliographies 88
  Chinese History - General and Specific by Period 88
  'Periodical' Bibliographies for Chinese History 95
  Chinese Literature 96
  Language 98
  Miscellaneous 98
   Classics 98
   Philosophy and Religion 98
   Law 99
   Art 100
   Social Sciences 100

GENERAL BIBLIOGRAPHIES

Cumulative

Teng Ssu-yü and Knight Biggerstaff, *An Annotated Bibliography of Selected Reference Works* [Cambridge, Mass., 1971; third edition (hereafter TB)].

> Although dated, this may be considered one of the most important bibliographies of Chinese research materials compiled; arranged according to the following categories: (1) bibliographies; (2) encyclopedias; (3) dictionaries; (4) geographical works; (5) biographical works; (6) tables (7) yearbooks; (8) sinological indexes.
> See Edgren's review of this work in *Acta Orientalia* 34 (1972): 213-219, which provides critical comments.

Ch'üan-kuo hsin shu-mu 全國新書目 (Beijing, 1951—).

> Although this work is not comprehensive (*nei-pu* publications were not listed), this is the most complete bibliographical record for the People's Republic publications from 1950, arranged by broad subjects and giving full bibliographical information, and sometimes a short annotation. Books in minority and Western languages are cited by their Chinese titles. Original titles and authors of books translated into Chinese are noted. Issued on an annual basis for 1950, semi-annually for 1951-52, annually for 1953, and monthly from 1954 to August 1958, when its frequency changed to three times a month. It was issued without interruption until the 1966 Cultural Revolution, with a total of 286 issues being published. The bibliography resumed publication in June 1972 as a bimonthly and starting from January 1973, its frequency has changed to monthly.

Ch'üan-kuo tsung shu-mu 全國總書目 (Beijing, 1956-58).

> This work was intended to become a 'national cumulated catalogue of books'. The first volume covered publications for the period 1949-1954. Succeeding volumes are for publications issued in 1955 to 1958. These annual volumes were more than a cumulation of the *Ch'üan-kuo hsin shu-mu*, since they contain 40% more titles. A wide range of publications were included, such as periodicals, textbooks, books for the blind, and books in minority and Western languages. Contained title index.

Ch'üan-kuo chu-yao pao-k'an tzu-liao so-yin, 1955-66 全國主要報刊資料索引 (Shanghai, 1967; reprint).

This is the national index to materials in important periodicals and newspapers, originally issued periodically (between 1955 and 1958, 38 issues appeared). Arranged by subject, then by newspaper and periodical title in which the article appeared. Date of publication, name of author, pagination, and volume are given. Each issue contained some 5,000 articles from approximately 300 periodicals and newspapers. In 1959 it was divided into two sections: philosophy and social sciences, and natural and applied sciences. From 1966 through 1972, publication of this index was suspended. Since 1972, issues have appeared under the title *Ch'üan-kuo pao-k'an so-yin* 全國報刊索引.

Chung-hua min-kuo t'u-shu tsung mu-lu 中華民國圖書總目錄 (Taipei, since 1974).

This was the first comprehensive "books in print" available in the Republic of China. It listed more than 30,000 books, pamphlets, periodicals, and audio-visual materials published in Taiwan. Entries were classified under nine major subject categories and 99 subcategories. Within each subcategory, items were grouped by publisher, and listed by title, author, publisher, and price, but without imprint date or pagination. Western language publications were also listed.

Min-kuo shih-ch'i tsung shu-mu (1911-1949) 民國時期總書目 (1911-1949) (Beijing, since 1986) six volumes to date, projected 20 volumes.

A comprehensive listing of *all* books published during those years in the title. Volume 1 specializes on works concerning linguistics; volume 2 on philosophy and psychology; volumes 3 and 4 on Chinese and world literature; volumes 5 and 6 on economics. Entries give place and date(s) of publication, and name of publisher. There is an alphabetical *pinyin* index based on the pronunciation of the first character in each title. Also, has a stroke index.

Annual

Chung-kuo ch'u-pan nien-chien 中國出版年鑒 (Beijing, since 1980)
This is a yearly publications annual, listing books and other ma-

terials. Since 1988 this work was divided into the following categories: books (including reprints), textbooks (also including reprints), pictorial materials, periodicals, and newspapers.

Chung-hua min-kuo ch'u-pan nien-chien 中華民國出版年鑒 (Taipei, since 1976).
In addition to listing exact references for both books and journals, published in Taiwan, including foreign titles, this work also lists publishers with their addresses, and telephone numbers. Has author index, but that for Westerners is listed alphabetically by given names!

Tôyôshi Kenkyû Bunken Ruimoku
(see description under 'General and Specific Bibliographies Western languages')

Han-hsüeh yen-chiu chung-hsin 漢學研究中心, comp. *T'ai-wan ti-ch'ü Han-hsüeh lun-chu hsüan-mu* 台灣地區漢學論著選目 (Taipei, since 1982).
Published annually, this bibliography lists both books and articles printed in Taiwan. Arrangement by subject with an author index. There is a single index for the contents of the five volumes published 1982-1986, entitled *T'ai-wan ti-ch'ü Han-hsüeh lun-chu hsüan-mu hui-pien pen* 台灣地區漢學論著選目彙編本 (Taipei, 1987; reprinted 1990).

Kuo-li chung-yang t'u-shu-kuan 國立中央圖書館 ed., *Chung-hua min-kuo ch'i-k'an lun-wen so-yin hui-pien* 中華民國期刊論文索引彙編 (Taipei, since 1970).
Although this index is not restricted to sinological literature (one will find publications about natural science as well), this is a good place to find what has been published in Taiwan for a given year. The index is arranged according to broad subjects, e.g. philosophy, religion, language and literature, and sub-divided further. There are author indexes (arranged by number of strokes) for East Asian writers and an alphabetical listing for Western writers.

Kung-chü-shu

Wu-han ta-hsüeh t'u-shu-kuan hsüeh hsi "Chung-wen kung-chü-shu shih-yung fa" pien-hsieh tsu 武漢大學圖書館學系 "中文工具書使用法" 編寫組, ed.,

Chung-wen kung-chü-shu shih-yung fa 中文工具書使用法 (Beijing, 1982).

> In two parts. The first part is an annotated bibliography of reference works. The second part is composed of essays on how to do different kinds of research (e.g. biographical, legal, statistical, etc.). No index.

Nan-ching ta-hsüeh t'u-shu-kuan, Chung-wen hsi, li-shih hsi, pien-hsieh tsu 南京大學圖書館，中文系，歷史系，編寫組 ed., *Wen shih che kung-chü-shu chien-chieh* 文史哲工具書簡介 (Tianjin, 1981).

> This is the expanded edition of the 1980 original work. Covers PRC publications, including pre-1949 works and some Japanese references, but no Western publications. Arranged by category (chronology, biography, etc.), and has title index by number of strokes in the first character.

Lin T'ieh-sen 林鐵森, *Chung-kuo li-shih kung-chü-shu chih-nan* 中國歷史工具書指南(Beijing, 1992).

> Examines more than 2500 works, including those in Western languages. Arranged according to subject, and sub-divided chronologically, and by subject. Includes a useful separate chapter for finding other *kung-chü-shu*, incorporating those written in the Republican period. Has separate chapters for subjects like economic, military, and legal history, foreign relations, cultural history, history of science, religion, women's history, archaeology, history of minorities. This work is also good on local history. Indices for Chinese works (arranged in alphabetical *pinyin* order), Japanese, Western language, and Russian publications. This is one of the few Chinese works that incorporates Western language scholarship on China with Chinese scholarship.

Yamane Yukio 山根幸夫 ed., *Chûgoku shi kenkyû nyûmon* 中国史研究入門 [Tokyo, 1983 two volumes; rev. ed. 1991; edition updated for Hong Kong and Taiwan by Kao Ming-shih 高明士 ed., *Chung-kuo shih yen-chiu chih-nan* 中國史研究指南 (Taipei, 1990, 5 vols.); PRC edition announced].

> This a collection of detailed bibliographical essays by specialists, arranged chronologically from antiquity to the present, and further sub-divided by subject. Both primary and secondary sources (in all languages) published through 1990 are included. Japanese version has an appendix describing Japan's major sinological libraries, journals, bookstores (including addresses and phone numbers). Each volume has title index.

SPECIALIZED BIBLIOGRAPHIES

Chinese History

General

Chung-kuo ku-tai-shih lun-wen tzu-liao so-yin 中國古代史論文資料索引
(Shanghai, 1985), 2 vols.

A systematic bibliography on premodern Chinese history, includes both scientific and non-scientific publications that were
produced between October 1949 and September 1979 in the
PRC. Volume 1 is arranged by subject (including local history).
Volume 2 arranged chronologically, and then by subject (including biography). Has an author index.

Pa-shih-nien lai shih-hsüeh shu-mu, 1900-1980 八十年來史學書目
(Beijing, 1984).

Arranged by subject, this bibliography contains references to
over 12,400 Chinese books (including Chinese translations),
published 1900-1980 on all historical subjects (archaeology
too). With author index.

Chung-kuo she-hui ching-chi shih lun-chu mu-lu, 1900-1984
中國社會經濟史論著目錄 (Jinan, 1988).

This is an excellent, systematic bibliography on Chinese social
and economic history. Covers some 20,000 books and articles,
including works published in Hong Kong and Taiwan. There
are two separate bibliographical lists on the history of Chinese
economic thought, and on 'theoretical problems of Chinese
socio-economic history'.

Chung-kuo li-shih ti-li hsüeh lun-chu so-yin (1900-1980) 中國歷史地理學論
著索引 (Beijing, 1986).

A systematic bibliography about historical geography in some
23,000 articles and books in Chinese, including those published in Hong Kong and Taiwan, and in Japanese, until 1982.

Shih-hsüeh lun-wen fen-lei so-yin 史學論文分類索引 (Beijing, 1990)

Updates other general historical bibliographies. Arranged according to subject, with author and title indexes at the end.

Feng Erh-k'ang   馮爾康, *Chung-kuo she-hui shih yen-chiu kai-shu* 中國社會史研究概述 (Tianjin, 1989).

Surveys all of Chinese social history up to 1985 and includes important Japanese publications. Especially useful for early Republican period scholarship. Contains listings for both books and articles, and on a variety of topics, e.g. 'everyday life'.

Chien-kuo i-lai Chung-kuo shih-hsüeh lun-wen-chi p'ien-mu so-yin 建國以來中國史學論文集篇目索引 (Beijing, 1992).

Conveniently arranged index to principal historical collected writings from 1949 to 1982. Includes author index, based on stroke-counts, and subject index. The table of contents is based on similar categories as those in the yearbook *Chung-kuo li-shih-hsüeh nien-chien* 中國歷史學年鑒 categories [see below, under *'Periodical' Bibliographies for Chinese History*].

Specific by Period

Pre-Ch'in to Sung

Chan-kuo Ch'in Han shih lun-wen so-yin 1900-1980 戰國秦漢史論文索引 (Beijing, 1983).

Arranged by subject, with no index.

Sanae Yoshio 早苗良雄,
Kandai kenkyû bunken mokuroku—hôbun hen 漢代研究文献目録・邦文篇 (Kyoto, 1981).

A systematic listing of Japanese publications concerning every aspect of both former and later Han dynasty developments. Includes an author index.

Wei Chin Nan-pei ch'ao shih yen-chiu lun-wen shu-mu yin-te 魏晉南北朝史研究論文書目引得 (Taipei, 1971).

Bibliography of Chinese and Japanese works published 1912-1969. Arranged by subject, with stroke-count author and article title indexes.

Sui T'ang Wu-tai shih lun-chu mu-lu 1900-1981 隋唐五代史論著目録 (Suzhou, 1985).

A systematic bibliography about the Sui, T'ang, and Five Dynasties periods of Chinese publications (including those from Taiwan and Hong Kong) and Japanese publications from 1900 to 1981. Contains author index.

Sung

Sung Hsi 宋晞,
Sung-shih yen-chiu lun-wen yü shu-chi mu-lu 宋史研究論文與書籍目錄 (Taipei, 1983).
> Systematic bibliography about the Sung period. Includes publications from the PRC, Taiwan, and Hong Kong from 1905 to 1981. There is an author index.

Ch'en Ch'ing-hao 陳慶浩,
Sung Liao Chin shih shu-chi lun-wen mu-lu t'ung-chien, Chung-wen pu-fen (1900-1975) 宋遼金史書籍論文目錄通檢，中文部份 "Bibliographie et index des travaux en chinois sur les Sung 1900-1975" (Paris, 1979).
> Arranged by subject, with subject and author indexes.

Sung Liao Hsia Chin shih yen-chiu lun-chi so-yin 宋遼夏金史研究論集索引 (Hangzhou, 1985).
> Unannotated bibliography of works appearing between 1900-1982, with emphasis on post-1949 scholarship.

Sôdai kenkyû bunken teiyô 宋代研究交献提要 (Tokyo, 1961).
> An invaluable listing of selected books and articles, arranged separately, published before 1961. There is an author index.

Sôdai kenkyû bunken mokuroku 宋代研究文献目録 (Tokyo, 1957; 1959; 1970).
> Three unannotated but classified bibliographies covering Japanese scholarship from the Meiji period (1868-1912) to 1970.

Yüan

Yang Chih-chiu 楊志玖 et al., *Yüan-shih hsüeh kai-shuo* 元史學概說 (Tianjin, 1989).
> Assesses the 'state of the field' for Yüan Studies, covering a vast range of topics, followed by a comprehensive list of publications in Chinese, Japanese, Russian, and Western languages, since the 19th century.

Ming

Chung-kuo chin pa-shih nien Ming-shih lun-chu mu-lu 中國近八十年明史
論著目錄 (Nanjing, 1981).
Systematic bibliography about the Ming in Chinese publications from the PRC, Taiwan, and Hong Kong between 1905-1981.

Li Hsiao-lin 李小林 and Li Sheng-wen 李晟文,
Ming-shih yen-chiu pei-lan 明史研究備覽 (Tianjin, 1988).
This is both a bibliography and a research guide. It includes a 107-page annotated bibliography of primary sources, and a 122-page bibliography of articles, an annotated bibliography of book-length studies, listing works from published in the PRC, Taiwan, Hong Kong, Japan, and the West. There are also a series of bibliographical "state of the field" essays on key topics in Ming history.

Richard T. Wang, *Ming Studies in Japan 1961-1981: A Classified Bibliography* (Minneapolis, 1985).
This is an "update" of Yamane Yukio, *Mindai shi kenkyû bunken mokuroku* 明代史研究文献目録 (Tokyo, 1960). Has author index.

Wu Chih-ho, "A Classified List of Articles and Books on Ming China [parts I-VI]." *Chinese Culture* 20.2(1979)129-165; 20.3 (1979):91-144; 20.4(1979):81-143; 21.1(1980)93-150; 21.2(1980): 115-144; 21.3(1980):121-140.
Contains more than 5500 entries, arranged by subject.

Feng Hui-min 馮惠民 and Li Wan-chien 李萬健, comp., *Ming-tai shu-mu t'i-pa ts'ung-k'an* 明代書目題跋叢刊 (Beijing, 1994), 2 vols.

Ch'ing and Later

G.W. Skinner, *Modern Chinese Society 1644-1972: An Analytical Bibliography* (Stanford, 1973), Vols. II and III.
The volumes for Chinese and Japanese references are arranged similarly to the one in Western languages, according to the local systems macro-regions approach. Indispensable for Ch'ing and Republican social and economic history.

Ch'ing-shih lun-wen so-yin 清史論文索引 (Beijing, 1985).
Lists some 20,000 books/articles published from 1900 until

June 1981. Includes publications from Taiwan and Hong Kong, arranged by subject, but no indexes.

Ch'en Sheng-hsi 陳生璽 et al., *Ch'ing-shih yen-chiu kai-shuo* 清史研究概說 (Tianjin, 1991).
This guide to all aspects of Ch'ing history presents a useful introduction to the study of the period by giving a history of Ch'ing studies, all listing secondary publications.

Chung-kuo chin-tai shih lun-chu mu-lu (1949-1979) 中國近代史論著目錄 (Shanghai, 1980).
Covers the period from the Opium War to the Northern Warlords, and arranged according to subject (including biography and local history). Citations to PRC journal and newspaper articles, and books. No index.

Chung-kuo chin-tai shih lun-wen tzu-liao so-yin 1949-1979 中國近代史論文資料索引 (Beijing, 1983).
Lists PRC articles only about the period from the Opium War to the eve of the May 4th Movement. Arranged by subject, with a separate bibliography for biographies (arranged by stroke order of the subject's surname).

Ch'ing-tai pien-chiang shih ti lun-chu so-yin 清代邊疆史地論著索引 (Beijing, 1988).
Index to articles on the history and geography of border regions in China.

Hsi-shih ch'i-shih-lu: Chuan-chia t'an ju-ho hsüeh-hsi Chung-kuo chin-t'ai shih 習史啓示錄：專家談如何學習中國近代史 (Tianjin, 1988).
Detailed bibliographical essays about Chinese history on different aspects of the late Ch'ing, such as the Opium War, Taiping Rebellion, Self-strengthening, etc.. Different authors evaluate the existing literature and summarize it. This work is useful because it contains abstracts about the many Chinese primary source publications that have appeared since 1949.

John Fairbank, Masataka Banno, and Sumiko Yamamoto, comp., *Japanese Studies of Modern China: A Bibliographical Guide to Historical and Social Science Research on the 19th and 20th Centuries* (Rutland, Vt., 1955; reissued Cambridge, Mass., 1971).
This is a guide to the major Japanese secondary materials on

19th and 20th century China. Lists and describes over 1,000 Japanese books and articles, with detailed summaries of all aspects of Chinese development. Especially strong on economic and social topics.

Kamachi Noriko, John K. Fairbank, and Ichiko Chûzô, *Japanese Studies of Modern China since 1953: A Bibliographical Guide to Historical and Social Science Research on the Nineteenth and Twentieth Centuries, Supplementary Volume for 1953-1969* (Cambridge, Mass., 1975).
Revision of 1955 (1971) work. Complete and easy to use.

Yamane Yukio, ed.   *Shinpen shingai kakumei bunken mokuroku* 新編辛亥革命文献目録 (Tokyo, 1983).
Contains citations to 425 books and 6192 articles in Chinese and Japanese. This work interprets "1911 Revolution" broadly to include late Ch'ing socio-economic, political, and intellectual history. Has a local history section, author indexes.

Jung T'ien-lin   榮天琳, Ch'eng Han-ch'ang   成漢昌   et.al., eds., *Chung-kuo hsien-tai-shih lun-wen chu-tso mu-lu so-yin 1949-1981* 中國現代史論文著作目錄索引 (Beijing, 1986).
Bibliographic broad survey of Republican history and later for publications appearing in the PRC from 1949-81. There is a continuation of this work, compiled by Ch'eng Han-ch'ang, et.al., *Chung-kuo hsien-tai-shih lun-wen chu-tso mu-lu so-yin, 1982-1987* (Beijing, 1990). Both volumes are arranged according to topics, e.g. historical writing, social history, economic history, with further sub-divisions. Includes sections for the Guangzhou government, Northern warlords, and Wuhan government. Contains two separate appendices: one for authors, arranged alphabetically by pinyin spelling, and one for titles, also alphabetical, according to the first word in the title.

Chang Chu-hung   張注洪, *Chung-kuo hsien-tai ko-ming-shih shih-liao-hsüeh* 中國現代革命史史料學 (Beijing, 1987).
This is a good introduction to the history of the Chinese communist movement before 1949. Parts of this work have been translated into English and have appeared is issues of *Chinese Studies in History,* and *Chinese Studies in Sociology and Anthropology* [see Chapter XI 'Translations'].

Chung-kuo hsien-tai-shih lun-wen shu-mu so-yin 中國現代史論文書目索引 (Henan, 1986).

　　Bibliography of publications on Chinese history for the period 1911-1949, published between 1949 and 1984. Separate sections for books and articles, with detailed summaries per item.

Chieh-fang-ch'ü ken-chü-ti t'u-shu mu-lu 解放區根據地圖書目錄 (Beijing, 1989).

　　Extensive bibliography of books published in "liberated areas" before October 1949. For the most part, each entry includes title, author, date and place of publication, and publisher. Arranged according to subject, and includes Marxist-Leninist and Maoist thought, philosophy, social sciences, history, military matters, law, and culture. Coverage also extends to literature and writers. Also has a general section for biographies.

Li Yung-p'u 李永璞 ed., *Ch'üan-kuo ko-chi cheng-hsieh wen-shih tzu-liao p'ien-mu so-yin, 1960-1990* 全國各級政協文史資料篇目索引 (Beijing, 1992), 5 vols..

　　This work, containing some 300,000 entries, is a guide for collections of documents on Chinese developments in the following topics: politics, military matters, trade (vol.1); economy, culture (vol.2); society, local matters (vol.3); biography (vols. 4 and 5). Vol.5 is an index to all the collections used. This work is also useful for tracing the activities of particular political figures over time.

Chung-kuo chin-tai ching-chi shih lun-chu mu-lu t'i-yao 中國近代經濟史論著目錄提要 (Shanghai, 1989).

　　This collection of 298 abstracts (each about one page in length) and a bibliography of some 2,293 items gives a useful insight into PRC historiography on the subject on economic history.

Ma Wei-yi, *A Bibliography of Chinese-language Materials on the People's Communes* (Ann Arbor, 1982).

　　A bibliography of about 2800 Chinese language articles about the communes, published between 1957 and 1966. There is a translation of each title, and a brief description of each entry. There is an index according to commune name.

'Periodical' Bibliographies on Chinese History

Chung-kuo li-shih-hsüeh nien-chien 中國歷史學年鑒 (Beijing, since 1979).

A 'yearbook' on Chinese historiography and history, arranged according to the periods of Chinese history. Each volume covers scholarly publications (books and journal articles) that appeared the year before on the cover, so that the 'yearbook' for 1993 is in actual fact, an index to the work published in 1992. The exception to that arrangement is the 'yearbook' for 1979, which does include publications in that year (and thus, there is no 'yearbook' for 1980). Also contains a systematic bibliography according to period. Lists historical congresses for the given year.

Shih-hsüeh ch'ing-pao 史學情報 (since 1982).

A quarterly publication which summarizes important articles, reviews, and bibliographies of Chinese history in the PRC.

Shigaku zasshi 史学雑誌 (May issue).

This Japanese journal in its May issue contains extensive bibliographical essays, arranged by period, on publications about Chinese history (mainly Japanese works, but also some Chinese works) from the year before issue.

There are published two volumes of translations of some of these essays. See Joshua A. Fogel, ed. and trans., *Recent Japanese Studies of Modern Chinese History: A Special Issue of Chinese Studies in History* 18.1-2 (Fall-Winter, 1984-85). This volume contains translations of the sections 'Ming-Ch'ing Studies' (1978-81), and 'Post-Opium War China' (1979-81), which covers the May Fourth Period. Also, Joshua Fogel, *Recent Japanese Studies of Modern Chinese History: Translations from Shigaku Zasshi for 1983-86* (Armonk, N.Y., 1989) [published simultaneously as volume 22.1-2 of *Chinese Studies in History*]. Translations for more recent issues of *Shigaku zasshi* summaries may be found in the *Journal of Sung Yuan Studies* for the Sung and Yüan periods, and *Late Imperial China* for the Ming and Ch'ing dynasties.

Chinese Literature

Yüan Hsüeh-liang 袁學艮, *Chung-kuo ku-tien wen-hsüeh wen-hsien chien-so yü li-yung* 中國古典文學文獻檢索與利用(Chengdu, 1988).

This guide for the study of traditional Chinese literature contains chapters for the different dynasties and the literature of these periods, followed by chapters about traditional literary criticism, references, dictionaries, bibliographies, and catalogues. Includes some Japanese reference works, but nothing on those in Western languages.

Chung-kuo ku-tien wen-hsüeh yen-chiu lun-wen so-yin (1949-1980) 中國古典文學研究論文索引 (Guangxi, 1984).

A systematic bibliography for both books and articles about traditional Chinese literature which surveys all Chinese publications, for this period, including those from Hong Kong and Taiwan. Arranged historically, and sub-divided by genre. Includes publications about literature from the Ch'ing and Republican periods.

Chung-kuo ku-tien wen-hsüeh yen-chiu lun-wen so-yin 中國古典文學研究論文索引 (Hong Kong, 1980).

Covers publications in two parts: 1949-1962; and 1963-June 1966.

Chung-kuo ku-tien wen-hsüeh yen-chiu lun-wen so-yin 中國古典文學研究論文索引 [(Beijing, 1985) for the period January 1980-December 1982; (Beijing, 1988) for the period January 1981-December 1983.].

Ou-yang Chien 歐陽健, comp. *Chung-kuo t'ung-su hsiao-shuo tsung-mu t'i-yao* 中國通俗小說總目提要 (Beijing, 1990; second imprint 1991).

As the title suggests, this work is an annotated comprehensive bibliography of Chinese popular fiction. Entries provide alternate titles, publication histories, locations of rare editions, synopses, references to other texts sharing the same subject matter, and general comments. This publication should be used in conjunction with the following work.

Otsuka Hidetaka 大塚秀高, *Zôho Chûgoku tsûzoku shôsetsu shomoku* 増補中国通俗小説書目 (Tokyo, 1987).

> Lists all editions for novels (except the "six classic novels") and a great number of collections of stories. Because the author has consulted so many library catalogues and reference works to check his listings, this work is a reliable source for publication details of individual titles. Includes information on number of printings and names of publishers.

Chu I-hsüan 朱一玄, Tung Tse-yün 董澤雲, and Liu Chien-tai 劉建岱, eds., *Ku-tien hsiao-shuo hsi-ch'ü shu-mu 1949-85* 古典小說戲曲書目 (Changchun, 1991).

Chung-kuo ku-tien hsi-ch'ü yen-chiu tzu-liao so-yin 中國古典戲曲研究資料索引 (Hong Kong, 1989).

Chung-kuo ku-tien wen-hsüeh li-lun p'i-p'ing shih tzu-liao so-yin 1949-1979 中國古典文學理論批評史資料索引 (Shanghai, n.d.).

Chung-kuo ku-tien wen-hsüeh yen-chiu nien-chien 中國古典文學研究年鑒 (Shanghai, 1987).

> Although this work contains 'yearbook' in the title, it is in fact a publication that lists the secondary studies about Chinese traditional literature, including that in Japanese, for the year 1984, only.

Chou Chin 周錦, comp. *Chung-kuo hsien-tai wen-hsüeh tso-p'in shu-ming ta-tz'u-tien* 中國現代文學作品書名大辭典 (Taipei, 1986) 3 vols.

> This "encyclopedic dictionary" lists the titles of literary publications dating from 1911-1949, and Taiwanese literature since 1949. Arranged according to number of strokes. There is a thematic index of the entries, index of authors, and chronological summary of all the given titles.

Chung-kuo wen-hsüeh yen-chiu nien-chien 中國文學研究年鑒 (Beijing, since 1981).

> A 'yearbook' that discusses the most important PRC publications in modern literature. Includes an extended bibliography of secondary studies on modern literature.

Chung-kuo hsien-tai tang-tai wen-hsüeh yen-chiu 中國現代當代文學研究
(Beijing, since 1981).

This twice-monthly issue in the *Fu-yin pao-k'an tzu-liao* reprint
series [see under Chapter III 'Journals and Newspapers'] is the
most convenient way to keep up with publications about contemporary literature in the PRC. In addition to reprints of important articles, each issue contains a systematic bibliography
of articles and books appearing in the field, according to subject and writers.

Language

Chung-kuo yü-yen-hsüeh lun-wen so-yin: 1950-1980 中國語言學論文索引
(Changchum, 1983).

Index to articles on Chinese linguistics appearing in the PRC
from 1950-1980.

Yang Hsiu-chün 楊秀君, ed., *Chung-kuo yü-yen-hsüeh lun-wen so-yin:
1981-1985* 中國語言學論文索引 (Changchun, 1986).

Continuation of above work for the period 1981-1985.

Miscellaneous

Classics

Ching-hsüeh yen-chiu lun-chu mu-lu 1912-1987   經學研究論著目錄
(Taipei, 1990) 2 vols.

Philosophy and Religion

Chung-kuo che-hsüeh nien-chien 中國哲學年鑒 (Shanghai, since 1982).
A 'yearbook' about current research in philosophy, which includes traditional Chinese thought (Buddhism and Taoism),
but not Marxism. Contains general discussions and a systematic bibliography.

Fang K'o-li 方克立, et al., *Chung-kuo che-hsüeh-shih lun-wen so-yin*
中國哲學史論文索引 (Beijing, 1988) 4 vols.

Covers the period since 1950, on Chinese history of philosophy.

K'ung-tzu yen-chiu lun-wen chu-tso mu-lu 1949-1986   孔子研究論文
著作目錄 (Jinan, 1987).

Gives overview of PRC publications on Confucian studies.

Chung-kuo ssu-hsiang, tsung-chiao, wen-hua kuan-hsi lun-wen mu-lu
中國思想宗教文化關係論文目錄 (Taipei, 1981).
  A very useful indexed bibliography of Japanese articles and
  books concerning Chinese thought and religion published
  since the Meiji period. Includes an author index.

Lin Mei-jung 林美容, *T'ai-wan min-chien hsin-yang yen-chiu shu-mu*
台灣民間信仰研究書目 (Taipei, 1991).
  A bibliography of Taiwanese folk belief, includes 'Confucian
  festivals' as well. Has author index by strokes.

Chung-kuo Chi-tu-chiao-shih yen-chiu shu-mu   中國基督教史研究書目
(Taipei, 1981).
  Indexes both Chinese and Japanese references on the history
  of Christianity in China from 618 through post 1949 developments. Includes Western writers as well as Chinese and Japanese.

Oriental History Seminar of Tsukuba University,   *Min, Shin
shûkyôshi kenkyû bunken mokuroku (kô)* 明清宗教史研究文献目録 (稿)
(Tsukuba, 1989).
  Works in Japanese and Chinese cited in books and journals
  since the beginning of this century. Includes all religions, both
  domestic and foreign, with an extensive section on Christianity,
  including that of the Taipings. Has an author index.

Law

Chung-kuo cheng-fa ta-hsüeh t'u-shu-kuan   中國政法大學圖書館
ed., *Chung-kuo fa-lü t'u-shu tsung-mu (1911-1990)* 中國法律圖書總目
(Beijing, 1991).
  'Comprehensive Table of Contents of Chinese Law Books'.
  Broadly arranged according to topics, e.g. civil law, penal law,
  economic law, etc.. Includes both journal articles and books on
  these subjects since 1911. There are two separate appendices:
  one for references on the history of law from the Ch'in onward
  through the Ch'ing dynasty, and a separate appendix for law
  related to Taiwan and Hong Kong. At the end are located six
  indices for authors and book titles (including two separate
  ones for Taiwan and Hong Kong authors and titles).

Chang Wei-jen 張偉仁, *Chung-kuo fa-chih shih shu-mu* 中國法制史書目 (Taipei, 1976), 3 vols.

> Gives detailed descriptions of 2352 primary and secondary sources held by 14 libraries in Taiwan. Materials date from the pre-Ch'in through the Ch'ing periods. This work defines 'legal history' very broadly to include institutional, economic, and social history. Has a stroke-count author and title indexes.

Art

Chung-kuo kung-i mei-shu ta-tz'u-tien 中國工藝美術大辭典 (Nanjing, 1989; note there is an "improved edition" of this work, with the same title, published in Taipei by Hsiung-shih t'u-shu, 1991).

> This encyclopedic dictionary which covers every kind of art, from fine arts to applied (including furniture, clothing and headresses, and dolls) is arranged according to subject. Entries include extensive primary references, and therefore this work may certainly be the starting point for finding documentation on any aspect of Chinese art and artists. Much emphasis on local specialities. There are several appendices which include essays summarizing special characteristics of Chinese art, e.g. paper-making. Character index based on number of strokes of first word. Indispensable.

Social Sciences

Chung-kuo she-hui k'o-hsüeh wen-hsien t'i-lu 中國社會科學文獻題錄 (Beijing, since 1986).

> A bi-monthly publication that lists PRC social science journal articles, with about 6000 to 7000 citations per issue, arranged by subject: Marxism-Leninism-Mao Tse-tung Thought, philosophy, politics, law, "general social science" (statistics, sociology, demography, management, human resources), economics, culture, "the enterprise of science and scientific research", education, language, literature, history, and archaeology. No index.

Kuang-fu i-lai T'ai-wan ti-ch'ü ch'u-pan jen-lei-hsüeh lun-chu mu-lu 光復以來臺灣地區出版人類學論著目錄 (Taipei, 1983).

> Bibliography of anthropological works published in Taiwan, 1945-1982.

CHAPTER THREE

JOURNALS AND NEWSPAPERS

Introduction

Western Language Journals

The history of journals (or periodicals) in Western languages about China began with the Jesuits who published the *Lettres édifantes et curieuses,*[1] in 34 volumes in Paris from 1703 to 1776 (about a third dealing with China), and later, *Mémoires concernant l'histoire, les sciences, les arts, les moeurs, les usuages etc., des Chinois*[2] (17 volumes; Paris, 1776-1814). European scholarly journals that incorporated material on China included *Journal des savants* (from 1665), *Année littéraire* (1754-90), and the *Journal encyclopédique* (1756-93). In the 19th century periodical publications containing information on China were sponsored either by specific missions,[3] or later, by research societies such as the Société Asiatique (founded in 1822), the Royal Asiatic Society[4] (founded in 1823), the American Oriental Society (founded in 1842), or the Deutsche Morgenländische Gesellschaft (founded in 1844). In general, the purpose of these learned societies was to promote

---

[1] The full title of this collection is *Lettres édifantes et curieuses écrites des missions étrangères par quelques missionnaires de la Compagnie de Jésus.* The series was continued in the nineteenth century, first by the *Nouvelles lettres édifantes des missions de la Chine et des Indes Orientales,* 8 vols. (Paris, 1818-23), and then by the *Association de la Propagation de la Foi, Annales...Collection faisant suite à toutes les éditions des Lettres édifantes* (Lyon, 1827). For further details about the contents, see Cordier, *Bibliotheca sinica,* vol. 2, cols. 957-80 (covering the years 1826-1903) and vol. 5, cols. 3601-12 (covering 1903-21).

[2] For the contents of the individual volumes, see Cordier, *Bibliotheca sinica,* vol.1, cols. 54-6.

[3] The first English periodical about China, the *Chinese Repository,* was established in Canton in 1832 by an American, Elijah C. Bridgman. Its purpose was the dissemination among foreigners of mission news and news concerning China. The *Repository* was published until 1851, and after 1867 the *Chinese Recorder* continued its predecessor's objectives until the late 1940s. The most complete listing of 'religious periodicals', including those in Chinese, in issue either before or until 1940, may be found in Rudolf Löwenthal, *The Religious Periodical Press* (Peking, 1940).

[4] For the history of this institution, see Stuart Simmonds and Simon Digby, eds., *The Royal Asiatic Society: Its History and Its Treasures* (London and Leiden, 1979).

the appreciation of non-Western languages and cultures, and thus the publication of their members' research was a constant expression of that interest. In the second half of the 19th century government-sponsored colonial institutions also began to issue learned journals to which both civil servants and scholars contributed, e.g. *Bulletin de l'École française d'Extrême-Orient*.

In the twentieth century, as the study of China became an acceptable academic subject in several learned institutions, such as Harvard University in the United States and Leiden University in the Netherlands, professors attached to these places established journals to promote sinological study. The two most famous of these journals, both still publishing, are the *Harvard Journal of Asiatic Studies* by Harvard University, and *T'oung Pao* by the publisher E.J. Brill, issued from Cambridge, Massachusetts, and Leiden, respectively. In China too, there developed a number of English-language periodicals that provided scholarly and statistical information on the economy and society, such as the *Chinese Social and Political Science Review*, issued quarterly from Peking, 1916-1941, the *Nankai Social and Economic Quarterly*, published by the Nankai Institute of Economics, Nankai University, from 1935 through the 1940s, or *T'ien-hsia Monthly*, printed in Shanghai and Hong Kong, 1935-41.[5]

Since World War II, both the study of 'premodern China', i.e. China before 1800, and modern China have become favorite subjects in university curricula in the West. This has resulted in another wave of new periodicals being founded, the most important of which is the *Journal of Asian Studies*. Although not specifically directed on China, its foci including South and Southeast Asia, Japan, and Korea, this journal serves as a important indicator of current trends in the field of China study. The *Journal* is published by the Association for Asian Studies, which is the leading American institution for the study of Asia. It hosts an annual convention, attended by some 3000 members, and sponsors regional conferences all over the United States to help support younger scholars to keep in contact with each other. In 1960 another important journal, the *China Quarterly* began publication. It was the first Western language journal to take a "serious look" at the PRC,

---

[5] For an annotated listing of 189 Western-language periodicals published in China, as well as those published on China in the West until 1949, see Richard Walker, *Western Language Periodicals on China (A Selective List)* (New Haven, 1949).

providing specialists an opportunity to expressive diverse views on all aspects of Chinese development.[6]

Another recent development in the publication of periodicals is the popularity of the 'newsletter'. This is usually a journal specializing on the history of one or two Chinese dynasties (e.g. *Journal of Sung Yuan Studies*), or on a particular aspect of Chinese civilization (e.g. *Chinese Science*). Newsletters usually publish specialized research results, and for that reason, attract the interest of younger scholars who may have just completed Ph.D. dissertations. Newsletters provide an important medium for these younger scholars to make known to colleagues what they have achieved. In addition to articles about China, many journals contain book reviews of recent publications. Looking at current book reviews is one way of 'keeping up with the field', and learning about current themes of interest. A certain way to know what is being published is to examine *Current Contents of Foreign Periodicals in Chinese Studies* (Taipei, since 1984), which appears quarterly. This listing of Western language and Japanese articles, as well as book reviews, for both premodern and modern China studies, arranged alphabetically by journal title, is referred to in chapter II 'General Bibliographies in Western Languages' - in the section *Annual*. The most recent publication that regularly produces book reviews is the semi-annual *China Review International*, first issued in Spring, 1994 by the University of Hawai'i Press.

For up-to-date information on current events in the East Asia region, a number of journals are recommended. The weekly *Far Eastern Economic Review*, although not specially oriented toward China, gives in-depth coverage on all aspects of Chinese development. The bi-monthly *China News Analysis* is an excellent source on PRC happenings, and the monthly, *China aktuell* specializes in the most current information on changing political and economic developments in East Asia (includes coverage of Taiwan and Hong Kong).[7] Its monthly and annual indexes, arranged by subject, are extremely useful. Last, we should not fail to mention that the PRC publishes a number of English language periodicals.

---

[6] For an interesting account of the founding of the *China Quarterly*, see Peter Coleman, *The Liberal Conspiracy: The Congress for Cultural Freedom and the Struggle for the Mind of Postwar Europe* (New York, 1989), pp.195-96. According to Coleman, the first editor Roderick MacFarquhar, did his best to keep its pages open to people ranging from a CIA sinologist to Owen Lattimore.

[7] Since 1983, this bibliography has been issued from Hamburg separately as *Bibliography of Chinese Studies* [see chapter II General Bibliographies in Western Languages Annual]

Among the most well-known are *China Reconstructs, Beijing Review* (formerly, 'Peking Review'), and *Chinese Literature.*

Western Language Newspapers

Western language newspapers published in China, including Hong Kong and Macao, form a rich source of information about 19th and 20th century China. Newspapers may be utilized as a research tool, not only for the info they tell about the foreign community in China, but also for the history of Chinese journalism. Although Western language newspapers at first sight may seem limited to the exclusive interests of foreigners, there were enough notable exceptions to this pattern. The larger newspapers contained articles by "professional" correspondents whose eye-witness to particular events gave unique insight into the events and changes of the Ch'ing period. The *South China Morning Post,* for example, was founded in 1903 with the avowed purpose of supporting the reform movement in China.[8]

The first English newspaper issued from the China coast was the *Canton Register,*[9] published from 1828-1843. It was established by the Englishman James Matheson, edited by the American William Wood, with the Protestant missionary Robert Morrison, the chief contributor. But the *Canton Register* like other publications until the 1880s, when "professional journalism" became a dominating mode of discourse, was more a voice of their owners and editors than an objective source of news. This newspaper was mainly a vehicle of expression for British interests, and in particular those of the British East India Company, in the Canton region. From 1844 to 1911 Hong Kong dominated South China journalism, and from 1860 onward, Shanghai's growing importance also influenced the impact of Hong Kong based newspapers. From then onward, Hong Kong newspapers gave more attention to events and news in the colony and South China while Shanghai

---

[8] It is still publishing, and is considered the leading Hong Kong English newspaper.

[9] This was not the first Western language China coast newspaper. Two Portuguese newspapers, the *A Abelha da China* (1822-1823) and the *Gazeta de Macau* (1824-1826), both under Roman Catholic sponsorship, supporting ruling groups in the Macao government, ceased publication for lack of support.

publications gave more coverage to contemporary struggles between China and foreign powers, including diplomatic developments in Peking. But it was in Hong Kong where Chinese journalists first began to develop the Chinese language press, and it was there also that the first investment of Chinese capital in English-language newspapers took place.

In Shanghai, the *North China Herald and Supreme Court and Consular Gazette*, founded in 1850, became the leading journalistic publication.[10] Over time it gained a reputation for its authorativeness and completeness. The paper began as a 'weekly', containing extracts from other Western language newspapers, a summary of the week's news, and commercial info. From its earliest beginnings, the newspaper was open to 'differing' views, and its list of correspondents included a variety of officials, bureaucrats, and missionaries. Although the founder of the *North China Herald*, Henry Shearman (d.1856) was a devout man, who supported Protestant missionaries in China, the paper did entertain criticism of missionaries. The paper's first notices of the Taiping Rebellion in 1851 and 1853 saw at first sympathy because of the Christianity of the rebels, then became anti-Taiping in 1856, and severely so from 1861. The *North China Herald* was not the only Shanghai newspaper, but over time it gained a reputation for comprehensiveness.[11]

As the foreign population in Shanghai grew, the number of newspapers publishing also increased. Newspapers in French and German began to appear, and other cities besides Hong Kong and Shanghai gained a Western language press. These included Tientsin, Tsingtao, Peking, Harbin, Amoy, Chefoo, Foochow, Hankow, and Weihaiwei.[12]

---

[10] Many libraries all over the world hold a reproduction of this newspaper in microfilm form from as far back as the 1860s.

[11] In the 1880s, the *Herald*, issued weekly, became a daily, with the name *North China News*.

[12] For a complete listing of all known China-coast newspapers up to 1911, see Frank H.H. King and Prescott Clark, *A Research Guide to China-Coast Newspapers, 1822-1911* (Cambridge, Mass., 1965) which identifies, locates, and evaluates some 200 newspapers of that era. The guide also includes a valuable biographical dictionary of persons involved in newspaper publishing. For newspapers after 1911, refer to the list of 'daily' periodicals in John Fairbank, *The Cambridge History of China: volume 12. Republican China 1912-1949 Part I* (Cambridge, 1983), p.834.

Chinese Language Journals

It is interesting to note that the first journal in Chinese was published not in China, and not by a Chinese.[13] The Protestant missionaries Robert Morrison and W.C. Milne started periodicals in Malacca, and later Hong Kong and Shanghai. In the latter two places the Chinese learned the methods of periodical and newspaper production and later started their own newspapers. While the first Chinese magazine, called *Ch'a shih-su mei-yüeh t'ung-chi chuan* 察世俗每月統計傳 [A General Monthly Record, containing an Investigation of the Opinions and Practices of Society], founded by Morrison in 1815, appeared on Malacca, it was soon followed by China's first modern 'native' magazine, *Tung-hsi yang k'ao mei-yüeh t'ung-chi chuan* 東西洋考每月統計傳 [Eastern Western Monthly Magazine], established by Karl Gützlaff in Canton in 1833. This magazine was "periodical apologia for Western civilization", introducing general Western knowledge of astronomy, geography, and machinery to demonstrate the superiority of Western civilization.

The history of the missionary press included among its pioneers a list of foreign sinologists who did try to understand Chinese civilization. Robert Morrison, for example, composed the first Chinese-English dictionary, and one must not forget that James Legge, the first translator of the Classics, was also a missionary. Until 1895, when a new group of Chinese periodicals advocating radical social and political reform started, the majority of these journals was dominated by Protestant missionaries.[14] Thus, scholar-missionaries like Alexander Wylie, founder of the Shanghai-based *Liu-ho ts'ung-t'an* 六合叢談 (Sundry Talks on the Six Di-

---

[13] An historical introduction to the Chinese periodical press is Roswell S. Britton, *The Chinese Periodical Press, 1800-1912* (Shanghai, 1933); further information on the history of the Chinese press may be found in Lin Yutang, *A History of the Press and Public Opinion in China* (Shanghai, 1936). See also Rudolf Löwenthal, "Western Literature in Chinese Journalism: A Bibliography," *Nankai Social and Economic Quarterly*, 9.4 (1937):1007-1066. This article is especially helpful on censorship problems in the Chinese press.

[14] The Catholics were late in beginning periodicals. The French Jesuit establishment at Zikawei, near Shanghai, in 1878 began the *I wen lu* 益聞錄, at first semimonthly, later weekly and then semi-weekly. In 1898 this magazine absorbed one of the Chinese reviews which had begun to fail after a number of issues. This is perhaps the only case of a foreign missionary journal merging with a purely Chinese journal. For a list of Protestant missionary journals, see Archie Crouch, et. al., *Christianity in China: A Scholar's Guide to Resources in the Libraries and Archives of the United States* (New York, 1989). See 'Serial titles', pp.407-486.

rections), or Young J. Allen,[15] publisher of *I-chih hsin-pao* 益智新報 (A Miscellany of Useful Knowledge), attempted to spread knowledge about Western countries (including history, philosophy, and cultural institutions) while they worked in the interest of Christian missions.

After China's defeat in the Sino-Japanese War in 1895, the Chinese periodical press came of its own. Periodicals, both journals and newspapers, were the chief means of expression for political reforms. In the era between 1895 and 1911, a number of important journals were begun by leading intellectuals, despite the fact that the authorities often tried to ban these publications. *Tung-fang tsa-chih* 東方雜誌 (Eastern Miscellany), published in Shanghai by the Shang-wu yin-shu kuan 商務印書館 from 1904 until 1949, has had the longest existence of any modern Chinese magazine.[16] It is also a rich source for historical information on the first half of the 20th century. Much of what was written about Chinese history, literature, or linguistics before 1937 appeared in journals (as opposed to books), and after that year, scholars had difficulty publishing anything, least of all in book form.

The Chinese periodicals of the pre-1949 era represent a great variation of interests. In general, they fall into four main categories:

(1) National magazines of news and essays. Examples:

Tung-fang tsa-chih; Kuo-wen chou-pao 國聞週報 (Kuo-wen Weekly, Illustrated) [Shanghai, 1924-1937];[17] *Sheng-huo* 生活 (Life) [Shanghai, 1925-1933].

(2) Scholarly journals which dealt both with contemporary social and economic issues, but also investigated new modes in historical writing, and literary and linguistic research. Examples:

She-hui k'o-hsüeh tsa-chih 社會科學雜誌 (Quarterly Review of Social

---

[15] Adrian A. Bennett, *Missionary Journalist in China: Young J. Allen and His Magazines, 1860-1883* (Athens, Georgia, 1983) gives an account of this man's life in China.

[16] Lin Yutang, *A History of the Press and Public Opinion in China*, pp.91-93, 107-113, 127-130 lists important 19th and 20th century Chinese periodicals.

[17] There are cumulative tables of contents for these two journals: *Tung-fang tsa-chih tsung-mu* 東方雜誌總目 (Beijing, 1957); *Kuo-wen chou-pao tsung-mu* 國聞週報總目 (Beijing, 1957).

Sciences) [Peiping, Nanking, Institute of Socal Sciences, Academia Sinica, 1930-37; 1947-48]; *Kuo-hsüeh chi-k'an* 國學季刊 (Sinological Quarterly) [Peking, Sinological Institute of Peking National University, 1923-1949]; university *hsüeh-pao* which gave both information on scholarly discussion but also provided commentaries on contemporary problems.[18]

(3) Magazines of specialized professional communities, such as bankers or economists.

Examples:

Shanghai tsung shang-hui yüeh-pao 上海總商會月報 (Journal of the General Chamber of Commerce of Shanghai) [Shanghai, General Chamber of Commerce, 1921-1927]

Yin-hang chou-pao 銀行週報 (The Banker's Weekly) [Shanghai, 1917-1950]; the most important of the Shanghai banking publications, issued a weekly review of the money market, and thus contains much information on the state of trade and prices,over a long period of time.

Chung-hang yüeh-k'an 中行月刊 (Bank of China monthly review) [Shanghai, 1930-38]; this was the major economic journal of the 1930's, with articles and statistics on all aspects of the economy.

(4) Publications representing particular intellectual trends and factions, such as those concerning the reform movement,[19] the May Fourth era,[20] and intellectual life during the Nanking Decade.

Examples:

I-lin 譯林 [Shanghai, 1901-?]; a journal of translations, edited by a group of Foochow scholars, headed by Lin Shu 林紓.

Kuo-ts'ui hsüeh-pao 國粹學報 (Journal of National Essence) [Shanghai, 1904-1911]; an important monthly for the preservation of the

---

[18] More examples of these scholarly journals may be found in Fairbank and Liu, eds., *Modern China: A Bibliographical Guide to Chinese Works 1898-1937*, Chapter 9 "Selected Learned Journals".

[19] Many of the best known reform journals have photolithographed reprint editions. These include *Shih-wu pao* 時務報 (Current Affairs), *Ch'ing-i pao* 清議報 (Upright discussion), and *Yung-yen* 庸言 (Justice), all edited by Liang Ch'i-ch'ao.

[20] For a guide to periodicals of this era, see *Wu-ssu shih-ch'i ch'i-k'an chieh-shao* 五四時期期刊介紹 (Beijing, 1958-59), 3 volumes; reprinted (Beijing, 1979). This collection examines 240 May Fourth periodicals. Each selection receives an historical sketch, a summary of its contents. Appendices reprint initial editorials and tables of contents. Also refer to Chow Tse-tung, *Research Guide to the May Fourth Movement: Intellectual Revolution in Modern China, 1915-24* (Cambridge, Mass., 1963) which describes some 600 periodicals of the 1915-23 period.

Chinese heritage, headed by Chang Ping-lin and Liu Shih-p'ei 劉師培.[21]

Since the founding of the PRC, there have been few periodical publications that have had a continuous span through the country's history. Three prominent exceptions are two newspapers, *Jen-min jih-pao* 人民日報 (People's Daily), the Shanghai based *Wen-hui pao* 文滙報 (Wen-hui Daily) [both discussed in the section 'A Partial Listing of Chinese Newspapers'], and the government gazette *Hsin-hua yüeh-pao* 新華月報 (New China Monthly), published as *Hsin-hua pan-yüeh-k'an* 新華半月刊 (New China semi-monthly) from 1956 to 1961. Since 1949 *Hsin-hua yüeh-pao* served as a compendium of major newspaper and journal articles. Averaging between 200 and 250 pages in length, this publication contained major directives, speeches, editorials, commentaries, and news dispatches as well as a chronology of major events of the month. In 1979 this journal split into two publications, one retaining the former name and remaining a semi-official government gazette, and the other, *Hsin-hua wen-chai* 新華文摘 a "reprint organ", duplicating already published articles on history, economics, philosophy, culture, and politics.

Many journals and newspapers ceased availability to foreigners after the Great Leap Forward, and other publications simply stopped during the Cultural Revolution. The leading theoretical journal of the PRC was *Hung Ch'i* 紅旗 (The Red Flag), published from 1958-1968, began as a semi-monthly, but its editions became irregular after early 1963. The substantative contents of *Hung Ch'i* included the major issues of the time and reflected how policies changed and were communicated through the society. *Hung Ch'i* ended publication in 1988 and was replaced by another theoretical journal *Ch'iu shih* 求實 (Seeking Truth).

Since the 'reform era' of the 1980s, official theoretical journals have had to stand up to the competition of 'popular magazines' which draw a large readership because they provide 'leisure reading', e.g. *Chung-kuo fu-nü* 中國婦女 for women, or the 'men's magazine' *Nan-tzu-han* 男子漢, or journals about film, such as the popular *Ta-chia tien-ying* 大家電影. There are also "watchdog" journals about the PRC, issued from both Hong Kong and Taiwan, which

---

[21] For reprints of learned journals (and newspapers) of the Republican period, see P.K. Yu, *Research Materials on Twentieth-Century China: An Annotated List of CCRM Publications* (Washington, 1975).

are discussed in a sub-section of the section 'A Partial Listing of
Important Current Chinese Journals' in the *References* of this chapter.

For a complete listing of existing (and non-existing) Chinese
periodicals, the reader is advised to turn to the section 'Union
Catalogues of Chinese Journals and Newspapers', and for the contents of journals, to the section 'Indexes to Chinese Journals'. The
union lists of Chinese periodicals may include as many as 8000 titles of works that flourished between 1864 and 1991. For literary
journals, it is indispensable to consult union catalogues, since
there were so many publications of this genre with an irregular
span. It is impossible to cite one particular journal, even among
those long-standing, that is representative of the Chinese periodical press as a whole. To find those journals which may be most relevant for a particular subject, one should utilize the indexes listed
in this chapter, as well as those in chapter II Chinese and Japanese
Bibliographies, in the section 'Specialist Bibliographies'. For example, the yearly *Chung-kuo li-shih-hsüeh nien-chien* lists by dynastic
period, and for 'modern history', according to the sub-divisions of
economic, governmental, social, educational, intellectual, and local history, the most outstanding articles, with full citation to author, journal, and volume, for the year preceding its publication.[22]

Another important aid for gaining control of current publications is the *Fu-yin pao-k'an tzu-liao* 複印報刊資料 (Duplication of
Press Material) reprint series.[23] This series began publication in
the 1950s for internal use and was made available for foreign sub-
scription in 1978. Originally covering only 22 topics, these facsimile reprints have been expanded to cover over 100. The articles are selected from 2000 newspapers and periodicals published
in the PRC. While articles on all aspects of contemporary Chinese
affairs are included, those concerning military affairs were omit-

---

[22] Indexes to Chinese periodical literature may also be found now on CD-
ROMs (Compact Disk-Read-Only-Memory). They are usually commercially produced and require a computer with a certain high memory for installation. For
example, the Program *Chinese Periodical Literature on CD-ROM* (Hsinchu, Taiwan)
provides a general index of Chinese periodicals for more than 1,255 periodicals
and journals in all disciplines from January, 1982 through December, 1992. At the
moment programs like these are expensive to purchase but presumably will develop into a more common tool for library users to consult.
[23] Formally known as 'Chung-kuo Jen-min ta-hsüeh Fu-yin pao-k'an tzu-liao'
series.

ted from the public offering until 1989. Most volumes in the series are monthly publications, and each issue carries its own index. There is also a cumulative annual index. Although the series was designated *nei-pu* in 1982-83, it was re-opened to foreigners in 1984. For every aspect of Chinese development (including cultural matters), there may one or more specific titles in the *Fu-yin pao-k'an tzu-liao* series that are pertinent. For example, with regard to contemporary law and politics, there are *Chung-kuo cheng-chih* 中國政治 or *Fa-lü* 法律, or for contemporary literature, *Chung-kuo hsien-tai tang-tai wen-hsüeh yen-chiu* 中國現代當代文學研究. In this chapter's reference section 'A Partial Listing of Important Current Chinese Journals', those publications belonging to this series are noted with an (F).

Major Chinese universities also issue journal publications, and often these university journals are divided into two different editions, one for the humanities and social sciences, and the other for the natural sciences. Thus, Che-chiang University's journal appears in two editions: *Che-chiang ta-hsüeh hsüeh-pao (she-k'o); (tzu-jan)* 浙江大學學報（社科）（自然）.

As in the West, there exists in East Asia, *t'ung-hsün* 通訊 (newletter) type of journals which bring up-to-date information concerning the 'state-of-the-field', most recent publications, international seminars, and meetings. For example, *Chung-kuo k'o-hsüeh shih t'ung-hsün* 中國科學史通訊, issued from Taiwan, is a semi-annual publication that covers very thoroughly everything going on in the history of Chinese science in Taiwan, Japan, the USA, Europe, as well as the PRC. Such publications indicate the extensive international links of present day Chinese studies.

Last, a word must be said about Japanese sinological journals. Not all the publications listed in the section 'A Partial Listing of Important Japanese Journals for Sinology' are specifically orientated toward Chinese studies, but they all form a rich source of information. Japanese scholars, often working for years on a specific topic, will usually publish their results in the form of a journal article rather than a definitive book. In recent years the most important Japanese journals such as *Shigaku zasshi* or *Tôyôshi Kenkyû* 東洋史研究 incorporate current sinological research in the PRC into their agendas, including translations into Japanese of Chinese publications.

Chinese Newspapers

The beginnings of the Chinese daily press date to the 1850s and 1860s, but one may argue that there was a "press" of sorts as early as the Han period. At that time "official bulletins or gazettes" were issued from the capital, for the exclusive use of the bureaucracy. These bulletins, known usually under the name *ti-pao* 邸報 (metropolitan gazettes) were originally a kind of newsletter sent to provincial authorities by their correspondents in the capital. A turning point in the evolution of the *ti-pao* came during the T'ang, when the Bureau of Official Reports (Chin-tsou yüan 進奏院) was established. This office was responsible for transmitting imperial edicts to the local authorities through their 'residences' in the capital, and also for transmitting, in the same way, reports and other official documents from the provinces to the Court. The character of the *ti-pao* changed, consequently, from the former semi-private newsletters into regular official bulletins. During the Sung, the growing numbers of scholar-gentry took even greater interest in these newsletters, there developed in addition to the 'official gazettes' a kind of 'unofficial tabloid' gazette, known as *hsiao-pao* 小報. Official gazettes continued to exist and develop under subsequent dynasties until the 19th century when they were gradually replaced by the modern Chinese press modelled on the Western formation.

The first Chinese newspapers, issued daily, dates from the 1850s and 1860s. *Chung-wai hsin-pao* 中外新報, the first Chinese newspaper, was founded by Wu T'ing-fang 伍廷芳 in Hong Kong in 1858 (and flourished until 1919), and published as the Chinese edition of the local English journal *Daily Press*.[24] The first newspaper published in China was the *Shang-hai hsin-pao* 上海新報, the Chinese edition of the famous *North China Herald*, first issued as a weekly from November 1861, and then as a daily from July 1872, but shortly thereafter ceased publication. Probably, the most famous Chinese newspaper that had a continuous existence was *Shen-pao* 申報, founded in 1872, which ceased publication in 1949.[25] *Shen-pao* was originally owned by the English firm of Major

---

[24] For the most complete discussion about the development of the Chinese press, see Wolfgang Mohr, *Die Moderne Chinesische Tagepresse: ihre Entwicklung in Tafeln und Dokumenten* (three volumes) (Wiesbaden, 1976).

[25] An index series for this newspaper has been issued. See *Shen-pao so-yin* 申報索引 *1919-1920* (Shanghai, 1987), which has been followed by that for 1921-22, 1923-24, 1925-26, etc..

Brothers Limited, and in the first decades of its existence was more a "commercial newspaper", basically a translation of the Western press, inclusive of missionary propaganda, than a source of information for international or local developments. After the use of the telegraph became common from 1884, the contents of *Shen-pao*, like other newspapers became more varied, and political and military news was reported.

In general, historians divide the development of the modern Chinese press into four periods: (1) newspapers founded before 1895, and written in *wen-yen*; (2) newspapers of the 1895-1911 period; (3) newspapers of the Republican period; (4) newspapers of the PRC, since 1949. See the section 'A Partial Listing of Important Chinese Newspapers Past and Present' among the References in this chapter. Despite a long and predominating tradition of censorship,[26] Chinese newspapers represent a formidable source of information for the study of modern China. Late Ch'ing newspapers are a reliable source for the study of intellectual history, and the Republican period press is still the foundation for understanding all aspects of Chinese development in this period: social, economic, political, financial, and urban change.

After 1949, the PRC set new censorship standards on the release of information, both for its own citizens and for the foreign community. News was controlled through the Chinese news agency Hsin-hua she 新華社, and the Communist Party held a monopoly on the spread of information until a new liberalization in the control of the media occurred in the 1980s. Until then, a foreigner had access to published news only through *Jen-min jih-pao*, and *Kuang-ming jih-pao* 光明日報. The last fifteen years has witnessed an explosion in the number of newspapers, from an average of 182 for all of China in 1976 to at least 1,200 nowadays.[27]

---

[26] For an introduction to this subject for 20th century developments, see Lee-hsia Hsu Ting, *Government Control of the Press in Modern China 1900-1949* (Cambridge, Mass., 1974); and Terry Narramore, "Journalism as a Profession in China, 1912-1937: Ideology and Commercialization," *Transactions of the International Conference of Orientalists in Japan*, 35 (1990):111-136.

[27] To date, the largest and most complete collection of Chinese local newspapers available anywhere outside of China is located at the Universities Service Centre (USC), now a part of the Chinese University of Hong Kong. In 1987, USC managed to acquire from China complete sets of 39 Chinese national, provincial, and municipal newspapers from 1950 to 1987 (some date from 1949). For a guide to PRC newspapers before the 1980s explosion, see David Goodman, *Research Guide to Chinese Provincial and Regional Newspapers* (London, 1976).

The rise in numbers is related to the formation of the regional press: as more and more localities in the PRC enact policies *de facto* independent from the central government, local media agencies take on growing influence.[28]

Nevertheless, one must be cautious in using the PRC press. Whether the focus is on a specific locale, policy issues, or institutions, the press, in general, is more prescriptive of structure than analytical of process. The Chinese press often conveys a sense that Chinese organizations work efficiently and that there is a kind of consensus about all government operations.

To find complete listings of newspaper holdings in China, one is advised to turn to the union catalogues, as listed in the reference section in this chapter.

---

[28] Since March 1, 1988, an index of all PRC newspapers including *nei-pu* works has been made. See *Tang-tai Chung-kuo pao-chih ta-ch'üan* 當代中國報紙大全 (Yin-chuan, 1988).

References—Journals and Newspapers

Western Language Journals: Premodern China 116
Western Language Journals: Modern China 118
A Partial Listing of Important Current Chinese Journals 120
A Partial Listing of Important Chinese Newspapers Past and
   Present 125
A Partial Listing of Important Japanese Journals for Sinology 128
Union Catalogues of Chinese Journals and Newspapers 131
Indexes to Chinese Journals—General and Specialized 134

WESTERN LANGUAGE JOURNALS: PREMODERN CHINA

(N) denotes a 'newsletter'
* denotes journal may contain info on modern China

Acta Asiatica (1963 ≥...) Tokyo; often contains translations of leading Japanese sinologists.

Asia Major, three series (1924-1934) Leipzig; (1949-1974) London; (1988 ≥...) Princeton.

Ars Orientalis (1954 ≥...) USA; for information on Chinese art.

Bulletin de l'École française d'Extrême-Orient (1901 ≥...) Hanoi and Paris.

Bulletin of the Museum of Far Eastern Antiquities (1929 ≥...) Stockholm.

Bulletin of the School of Oriental and African Studies (1917 ≥...) London.

Cahiers d'Extrême-Asie (1985 ≥...) Kyoto; very informative on the history of Chinese religions.

Cahiers de linguistique—Asie orientale (1978 ≥...) Paris.

Chinese Culture (1957 ≥...) Taipei; concentrates on Chinese history.

Chinese Music (1978 ≥...) USA

Chinese Science (N) (1975 ≥...) USA.

CLEAR: Chinese Literature: Essays, Articles, Reviews (1979 ≥...) USA.

Early China (N) (1975 ≥...) USA; incorporates "Society for the Study of Pre-Han China Newsletter" (1969).

East Asian History * (1991 ≥...) Canberra; formerly "Papers on Far Eastern History" (1970-1990).

Etudes chinoises * (1983 ≥...) Paris; informative about sinology in France.

Extrême-Orient Extrême-Occident * (1982 ≥...) Paris.

Harvard Journal of Asiatic Studies (1936 ≥...) USA; America's leading sinological journal.

Journal of the American Oriental Society (1849 ≥...) USA.

Journal of Asian History (1968 ≥...) USA.

Journal of Asian Studies * (1955 ≥...) USA; formerly "Far Eastern Quarterly" (1941-1955).

Journal Asiatique (1822 ≥...) Paris. Issued by the Société Asiatique.

Journal of the Chinese Language Teachers Association * (1965 ≥...) USA.

Journal of Chinese Linguistics * (1973 ≥...) USA.

Journal of Chinese Philosophy (1973 ≥...) USA.

Journal of Chinese Religions (N) (1983 ≥...) USA; formerly "Journal of the Society for the Study of Chinese Religions" (1976-1982).

Journal of the Economic and Social History of the Orient (1957 ≥...) Leiden.

Journal of Oriental Studies (1954 ≥...) Hong Kong.

Journal of the Royal Asiatic Society (1823 ≥...) London.

Journal of Sung Yuan Studies (1970 ≥...) USA; formerly "Bulletin of Sung-Yüan Studies"; and "Sung Studies Newsletter".

Late Imperial China (N) (1985 ≥...) USA; formerly "Ch'ing-shih wen-t'i" (1975-84).

Mélanges chinois et Bouddhiques (1931 ≥...) Bruxelles.

Ming Studies (N) (1975 ≥...) USA.

Monumenta Serica (1935 ≥...) Köln.

Oriens Extremus (1954 ≥...) Hamburg.

Papers on Chinese History (1992 ≥...) USA; reproduces Harvard University seminar papers.

Sinologica (1947 ≥...) Bâsle.

Sino-Western Cultural Relations (N) (1979 ≥...) USA; formerly "China Mission Studies Bulletin".

T'ang Studies (N) (1985 ≥...) USA.

Taoist Resources (N) (1988 ≥...) USA.

T'oung Pao (1890 ≥...) Leiden; leading sinological journal in Europe.

WESTERN LANGUAGE JOURNALS: MODERN CHINA

(N) denotes a 'newsletter'

Australian Journal of Chinese Affairs (1979 ≥...) Canberra; scholarly analysis of current topics.

Asian Survey (1961 ≥...) Berkeley; monthly journal on contemporary Asian history.

Beijing Review (1979 ≥...) Beijing; formerly *Peking Review* (1958-1979), appears weekly.

Bulletin of Concerned Asian Scholars (1969 ≥...) USA; contains extensive book reviews, sometimes.

CCP Research Newsletter (N) (1988 ≥...) USA; twice yearly, begun by a group of younger scholars interested in Party history.

China aktuell (1971 ≥...) Hamburg; features monthly and yearly indexes on all aspects of PRC developments. Very up-to-date.

China Business Review (1974 ≥...) Washington; irregular.

China City Planning Review (1984 ≥...) Beijing; three times per year.

China Environmental News (1988 ≥...) Beijing; monthly.

China Exchange News (1978 ≥...) Washington; quarterly, with most up to date info on American and PRC joint-educational programs.

China Information (1986 ≥...) Leiden; quarterly informative journal on Chinese developments, including cultural matters.

China Law Reporter (1980 ≥...) Chicago; quarterly.

China Monthly Data (1993 ≥...) Hamburg; monthly.

China News Analysis (1953 ≥...) Hong Kong; bi-monthly 'watchdog' commentary.

China Newsletter (1979 ≥...) Tokyo; bi-monthly information on the Chinese economy.

China Quarterly (1960 ≥...) London; quarterly, leading academic journal on contemporary China, sometimes includes info on Hong Kong and Taiwan.

China Statistics Monthly (1988 ≥...) USA; monthly statistics on trade and prices.

China Trader (1978 ≥...) Hong Kong; monthly.

China's Foreign Trade (1956 ≥...) Beijing; monthly, sponsored by Chinese Council for the Promotion of International Trade.

Far Eastern Economic Review (1946 ≥...) Hong Kong; weekly up-to-date analysis of current events in China, among other Asian regions.

Issues and Studies (1964 ≥...) Taipei; monthly journal, with some good writing on current events in the PRC, propagandist in tone.

Journal of Contemporary China (1992 ≥...) Princeton; biannual, focuses on post T'ien-an-men issues, in particular, politics.

Modern Asian Studies (1967 ≥...) Cambridge; often contains historical articles on China during the 19th and 20th centuries.

Modern China (1975 ≥...) USA; leading US journal on modern Chinese history.

Modern Chinese Literature (N) (1986 ≥...) USA.

Pacific Affairs (1928 ≥...) Vancouver; quarterly scholarly journal on modern Asian history, with good book reviews.

Problems of Communism (1951 ≥...) USA; has interesting information on China, occasionally.

Positions: East Asia Cultures Critique (1993 ≥ ...) USA; publishes critical, reflexive articles on East Asia.

Republican China (1976 ≥...) (N) USA; formerly known as "Chinese Republic Studies Newsletter".

Summary of World Broadcasts, BBC—The Far East (1977 ≥...) England; good for 'China watching'.

Note:
China Daily (since 1981 ≥...) Beijing; China's leading English language newspaper.

A Partial Listing of Important Current Chinese Journals

Note: These include Taiwan/Hong Kong based journals, where relevant. Those journals marked with a (F) may be found in the *Fu-yin pao-k'an tzu-liao* reprint series.

For those journals whose titles are not explicit, the principal subject matter is indicated.

(1) Scientific journals (for research in particular subjects; examples, there are several thousands of this kind):

Ch'eng-shih ching-chi 城市經濟 (F)
Chiang-han k'ao-ku 江漢考古
Chiang-han lun-t'an 江漢論壇 (history)
Chiang-huai lun-t'an 江淮論壇 (history)
Chiao-t'ung yün-shu ching-chi 交通運輸經濟 (F)
Chien-chu li-shih yen-chiu 建築歷史研究
Chin-tai Chung-kuo shih yen-chiu t'ung-hsün　近代中國史研究通訊 (Taiwan; newsletter for modern Chinese history)
Chin-tai shih yen-chiu 近代史研究
Ching-chi shih 經濟史(F)
Ching-chi tao-pao 經濟導報(Hong Kong)
Ching-chi yen-chiu 經濟研究[1]
Ch'ing-hua hsüeh-pao 清華學報 (1924-1947; n.s. 1956 Taiwan)
Ch'ing-shih yen-chiu 清史研究
Chung-kuo che-hsüeh shih 中國哲學史(F)
Chung-kuo cheng-chih 中國政治 (F)
Chung-kuo chin-tai shih 中國近代史 (F)
Chung-kuo ching-chi-shih yen-chiu 中國經濟史研究
Chung-kuo ching-nei yü-yen chi yü-yen-hsüeh 中國境內語言及語言學
Chung-kuo hsien-tai shih 中國現代史 (F)
Chung-kuo hsien-tai tang-tai wen-hsüeh yen-chiu　中國現代當代文學研究 (F)
Chung-kuo huan-ching k'o-hsüeh 中國環境科學
Chung-kuo k'o-chi shih-liao 中國科技史料
Chung-kuo kung-ch'an-tang 中國共產黨(F)

---

[1] The present journal should not be confused with an earlier version of this publication with the same title. *Ching-chi yen-chiu* was the principal theoretical economic journal published in the PRC between 1955 and 1966. It has been indexed by James Nickum, *A Research Guide to Jingji Yanjiu (Economic Studies)* (Berkeley, 1972), which provides both a listing of articles in both Chinese and English, as well as a subject index and an author index.

Chung-kuo nung-shih 中國農史

Chung-kuo nung-yeh k'o-hsüeh 中國農業科學

Chung-kuo shao-shu min-tsu 中國少數民族 (F)

Chung-kuo she-hui ching-chi shih yen-chiu 中國社會經濟史研究

Chung-kuo she-hui k'o-hsüeh 中國社會科學

Chung-kuo shih yen-chiu 中國史研究

Chung-kuo tang-shih t'ung-hsün 中國黨史通訊

Chung-kuo ti-li 中國地理 (F)

Chung-kuo t'ung-chi 中國統計

Chung-kuo t'ung-chi yüeh-pao 中國統計月報

Chung-kuo wen-che yen-chiu chi-k'an 中國文哲研究集刊 (Taiwan)

Chung-kuo yü-wen 中國語文

Chung-wai fa-hsüeh 中外法學 (Beijing University Law School Journal)

Chung-yang yen-chiu-yüan li-shih yü-yen yen-chiu-so chi-k'an 中央研究院歷史語言研究所集刊 (Bulletin of the Institute of History and Philology, Academia Sinica, Taiwan)

Chung-yang yen-chiu-yüan chin-tai shih yen-chiu-so chi-k'an 中央研究院近代史研究所集刊 (Bulletin of the Institute of Modern History, Academia Sinica, Taiwan)

Fu-chien lun-t'an 福建論壇

Fa-lü 法律 (F)

Fu-nü tsu-chih yü huo-tung 婦女組織與活動 (F)

Han-hsüeh yen-chiu 漢學研究 (Taiwan)

Han-hsüeh yen-chiu t'ung-hsün 漢學研究通訊 (Taiwan)

Hsi-ch'ü yen-chiu 戲曲研究 (F)

Hsiang-kang Chung-wen ta-hsüeh hsüeh-pao 香港中文大學學報 (Hong Kong)

Hsin shih-hsüeh 新史學 (Taiwan; innovative and internationally-oriented history journal)

Hsin-hua wen-chai 新華文摘

Hung-lou-meng yen-chiu 紅樓夢研究 (F)

Jen-k'ou hsüeh 人口學 (F)

Jen-wen chi she-hui k'o-hsüeh chi-k'an 人文及社會科學季刊 (Taiwan)

Jen-wen tsa-chih 人文雜誌

K'ao-ku 考古

K'ao-ku hsüeh-pao 考古學報

K'ao-ku yü wen-wu 考古與文物

K'o-chi kuan-li yü ch'eng-chiu 科技管理與成就 (F)

K'o-hsüeh chi-shu 科學技術 (F)

Ku-kung hsüeh-shu chi-k'an 故宮學術季刊 (Taiwan; National Palace
  Museum Quarterly)
Ku-kung po-wu-yüan yüan-k'an 故宮博物院院刊
Kung-yeh ching-chi 工業經濟 (F)
K'ung-tzu yen-chiu 孔子研究
Kuo-chi mao-i wen-t'i 國際貿易問題 (international trade)
Kuo-min ching-chi chi-hua yü kuan-li 國民經濟計劃與管理 (F)
Lao-tung ching-chi yü jen-k'ou 勞動經濟與人口 (F)
Li-shih chiao-hsüeh 歷史教學
Li-shih hsüeh-pao 歷史學報
Li-shih tang-an 歷史檔案
Li-shih ti-li 歷史地理
Li-shih yen-chiu 歷史研究[2]
Lin-shih wen-chi 林史文集
Mei-shu-shih lun 美術史論
Min-tsu yü-wen 民族語文
Ming Ch'ing shih 明清史(F)
Ming Ch'ing shih chi-k'an 明清史集刊
Nan-k'ai shih-hsüeh 南開史學
Nung-yeh ching-chi 農業經濟(F)
Nung-yeh k'ao-ku 農業考古
San-kuo Liang Chin Sui T'ang shih 三國兩晉隋唐史(F)
She-hui hsüeh 社會學 (F)
Shih-hsüeh-shih yen-chiu 史學史研究
Shu-fa 書法
Shui-ch'an-yeh ching-chi 水產業經濟(F)
Sung Liao Chin Yüan shih 宋遼金元史(F)
Ta-hsüeh chiao-yü 大學教育(F)
Tang-an yü li-shih 檔案與歷史
T'e-ch'ü yü k'ai-fang-shih ching-chi 特區與開放市經濟(F)
Tsung-chiao 宗教(F)
T'u-shu-kuan-hsüeh 圖書館學 (F)
T'u-shu p'ing-chieh 圖書評介(F)
Tun-huang yen-chiu 敦煌研究
Tung-pei ti-fang shih yen-chiu 東北地方史研究
Tzu-jan k'o-hsüeh shih yen-chiu 自然科學史研究

---

[2] Has an index: Tanaguchi Fusao 谷口房男, *'Rekishi kenkyû' sômuku, sakuin*
歷史研究総目, 索引 (Tokyo, 1981); includes all issues up to 1980, with a separate listing of titles per issue, and an author index, arranged according to the number of
strokes of authors' names.

Wen-hsien 文獻
Wen-hsüeh i-ch'an 文學遺產
Wen-hsüeh p'ing-lun 文學評論
Wen-i li-lun 文藝理論 (F)
Wen-wu 文物[3]
Wen Shih Che 文史哲
Wu-shen-lun 無神論(F)
Wu-tzu ching-chi 物資經濟(F)
Yü-yen chiao-hsüeh yü yen-chiu 語言教學與研究
Yü-yen-hsüeh lun-ts'ung 語言學論叢
Yü-yen wen-hsüeh hsüeh 語言文學學(F)
Yü-yen yen-chiu 語言研究

(2) *University journals* (again, only examples):
　　An-hui shih-ta hsüeh-pao 安徽師大學報 (University Journal from Anhui Normal University)
　　Hang-chou ta-hsüeh hsüeh-pao 杭州大學學報
　　Hsia-men ta-hsüeh hsüeh-pao 廈門大學學報
　　Pei-ching ta-hsüeh hsüeh pao 北京大學學報
　　Tan-chiang hsüeh-pao 淡江學報 (Taiwan)

(3) *Cultural journals* (again, only a few examples out of the many thousands):
　　Ch'un-feng 春風(short story magazine)
　　Hsiao-shuo yüeh-pao 小說月報 (leading PRC monthly publishing short stories and novellas)
　　Lien-ho wen-hsüeh 聯合文學 (the major literary magazine in Taiwan)
　　Pao-kao wen-hsüeh 報告文學 (a journal of reportage literature)
　　Shih-chieh chih-shih 世界知識 (foreign politics, presented in an "easy" informal format)
　　Shih-yüeh 十月 (literary)
　　Shou-huo 收獲 (literary)
　　Ta-chung tien-ying 大衆電影 (popular journal about films)
　　Tien-ying wen-hsüeh 電影文學 (films and filmmaking)

---

3 Has an index: *Wen-wu san-wu-ling ch'i tsung-mu so-yin* 文物三五零期總目索引 (1950.1-1985.7) (Beijing, 1986).

(4) Leisure journals
    Chung-kuo ch'ing-nien 中國青年 (Chinese youth)
    Chung-kuo fu-nü 中國婦女 (women's magazine)
    Chung-kuo lao-nien 中國老年 (for the "over 60's")
    Hsien-tai chia-t'ing 現代家庭 (family life)
    Hsin t'i-yü 新體育 (sport)
    Lü-yu 旅遊 (travel and tourism)
    Mei-hua sheng-huo 美化生活 (housekeeping)

(5) Summary publications
    Hsin-hua wen-chai 新華文摘 (1979-present; the successor of *Hsin-hua yüeh-pao*) Monthly journal that reproduces parts of, or entire articles out of journals and newspapers. The subjects include matters concerning economy, ideology, literature, and scientific research.

(6) "Watchdog" journals about the PRC
    from Hong Kong:
    Chiu-shih nien-tai 九十年代
    Cheng ming 爭鳴
    Both these monthly journals give information on "anti-Communist" groups (i.e. those not attached to Taiwan), high party officials from the CCP, and "inside-information" on important overseas Chinese figures. Much of what is written here is "taboo" in both the PRC and in Taiwan!

    from Taiwan:
    Chung-kung yen-chiu 中共研究
    A monthly from Taiwan which discusses developments in the PRC. Often presents "new" information and insights on Chinese political happenings; until 1969, was known as *Fei-ch'ing yen-chiu* 匪情研究

A PARTIAL LISTING OF IMPORTANT CHINESE NEWSPAPERS
PAST AND PRESENT

Note: In many cases, these newspapers are available in the form of re-prints and/or microfilms. In either case, an indication is given for which period one form or another of reproduction is known with an (R) and the dates.

(1) Those newspapers founded before 1895 (and written in *wen-yen*):
Shen-pao 申報 Shanghai, daily, founded 1872; for many years the most influential newspaper, ceased publication in 1949.
(R) for entire set plus indexes in the *Shen-pao so-yin 1872-1949* [see discussion in this chapter '*Chinese Newspapers*'].

Hsin-wen pao 新聞報 Shanghai, from 1893 until 1959?, competed with *Shen-pao*, with stress upon the commercial and economic problems of the country.
(R) available for period 1893 through May 27, 1949.

Hua-tzu jih-pao 華字日報, appeared in Hong-Kong from 1864 to 1941.

Shang-hai hsin-pao 上海新報, founded in 1861 as a 'weekly', and then became a daily from 1872, but stopped in the same year. This was the Chinese edition of the well-known British publication, *North China Herald.*
(R) available from May 24, 1862 to December 31, 1872.

(2) Newpapers 1895-1911 (considered by some scholars as one of the most brilliant epochs in the history of modern Chinese jour-nalism):
a) Those newspapers connected with the reform movement and the idea of a constitution:

Shih-wu pao 時務報, from July 1886 to May 1898; an organ of the Shanghai branch of a reform society called Ch'iang-hsüeh hui 強學會, published in Shanghai 3 times a month.

Ch'ing-i pao 清議報, edited by Liang Ch'i-ch'ao, issued in Yoko-hama 3 times a month from Dec. 13, 1898 until the end of 1901.

Hsin-min ts'ung-pao 新民叢報, a successor of the *Ch'ing-i pao* and also edited by Liang Ch'i-ch'ao, published fortnightly in Yoko-hama from Feb. 2, 1902 to July, 1907.

b) Those newspapers connected with and advocating the republican revolution:

Chung-kuo jih-pao 中國日報, the first Chinese revolutionary daily, edited by Sun Yat-sen's partisans, published in Hong Kong from Dec. 1899 until 1913.

Su-pao 蘇報 Shanghai, from 1896 to June 1903. Well-known because of its association with Chang Ping-lin. Very anti-Manchu.

Min-pao 民報 Tokyo, from Nov. 26, 1905 to Oct. 1908 as a monthly; the most important Chinese revolutionary periodical before 1911 and the organ of Sun Yat-sen's T'ung-meng hui 同盟會.

(3) Republican period—there were *thousands* of newspapers published in this period. According to one incomplete source of statistical data, in Peking alone some hundred newspapers were published. Some of the most important include:

Ch'en-pao 晨報 (The Morning Post), Peking, 1918-1943.
(R) available for 1918-June 5, 1928; October 16,1937-December 30, 1943.

Shih-pao 實報 (Truth Post), Peking, 1928-1944 (published during the Japanese occupation as well).

Shih-chieh jih-pao 世界日報, Peking, 1925-49.
(R) available for all issues.

Ta-kung-pao 大公報 ("L'Impartial"), Tientsin 1902 →, Shanghai 1935 →, Hong Kong 1938 →. considered by Fairbank the best source on the 1920s and 1930s.
(R) available for entire series.

Min-kuo jih-pao 民國日報 Shanghai and Canton 1914 , spiritual successor to the T'ung-meng hui newspapers, superseded by the following newspaper.

Chung-yang jih-pao 中央日報 (The Central Daily News), from 1928 in Shanghai, then Nanking, then Chungking, now Taipei. Official KMT organ from 1929 .
(R) available for entire period 1928-December 15, 1948.

Chieh-fang jih-pao 解放日報 (Liberation Daily), Yenan. The official CCP organ of the pre-1949 period.

(4) Newspapers of the Chinese People's Republic, 1949—
For an introduction to newspaper publishing until 1967, see
Berton and Wu, *Contemporary China: A Research Guide*, Chapters II,
III, and XVII.
Present day leading newspapers include:

Jen-min jih-pao 人民日報 is not a newspaper in the Western sense of
the word. Its function is to make clear the authoritative Party
standpoint on certain issues, and to throw open subject for debate
within clearly demarcated political lines. It is therefore, very heavy
reading (has an index). Since 1982 there exists (R) in the convenient form of a book-like photocopy.

Kuang-ming jih-pao 光明日報, not affiliated with the Party, contains
much cultural and intellectual news (has an index).

Chieh-fang-chün pao 解放軍報, an organ of the People's Republic
Army.

Kung-jen jih-pao 工人日報, the newspaper of the All China Federation of Trade Unions.

Wen-hui pao 文滙報, non-Party paper. This work has been indexed
for the period 1949-1966. See Phyllis Wang and Donald Gibbs,
eds., *Reader's Guide to China's Literary Gazette, 1949-1966* (Berkeley,
1991). Indexed by author's name (both in *pinyin* and in Wade-
Giles romanization).

The Hsinhua News Agency provides a daily release in English and
Chinese containing major items from the Chinese press. They are
widely available.

A Partial Listing of Important Japanese Journals

Note: Not all the following Japanese journals are directed exclusively toward China, but all of them do include on a regular basis scholarly articles concerning some aspects of Chinese history, literature, or contemporary affairs. These titles are considered the major Japanese periodical publications for China, but often there are articles or essays appearing in other journals, not listed here. To find these, one should consult the *Chûgoku kankei ronsetsu shiryô* 中国関係論説資料 (Tokyo, since 1964) series. These series appear in three parts: (1) philosophy and religion; (2) literature, linguistics, and the arts (in the broadest sense); (3) history, politics, and economics, and each part is published in a double set of volumes per year. Each volume reproduces important journal publications for that given year. As these volumes are released fairly quickly, one may find what work has been published the previous year. In general, the following titles conforms to the journals surveyed in the *Current Contents of Foreign Periodicals in Chinese Studies* (see the section *General Bibliographies* in Chapter II).

Ajia Bunka アジア文化 (Tokyo)
Ajia Keizai アジア経済 (Tokyo)
Ajia Kenkyû アジア研究 (Tokyo)
Ajia Kenkyûjo Kiyô アジア研究所紀要 (Tokyo)
Aoyama Shigaku 青山史学 (Tokyo)
Bijutsu Kenkyû 美術研究 (Tokyo)
Bungaku Kenkyû 文学研究 (Fukuoka)
Bunka 文化 (Sendai)
Chûgoku–Shakai to Bunka 中国‐社会と文化 (Tokyo)
Chûgoku Bungaku (Geppô) 中国文学 (月報) (Kyoto)
Chûgoku Bungaku Ronshû 中国文学論集 (Fukuoka)
Chûgoku Bungakuhô 中国文学報 (Kyoto)
Chûgoku Chûsei Bungaku Kenkyû 中国中世文学研究 (Hiroshima)
Chûgoku Joseishi Kenkyû 中国女性史研究 (Tokyo)
Chûgoku Kenkyû Geppô 中国研究月報 (Tokyo)
Chûgoku Koten Kenkyû 中国古典研究 (Tokyo)
Chûgoku Shibun Ronsô 中国詩文論叢 (Tokyo)
Chûgoku Shigaku 中国史学 (Tokyo)
Chûgoku Shisôshi Kenkyû 中国思想史研究 (Kyoto)
Chûgoku Tetsugaku 中国哲学 (Sapporo)
Chûgoku Tetsugaku Kenkyû 中国哲学研究 (Tokyo)
Chûgoku Tetsugaku Ronshû 中国哲学論集 (Fukuoka)
Chûgoku Zokubungaku Kenkyû 中国俗文学研究 (Tokyo)

Gakurin 学林 (Kyoto)

Gendai Chûgoku 現代中国 (Tokyo)

Hikaku Bungaku Kenkyû 比較文学研究 (Tokyo)

Indogaku Bukkyôgaku Kenkyû 印度学仏教学研究 (Tokyo)

Kansai Daigaku Tôzai Gakujutsu Kenkyûjo Kiyô 関西大学東西学術研究所
　紀要 (Osaka)

Kindai Chûgoku 近代中国 (Tokyo)

Kindai Chûgoku Kenkyû Ihô 近代中国研究彙報 (Tokyo)

Kyoto Daigaku Bungakubu Kenkyû Kiyô 京都大学文学部研究紀要
　(Kyoto)

Kyûshû Chûgoku Gakkaihô 九州中国学会報 (Fukuoka)

Mimei 未名 (Kobe)

Mindaishi Kenkyû 明代史研究 (Tokyo)

Mondai to Kenkyû 問題と研究 (Tokyo)

Nagoya Daigaku Jinbun Kagaku Kenkyû 名古屋大学人文科学研究
　(Nagoya)

Nihon Chûgoku Kôkogakkai Kaihô 日本中国考古学会会報 (Tokyo)

Nippon Chûgoku Gakkaihô 日本中国学会報 (Tokyo)

Osaka Daigaku Bungakubu Kiyô 大阪大学文学部紀要 (Osaka)

Rekishi Kenkyû 歴史研究 (Osaka)

Rekishigaku Kenkyû 歴史学研究 (Tokyo)

Risshô Daigaku Tôyôshi Ronshû 立正大学東洋史論集 (Tokyo)

Shakai Bunka Shigaku 社会文化史学 (Tokyo)

Shakai Keizai Shigaku 社会経済史学 (Tokyo)

Shichô 史潮 (Tokyo)

Shien 史苑 (Tokyo)

Shigaku Kenkyû 史学研究 (Hiroshima)

Shigaku Zasshi 史学雑誌 (Tokyo)

Shikyô Kenkyû 詩経研究 (Tokyo)

Shirin 史林 (Kyoto)

Shisen 史泉 (Osaka)

Shisô 思想 (Tokyo)

Shiteki 史滴 (Tokyo)

Tenri Daigaku Gakuhô 天理大学学報 (Tenri)

Tôhô Gakuhô 東方学報 (Kyoto)

Tôhô Shûkyô 東方宗教 (Tokyo)

Tôhôgaku 東方学 (Tokyo)

Tôyô Bunka 東洋文化 (Tokyo)

Tôyô Bunka Kenkyûjo Kiyô 東洋文化研究所紀要 (Tokyo)

Tôyô Gakuhô 東洋学報 (Tokyo)

Tôyô Kenkyû 東洋研究 (Tokyo)

Tôyô Shien 東洋史苑 (Kyoto)

Tôyôgaku Ronsô–Tôyô Daigaku Bungakubu Kiyô 東洋学論叢 - 東洋大学 文学部紀要 (Tokyo)

Tôyôshi Kenkyû 東洋史研究 (Kyoto)

Yamagata Daigaku Kiyô–Jinbun Kagaku 山形大学紀要 - 人文科学 (Yamagata)

UNION CATALOGUES OF CHINESE JOURNALS AND NEWSPAPERS

Journals

Ch'üan-kuo Chung-wen ch'i-k'an lien-ho mu-lu tseng-ting pen 1833-1949 全國中文期刊聯合目錄增訂本 (Beijing, 1981).

This Chinese union list is a revision of the 1961 original edition, and lists the titles of some 20,000 Chinese journals of 'scholarly value', held in fifty PRC libraries. Arranged by stroke count of title. Has *pinyin* and stroke-count indexes to the first character of the title. Since the scope is from 1833 to 1949, it is an indispensable reference tool for the identification of Chinese periodicals.

Chung-kuo pao-k'an ta-ch'üan 中國報刊大全 (Beijing, 1987), 2 vols.

Lists 1600 newspapers and 5300 periodicals published in 1987, complete with bibliographical information for each entry, including the name of the sponsoring organization, a brief account of the history of the publication and its scope, and whether it is a *nei-pu* publication.

Huang Han-chu and David Hsu, *Chinese Periodicals in the Library of Congress: A Bibliography* (Washington, D.C., 1988).

Revised and expanded edition of 1978 original. Gives information on some 8000 Chinese periodicals published from 1864-1986. Arranged alphabetically by title.

Périodiques en langue chinoise de la Bibliothèque nationale (Paris, 1972).

The first printed catalogue of this library's rich collection of Chinese journals, up to 1969. This work is divided into several different lists which allows the non-French reader to make use of its contents. Includes the following lists of journals, according to: (1) romanized alphabetical order [based on the French transliteration system], Chinese characters [arranged by stroke count order], subject or title in English, French, and Chinese. There is also a systematic listing according to topic (e.g. philosophy, or library science), and according to place of issue. Although a similar catalogue was issued in 1984, *Inventaire des périodiques chinois dans les bibliothèques francaises*, this later work is only an alphabetical list (in *pinyin*) of the titles and particular French library holdings of each periodical.

Chung-wen ho-hsin ch'i-k'an yao-mu tsung-lan 中文核心期刊要目總覽 (Beijing, 1992).

'A Guide to the Core Journals of China'. In 125 categories, lists some 10,000 journals which cover fields including philosophy, social sciences, humanities, natural science, medicine, agriculture, and engineering. Each entry is given a bibliographical description (title and its English translation, publisher, etc.). There is a title index at the end of the book.

Chung-kuo pao-k'an mu-lu 中國報刊目錄 (Beijing, 1993).

This is a guide to 2970 journals (and 243 newspapers), arranged according to subject (philosophy, social sciences, history, etc.). Gives titles in Chinese and English, and notes frequency of issue (quarterly, weekly).

Newspapers

The Contemporary China Institute, *A Bibliography of Chinese Newspapers and Periodicals in European Libraries* (Cambridge, 1975).

Gives information about 102 collections, comprising more than 1000 periodicals, including those in Eastern Europe and the former Soviet Union.

Huang Han-chu and David Hsu, *Chinese Newspapers in the Library of Congress: A Bibliography* (Washington, D.C., 1985).

Gives information on some 1200 newspapers published from the 1870s to the present. Arranged alphabetically by title. Has localities index and stroke-count index for first character in title.

Pei-ching t'u-shu-kuan kuan-ts'ang pao-chih mu-lu   北京圖書館館藏報 紙目錄 (Beijing, 1981).

Gives locational information for some 1800 Chinese and 1000 foreign-language newspapers. Chinese-language titles are grouped into pre- and post-1949 sections and then arranged by province. There is a separate section for Hong Kong, Macao, and overseas Chinese titles, arranged by country. Foreign-language titles are also arranged by country. Has stroke-count title indexes.

Shang-hai t'u-shu-kuan kuan-ts'ang Chung-wen pao-chih mu-lu (1862-1949) 上海圖書館館藏中文報紙目錄 (Shanghai, 1982).

Gives holding information on 3543 Chinese newspaper titles, arranged by stroke order. Has romanized (*pinyin*) index to the first character of each title. Has index of titles arranged according to place of publication.

Shang-hai t'u-shu-kuan kuan-ts'ang Chung-wen pao-chih fu-k'an mu-lu (1898-1949) 上海圖書館館藏中文報紙副刊目錄 (Shanghai, 1985).

Complements the last work above. Provides holding information on 7078 titles of supplements (special issues, magazine sections) to over 1400 newspapers. Titles are arranged according to stroke order. Has romanized (*pinyin*) index to the first character of the title. Also has index of titles arranged by subject, and an index of titles arranged by the title of the newspaper in which the supplements appeared.

Chung-kung ti-hsia tang-shih ch'i-pao-k'an tiao-ch'a yen-chiu 1919-1949 中共地下黨史期報刊調查研究 (Taipei, 1991).

An annotated list of newspapers and periodicals of the Chinese Communist Party, 1919-1949.

Current Chinese Newspaper Holdings in the Asian Library Collection of the University of California System and the Hoover Institution, Stanford University
(Berkeley, 1991).

INDEXES TO CHINESE JOURNALS

Aside from the specific bibliographies listed in chapter II for works in either Western languages or Chinese and Japanese, the following works may also prove useful for determining the contents of journal articles relevant to a particular topic. While many of these works may seem dated, they do in effect still give important information. For the names and the contents of a number of indexes specializing in articles related to sinology, literature, geography, education, and agriculture before 1949, one should turn to the section 'Indexes to Periodicals and Newspapers' in TB.

General Indexes

Yü Ping-ch'üan 余秉權,
Chung-kuo shih-hsüeh lun-wen yin-te 中國史學論文引得 Volume I:1901-1962 (Hong Kong, 1963) and Volume II:1905-1964 (Cambridge, Mass., 1970).

Analyses the contents of 954 periodicals published between 1902 and 1964. It is necessary to use both volumes in the index. The first was compiled from only those journals available in Hong Kong libraries, and the second from those in Europe and the US. Arranged by author; volume one has a subject index, but it is difficult to use.

Chung-kuo shih-hsüeh lun-wen so-yin 中國史學論文索引 (Beijing, 1957-58), two volumes.

The period covered by this index is circa 1900-37. The entries are arranged according to 13 subject categories. Contains over 30,000 entries from over 1300 periodicals; an index lists titles, names, and places. Deals with both premodern and modern history.

Chung-kuo chin erh-shih nien wen-shih-che lun-wen fen-lei so-yin 中國近二十年文史哲論文分類索引 (Taipei,1970)

Subject index to Taiwan periodicals, 1948-1968, on Chinese literature, history, and philosophy. Arrangement is by a helpful and detailed subject classification index. There is also an author index.

Howard, Richard comp., *Index to Learned Chinese Periodicals (1927-54)* (Boston, 1962).

Although this index examines the contents of only 14 titles, they are probably the most important for the Republican period. Most of the subjects covered concern premodern history, and thus this work is an outstanding source to examine the development of the modern historiography of premodern China. There are separate author and subject listings. Each entry contains the author's name, title (with an English translation), and reference to journal (title, volume, year, pages). Some entries have an English abstract.

Specialized Indexes

Sun, E-tu Zen and John DeFrancis, *Bibliography of Chinese Social History: A Selected and Critical List of Chinese Periodical Sources* (New Haven, 1952).

Covers 176 articles in Chinese on social history appearing mainly during the 1930's. Annotated.

Chung-kuo hsien-tai wen-hsüeh ch'i-k'an mu-lu ch'u-kao 中國現代文學期刊目錄（初稿）(Shanghai, 1961).

This is an index to more than 1582 Chinese literary periodicals published between 1902 and 1949, including those in Communist-held areas and areas under Japanese occupation.

T'ang Yüan 唐沅, et. al., *Chung-kuo hsien-tai wen-hsüeh ch'i-k'an mu-lu hui-pien* 中國現代文學期刊目錄滙編 (Tianjin, 1988), two volumes.

Supersedes the above work. Volume I lists the contents of some 1800 literary journals, arranged according to first date of appearance, cross-refenced with a listing of titles according to stroke counts. The first half of Volume II continues the journal contents, and includes a separate author index, based on stroke counts, and an institutional holding index. At the end of Volume II, there is a table listing all journals examined, their frequency and place of publication, principal editors, and publishers. Indispensable for 20th century literature studies.

Liu Chun-jo, *Controversies in Modern Chinese Intellectual History: An Analytical Bibliography of Periodical Articles, Mainly of the May Fourth and Post-May Fourth Era* (Cambridge, Mass., 1964).
    Discusses some 500 articles, grouped by issue. Annotated. Includes literary, social, political, and intellectual matters.

Soong, James C.Y., *Red Flag, 1958-1968: A Research Guide* (Washington, D.C., 1969).
    Lists articles by topic, notes translations, if they exist, and has separate indexes for authors and people cited. Reproduces tables of contents and *Hung-ch'i*'s own annual subject index.

Pao-k'an tzu-liao so-yin 報刊資料索引 (Beijing, since 1984).
    Can be used in conjunction with the 'Fu-yin pao-k'an tzu-liao' reprint series.

CHAPTER FOUR

BIOGRAPHY IN CHINA: PAST AND PRESENT

Introduction

The writing of biography in China has been and continues to be a different genre than that in the West. In China, the biography represents the public record of a person, and not an investigation of his/her particular personality. The 'Standard' or Dynastic Histories contain thousands of biographical entries, and there are collections of specialized biographies in local gazetteers so that the total number of life histories may be an enormous figure. In addition, epitaphs which were very often commissioned by the family of a deceased member, form a rich source of biographical information.[1] Nevertheless, in all these works, biographies generally were highly formal, and often nothing more than a series of near clichés, and without much personal information. The purpose of biography was didactic: the subject's success (or failure) was an illustration for future generations to follow, or as the case may be, to avoid. The emphasis was on a person's virtue, and most commonly, how that virtue related to administrative success.

There has also been a Chinese tradition of 'rebel-reformer' in biographical writing, but the subjects of these studies were usually classifed as 'villains', and relegated to the back pages of standard histories.[2] In the twentieth century the 'rebel-reformer' took on

---

[1] A very good summary of what worthwhile has been written about the genre of Chinese biography in both English and Chinese may be noted in the excellent article by Brian Moloughney, "From Biographical History to Historical Biography: A Transformation in Chinese Historical Writing," *East Asian History*, 4 (1992):1-30. This article brings up to date other important studies of biographical writing for the premodern period: Peter Olbricht, "Die Biographie in China," *Saeculum* 8 (1957):224-35; Denis Twitchett, "Chinese Biographical Writing," in *Historians of China and Japan*, ed.by W.G.Beasley and E.G. Pulleyblank (London, 1961),pp.95-114; *idem.*, "Problems of Chinese Biography," in *Confucian Personalities*, ed. by A.F.Wright and D.Twitchett (Stanford, 1962), pp.24-39; David S.Nivison, "Aspects of Traditional Chinese Biography," *Journal of Asian Studies* 21 (1962):457-63.

[2] Two clear examples of this phenomenon are the biographies of the late Ming rebels Li Tzu-ch'eng 李自成 (1605?-45) and Chang Hsien-chung 張獻忠 (1605-47) in the Ming dynastic history. See the excellent discussion of the 'rebel-reformer' tradition by Wang Gungwu, "The Rebel-Reformer and Modern Chinese Biography," in his, *The Chineseness of China: Selected Essays* (Hong Kong, 1991), pp.187-206.

heroic status [see below], but despite this development, modern biographical writing in China still lacks the depth and personal reflections of its counterpart in the West. One will find little to no personal information in 'official' PRC or Taiwan sources about contemporary persons.[3]

The form of the biography in traditional China is modelled on the *lieh-chuan* 列傳 of the Dynastic Histories. This form was fixed by two of China's earliest historians, Ssu-ma Ch'ien 司馬遷 (145-90 B.C.) and Pan Ku.[4] It was imitated in later histories and in various 'unofficial' compilations—such as local gazetteers—and information was often excerpted from it for inclusion in the chronological charts (*nien-p'u* 年譜) which outline, year by year, the important events in an individual's life. In the term *lieh-chuan, chuan* means "transmission" or "account", while *lieh* "rank" or "series" refers to the manner in which they are arranged in each of the histories.[5] The evaluation of a person's deeds was for the public record, and a series of these biographies, or *lieh-chuan* ("ordered or connected traditions") would make a full didactic impact.[6]

In general, the life history of an individual in a dynastic or local history usually contains information in the following order: person's name; other names (including style, pen names); native place; names of father, grandfather, or distinguished ancestors with the offices they held; anecdotes about the person's youth, especially his learning record; record of official posts and honors; date of death, with possible age; sons, and their offices; publications by the deceased. There might be interspersed with the above, mention of some important events in which s/he took place and some famous people with whom s/he had contact, but none of this will be in depth, and it is unlikely that one may gain

---

[3] For an overview on biographical writing in this century, see, Moloughney, *ibid.*, and Richard Howard, "Modern Chinese Biographical Writing," *Journal of Asian Studies* 21 (1962):465-73; and William Ayers, "Current Biography in Communist China," *Journal of Asian Studies* 21 (1962):477-85.

[4] For the earliest references on the *lieh-chuan* writing, see Moloughney, *ibid.*, pp.1-4. An interesting recent account of Ssu-ma Ch'ien's contribution to historical writing, is Grant Hardy, "Can an Ancient Chinese Historian Contribute to Modern Western Theory? The Multiple Narratives of Ssu-ma Ch'ien," *History and Theory*, 33 (1994):20-38,

[5] Pierre Ryckmans, "A New Interpretation of the Term *lieh-chuan* as used in the *Shih-chi*," *Papers on Far Eastern History* 5 (1972):135-47 gives an interesting account of *lieh-chuan*, and translates them as 'exemplary lives'.

[6] The exemplary nature of early biography was prominent in the brief 'pseudo-biographical' anecdotes collected to form the *Lieh-nü chuan* 列女傳 (Biographies of Women) circa 16 B.C..

an idea of the person's personality or her/his relationship with those around her/him.

Genealogical writings, *chia-p'u* 家譜 or *tsung-p'u* 宗譜, which became common from the Sung onward also give only this kind of formal information about individuals and their families. Two types of sources complement this type of traditional biographical writing. *Pi-chi* 筆記 (miscellaneous notes, or notebooks) may contain short anecdotes on someone's character, although often these are based on heresay, and tend to "fictionalize" the person's life into historical romance. On the other hand, *pieh-chuan* 別傳 (unofficial biography) which became popular in the Ch'ing may give much insight into the subject's character. They were most often composed by a close friend of the deceased, and commemorated the intimacy between subject and author.

Since the 1930s, there have been enormous efforts made to incorporate existing Chinese biographical records into the mainstream of modern historiographical writing. In 1934 Chinese and Western scholars began work on the first 'modern' biographical dictionary of persons active in the period 1600-1911. The project was completed in 1942 under the leadership of Arthur Hummel, and published by the US Library of Congress. The two volume *Eminent Chinese of the Ch'ing Period* (hereafter, ECCP) was the product of joint efforts by both well-trained Chinese and Western historians; ECCP has remained the 'model biographical dictionary' in the English language. Since its publication, other biographical dictionary projects were initiated. We now have biographical dictionaries in English for the Sung (appearing in 1976), the Yüan (recently published in 1993), and the Ming (also completed in 1976) dynasties. For the twentieth century, two major publications have been published, the five-volume *Biographical Dictionary of Republican China* (1967-71) and the *Biographic Dictionary of Chinese Communism (1921-65)* (1971).[7] A future "ECCP" type dictionary project is a five-volume set on Chinese women from the Han dynasty to the present.

Perhaps, one of the most important contributions of 20th century biographical writing was that the phenomenon of the 'rebel-reformer' was cast in a new light.[8] Sun Yat-sen's autobiographical

---

[7] There have been some other recent biographical dictionaries for PRC figures, but these do not measure in depth to those mentioned above.

[8] Wang Gungwu, "The Rebel Reformer," p.192.

account of his kidnapping, published in 1897, and his 'reminiscences' which appeared in the London-based *Strand Magazine* in 1912 ushered in a certain transformation in Chinese biographical writing. As Wang Gungwu has written, the changing images of the rebel leader could make such otherwise "detestable" individuals into (respectable) reformer heroes. A case in point is the 20th century image of the Taiping leader Hung Hsiu-ch'üan 洪秀全 (1812-64), who has been transformed from a rebel troublemaker into an inspiring peasant leader.[9] Another major change in biographical writing, occurring in the 20th century, was the growing popularity of autobiographical writing. For public figures in China to record information about themselves seemed to gain more and more acceptance in the first half of this century.[10] The result was a steady stream of self-prepared *nien-p'u* biographies, culminating in the young historian Ku Chieh-kang's personal account of how he came to write ancient Chinese history.[11]

The nationalism of the 1930s and 40s inspired another new interest in biographical writing in China: the translation of Western biographies about 'nationalistic heroes' into Chinese.[12] These included biographies of Bismarck, Napoleon, Hitler, Tolstoy, Gandhi, George Washington, Woodrow Wilson, Marx and Lenin(!), and even Henry Ford. Interestingly, this was also a time when Chinese historians began to look at the individuality of certain figures who had played an important role in Chinese politics in the past. One figure who captured the attention of a number of writers was the Ming Grand Secretary Chang Chü-cheng 張居正 (1525-82). Chu Tung-yun's biography of the late Ming figure was the second known investigation.[13] According Wang Gungwu, Chu had been

---

[9] This image has become 'standard'. See, for example, the portrait of Hung in Frederic Wakeman, *The Fall of Imperial China* (New York, 1975).

[10] Wu Pei-yi in his *The Confucian's Progress: Autobiographical Writings in Traditional China* (Princeton, 1990) makes the point that in imperial times it was not until, and only during the late Ming, that Chinese literati engaged in any form of self-revelatory writing.

[11] See Chapter I, 'A Brief History of Chinese Studies and Sinology'. One may argue, as does Moloughney, *ibid.*, pp.15-22, that Liang Ch'i-ch'ao also created another form of biographical writing in which the individual has an 'independent life'. His studies of Li Hung-chang 李鴻章 (1823-1901), K'ang You-wei, and Wang An-shih 王安石 (1025-86) were supposed to reflect the tension of 'life' and 'times'.

[12] This phase of modern biographical writing is well-discussed in Ch'en Shih-hsiang, "An Innovation in Chinese Biographical Writing," *Far Eastern Quarterly* 13.1 (1953):44-62.

[13] Chu Tung-jun 朱東潤, *Chang Chü-cheng ta-chuan* 張居正大傳 (1945). The other

inspired by his reading of Boswell, Morley's *Life of Gladstone,*
Monypenny's *Life of Disraeli,* and Lytton Strachey's *Queen Victoria*
and *Eminent Victorians.*[14] In Chu's biography, Chang Chü-cheng
emerges as an 'individual' caught up in the sordid world of mid-
16th century politics, and not always as a 'super master politician'.
He had his "problems" as well.[15]

Despite all these promising new trends in 20th century historiography, biographical writing continues to remain a limited enterprise in China. In the words of Wang Gungwu, "the tradition to
commemorate, to eulogize, dutifully to show respect for the
dead" dominates both past and present biography.[16] The many
reasons given for phenomenon include China's "strong collective
tradition", and the tendency to utilize history, and therefore biography, as a method of teaching political example. It is probably
this purpose that provides the link in the writing of Chinese biography from past into present so that one may draw a line of continuity from historical times to now.

Chinese Names and their Alternatives

Chinese names consist of a surname (family name, *hsing* 姓) and
one fixed given name (*ming* 名), usually given in that order. The
surname is usually composed of one character, but there are a
number with two characters, such as Ou-yang, as in Ou-yang Hsiu,
or Ssu-ma, in Ssu-ma Kuang. In addition, in imperial China, people were also identified by the following:

shih 氏   clan or family name (particularly for women)
hsiao-ming 小名 childhood name, also *ju-ming* 乳名 or *nai-ming* 奶名
tzu 字   style, courtesy name used by person's friends
                   (usually given by his family)

---

attempt was by Ch'en I-lin 陳翊林 in 1934, and there was a *nien-p'u* published by
Yang Tu 楊度 in 1938. See Wang Gungwu, "The Rebel-Reformer," p.323 (note
#52).

[14] Wang Gungwu, *ibid.,* p.204.

[15] Compare with a more recent portrait drawn of this individual by Ray
Huang in his book *1587, A Year of No Significance: The Ming Dynasty in Decline* (New
Haven, 1981). Huang's book is a strong contrast to more conventional biographi-
cal writing, and a delight to read.

[16] Wang Gungwu, p.205. The political reform campaigns of the 1950s in the
PRC introduced another form of biographical writing, i.e. the "confession",
whereby well-known intellectuals were forced to write self-criticisms in the guise
of autobiography.

hao 號	fancy name (usually given by friends)
pieh-hao 別號	studio name, poetic name (chosen by person himself/herself)
pi-ming 筆名	pseudonym of writers, nom-de-plume
wai-hao 外號	nickname, also *ch'o-hao* 綽號, *hun-hao* 混號, *hun-hao* 諢號
nien-hao 年號	reign name of emperors
shih 謚	posthumous name or emperor or high official
hui 諱	taboo name, personal name or respected person, such as emperor, father

There about 200 common surnames in China, although some sources list as many as 4000. The Sung text *Pai chia hsing* 百家姓 was used in imperial times to teach characters to pupils at the elementary level of education. It lists, in no apparent order, 406 single-character and 30 double-character names.

As for given names, there seems to have been no limit to parental imagination. There was also the customary use of *meng* 孟, *chung* 仲, *shu* 叔, and *chi* 季 for oldest, second, third and youngest sons. In most families a generation order is expressed by one common character in the personal names of the same generation, the so-called *p'ai-hang* 排行 order.

Chinese literati were often cited in both official and non-official publications by names other than their *hsiao-ming*, and thus it is often necessary to use a guide to alternative names to find their name assigned at birth. Common people rarely had alternative names, and they were often referred to simply by number, e.g. Hu San 胡三 or Ma Wu 馬五. Women of the common classes did not have names and were assigned recognition by their married name, their natal surname, and the word *shih*, e.g. Hu Ma *shih* 胡馬氏, "Mrs. Hu, née Ma". Monks and priests usually abandoned their family names and were known by their religious names, e.g. Fa-hai or P'u-tu 普度.

More information about the Chinese naming process, both for Han Chinese and the 56 minorities that inhabit the geographical regions under Chinese suzerainty may be found in:
Chang Lien-fang 張聯芳 ed., *Chung-kuo jen ti hsing-ming* 中國人的姓名 (Beijing, 1992). Arranged in a series of separate essays covering these 57 groups, all authored by different individuals, this collection aims to explain the history and nature of the naming process.

Also useful for further understanding of the Chinese naming

process is an 'appellation dictionary'. See for example, Chang Hsiao-chung 張孝忠 et.al. eds. *Ku-chin ch'eng-wei-yü tz'u-tien* 古今稱謂語詞典 (Beijing, 1988). This work is a guide to expressions concerning names of persons. It is arranged according to *pinyin* spelling of the first word of the expression. For each entry in the dictionary, the origins of the term and examples of its usage are given. The book ends with a series of three charts demonstrating the characters which one employs in expressing familial relations.

References—Biography in China

Guides to Alternative Names 145
Comprehensive Biographical Dictionaries 147
Biographical Dictionaries Specific by Period 149
     Western Languages 149
     Chinese 152
Biographical Dictionaries—Topical 162
Other Biographical Aids 167

GUIDES TO ALTERNATIVE NAMES

Ch'en Te-yün 陳德芸, *Ku-chin jen-wu pieh-ming so-yin* 古今人物別名索引 (original Canton, 1937; Taiwan reprint, 1965).

> This work gives some 60,000 alternative names (both *tzu* and *hao*) for persons from earliest times to the Republican period. There is a stroke index at the end, which is based on number of strokes and classifier.

Ch'en Nai-ch'ien 陳乃乾, *Shih-ming pieh-hao so-yin* 室名別號索引 [(Beijing, 1957); revised in cooperation with Ting Ning 丁寧, et.al. (Beijing, 1982)].

> The revised edition contains some 35,000 entries, arranged by stroke and classifier, with a stroke index at the end. Each entry is identified by dynasty, native place, and full name.

Yang T'ing-fu 楊廷福, and Yang T'ung-fu 楊同甫, *Ch'ing-jen shih-ming pieh-ch'eng tzu-hao so-yin* 清人室名別稱自號索引 (Shanghai, 1988), 2 volumes.

> The first volume converts some 106,000 alternative names to regular names, and the second volume arranges some 40,000 regular names, and gives native place and alternative names.

Wang Te-i 王德毅, *Ch'ing-jen pieh-ming tzu-hao so-yin (fu i-ming piao)* 清人別名字號索引（附異名表）(Taipei, 1985).

> Gives the regular names for some 36,000 alternative names, but does not give native place.

Chu Pao-liang 朱保樑, comp. *Twentieth Century Chinese Writers and their Pen Names* (Boston, 1977; revised edition, Taipei, 1989)).

> An index to the pseudonyms of 20th century writers, alphabetically arranged according to Wade-Giles. The real name is given in capital letters, and the pseudonym(s) in ordinary letters. There is a stroke index, and a bibliography. This work incorporates past indexes for this subject [including Austin Shu, *Modern Chinese Authors: a List of Pseudonyms* (Taipei, 1971)].

Tseng Chien-jung 曾健戎 and Liu Yao-hua 劉耀華 comp., *Chung-kuo hsien-tai wen-t'an pi-ming lu* 中國現代文壇筆名錄 (Chongqing, 1986).

> Index for the pseudonyms of about 7,000 writers for the period 1911-1949. Section one lists pseudonyms and gives real names,

section two vice-versa. Arranged according to 4-corner system. Index based on number of strokes, and *pinyin* spelling of surname. There is also an appendix which lists the principal publications of each writer according to his/her pseudonym.

COMPREHENSIVE BIOGRAPHICAL DICTIONARIES

Western Language

Herbert Giles, *A Chinese Biographical Dictionary* (London, 1898; reprint Taipei, 1962).

This is the classic 19th century biographical dictionary, containing the names of some 2,579 prominent Chinese from ancient times to the late Ch'ing. The arrangement is alphabetical, according to Wade-Giles romanization. As the primary purpose of this dictionary was to identify names used in literary allusions, it is full of anecdotes, and highly inaccurate.

Chinese

Fang I 方毅 et.al.. *Chung-kuo jen-ming ta tz'u-tien* 中國人名大辭典 (Shanghai, 1921; many reprints, including Taiwan, 1977).

This is the largest, most extensive biographical dictionary available for China, and has been the standard reference since its appearance (see TB). It includes over 40,000 persons from oldest antiquity to the end of the Ch'ing. The latest Taiwan edition has a supplement for the period 1911-1976 with a separate 4-corner index. The arrangement is by number of strokes and then by classifier. The name of the individual is followed by dynasty, native place, alternative names, and a short biographical notice, which generally consists of short passages from other sources.

Li Pao-yin 李寶印, *Jen-wu kung-chü-shu tz'u-tien* 人物工具書詞典 (Changchun, 1989).

A 'reference work' on biographical references.

Chiang Liang-fu 姜亮夫, *Li-tai jen-wu nien-li pei-chuan tsung-piao* 歷代人物年里碑傳綜表 (Shanghai, 1937; revised and reprinted, in Beijing 1959, in Hong Kong 1961, and Taipei 1965).

Gives the birth and death dates of some 10,000 persons. In the Beijing edition, persons are arranged chronologically by birth date, but those for whom only a death date is known are placed after those born that year. There is a stroke and classifier index with a reference to the year of birth.

In recent years, there have appeared a rather large number of *ming-jen tz'u-tien* 名人辭典 (dictionaries of famous people). Among the best known are:

Wu Hai-lin 吳海林 and Li Yen-p'ei 李延沛, *Chung-kuo li-shih jen-wu tz'u-tien*中國歷史人物辭典 (Harbin, 1983).
> Arranged chronologically by year of birth. Contains an index of some 12,000 names.

Wu Hai-lin and Li Yen-p'ei, *Chung-kuo li-shih jen-wu sheng-tsu nien-piao*中國歷史人物生卒年表 (Harbin, 1981).
> Contains names, alternative names, native places, and dates for 6623 persons.

Chung-kuo jen-ming ta tz'u-tien 中國人名大詞典 (Shanghai: Shang-hai tz'u-shu ch'u-pan-she, 1989) 3 vols.
> The first volume is historical, and contains biographies of some 700 persons from antiquity to October 1, 1949. The second volume concerns persons active in the period from October 1, 1949 through December 1986. This volume contains pictures of the subjects, and short summaries of his/her career, both before and after Liberation. The third volume focuses upon present-day officials, both civil and military, who were active until December 31, 1988 in either provincial, county, or municipal government. The third volume has no pictures.

BIOGRAPHICAL DICTIONARIES SPECIFIC BY PERIOD

Western Languages

Premodern Period

Herbert Franke, ed., *Sung Biographies* (Wiesbaden, 1976) four volumes.

> Gives information on 440 persons from the Sung period (976-1260); arranged alphabetically, in Wade-Giles, by surname. There is a a separate volume for artists. Notices are of varying length and quality, since the authors have various national origins. Entries may be in English, German, or French.

Igor de Rachewitz, Hok-lam Chan, Hsiao Ch'i-ch'ing, and Peter W. Grier, eds., *In the Service of the Khan: Eminent Personalities of the Early Mongol-Yüan Period (1200-1300)* (Wiesbaden, 1993).

> Offers extensive biographies of some 37 'imperial servants', prominent during the first five reigns of the Mongol period. The selection is based on what the editors consider 'representative types', but as they admit, their choice leaves out members of the imperial clan, southern Chinese, and women (with the exception of empresses). Biographies are divided by period and arranged according to professional category (military leaders, advisers, and administrators, etc.). Entries include various names, styles, offices and titles in translations, and relevant dates according to the Western calendar. There is a separate bibliography, covering all important primary and secondary sources up to 1990-91. There are Chinese character indices for topics and terms, offices and titles, proper names, and place names. There is also a general index for page references to people and subjects, and major cities.

L.C. Goodrich and Chao-ying Fang, eds., *Dictionary of Ming Biography 1368-1644* (New York, 1976) two volumes.

> Contains 659 biographies, including those of emperors, the emperor's family, bureaucrats, military leaders, eunuchs, envoys and travellers, cultural leaders. The biographical entries, arranged alphabetically in Wade-Giles transcription, provide known dates of birth and death according to the Western calendar system, as well as Chinese characters for most proper

nouns placed in the text, and usually include a summary of the career of the subject, some consideration of the subject's writings, and mention of members of his or her family. Each entry also contains a bibliographical appendix giving references to primary and secondary literature. There are indexes of names, books, and subjects, and there are frequent references to ECCP.

A.W. Hummel, ed., *Eminent Chinese of the Ch'ing Period* (Washington, 1943-44; Taiwan reprint, 1964) two volumes.
Includes biographies of about 800 famous officials,writers, active during the Ch'ing. The format of the *Dictionary of Ming Biography* was based on this work. There is also a long essay by Hu Shih on matters of Ch'ing scholarship.

Modern Period

Howard Boorman and Richard C. Howard, eds., *Biographical Dictionary of Republican China* (New York, 1967-1971) five volumes.
A useful work, containing 600 in-depth biographies on the pattern of ECCP. It has been criticized for its heavy stress on the KMT period, and the interpretation of some of those written about is uncritical. Volume 4 contains a bibliography, volume 5 is the index to the entire work.

Donald W. Klein and Anne B. Clark, eds., *Biographical Dictionary of Chinese Communism, 1921-1965* (Cambridge, Mass., 1971) two volumes.
This is an indispensable reference work on the participants in the communist movement. There are 433 biographies, some as long as 15 pages, with excellent bibliographical references. The appendices and bibliographies give access to information about some 1300 more leaders. Another strong point is the careful coverage of Party history before 1949, as well as that between 1949-1965, when coverage ends.

Who's Who in Communist China (Hong Kong, 1969-70) two volumes.
Gives short biographical sketches on some 2800 Chinese leaders with an emphasis on official positions, and little to no information about the subjects' pre-1949 experiences. No one who

died before 1949 is included; the cut-off date for information is 1968, and thus some information about the Cultural Revolution may be found here.

Chinese Communist Who's Who (Taipei, 1970) two volumes. This a revision and translation of *Chung-kung jen-ming lu* 中共人名錄 (Taipei, 1967).

It presents in summarized form the careers of some 3800 leaders, and may be considered accurate and inclusive.

Wolfgang Bartke, *Who's Who in the PRC* (München, 1991) two volumes, third edition.

Contains information on some 4120 persons, arranged alphabetically, according to pinyin. Although this edition "updates" those of 1990 and 1985 [see below], it does not include persons who died between 1985 and 1991. However, there is a list of 1340 persons found in the 1985 edition, not included in the third edition. It also includes some Democracy Movement figures, but for the main, remains a biographical dictionary (with photos) of important cadres.

Wolfgang Bartke, *Biographical Dictionary and Analysis of China's Party Leadership 1922-1988* (München, 1990).

Divided into two parts. The first part gives the biographies, in listed form, of 1094 members and alternative members of the second through thirteenth Central Committees, 1922-1988, in *pinyin* order, some with photos. The second part gives an analysis, both in written and chart form of the Central Committees.

Wolfgang Bartke, *China's New Party Leadership: Biographies of Members and Anaylsis of the Twelfth Central Committee of the Chinese Communist Party* (New York, 1985).

Arranged according to *pinyin* with photos, biographies in list form of members' positions and past political appointments. Gives an excellent overview of the leadership positions in the PRC Government and the Communist Party. As the preface notes, the Twelfth Party Congress, held in 1982, marked the decisive victory of Teng Hsiao-p'ing's faction over its Maoist opponents within the Party. It comprises in the main the victims of the Cultural Revolution in the Party, the state bureaucracy, and the Army.

Editorial Board of *Who's Who in China, Who's Who in China: Current Leaders* (Boulder, Colo., 1994).

A comprehensive listing of some 2,000 biographies on CD-ROM in both Chinese and English, with matching photographs. Up-to-date to 1994. Users can find persons according to name, title, institution, educational background, age, nationality, and many other criteria. There is also a government organization chart that locates all individuals by title. With this program, one may find the mayors of China's Special Economic Zones, the commander of the Beijing Military Area, all ministers under the age of sixty who attended the same school, all the natives of Guangdong Province now in leadership positions, or all political figures with backgrounds as historians, soil scientists, or actors. With this system, one may easily search and cross-reference the available data. The publishers promise to make "up-dates" available every spring of a given year.

Chinese

The reprinted Dynastic Histories, published in the PRC by Chung-hua shu-chü in the 1970s and 80s, have a cumulative index for the biographical section of each of the dynastic histories. See Chang Ch'en-shih 張忱石, *Erh-shih-ssu shih chi-chuan jen-ming so-yin* 二十四史記傳人名索引 (Beijing, 1980). Only the reference to a biography is given, according to the page number of the Beijing edition, but also according to *chüan*, and thus can be used with other editions. This volume is arranged according to the four-corner system, with a stroke index.

Han

Chung Hua 鍾華, comp., *Shih-chi jen-ming so-yin* 史記人名索引 (Beijing, 1977).

Wei Lien-k'o 魏連科 comp., *Han-shu jen-ming so-yin* 漢書人名索引 (Beijing, 1979).

Li Yü-min 李裕民 comp., *Hou Han-shu jen-ming so-yin* 後漢書人名索引 (Beijing, 1979).

Shih-chi chi chu-shih tsung-ho yin-te 史記及注釋綜合引得 (Combined Indices to *Shih-chi* and the Notes of P'ei Yin, Ssu-ma Cheng, Chang Shou-chieh, and Takigawa Kametaro)

Published as Index No. 40 in the Harvard-Yenching Institute Sinological Series (1947). Indexes persons' names, place names, offices, titles and other technical terms in the text and commentaries. There is a stroke index, and alphabetical index, according to Wade-Giles.

Wong Fook-luen 黃福鑾 ed., *Shih-chi so-yin* 史記索引 (Hong Kong, 1963).

A subject index, of persons, place names, and terms. There is a brief explanation of names and terms. Arranged according to 24 categories, each of which is indexed by total stroke count.

Han-shu chi pu-chu tsung-ho yin-te 漢書及補注綜合引得 (Combined Indices to Han Shu and the Notes of Yen Shih-ku and Wang Hsien-chien).

Published as Index No. 36 in the Harvard-Yenching Insititute Sinological Series (1940). Indexes persons' names and alternative names, place names, titles, and other technical terms occurring in the text of the *Han shu* and its two major commentaries. With stroke index, and alphabetical finding list, according to Wade-Giles.

Wong Fook-luen ed., *Han-shu so-yin* 漢書索引 (Hong Kong, 1966).

Indexes persons' names and place names in the *Han-shu*, according to 25 categories, indexed by stroke count. Brief identification of explanation of names is given, sometimes.

Hou Han-shu chi chu-shih tsung-ho yin-te 後漢書及注釋綜合引得 (Combined Indices to Hou Han-shu and the Notes of Liu Chao and Li Hsien).

Published as Index No.41 in the Harvard-Yenching Indexes (1949). Indexes persons' names, place names, offices, titles and other technical terms in the text and commentaries. There are finding indexes based on stroke- count, and Wade-Giles alphabetical order.

Wong Fook-luen, ed., *Hou Han-shu so-yin* 後漢書索引 (Hong Kong, 1971).

Indexes persons' names and places in the *Hou Han-shu*, according to 25 categories, indexed by stroke count. With some brief explanations.

Three Kingdoms (221-265/280)

San-kuo-chih chi P'ei chu tsung-ho yin-te 三國志及裴注綜合引得 (Combined Indices to San Kuo chih and the Notes of P'ei Sung-chih) Harvard-Yenching Index No.33 (1938).

Indexes proper names, place names, offices, titles, technical terms, and titles of works quoted in the commentary.

Chin (265-419)

Chang Ch'en-shih 張忱石 comp., *Chin-shu jen-ming so-yin* 晉書人名索引 (Beijing, 1977).

Northern Dynasties (386-580)

Ch'en Chung-an 陳仲安 et.al., *Pei-ch'ao ssu-shih jen-ming so-yin* 北朝四史人名索引 (Beijing, 1988).

Indexes to the Chung-hua shu-chü editions of the dynastic histories of the Northern Wei, Western Wei, Northern Ch'i, and Northern Chou dynasties.

Southern Dynasties (420-589)

Chang Ch'en-shih comp., *Nan-ch'ao wu-shih jen-ming so-yin* 南朝五史人名索引 (Beijing, 1985).

Indexes to the Chung-hua shu-chü editions of the *Sung shu, Nan Chi shu, Liang shu, Ch'en shu,* and *Nan shih.*

Sui (589-617)

Teng Ching-yüan 鄧經元, *Sui-shu jen-ming so-yin* 隋書人名索引 (Beijing, 1979).

T'ang (618-906) and Five Dynasties (906-960)

Fu Hsüan-ts'ung 傅璇琮 et.al. comp., *T'ang Wu-tai jen-wu chuan-chi tzu-liao tsung-ho so-yin* 唐五代人物傳記資料綜合索引 (Beijing, 1982)

Indexes the biographies in 86 primary sources, including existing local gazetteers from the Sung period. Names arranged according to four-corner index number, also with indexes according to person's *tzu* and *hao* name.

Chang Wan-ch'i 張萬起 comp., *Hsin-chiu T'ang-shu jen-ming so-yin* 新舊唐書人名索引 (Shanghai, 1986), three volumes.

Chang Wan-ch'i comp., *Hsin-chiu Wu-tai shih jen-ming so-yin* 新舊五代史人名索引 (Shanghai, 1980).

Hiraoka Takeo 平岡武夫 comp., *Tôjin no denki sakuin* 唐人の伝記索引 (Kyoto, 1951).
> Indexes 17 works containing biographical information on T'ang figures, in four categories: poets, Buddhists, Taoists, and painters. Entries are listed in four-corner sequence, with supplementary indexes for stroke count, and Wade-Giles alphabetical order.

Chang Ch'en-shih 張忱石, *T'ang hui yao jen-ming so-yin* 唐會要人名索引 (Beijing, 1991).

Sung (960-1276)

Ch'ang Pi-te 昌皮得 et.al. comp., *Sung-jen chuan-chi tzu-liao so-yin* 宋人傳記資料索引 (Taipei, 1972-1982), six volumes. Index in the 6th volume.
> Index of some 15,000 persons based on 490 different sources. Gives short biographies, alternative names, and other important family members.

Ssu-shih-ch'i chung Sung-tai chuan-chi tsung-ho yin-te 四十七種宋代傳記綜合引得 (Combined Indices to Forty-seven Collections of Sung Dynasty Biographies).
> Published as No. 34 of the Harvard-Yenching Index Series (1939). Indexes' persons' names in the *hsing-ming* form where possible, entering *tzu* and *hao* next to them, and reference to any of the 47 texts. Has total stroke and Wade-Giles supplementary indexes.

Aoyama Sadao 青山定雄 general editor, *Sôjin denki sakuin* 宋人伝記索引 (Tokyo, 1968).
> Indexes some 8,000 persons, not in the Harvard-Yenching index above. The figures included are those of Chinese serving the Liao and Chin courts. Under each subject, entered in *hsing-ming* form, is his *tzu*, place of origin, dates, great-grandfather's,

grandfather's, and father's names, when available. Entries are
arranged according to total stroke count order, and there are
Japanese *kana*, as well as, Wade-Giles alphabetical indexes.

Chu Shih-chia 朱士嘉 comp., *Sung Yüan fang-chih chuan-chi so-yin*
宋元方志傳記索引 (Beijing, 1963).
This is an index to the biographical materials of 3949 men contained in 33 Sung and Yüan gazetteers. The names are arranged by stroke and classifer. The *tzu* and other names given
in these sources are also entered after the full name. There is a
list of the gazetteers, with names of compilers, editions, and
abbreviations used in the book. There is also a four-corner index to the names.

Wang Te-i, comp., *Sung hui-yao chi-kao jen-ming so-yin*
宋會要輯稿人名索引 (Taipei, 1978) .
This is an index to persons in one of the most important
sources to Sung history, the *Sung hui-yao.*

Yü Ju-yün 兪如雲, *Sung-shih jen-ming so-yin* 宋史人名索引 (Shanghai,
1992) 4 vols.

Liao (907-1125), Chin (1115-1234), Yüan (1260-1368)

Tseng I-fen 曾眙芬 and Ts'ui Wen-yin 崔文印, *Liao-shih jen-ming so-
yin* 遼史人名索引 (Beijing, 1982).

Ts'ui Wen-yin, *Chin-shih jen-ming so-yin* 金史人名索引 (Beijing,
1980).

Yao Ching-an 姚景安, *Yüan-shih jen-ming so-yin* 元史人名索引 (Beijing,
1982).

Liao Chin Yüan chuan-chi san-shih chung tsung-ho yin-te
遼金元傳記三十種綜合引得 (Combined Indices to Thirty Collections
of Liao, Chin, and Yüan Biographies).
Published as Index No. 35 of the Harvard-Yenching Indexes
(1940). Indexes thirty works, containing biographical material
for Liao, Chin, and Yüan dynasty figures. Names are indexed
according to name given at birth, with alternative names given,
as well.

Chin Yüan jen wen-chi chuan-chi tzu-liao so-yin 金元人文集傳記資料索引 (Index to Biographical Material in Chin and Yüan Literary Works) compiled by Igor de Rachewiltz and Miyoko Nakano (Canberra, 1970, 1972, 1979), three volumes.

This index supplements the biographies given in the above Harvard-Yenching index. The texts here are literary, and not historical.

Igor de Rachewiltz and May Wang, *Repertory of Proper Names in Yüan Literary Sources* (Taipei, 1988), three volumes.

Wang Te-i et.al., *Yüan-jen chuan-chi tzu-liao so-yin* 元人傳記資料索引 (Taipei, 1982), five volumes.

For each person this reference gives birth and death dates, alternate name(s), native place, short biographical sketch, citations to references in primary sources, including local gazetteers from the Yüan and Ming periods. Arranged by stroke count of name. Volume 5 contains stroke-count index of alternate names.

Umehara Kaoru 梅原郁 and Kinugawa Tsuyoshi 依川強 comp., *Ryô Kin Genjin denki sakuin* 遼金元人伝記索引 (Kyoto, 1972).

Indexes biographical information for 3186 persons of the Liao, Chin, and Yüan periods from 130 literary collections and other sources. The sources are listed by title, and their abbreviated title, at the beginning to the index. Entries are listed according to stroke count order, and for each entry, the person's alternative names, place of origin, dates, the names of his father, grandfather and great-grandfather, his sons' and grandsons' names, his sons-in-law, and the source from which the info is taken. There are biographies of Buddhist and Taoist monks, and women.

Ming (1368-1644)

Li Yü-min 李裕民 comp., *Ming-shih jen-ming so-yin* 明史人名索引 (Beijing, 1985), 2 volumes.

Ch'ang Pi-te comp., *Ming-jen chuan-chi tzu-liao so-yin* 明人傳記資料索引 (Taipei, 1966), 2 volumes.

Utilizing some 600 sources (528 literary collections and 65 historical works), this index contains information on some 8500 people from the Ming. Under each name indexed there is a condensed biography, with date where possible, and citation of sources from which the information is drawn. There is a separate listing of alternative names. The entire index is arranged according to total number of strokes in the person's surname, with a finding index for surnames at the front of each volume. There is also a listing in alphabetical order based on Wade-Giles romanization for all entries, giving reference to the main index. See also, Wang Te-i, "Supplement to *Ming-jen chuan-chi tzu-liao so-yin*," *Mindaishi kenkyu* 7 (1979):47-54.

Pa-shih-chiu chung Ming-tai chuan-chi tsung-ho yin-te 八十九種明代傳記 總和引得 (Combined Indices to Eighty-nine Collections of Ming Biographies).

Published as Index No. 24 in the Harvard-Yenching Indexes (1935), in three volumes. Indexes 89 works, mainly historical texts (including the *Ming-shih* and collections of biographies, but no local histories. Volume I indexes names in the *tzu* and *hao* form, providing information in the *hsing-ming* form. Volumes II and III indexes names in the *hsing-ming* form, and provide references to the 89 texts listed in the introduction in Volume I. There are supplementary finding indexes for the total stroke count and Wade-Giles alphabetical orders. In total some 30,000 persons are referred to here.

Ming-tai ti-fang-chih chuan-chi so-yin (Chung Rih hsien-ts'ang san-pai chung) 明代地方志傳記索引（中日現藏三百種）(Taipei, 1986), two volumes.

Each person's entry, arranged by surname in stroke count order indicates his highest examination degree (if *chü-jen* or *chin-shih*), native province, and citation to gazetteer biography. This is an expansion of Yamane Yukio's *Nihon genzon Mindai chihôshi denki sakuin kô* 日本現蔵明代地方志伝記索引稿 (1964), which included some 30,000 names. The present work includes the holdings of 7 major collections in Taiwan and 5 major reprint series published in Taiwan and Hong Kong, in addition to the holdings of 12 major Japanese collections.

Li Kuo-hsiang 李國祥, ed., *Ming shih-lu lei-tsuan. Jen-wu chuan-chi* 明實錄類纂人物傳記 (Wuhan, 1990).
  Biographies of 2,350 persons included in the *Ming shih-lu*. Arranged chronologically. With a stroke order index.

T'ien-i-ko ts'ang Ming-tai fang-chih hsüan k'an jen-wu chuan-chi tzu-liao jen-ming so-yin 天一閣藏明代方志選刊人物傳記資料人名索引 (1989)
  Indexes the biographies in the reprint series of (done in the early 1980's) of Ming gazetteers held by the T'ien-i-ko Library in Ningbo.

Ch'ing (1644-1912)

San-shih-san chung Ch'ing-tai chuan-chi tsung-ho yin-te 三十三種清代傳記綜合引得 (Index to Thirty-three Collections of Ch'ing Dynasty Biographies).
  Index No.9 in the Harvard-Yenching Index Series (1932; re-issued with corrections in Tokyo, 1960). Indexes names of persons in 33 collections of Ch'ing dynasty biographies, comprising mainly historical works, but also biographies of poets and painters. There are supplementary indexes for the total stroke count and Wade-Giles alphabetical order.

Ts'ai Kuan-lo 蔡冠洛, *Ch'ing-tai ch'i-pai ming-jen chuan* 清代七百名人傳 (Shanghai, 1937), three volumes.
  Biographies of 700 men, with useful appendices, including classification by native place.

Ch'en Nai-ch'ien 陳乃乾 comp., *Ch'ing-tai pei-chuan-wen t'ung-chien* 清代碑傳文通檢 (Beijing, 1959).
  Indexes the contents of 1025 collections of epitaphs of those persons inscribed on tombs or monuments or biographical material in prefaces, sacrificial prayers, or other sources. The contents are arranged according to stroke and classifier. Each entry supplies *tzu* and *hao* when possible, place of origin and dates when known, and genre and author of biographical text from which this information is drawn. Three appendices note discrepancies in names and in dates, and another gives bibiographies.

Kuo-li ku-kung po-wu-yüan ts'ang 國立故宮博物院藏, comp. *Ch'ing-tai wen-hsien chuan-pao, chuan-kao jen-ming so-yin* 清代文獻傳包傳稿人名索引 (Taipei, 1986).

Indexes archival biographical materials, i.e. draft biographies and biographical "packets", held by Taiwan's National Palace Museum for over 10,000 Ch'ing persons. Also indicates if person, is indexed in HY Index no.9.

Chou Chün-fu 周駿富, *Ch'ing-tai chuan-chi ts'ung-k'an so-yin* 清代傳記叢刊索引(Taipei, 1986), three volumes.

The most complete index to Ch'ing biographies to date. Indexes the *Ch'ing-tai chuan-chi ts'ung-k'an*, a compendium of 150 separate biographical collections reprinted under Chou's editorship in 1985 in 202 volumes. This index gives citations to some 47,000 persons, in contrast to the HY index no.9 which indexes some 27,000.

Ch'ing-shih wei-yüan hui 清史委員會 ed., *Ch'ing-tai jen-wu chuan kao* 清代人物傳稿 (Beijing, 1984—; in two series, "A" and "B", with some volumes in "B" published in Shenyang).

Well-annotated biographies for persons from the entire Ch'ing dynasty. Includes extensive bibliographical material. As of 1994, a total of 10 volumes have appeared. Both series seem to be part of a long term project to produce a new *Ch'ing-shih*.

Republic and later (1912...)

Min-kuo jen-wu chuan 民國人物傳 (Beijing, 1978-1987), six volumes.

Short biographies of Chinese who were active during the Republic.

Hu Hua 胡華 comp., *Chung-kung tang-shih jen-wu chuan* 中共黨史人物傳 (Xian, since 1980), projected more than 40 volumes.

Biographies of personalities in the history of the Chinese Communist Party. Each volume contains more than 10 long biographies, each written by different authors, based on documents, archival research, and personal memory (with some interesting details). There are footnotes and some bibliographical references.

Ho Tung 何東, et.al. comp., *Chung-kuo ke-ming shih jen-wu tz'u-tien* 中國革命史人物詞典 (Beijing, 1991).

Chung-kuo tang-tai ming-jen lu 中國當代名人錄 (Shanghai, 1991).
Contemporary 'Who's Who' of China.

Chung-hua min-kuo tang-tai ming-jen lu 中華民國當代名人錄 (Taipei, 1985), five volumes.
A 'who's who' of the present Republic of China.

Wang Chi-hsiang 王繼祥 et.al., *Chung-kuo chin-hsien-tai jen-wu chuan-chi tzu-liao so-yin* 中國今現代人物傳記資料索引 (Changchun, 1988).
Index to biographical material on modern and contemporary Chinese individuals.

Art

James Cahill, *An Index of Early Chinese Painters and Paintings: T'ang, Sung, and Yüan* (Berkeley, 1980).
    Contains extensive biographical material on Chinese painters. See chapter II 'Bibliographies in Western Languages' under *Miscellaneous*.

Nancy N. Seymour, *Index Dictionary of Chinese Artists* (Methuen, New Jersey, 1988).
    Contains entries about more than 5000 persons from the T'ang onward.

Sun T'a 孫鵠, *Chung-kuo hua-chia jen-ming ta tz'u-tien* 中國畫家人名大辭典 (Shanghai, 1934; Taiwan reprints 1959, 1962).
    Contains brief biographical summaries of Chinese artists through the Ch'ing, based on the *Li-tai ming-hua chi* 歷代名畫記. Each entry consists of the name with a dot to separate the surname from the remainder, the dynasty, native place, a discussion of his career and art, and a source. The arrangement is by stroke, and there is a table of contents for surnames covered in the volume.

Yü Chien-hua 俞劍華, *Chung-kuo mei-shu-chia jen-ming tz'u-tien* 中國美術家人名辭典 (Shanghai, 1987).
    Revises the 1981 original edition, to include 31,000 artists since antiquity. This biographical dictionary gives short life-history sketches, bibliographical sources, and alternative names. Arranged by stroke order of name, and thereafter by radical. There is a separate appendix for modern artists.

Li Shu-chi 李恕基, *Chung-kuo i-shu chia tz'u-tien: hsien-tai pu-fen* 中國藝術家辭典，現代部份 (Changsha, 1981) 5 volumes.
    A dictionary of contemporary artists

Music

Ts'ao Ch'ou-sheng 曹惆生, *Chung-kuo yin-yüeh wu-tao hsi-ch'ü jen-ming tz'u-tien* 中國音樂舞蹈戲曲人名辭典 (Beijing, 1959).
    Gives rather short biographical notices, usually no more than

one or two lines, of 5201 persons connected with dance, drama and music throughout Chinese history until the end of the Ch'ing. Sources are given but no chapters or page references. Arranged according to stroke and classifier.

Literature

One should turn first to Nienhauser, ed., *The Indiana Companion to Traditional Chinese Literature* for quick reference.

T'an Cheng-pi 譚正璧, *Chung-kuo wen-hsüeh-chia ta tz'u-tien* 中國文學家大辭典 (Shanghai, 1934; revised Shanghai, 1981).

    Features the biographical notices of 6850 persons related to the history of literature in China. The entries are arranged chronologically, from Lao-tzu to the early Republican period. There is an index in the back, arranged by stroke and classifier. Each notice contains the dates of the individual, alternative names, something of the person's career and activities, and most famous works.

Miao Chuang 苗壯, ed. *Chung-kuo ku-tai hsiao-shuo jen-wu tz'u-tien* 中國古代小說人物辭典 (Jinan, 1991).

    A 'Dictionary of Characters in Old Chinese Fiction' is a guide to names of "fictitious" persons in Chinese fiction, from stories, novels, heroic tales, etc.. Includes some 1700 persons, arranged according to genres.

Wu Ju-yü 吳汝煜 and Hu K'o-hsien 胡可先, comp. *Ch'üan T'ang shih jen-ming k'ao* 全唐詩人名考 (Nanjing, 1990).

    This is a handy reference book for identifying all the historical personal names that have appeared in the titles, prefaces and annotations of the poems collected in the *Ch'üan T'ang shih*. The layout of this reference work is similar to a dictionary. Under each name entry, the volume number, the *chüan* number and the page number of each appearance in the 1979 edition of the *Ch'üan T'ang shih* published by the Chung-hua shu-chü are indicated by Arabic numerals in parentheses. Sometimes a brief biography is supplied. An index to personal names arranged by *pinyin* romanization may be found at the end of this work.

Buddhism

Chang Chih-che 張志哲, *Chung-hua fo-chiao jen-wu ta tz'u-tien* 中華佛教人物大辭典 (Shanghai, 1993).
> Over 14,000 names in 12,300 entries from the Han dynasty to the present with personal data and activities. Has 4-corner index.

Women

Yüan Shao-ying 袁韶瑩 and Yang Kui-chen 楊瑰珍, *Chung-kuo fu-nü ming-jen tz'u-tien* 中國婦女名人辭典 (Changchun, 1989).
> Gives info on some 4100 women from all periods of Chinese history. Arranged by stroke count of name, and contains a stroke-count name index, arranged by occupation.

Hu Wen-k'ai 胡文楷, *Li-tai fu-nü chu-tso k'ao* 歷代婦女著作考 (Shanghai, 1985).
> Lists the works of women authors from the Han through Ch'ing, with the last dynasty receiving most information. Each dynastic period receiving one chapter, except the Ch'ing (with four chapters) and sub-divided according to number of strokes of author's name. Some biographical info, where known, such as author's birthplace, father's and husband's name.

Cho Ch'eng-yüan 卓承元, *Chung-kuo fu-nü ming-jen tz'u-tien* 中國婦女名人詞典 (Hebei, 1991).
> Gives short biographies of Chinese women over the sweep of history up to today. Arranged according to number of strokes, with an alphabetical index at the beginning according to *pinyin* spelling.

Miyamoto Katsu 宮本勝 and Mihashi Masanobu 三橋正信, *Retsujo-den sakuhin (fu honbun)* 列女伝索引 (附本文) [Lieh-nü-chuan so-yin] (Tokyo, 1982).
> As the title indicates, an index to various traditional 'biographies of virtuous women'.

Hua-hsia fu-nü ming-jen tz'u-tien 華夏婦女名人詞典 (Beijing, 1988).
> Gives brief biographies of women involved in the Communist revolution. There is a listing according to province or city of origin. Arranged by number of strokes.

Modern Intellectuals

Liang Kuei-chih　梁桂芝, *Chung-kuo po-shih jen-ming tz'u-tien* 中國博士人名辭典 (Nanchang, 1992).
Includes only those scholars born after 1949.

Chinese Historians

Ch'iu Shu-sen 邱樹森, *Chung-kuo shih-hsüeh-chia tz'u-tien* 中國史學家 辭典 (Shijiazhuang, 1990).
A dictionary of Chinese historians from earliest times to the present. Arranged according to number of strokes of person's surname. At end, there is a title index where the author's name is also supplied. Includes the authors of some local gazetteers.

Guides to Japanese Sinologists

John Timothy Wixted, *Japanese Scholars of China: A Bibliographical Handbook* (Lewiston, N.Y., 1993).
Difficult to use, but the only English language guide available for the study of twentieth-century Japanese sinologists. Refers to more than 1500 scholars from all fields of China study. The main text lists alphabetically scholars' names, gives short characterizations of their areas of specialization, and indexes references to them in other Japanese sinologist guidebooks. Attention is paid to bibliographies of their works, and includes *festschriften* about them. Special attention is also directed to English and other Western language material about their scholarship: book-length translations, book reviews, and summaries. This reference has eight indices: to scholars' surnames by Chinese reading, scholars listed by field of study, scholars' Western-language books; to names of non-Japanese cited in the volume; Chinese characters for journal titles, publishers, place of publication, phrases cited. Unfortunately, this work does not give birth/death dates, and it is difficult to determine whether a particular scholar is alive or not. This work should be used in conjunction with the following two works.

Teng Ssu-yü in collaboration with Masuda Kenji and Kaneda Hiromitsu, *Japanese Studies on Japan and the Far East: A Short Biographical and Bibliographical Introduction* (Hong Kong, 1961).
Although seemingly "out-dated", this bibliography is still quite useful. In this volume scholars are arranged by general field of

research, and thus it is easy to determine at a quick glance who are (were) the leading experts in a particular subject. The book gives the date of birth of each scholar, a short synopsis of his/her career and area of scholarly interest, and an ample listing of the person's publications. The title of each publication is given in Japanese, in romanization, and in English translation.

Yen Shao-t'ang 嚴紹璗, *Jih-pen ti Chung-kuo hsüeh-chia* 日本的中國學家 (Beijing, 1980).

More comprehensive than Wixted's volume (includes politicians, journalists, and novelists), but this reference lists a particular Japanese scholar's work in Chinese (both books and articles), therefore making it difficult to determine the publication in Western or Japanese libraries. Scholars are listed alphabetically according to the *pinyin* romanization of the first character of their surnames. This volume gives the date of birth, current institutional affiliation, and areas of interest for each entry. There follows a long section outlining the career and activities of the person, and finally his/her publications.

Other Biographical Aids

Nien-p'u (Chronological Biographies)

Hsieh Wei 謝巍 ed. *Chung-kuo li-tai jen-wu nien-p'u k'ao-lu* 中國歷代人物年譜考錄 (Beijing, 1992).
Supersedes the following *nien-p'u* listings.

Wang Pao-hsien 王寶先, *Li-tai ming-jen nien-p'u tsung-mu* 歷代名人年譜綜目 (Taichung, 1956).

Wang Te-i, *Chung-kuo li-tai ming-jen nien-p'u tsung-mu* 中國歷代名人年譜總目 (Taipei, 1979).
Revision and expansion of Wang Pao-hsien's work. Covers 1325 persons.

Yang Tien-hsün 楊殿珣, *Chung-kuo li-tai nien-p'u tsung-lu* 中國歷代年譜總錄 (Beijing, 1980).
Includes 1829 persons.

Examination Candidates

Chu Pao-chiung 朱保炯 and Hsieh P'ei-lin 謝沛霖, *Ming Ch'ing chin-shih t'i-ming pei-lu so-yin* 明清進士題名碑錄索引 (Shanghai, 1980), 3 vols.
Guide to the 51,624 Ming and Ch'ing *chin-shih*. Arranged by name. Gives native place, date of degree, and quality of degree (i.e. rank in that year's class of passers). Volume 3 lists candidates by date and quality of degree.

Genealogies

See general discussion about genealogies as a source of information on China, in Otto B. van der Sprenkel, "Genealogical Registers," in Donald Leslie, et.al., *Essays on the Sources for Chinese History* (Canberra, 1973), pp.83-98.

Taga Akigorô 多賀秋五郎, *Chûgoku sôfu no kenkyû* 中国宗譜の研究 (Tokyo, 1981-82), two volumes.
A supplement to, but not a replacement for Taga's *Sôfu no*

kenkyû: shiryô hen 族譜の研究, 史料編. Volume 1 presents an historical study of the development of Chinese genealogies, closing with a discussion of the present-day compilations in Kowloon. Volume 2 contains detailed listings: (1) 1276 genealogies in Japanese collections (with call numbers for those in major collections); (2) 1247 genealogies held by Columbia, Harvard, Library of Congress, Berkeley, Stanford, and Chicago (also with call numbers); (3) 873 genealogies held by six institutions in the PRC, Hong Kong, and Taiwan (also with call numbers). There are surname and title indexes, but no locality index, chronological index, or institution index (unlike the 1960 volume).

Ted A. Telford et al., *Chinese Genealogies at the Genealogical Society of Utah: An Annotated Bibliography* (Taipei, 1983).
    This is a detailed catalogue of more than 3100 microfilmed genealogies at the Genealogical Society. Covers collections of genealogies in Taiwan, Japan, Korean, the US, and Great Britain, and includes locality and title indexes.

Chao Chen-chi 趙振績 and Ch'en Mei-kui 陳美桂, *T'ai-wan ch'ü tsu-p'u mu-lu* 台灣區族譜目錄 (Taipei, 1987).
    This is a union catalogue of 10,613 genealogies (both PRC and Taiwan). If a genealogy is in Taiwan or Utah collections, a call number is given. Arranged by stroke count of surname. Updates the Telford catalogue.

Biographies in Local Gazetteers

P'an Ming-shen 潘銘燊, *Kuang-tung ti-fang-chih chuan-chi so-yin* 廣東地方傳記索引 (Hong Kong, 1989) two volumes.
    Indexes the biographies of 10,222 persons in 11 Ch'ing gazetteers.

Ch'ih Hsiu-yün 池秀雲, *Shan-hsi t'ung-chih jen-wu chuan so-yin* 山西通志人物傳索引 (Taiyuan, 1984).
    Gives name, dynasty, native place, and page citation to the biographies of 15,808 persons.

Kao Hsiu-fang 高秀芳, *Pei-ching T'ien-chin ti-fang-chih jen-wu chuan-chi so-yin* 北京天津地方志人物傳記索引 (Beijing, 1987).
> Indexes the biographies in 73 gazetteers. Each entry gives name, alternate name(s), dynasty, native place, and biographical citation(s).

Jen I-min 任一民, *Ssu-ch'uan chin-hsien-tai jen-wu chuan* 四川近現代人物傳 (Chengdu, 1985-86), two volumes.
> Volume one contains 52 biographies, and volume two 62, for the period 1840-1986.

Other Aids to Biographical Info of Contemporary Persons

Since information on contemporary persons is so limited, it is advised to check, periodically, the indexes to the *China Quarterly*, and *China aktuell*, for those persons under investigation. Also, the yearly *China Directory* lists names of persons according to function. Ultimately, such a work as the *Who's Who in China* on CD-ROM [see 'Biographical Dictionaries Specific by Period—Western Languages] will become the easiest way to 'keep up' with activities of living personages.

CHAPTER FIVE

CHINA'S GEOGRAPHY: HISTORICAL AND MODERN SOURCES

Introduction

China, in addition to being the most populous country on earth, has the world's third largest area, 9.6 million square kilometers. This vast surface, both land and water, is highly varied and diverse, and through the ages the Chinese people have learned to exploit land and water resources to their great advantage. The continuity in the history of Chinese occupation of the same territory since the Shang dynasty is a tribute to the attainment of effective political control of such an immense and varied expanse. The success of the process by which China carved for itself a distinctive national region, administered by a central political/bureaucratic system, sanctioned by a powerful set of shared values and culture, may be measured in the continuity of the spatial system that lasted more than 2000 years. Answers to the why and how of China's political and cultural stability and permanence are historically interesting and are valuable for the insights they can provide into contemporary methods of environmental management and spatial organization.

Geographical science in China has a long and honorable history, comparable to the descriptive and cartographic traditions established by Anaximander, Eratosthenes, and Strabo in the West. This tradition can be seen in the enormous body of geographical material in China's dynastic histories and provincial, regional, and local gazetteers. The latter, of which a few date as far back as the T'ang-Sung period, describe local and regional flora, fauna, topography, hydrology, and natural catastrophes in China and include crude sketch maps. Both the *Shu-ching* and the *Shui-ching*, which are over 2000 years old, are even earlier examples of descriptive economic and physical geography texts. The *Yü Kung* 禹貢 chapter of the *Shu-ching* 書經 provides a primitive economic geography of the nine regions of early China. It has proved a source too, of endless speculation by Chinese scholars about the early geography of the country, and many later attempts have been made to reconstruct the landscape described.

From the earliest times the Chinese have appreciated the value of an exact knowledge of the country's geography.[1] In China, as elsewhere, map-making has served the various purposes of efficient tax-gathering, water conservancy, river transport, and defence against human enemies and natural disasters. In due course curiosity about the regions beyond China's immediate frontiers, fed by her always energetic travellers, became an added incentive to the cartographer. Surviving maps, such as that drawn on a pair of stone tablets at Xi'an, engraved in 1137, shows the coastline and the rivers of China with an astonishing degree of accuracy. This map is, moreover, drawn on the basis of a regular grid. Similar principles of scientific cartography were developed at about the same time by Ptolemy in the West and by Chang Heng 張衡 in China; but while Ptolemy's system passed to the Arabs, and was not rediscovered in Europe until the fifteenth century, the Chinese tradition, initiated already in pre-Han times is uninterrupted. The discovery in 1973 of several ancient maps dating to approximately 200 B.C. in Han dynasty tombs near the city of Changsha in Hunan province demonstrates that the Chinese had mastered surveying and scaling. Most of China's leading geographical writers in imperial history undertook geographical inquiry out of private speculation. These scholars include Chia Tan 賈耽 (729-805), Shen Kua 沈括 (1031-95), Hsü Hsia-k'o 徐霞客 (1586-1641), and the early Ch'ing k'ao-cheng scholar Ku Yen-wu.

But it was not until the twentieth century that geography became known as an academic discipline in China. Geography departments were established in several universities, and even the wartime capital at Chungking sponsored an Institute of Geography. After 1949 geographical study was organized in the Institute of Geography, which fell under the jurisdiction of the Chinese Academy of Sciences. During the 1950s, the Soviet model of geographical science was emulated. The Soviet approach was based on fieldwork, sound technical knowledge of the physical environment, and the interrelation of physical and economic geography. The Soviet influence proved a significant counterpoint to the large number of pre-liberation Western-trained geographic specialists in China (who were much more concerned with historical

---

[1] On the general history of Chinese geography and map-making, see Joseph Needham, "Geography and Cartography," in *Science and Civilisation in China*, vol. III, *Mathematics and the Sciences of the Heavens and Earth* (Cambridge, 1955), pp. 497-590.

and cultural geography), as can be seen by the numerous articles by Soviet geographers that appeared in China's main geographical journal, *Ti-li hsüeh-pao* 地理學報 (*Acta Geographica Sinica*), during that decade.

With the passing of Soviet influence, geographic activity continued to expand until the 1966-76 when all serious work stopped. Geography and its associated disciplines have a firm place in the modernization programs of the current regime, and in particular, the role of geographical study in agricultural production ('economic geography') has been especially promoted. Some of the numerous facets of contemporary geographical research in the PRC include: geomorphology (fluvial studies), climatology, hydrology, cartography, and not least, environmental protection.[2]

Basic Units of Territorial Administration: Past and Present

The basic geographical unit in China may be the village (*li* 里 or *ts'un* 村) or some other social grouping, but, through most of China's history (and until quite recently [see below]), administratively and descriptively, it is the *hsien* 縣. *Hsien* is translated variously as "county," "district" or "sub-prefecture." It consists of an administrative center, and during the imperial period was normally located in a walled city, which gives the *hsien* its name. Under its jurisdiction is an area of land containing other urban centers of varying size. The total number of *hsien* has remained remarkably constant through Chinese history, from the Han to Ming numbering between 1200 to 1500. The Ch'ing saw a great increase, numbering 1800 *hsien* in total, possibly because of new waves of population settlement in the south-west and north.

During China's imperial history, the *hsien* has consistently represented the lowest level of central control, but the higher levels of administrative organization differed from period to period. The "commandery" (*chün*) of the Ch'in was adopted by the Han, being increased from 36 to 103, but in later periods, the *chün* co-existed with or was replaced by the "prefecture" (*chou*). When co-existent,

<hr>

[2] For a general introduction to the reform programs concerning modern geography, see Lawrence C. Ma and Clifton W. Pannell, *China: The Geography of Development and Modernization* (London, 1983); and the more recent work by Roger Mark Selya, *The Geography of China, 1975-91: An Annotated Bibliography* (East Lansing, 1992).

one or the other had administrative precedence. The next step up the pyramid was the formation of "circuits" (*tao*) which came in the T'ang. In the Sung the term *lu* was used instead, but since the Yüan the term *sheng* has been used. In addition, other administrative units such as *fu* and *t'ing* have also occurred at levels equivalent to or superior to *chou*. But in effect, during the Ch'ing, and throughout most of the Republican period, at least when the government had effective control, there were three levels of administrative hierarchy: provinces, prefectures, and counties.

Basic Territorial Units in Chinese History

Ch'in	*chün* 郡 (commandery)		*hsien* 縣 (district)
Han	*chou* 州 (region)	*chün*	*hsien*
Six Dynasties	*chou*	*chün*	*hsien*
Sui	*chou*	*chün*	*hsien*
T'ang	*tao* 道 (circuit)	*chou* (prefecture) *fu* 府 (superior prefecture)	*hsien*
Sung	*tao* *lu* 路 (circuit)	*chou* *fu* *chün* 軍 (military prefecture)	*hsien*
Yüan	*sheng* 省 (province)	*fu* *chou* *chün*	*hsien*
Ming	*sheng* *chou*	*fu*	*hsien*
Ch'ing	*sheng*	*fu* *t'ing* 廳 (sub-prefecture)	*hsien*

For a complete discussion on the size and administrative details of each of these sub-divisions in Chinese history, see the sections

'Territorial Administration', dynasty by dynasty, given in the Introduction in Charles Hucker, *A Dictionary of Official Titles in Imperial
China* (Stanford, 1983).

The PRC Government continued the three-level administrative
hierarchy of province, prefecture, and county, but since 1984 the
system has undergone much change.[3] The essence of the new developments is the transfer of county-level units from the prefectures to which they formerly belonged, to the jurisdiction of
neighboring cities. The city (*shih* 市) has emerged as the key unit
of the administration of the economy. The purpose of this change
is to encourage the expansion of rural economy under the leadership of cities. In the new system, many (but not all) rural counties
have been transferred to cities at prefectural level, and the same
applies to many cities at county level. Moreover, all provincial
capitals have virtually become independent from their provinces'
adminstration.

China has 23 provinces (not counting Taiwan, but including
Hainan Island which was raised to provincial rank in 1988), three
great cities where administration reports directly to the central
government (Beijing, Shanghai, Tianjin) and 'five autonomous regions' (*tzu-chih-ch'ü* 自治區) representing national minorities (Inner Mongolia, Guangxi, Ningxia, Xinjiang and Tibet). The second level, the 'prefecture' in the former system remains the same,
but is now known as *ti-ch'ü* 地區 or *chuan-ch'ü* 專區. In the new system most large cities are separated for economic purposes from
prefectural government, and also made directly subordinate to
the central government. The third level units are either counties
(*hsien*) or cities (*shih* 市) with the rank of counties. An average
county in a typical province, such as Honan or Anhwei, is about
1200-2000 square kilometers in area, with a population between
600,000 and 700,000.

Formal administration in China ends at the county level. Below
this level, administration is the responsibility of local units, i.e.
townships (*hsiang* 鄉, at the level formerly represented by the
communes) and small towns. Below these are the villages, with village committees. At the end of 1986 there were 61,766 townships,
9755 small towns, and 848,000 village committees in China. There

---

[3] For a guide to administrative changes from 1820 to 1984, see: Chang Tsai-
p'u 張在普, *Chung-kuo chin-hsien-tai cheng-ch'ü yen-ko piao* 中國近現代政區沿革表
(Fuzhou, 1987).

are also five Special Economic Zones (SEZs): Shenzhen and Zhuhai in the Pearl River delta, Shantou in eastern Guangdong and Xiamen in southern Fujian, and since 1988, Hainan Province. In addition, there are 'Economic and Technological Development Zones', such as Pudong, part of the greater Shanghai region. These zones receive special tax privileges to attract high-tech and other enterprises, and will form the core of China's economic development in the future.

Chinese Historical Geographies and their Modern Guides

The basic material for tracing the historical geography of China is contained in the fourteen geographical monographs in the Standard Histories. In each of these the format is generally the same. Usually there is an introductory paragraph followed by a list of the administrative units, starting with the larger units and listing all the units under their jurisdiction. Often additional information is given, such as a description of each region of the territorial unit, the population of each *chou* or *chün*, or sometimes, even of each *hsien*, the rivers and mountains to be found within the borders of each *hsien*, and the past history of the changes in nomenclature and administrative organization.

The *Standard History of the Former Han (Han-shu)* was the first to include a Monograph on Administrative Geography and it is somewhat broader in scope than the Monographs in the other Standard Histories. It includes historical introductions on the regions of China; population figures (the census of A.D. 2) and the names and numbers of the districts in each province and fief; land under cultivation and brief economic profiles of each region (following the *Shih-chi* 129). For further information on the geographical section in the *Han-shu*, see N.L. Swann, "An Analysis of Structure of the Treatise on Geography," *Food and Money in Ancient China* (Princeton, 1950), pp. 71-75. There are also special indexes for the monographs on administrative geography: for the *Hou-Han-shu*, see B.J. Mansvelt-Beck, *The Treatises of the Later Han* (Leiden, 1990); for the old and new standard histories of the T'ang, Hiraoka Takeo, *Tôdai no gyôsei chiri* 唐代の行政地理 [vol. 2 of T'ang Civilization Reference Series (Kyoto, 1954)]; and for the Sung, H.M. Wright, *Geographical Names in Sung China* (Paris, 1956).

Wilkinson, pp.112-114, discusses 'early comprehensive geographical works' and 'comprehensive gazetteers of the Empire'. It should be stressed that one particular 17th century work, the *Tu-shih fang-yü chi-yao* 讀史方輿紀要 compiled by Ku Tsu-yü 顧祖禹 (1631-1692), is still a valuable reference today. It was first printed in 1811; there are many modern editions, including a punctuated 6-volume work. This study, which was compiled privately by Ku Tsu-yü, is a monumental study of historical-administrative and natural geography with special emphasis on the influence of to-pography on campaigns, battles, etc. Unlike the official geo-graphies, there are no sections on products, scenic spots, famous persons, and so on. Ku used over 100 geographical guides, the geographical monographs in the histories, and other works total-ling over 1000 titles. For these reasons, Ku's publication is useful to researchers working on any period.

There is an index to Ku's identification of the pre-17th century forms of no less than 30,000 places dealt with in the body of his work. See Aoyama Sadao 青山定男, *Tokushi hôyu kiyô sakuin, Shina rekidai chimei yôran* 讀史方輿紀要索引, 支那歷代地名要覽 (To-kyo, 1933).

For further bibliographic discussion on Chinese historical ge-ography, two recent Chinese works are recommended:[4]

Chang Chih-che 張志哲
Chung-kuo shih-chi kai-lun 中國史籍概論 (Jiangsu, 1988).
   This book is a descriptive guide to the contents of the most important texts on Chinese historical geography, including the contents of the SKCS.

Chin Sheng-ho 靳生禾
Chung-kuo li-shih ti-li wen-hsien kai-lun 中國歷史地理文獻概論 (Tai-yuan, 1987).
   An historical review of all the leading geographical texts in Chi-nese civilization, arranged chronologically.

Historical and Modern Atlases

The discovery in 1973 of several ancient maps in Han dynasty tombs near the city of Changsha in Hunan Province has caused a

---

[4] Also recommended is *Chung-kuo ti-li chu-tso yao-lan* 中國地理著作要覽 (Beijing, 1990) which surveys all PRC publications on geography (including those concern-ing outside China) from 1949-1988. Includes a survey of map collections.

reappraisal of the history of the development of Chinese cartography. The maps, which date to approximately 200 B.C., include two topographical and military maps and a plan for a prefectural administrative center. The topographical map, which depicts physical and relief features such as streams, lakes, and water bodies, shows that the Chinese had mastered surveying and scaling. The military map, which also to scale, depicts a variety of natural and cultural features and indicates that Chinese cartography had developed sufficiently to produce thematic maps with easily comprehensible and effective symbols.[5]

Quantitative cartography evolved slowly in China, but some of the basic principles were expressed by P'ei Hsiu 裴秀 (224-271). P'ei developed a method for indicating distances by a regular grid system (*chun-wang* 準望), coordinating locations on parallel lines in two dimensions. Although few Chinese cartographers followed P'ei's principles, some important quantitative maps were compiled between the eighth and sixteenth centuries. Chia Tan, the greatest T'ang cartographer, constructed for the government a map entitled *Hai-nei hua-i t'u* 海內華夷圖 (Map of Chinese and Barbarian Regions within the [four] Seas). The map was thirty feet long, thirty-three feet high, and used a grid scale of three centimeters for one hundred *li* 里 (Chinese mile). Joseph Needham has argued that Chia Tan's map must have been a map of Asia because of its huge scale.[6]

Chu Ssu-pen 朱思本 (1273-1337) inherited this grid format. Perhaps, the best known Chinese geographer until the 20th century, Chu, using grid-maps, was able to summarize the large body of new geographical information that the Mongol conquests in Asia had added to the earlier knowledge possessed by T'ang and Sung geographers. Chu's map became known as the "Mongol Atlas of China". In the 16th century, Lo Hung-hsien 羅洪先 (1504-1564) discovered a manuscript copy of Chu Ssu-pen's *Yü-ti t'u* 輿地圖 (Map of the Earth), which had been prepared between 1311 and 1320, but never printed. Lo revised and enlarged Chu's grid for-

---

[5] For further information about the discovery of these early maps and their significance for the study of early Chinese cartography, see Mei-ling Hsu, "The Han Maps and Early Chinese Cartography," *Annals of the Association of American Geographers*, 68.1 (1978):45-60.

[6] Further references about the history of cartography in imperial and republican China may be seen in Chen Cheng-hsiang, "The Historical Development of Cartography in China," *Progress in Human Geography*, 2.1 (1978):101-120.

mat in 1541 and entitled the result the *Kuang-yü t'u* 廣輿圖 (Enlarged Map of the Earth). The latter was printed about 1555.

The final stage in the cumulative development of traditional Chinese map-making came in the 18th century when French Jesuits during the K'ang-hsi era conducted systematic surveys of the entire Manchu realm between 1708 and 1718.[7] They drew up a series of maps of the Ch'ing empire and its border areas that surpassed earlier Jesuit surveys completed in the 17th century. Although Matteo Ricci (1552-1610) had introduced a system of longitude and latitude to China, Chinese geographers continued to employ the grid system. Interestingly, by the 19th century, Chinese maps utilized both systems. For example, the famous 1832 atlas entitled *Huang-ch'ao i-t'ung yü-t'u* 皇朝一統輿圖 (Comprehensive Atlas of the Ch'ing Empire) by Li Chao-lo 李兆洛 (1769-1841) displayed both grid and latitude/longitude lines on the same map.

The *Huang-yü ch'üan-t'u* 皇輿全圖 (Royal map of the Chinese empire), first completed in 1717 by the Jesuits, was revised by order of the Ch'ien-lung Emperor after he had successfully conquered Sinkiang and other regions in Central Asia. In both versions of the map, the place names appearing in China proper were in Chinese, while those appearing in frontier areas including Korea were in the Manchu language. Furthermore, both adopted a trapezoidal projection and regarded the parallel passing through Peking as the central parallel, and both were approximately at the scale of 1:1,400,000. Both maps were deposited in the imperial palace and remained unavailable to the public, but survey results of the French missionaries were transmitted to Paris, which were utilized by French scholars who produced maps and wrote geographical studies. Among the most famous of these were *Description géographique, historique, chronologique, politique, et physique de l'Empire de la Chine* (1735) by J.B. du Halde published in Paris, and *Nouvelle atlas de la Chine* (1737), published in Amsterdam. Both of these works had a wide and enduring circulation in Europe.

The Manchu government thereafter never took a very active interest in mapping activities, and some of the best maps made during the 19th century were those by foreign explorers such as Sven

---

[7] See Theodore N. Foss, "A Western Interpretation of China: Jesuit Cartography," in Charles Ronan and Bonnie Oh, eds., *East Meets West: The Jesuits in China, 1582-1773* (Chicago, 1988), pp. 209-251.

Hedin and Aurel Stein. In 1902 the Government did establish the Military Survey Institute which tried to begin a modern topographical mapping program, but after the Revolution of 1911, the chaotic political/military situation in China precluded any further mapping operations. Perhaps, the most successful mapping during the Republican period took place under the aegis of the Geological Survey of China, first set up to chart mining regions. The application of aerial surveying to cartography was begun in 1930 by a water conservancy commission. An important atlas was also produced during this period, the *Chung-hua min-kuo hsin ti-t'u* 中華民國新地圖 (New Atlas of the Republic of China), published by the leading Shanghai newspaper, *Shen pao*, in commemoration of its sixtieth anniversary in 1934. Originally consisting of 53 sheets, the atlas was condensed into a smaller edition, and reprinted in five editions until it was replaced by the *Atlas of the People's Republic of China* in 1958.[8] The *Atlas of the PRC* presented information up to 1956, and was finally updated in 1974. Thereafter, a series of handy atlases have appeared, the most popular of which is the *Chung-hua jen-min kung-ho-kuo fen-sheng ti-t'u chi* [see below, under 'Modern Atlases'].

---

[8] For more information on mapping in China in the last 100 years, including those by foreign countries, J.R. Williams, *China in Maps, 1890-1960: A Selective and Annotated Cartobibliography* (East Lansing, 1974). This work is particularly strong on pre-1949 cartography. It contains a bibliography plus an index for place names, and the addresses where the maps may be obtained.

References—China's Geography

Historical Atlases 181
Modern Atlases 183
Geographical Dictionaries 185

HISTORICAL ATLASES

T'an Ch'i-hsiang 譚其驤, ed., *Chung-kuo li-shih ti-t'u chi* 中國歷史地圖集 [(Shanghai, 1982-1989); Hong Kong: San-lien shu-tien, 1991-92)] in eight volumes, divided according to the following periods:

- vol. 1   Primitive Society, Hsia, Shang, Western Chou, Spring and Autumn, Warring States.
- vol. 2   Ch'in, Western Han and Eastern Han.
- vol. 3   Three Kingdoms, Western Chin.
- vol. 4   Eastern Chin, Sixteen Kingdoms, Northern and Southern Dynasties.
- vol. 5   Sui, T'ang, Five Dynasties.
- vol. 6   Sung, Liao, Chin.
- vol. 7   Yüan, Ming.
- vol. 8   Ch'ing.

In the Forward to volume one, there is a general overview of the history of historical cartography in China and an account of the compilation of this work. The set as a whole contains 304 maps, divided into 20 map-groups among the eight volumes. Each volume has an index arranged by the new radical system and a finding list ordered by number of strokes. It should be noted the original work is handicapped by the use of simplified characters, and this has been corrected by the Hong Kong version in traditional characters. Each volume has an introduction, table of contents (with the scale of the maps), and legend, all of these both in Chinese and English. On the maps, current names are printed in brown color, and those of the period being investigated are in black.

Ts'ao Wan-ju 曹婉如, *Chung-kuo ku-tai ti-t'u-chi* 中國古代地圖集 (Beijing, 1990–; one volume to date, 'From the Warring States Period to the Yüan Dynasty' 476 B.C. - A.D. 1368).

As the title notes, 'an atlas of ancient maps in China'. The format is large-size and therefore easier to read than many other atlases for this period. It is expected a number of more volumes will appear in this series.

Kuo Mo-jo   郭沫若, *Chung-kuo shih-kao ti-t'u chi*   中國史稿地圖集 (Shanghai, 1979) two volumes.

Volume I covers prehistoric times to Nan-Pei-ch'ao period, and Volume II the Sui to the end of the Ch'ing. The quality of these maps is not good, and one will find them difficult to read.

Yang Shou-ching 楊守敬 (1839-1915), comp., *Li-tai yü-ti yen-ko hsien-yao t'u* 歷代輿地沿革險要圖 (Taipei, 1981 reprint) 10 vols. Volume 11 (Taipei, 1981) is a place-name index, arranged according to number of strokes, for the preceding 10 volumes.

Some historians consider this work still to be the best historical atlas for China available. The first volume consists of a series of 71 general maps of specific periods in Chinese history from the nine regions of Yü to the Ming dynasty. Each map is in red, based on Ch'ing dynasty administration, and overprinted in black are the features of the particular period. The remaining volumes are each focused on one dynasty. Each volume has a brief preface and an outline of the chief administrative units with location symbols.

Chang Hai-p'eng 張海鵬, *Chung-kuo chin-tai shih-kao ti-t'u chi* 中國近代史稿地圖集 (Shanghai, 1984).

Includes 133 detailed maps covering the period from the Opium War to 1919, with accompanying discussions of historical events. Has a stroke index.

Chung-kuo chin wu-pai nien han-lao fen-pu t'u-chi   中國近五百年旱澇分佈圖集 (Beijing, 1981).

Atlas of droughts and floods over the past 500 years.

MODERN ATLASES

Chung-hua jen-min kung-ho-kuo fen-sheng ti-t'u chi 中華人民共和
國分省地圖集 (Beijing, 1974; many reprints).

This is a very convenient collection of provincial maps, each
displaying administrative divisions to the *hsien* level. Each provincial map is preceded by a short description of that region's
population, climate, industry, transportation. There is also a
series of maps for rivers, mountains, and other formations. All
names are indexed according to the radical of the first character; there is also an index based on number of strokes. This
atlas is also published in *pinyin*, subtitled *Han-yü p'in-yin pan*
漢語拼音版. The *pinyin* version has a complete alphabetical index, listing the place name's province, coordinates on the map,
and characters.

The Institute of Geography, Chinese Academy of Sciences and
State Planning Committee, comp., *The National Economic Atlas of
China* (Hong Kong and Oxford, 1994).

Contains 265 maps divided into ten groups. The descriptive
notes to the maps are bound separately in four handbooks
placed in the pockets inside the book's cover. Draws upon the
Industrial Census of 1985 and the Third and Fourth Population Censuses of 1982 and 1990 [and therefore, supersedes the
following work]. The division of the maps are: (1) geography
and administrative background; (2) resources; (3) population;
(4) general economy; (5) agriculture; (6) industry; (7) communications; (8) building, urban construction, and environmental protection; (9) commerce, foreign trade, tourism and
finance; (10) education, scientific research, culture, sports,
and health. There is also discussion of the regional comprehensive economy of each of China's provinces and major cities.
Invaluable: this the most comprehensive collection of data
available issued from the PRC.

Population Census Office of the State Council of the PRC and the
Institute of Geography of the Chinese Academy of Sciences, eds.,
The Population Atlas of China (Hong Kong, 1987).

This is the translation of the *Chung-kuo jen-k'ou ti-t'u chi*
中國人口地圖集 (Hong Kong, 1987). This work, based on the
1982 census, is more than a 'population atlas' for it provides

detailed information in the form of tables and diagrams of China's population, according to sex, profession, age, and education. It also contains eight maps of historical population distribution and density for the Western Han, Western Chin, Sui, T'ang, Yüan, Ming, Ch'ing, and Republican periods. It is now less than reliable for present-day population statistics, since publication of *The National Economic Atlas of China.*

Chung-kuo tzu-jan ti-li t'u-chi 中國自然地理圖集 (Beijing, 1984).
A collection of coloured maps, displaying the physical, social, and administrative geography of China. There is a detailed table of contents, arranged according to subject, but no index.

Nathan Sivin et.al., *The Contemporary Atlas of China* (London, 1988).
Less a collection of maps, more an excellent introduction to the history and culture of various regions of China.

P.J.M. Geelan and Denis Twitchett, *The Times Atlas of China* (New York, 1974).
Focuses on modern provinces, but contains 16 historical maps plus 35 city maps. Includes place name index in Wade-Giles romanization. With the 1984 changes in territorial administration, this collection is somewhat "outdated".

GEOGRAPHICAL DICTIONARIES

Hsiao Chien-chung 肖建中, et.al., *Chung-kuo hsien shih kai-lan* 中國縣市概覽 (Beijing, 1991).

Arranged according to provinces, with separate chapters for Beijing, Tianjin, and Shanghai. Subdivided by *hsien*. Information on *hsien* varies, but most entries include geographical data (weather, crops, etc.) and historical background (famous sites and persons originating from the location). At the end three indices for names of persons, shrines, and places, arranged according to number of strokes. Good for quick reference.

Chung-kuo ti-ming tz'u-tien 中國地名詞典 (Shanghai: Shanghai tz'u-shu, 1990).

Arranged according to number of strokes, with a stroke order index in the beginning. For each entry, including the names of mountains, rivers, and important historical sites, short historical sketches are provided. Past names, where relevant, are also supplied. In many cases up-to-date population information per entry is also recorded. There are a number of appendices for mountain-river systems, and major cities.

Li Han-chieh 李漢杰, et.al. *Chung-kuo fen sheng-shih-hsien ta tz'u-tien* 中國分省市縣大辭典 (Beijing, 1990).

Easy to read and use. Arranged according to province, then *ti-ch'ü*, or *shih*, and then *hsien*, with pinyin spellings for all entries. The table of contents reveals the order of provinces presented, and there is a stroke index at the end. Each entry includes information on natural geographical features, transport, industry, agriculture, cultural activities, and special features.

Yen Ch'ung-nien 閻崇年, ed., *Chung-kuo shih-hsien ta tz'u-tien* 中國市縣大辭典 (1991).

A dictionary of cities, arranged according to province (with the larger cities Beijing, Tianjin, and Shanghai having separate sections for the counties underneath their jurisdiction), and then *ti-ch'ü, shih,* and *hsien.* Includes 183 entries for cities on a prefectural level and 248 entries for cities on a county level, as well as, entries for 1936 *hsien.* Each entry includes information concerning historical development, political, social, cultural, and economic conditions, historical sites, and scenic spots. Has a stroke index at the back.

Tsang Li-ho 臧勵龢, et.al., *Chung-kuo ku-chin ti-ming ta tz'u-tien* 中國古今地名大辭典 (Shanghai, 1931; numerous reprints).

    A collection of some 40,000 names of geographical features and administrative units which have been noted during China's history, including the names of mountains and rivers, arranged according to stroke and radical. Under each name previous changes in name are given, and boundaries and geographical features are indicated; as a rule the modern name is also given, and in nearly half of the items there are quotations from other works, with sources cited. Modern place names are located according to larger or neighbouring places with a brief note on its administrative affiliation. Names which are associated with more than one place have entries added with a circle and dot to mark the change from one place to another.

Wei Sung-shan 魏嵩山, ed., *Chung-kuo li-shih ti-ming tz'u-tien* 中國歷史地名辭典(Nanchang, 1986).

    Gives the administrative status of some 20,000 present day places. Arranged according to number of strokes, with a stroke-number index.

Li Wen-fang 李文芳, *Chung-kuo ming-sheng so-yin* 中國名勝索引 (Beijing, 1987).

    Arranged by province, with three separate chapters for Beijing, Shanghai, and Tianjin. Makes clear which cities and *hsien* fall under which *ti-ch'ü.* Each entry receives a brief historical/geographical description; there is sometimes mention of a particular place's most notable characteristics. Good for quick reference.

Hiraoka Takeo 平岡武夫, *T'ang-tai ti Ch'ang-an yü Lo-yang so-yin* 唐代的長安與洛陽索引 (Shanghai, 1991).

    Although technically not a dictionary, this work is a valuable index to a number of contemporary studies of the two cities of Ch'ang-an and Lo-yang during the T'ang.

Shih-chieh ti-ming lu 世界地名錄 (Beijing, 1984) 2 volumes.

    250,000 foreign and 20,000 Chinese place names are given. At the end of volume 2, there are indices by place name, *pinyin*, characters, ad location. Important for finding the Chinese name of a foreign place.

For more detailed provincial geographical dictionaries, one
should turn to the series *Chung-hua jen-min kung-ho-kuo ti-ming tz'u-
tien* 中華人民共和國地名詞典 (Beijing, since 1987) which is issuing
volumes concentrating on each province.

Local Gazetteers

Introduction[9]

Local gazetteers (*ti-fang-chih* 地方志), sometimes also called "local
histories", are designated "local" to differentiate them from the
various kinds of comprehensive gazetteers (*tsung-chih* 總志), which
deal with the empire in general. The *Chia-ch'ing i-t'ung chih*, completed in 1820, was the largest and most accurate of this type of
gazetteer (see Wilkinson, p.113). Local gazetteers embrace all
types of information concerning the historical, geographical, economic, administrative, biographical, touristic, etc., aspects of a locality in China. Local gazetteers are usually subdivided into provincial gazetteers (*t'ung-chih* 通志), prefectural gazetteers (*fu-chih*
府志), and district gazetteers (*hsien-chih* 縣志). The provincial gazetteers were usually compiled by summarizing the information in
the prefectural gazetteers which were, in turn, abridged from previous editions and from the individual district gazetteers. There
are about 9,500 local gazetteers extant. They form one of the
most important sources for the study of Chinese civilization in the
last 1,000 years.[10]

Local gazetteers have a long pedigree, stretching back to the
time of the composition of the *Chou-li*, when "historians of the
outside" (*wai-shih* 外史) in charge of the "records of the four directions" (*ssu fang chih chih* 四方之志) were commanded to make
notes on the geography and administrative divisions of a number
of political units. During the first millennium of imperial history,
several regional political histories were composed, but most of

---

[9] The text of this introduction is based on Pierre-Étienne Will's monograph
Chinese Local Gazetteers: An Historical and Practical Introduction (Paris, 1992), originally presented to the Scandinavian Summer Course [see 'Preface', infra], as "Local Gazetteers". I thank Professor Will for allowing me to cite from this monograph.

[10] For specific examples of how gazetteers may be utilized for historical study
see, Pierre-Étienne Will, "Local Gazetteers as a Source for the Study of Long-term
Economic Change in China: Opportunities and Problems," *Han-hsüeh yen-chiu* ,
3.2 (1985):707-738.

them have been lost. In the Sui and the T'ang periods, the central government ordered the commanderies and prefectures of the empire to compile and submit dossiers called "Maps with explanations" (*t'u-ching* 圖經); according to an edict of 780, these compilations had to be submitted once every three years alongside population reports, and the practice seems to have been continued until, at least, up to the beginning of the Sung. Although some of these *t'u-ching* contained a combination of maps and information on local products, customs, population, administrative buildings, names of local officials, and degree holders, and thus, in this way resemble the genre of local gazetteers, for the most part, this was not so. The *t'u-ching* were not historical records; they served a different purpose, they were more like "administrative reports". It was the *t'u-ching* that provided source material for such geographical histories as the *Yüan-ho chün-hsien chih* (814), the *T'ai-p'ing huan-yü chi*, or the *Yüan-feng chiu-yü chih* (1080) (see Wilkinson, p.112).

The local gazetteer, in the format popularized in the thousands in the Ming and Ch'ing periods, was essentially a creation of the Sung period. By definition, a local gazetteer is a work, devoted to a given administrative unit, given in the title; it contains a series of sections on the land itself (topography, hydrology, toponymy, production, monuments), on its inhabitants (population, local customs, prominent families and local worthies, holders of academic titles, literary productions), and, most importantly, on its government (structure, personnel, fiscal, and other activities, biographical lists of officials); and it combines, in variable proportion, descriptions of the contemporary situation and historical accounts. A little more that 30 titles from the Sung (almost all of them from the Southern Sung, in fact), from a total of some 200, have survived. Yüan scholars are known to have compiled 60 gazetteers, of which only 11 are extant.

After the Sung, and mainly from the Ming onward, the output of local gazetteers expanded tremendously, particularly during the second half of the dynasty. The majority of Ming titles that have been preserved date from the two long reigns of Chia-ching (1522-66) and Wan-li (1573-1620). Although the claim made in some late Ming prefaces that "There is not a prefecture or district without a gazetteer" is slightly exaggerated, the Ming almost did not fall very short of this declaration. Many administrative units compiled more than one edition during the dynasty - up to six in some places. It has been calculated that around 3000 titles were compiled in the Ming, of which roughly 1000 are still extant. But, the golden age of gazetteer production is the Ch'ing dynasty, during which perhaps close to 7000 titles were published. The Ch'ing government was especially keen on maintaining a certain uniformity of style and control over the contents. There were numerous sets of directives concerning format, contents, and methodology issued in imperial edicts, circulars from the Board of Rites, and instructions from provincial governors or local officials.

Gazetteer production also continued during the Republican period. Under the Kuomintang regime, the Ministry of Interior edicted instructions aiming at modernizing the information presented in gazetteers and at making it less biased by local prejudice. The total number of gazetteers compiled in the 1920s and 1930s must hover between 600 and 700. Not a few are the result of new and thorough research into historical sources and are of very high quality. The period also saw the development of modern library science in China and, as a consequence, the first comprehensive attempts at locating and describing gazetteers.

Gazetteer compilation and publication practically came to a standstill during the Sino-Japanese and civil wars. However, post-1949 China has a rather remarkable revival of interest and activity in this domain. In 1956, the Science Program Planning Committee of the State Council launched a vast program to compile "new local gazetteers" (*hsin fang-chih* 新方志), a program in which the highest authorities of the Party and state expressed interest. Directives and proposals were drafted by various bodies, committees and "compiling units" were set up all over the country, and a considerable amount of data-collecting and writing was done. Numerous "new gazetteers" or fragments thereof, were published as early as the turn of the 1960s, usually in the form of drafts for restricted circulation (*nei-pu*).

Politics were much more present however than had been the case in previous periods, and in fact, these first efforts came under bitter attack at the time of the Socialist Education Movement of 1963-66 and during the Cultural Revolution. The program gradually resumed after the fall of the Gang of Four. In 1981, the Society for Research on Chinese Local History held its inaugural meeting in Taiyuan, and in general, the 1980s has been a period of tremendous activity in the field. These new *ti-fang-chih*, numbering some 150 by the end of 1991, run as long as 500 to 800 pages, and circulate as much as 3,000 copies. According to recent evaluations, these *ti-fang-chih* demonstrate a high degree of conformity so that the history of local developments rarely deviates from the dominant nationwide political and socioeconomic processes.[11]

One may well ask for whom and for what purpose local gazetteers were intended. In essence, the publication of gazetteers had two purposes: (1) aiding government (*tzu-chih* 資治), and (2) exalting local patriotism. The usefulness of gazetteers for administrators should be obvious. They provided in compact form a compendium of practically all the background knowledge a local official (who was, in most cases, a total stranger to the region where he ruled) needed. Local patriotism was also an important motivating factor behind the publication of local gazetteers, since *ai-hsiang* 愛鄉 was a dominant emotion in the writing of these works. As Pierre-Étienne Will notes in his study of local gazetteers, *ai-hsiang* was also a problem. It was recognized that 'love of locale' also "interfered" with the historical reliability of gazetteers. The public from which compilers were recruited and which, in any case *paid* to see them published, expected to find its locale shown off to advantage, that is, with more insistence on the *li* 利 than on the *ping* 病 (compare the title of Ku Yen-wu's well-known work, the *T'ien-hsia chün-kuo li-ping shu* 天下郡國利病書); or to use another frequently encountered phrase, to read more "praise" (*pao* 襃) than "censure" (*pien* 貶). Indeed, many prefaces candidly admit that, while the role of "history" proper is to distribute praise and blame and to warn future generations, that of gazetteers is to record things beautiful, and people outstanding, in order to "display the glory of a place" (*i chang i i chih sheng* 以彰一邑之盛).

While local gazetteers dating from the Sung were very often written by individuals (e.g. the famous gazetteer of Suzhou, the *Wu-chün chih* 吳郡志, was composed by the poet and traveller Fan Ch'eng-ta 范成大), those of the Ming and Ch'ing were collective enterprises, sometimes written under the authority of a bureau (*chü* 局), involving a team of officials and scholars whose names are listed on the title page. Although the combinations and the terminology may vary, the usual team included, at least, a com-

---

[11] There are two excellent studies on the development of *hsin fang-chih* in the PRC. Both articles contain detailed evaluations of specific gazetteers. See Eduard Vermeer, "New County Histories: A Research Note on their Compilation and Value," *Modern China*, 18.4 (1992):438-467; and Stig Thogersen and Søren Clausen, "New Reflections in the Mirror: Local Chinese Gazetteers (*Difangzhi*) in the 1980s," *Australian Journal of Chinese Affairs*, 27 (1992):161-184.

piler-in-chief (*chu-hsiu* 主修), who was the leading official of the administrative unit to which the gazetteer was devoted, and who more often than not was a sponsor rather than a real "author"; a senior editor (*tsung-tsuan* 總纂), or simply "editor" (*tsuan-hsiu* 纂修), who was the person actually in charge; and a host of assistant compilers (*fen-tsuan* 分纂 or *hsieh-tsuan* 協纂), data collectors (*ts'ai-fang* 採訪), collators (*chiao-tui* 校對), cartographers/artists (*hui-t'u* 繪圖). The sponsoring official was by definition a stranger to the area, and so was, in many cases, the chief compiler, who might be a noted scholar hired for the task; but the rank and file were all local scholar-gentry, and according to one author, if they were "most enthusiastic" to participate in the work, it was because of the glory that biographies of "loyal, filial, chaste, and virtuous persons" would bring to their locale and lineages. There is no doubt that these people set the tone of the gazetteers and that it was difficult for the editors to go against their wishes.

Finally, it is necessary to mention that, in addition to the "administrative" gazetteers devoted to the different sorts of administrative units - including county-level unit gazetteers, there were also "specialized gazetteers" (*chuan-chih* 專志), or what Timothy Brook has called "topographical and institutional gazetteers".[12] The specialized gazetteers, which are very close in format to the administrative gazetteers, are devoted either to topographical units such as rivers or mountains, or to institutions such as monasteries, shrines, and academies. As can be seen when browsing through the Brook bibliography, they cover in fact a very wide range of topics. Contrary to the conventional *fang-chih*, these specialized gazetteers were produced entirely by the gentry, and this may explain the high concentration of titles in Kiangsu and Chekiang. In this case the unifying efforts of the bureaucratic superstructure did not operate as they did where gazetteers describing administrative units were concerned.

Principal Subject Headings in Local Gazetteers

(1) Preface and general rules (*fan-li* 凡例), listing compilers and general editorial policy.

(2) Maps of the district, city plans, etc. (*yü-t'u* 輿圖, *t'u-k'ao* 圖考).

---

[12] Timothy Brook, *Geographical Sources of Ming-Qing History* (Ann Arbor, 1988). For further information about this volume, see below 'Other Aids for the Study of Local Gazetteers'.

This section may include: a general map of the area indicating the principal settlements and administrative boundaries and "districts" (*hsiang* 鄉); one or several maps of water control devices (*shui-li* 水利); pictures of official buildings, academies, monasteries, celebrated landscapes, and the like. The quality and detail of the maps varies widely. A few Ch'ing gazetteers adopted the grid-pattern introduced in China by Jesuit cartographers.

(3) Boundaries of the region (*chiang-yü* 疆輿) give a topographical description usually consisting of a list of distances from the administrative center of the territory to the subordinate centers (if any) and to the borders, arranged according to different points (such as, "80 *li* to the northeast, one reaches the border of such and such county," and so forth.) This section may also include "Successive Changes" (*yen-ko* 沿革) which may be presented in the form of a chronological table (*piao* 表) giving the successive names and administrative statuses of the place from its origins to the present.

(4) Main topographical features (*shan-ch'uan* 山川). Usually a lengthy enumeration of toponyms with localisation by distance (e.g. "so many *li* to the east of the county seat," etc.) or relative position ("to the northeast of such and such place just mentioned"). Watercourses are described step by step with the names of the places where they change direction, or receive a tributary, etc.

(5) Ancient monuments (*ku-chi* 古蹟). A list of remains of antiquarian or archaeological interest. In the same vein, there are usually sections or subsections on "Graves" (*ling-mu* 陵墓), "Ancestral shrines" (*tz'u-miao* 祠廟), "Buddhist and Taoist temples" (*ssu-yüan* 寺院), "Famous views" (*ming-sheng* 名勝), etc..

(6) Official buildings (*kung-shu* 公署) and city walls (*ch'eng-ch'ih* 城池) generally include historical data on these constructions. This section may also include data on granary storage (*ts'ang* 倉) and postal stations (*i* 驛).

(7) Water conservancy [*ho-fang* 河防 "river conservancy", or *chiang-fang* 江防 (same in the South), or *shui-li* 水利 "hydraulics", or *ho-ch'ü* 河渠 "streams and canals"]. Describes the various infrastructures and institutions related to water conservancy and irrigation. Contents vary with the nature of the terrain and hydrology. A great deal of historical material is sometimes included. There may be chronological lists of floods and construction works.

(8) Officials (*chih-kuan* 職官). Includes: (a) a list of the official posts attached to the administrative unit described in the gazetteer, and (b) for each post (or at least the top ones) a chronological list of the incumbents. This list may cover several centuries; each entry gives the name, place of origin, the academic qualification, date of arrival, sometimes the reason for departure, of the official; a short biographical notice listing what the official did when in the post may be attached.

(9) Examinations (*hsüan-chü* 選舉). A table listing in chronological order of examination years all the locals, past and present, who have won the provincial (*chü-jen*) or the metropolitan (*chin-shih*) degree, occasionally some information on their subsequent careers. *Kung-sheng* 貢生 and *chien-sheng* 監生 are also included, but it does not include the regular "students" (*sheng-yüan*): they are collectively dealt with in the section on state schools (*hsüeh-hsiao* 學校). Note that gazetteers are the only source to provide lists of *chü-ren* and *kung-sheng*.

(10) Population (*hu-k'ou* 戶口). Population figures in gazetteers are of very variable nature, quality, and detail. All Ch'ing gazetteers give figures of "male adults" (*jen-ting* 人丁), in fact fiscal units) dating from the beginning of the dynasty and based on late Ming quotas, sometimes later figures from the *pao-chia* 保甲 "censuses". Figures from previous periods are often included. What makes gazetteers unique is that they give demographic information below province level.

(11) "Land and taxes" (*t'ien-fu* 田賦). Statistical data, sometimes extremely detailed, on registered land, tax rates, and tax quotas. In most places these figures vary very little from the late 16th century on and should be used with caution when one wants to know the actual situation at any given time. Commercial and other taxes (*tsa-shui* 雜稅) are also given, and so are grain tribute and salt tax figures. This section may also include a detailed description of the administrative unit's budget in the form of quotas of receipts and expenses. The detail of amounts kept locally (*ts'un-liu* 存留) and amounts forwarded to superior units (*ch'i-yün* 起運) is usually given. There may be a chronological list of famine relief, tax exemptions and postponements, and the like, with indication of the disasters that caused them. Data on granary reserves are included either in this section or in a special section, normally called *ts'ang-ch'u* 倉儲.

(12) Market towns (*shih-chen* 市鎮). Lists the non-administrative towns, tolls, etc.

(13) Local products (*wu-ch'an* 物產, sometimes *t'u-ch'an* 土產). The usual format is a list of plants, animals, sometimes minerals, with various subsections (such as "cereals," "vegetables," "trees," and so on). The products are those supposed to be found in the locality at the time of compilation, but these lists have to be used with caution. Most of the time, the relative importance of the products listed (e.g. such and such cereal is more commonly grown, and so on) is not indicated.

(14) Local customs (*feng-su* 風俗). A section with very variable contents, ranging from vague considerations extracted from old sources to the effect that "The local people are pure (or violent) and like (or are little inclined to) learning," or precise ethnographic observations on festivals, marriage customs, etc.

(15) Personalities (*jen-wu* 人物), sometimes *lieh-chuan* 列傳 (biographies). These are biographical notices on local worthies, usually arranged under subheadings according to occupation and/or behavioral/moral group. A sample of the subsection headings might include "officials" (*huan-kuan* 宦官), "Confucian scholars" (*ju-lin* 儒林), "Belles-lettres authors" (*wen-hsüeh* 文學), "Artists" (*i-shu* 藝術), "Buddhists and Taoists" (*shih-lao* 釋老), "loyal and righteous" (*chung-i* 忠義) "filial and brotherly" (*hsiao-yu* 孝友), "philanthropic" (*hao-shan* 好善) or (*shan-jen* 善人), "chaste women" (*lieh-nü* 烈女), but there are many others.

(16) Literature (*i-wen* 藝文). This sometimes huge section is devoted to literature produced by local people, past and present. Although it may consist of (or include) a list of titles, as in the bibliographical chapters of dynastic histories, the more usual format, especially in Ch'ing gazetteers, is a series of texts quoted in full. In some cases the arrangement is prose then poetry, but there may be numerous subsections, such as memorials, accounts, discussions, stelae, and the like. Texts by non-locals writing on the locality, or for example county magistrates, may be included. This vast repository of information needs to be combed through systematically: it may conceal gems on any sort of topic.

(17) Miscellaneous (*tsa-chi* 雜記) or (*tsa-shih* 雜事). Often includes a chronological list of "disasters and strange events" (*tsai-i* 災異), "auspicious and strange events" (*hsiang-i* 祥異), "disasters and ca-

lamities" (*tsai-huo* 災禍), or the like, recording every kind of "extraordinary" occurrence, from a five-legged calf being born or a dragon being seen flying in the sky, to floods, droughts, famines, earthquakes, and other calamities. The same section occasionally includes a "record of events" (*chi-shih* 紀事) which is a chronology of historical, notably, military events having affected the locality.

References—Local Gazetteers

Catalogues of Local Gazetteers 197
Local Gazetteer Reprint Series... 198
Other Aids for the Study of Local Gazetteers........................ 199

CATALOGUES OF LOCAL GAZETTEERS

Chung-kuo k'o-hsüeh-yüan Pei-ching t'ien-wen-t'ai 中國科學院北京天文臺 comp., *Chung-kuo ti-fang-chih lien-ho mu-lu* 中國地方志聯合目錄 (Beijing, 1985).

Although this work is full of errors (which may in part be explained by the nature of the compiler), this volume remains the "ultimate catalogue" (Will's phrasing - Will also notes that the eminent local historian Chu Shih-chia 朱士嘉 was one of the chief compilers). Lists more than 8200 titles found in some 190 institutions. The arrangement follows the present-day official sequence of independent municipalities, provinces, and autonomous regions, and then areas (*ti-ch'ü*) and municipalities (*shih*). Locations of holding institutions are noted, including those in Taiwan. There is a title index as well as an index of some 10,000 authors/compilers.

Wang Te-i, comp., *Chung-hua min-kuo T'ai-wan ti-ch'ü kung-ts'ang fang-chih mu-lu* 中華民國台灣地區公藏方志目錄 (Taipei, 1985).

This work supersedes the earlier union catalogues of gazetteers held in Taiwan, published in 1957 and 1981 by the National Central Library. New acquisitions, reprints, and microfilms have been added. Gazetteers in *ts'ung-shu* collections are also included. Reprints and new printings done in PRC publishing houses are also given. An appendix lists Japanese gazetteers of places in Taiwan. For original editions the locations in 12 institutions are given. The arrangement follows the official list of administrative units as that in the *Ta Ch'ing i-t'ung-chih.*

Leslie, Donald and Jeremy Davidson, *Catalogues of Chinese Local Gazetteers* (Canberra, 1967).

This work is a bibliography of bibliographies concerning all information on local history research. Although "dated", there is much useful information for the beginning student to examine. There are three main parts: Union Lists, Individual Library Catalogues, and Special Topics.

For lists of catalogues of provincial holdings of gazetteers, and other regional history sources, see James Cole, *Updating Wilkinson*, pp. 90-111, valid to 1991.

LOCAL GAZETTEER REPRINT SERIES

Chung-kuo fang-chih ts'ung-shu 中國方志叢書 (Taipei, 1970 ...).
  The familiar "green volumes" of reprints that are the most
  popular in libraries outside the PRC. This reprint has been
  published in three series. As of 1993, only the first two series,
  including some 1370 titles, have been completed. This is the
  largest series of reprints.

Chung-kuo ti-fang-chih chi-ch'eng 中國地方志集成 (Beijing, 1992) 32
volumes.
  This is a new and large PRC reprint series. The bulk of the
  gazetteers date from the late Ch'ing and Republican periods

Jih-pen ts'ang Chung-kuo han-chien ti-fang-chih ts'ung-k'an 日本藏中
國罕見地方志叢刊 (Beijing, since 1991).
  Some 18 volumes have already been printed in this PRC reprint series of rare gazetteers in Japan.

Hsin-hsiu fang-chih ts'ung-k'an 新修方志叢刊 (Taipei).
  Second largest series of Taiwan based reprints.

Sung Yüan ti-fang-chih ts'ung-shu 宋元地方志叢書 (Taipei, 1987).
  Twelve volumes, including 37 titles.

T'ien-i-ko Ming-tai ti-fang-chih ts'ung-shu 天一閣明代地方志叢書 (Shang
hai, 1964 first edition; 1981, second edition).
  Includes 107 Ming gazetteers from the famous T'ien-i-k'e Library (Ning-po) collection. For a study of this collection, see Lo
  Chao-p'ing 駱兆平, *T'ien-i-ko ts'ang Ming-tai ti-fang-chih k'ao-lu*
  天一閣藏明代地方志考錄 (Beijing, 1982), which describes the
  original 435 gazetteers, of which 271 are still extant. This work
  is arranged by locale, and includes an index.

OTHER AIDS FOR THE STUDY OF LOCAL GAZETTEERS

Lai Hsin-hsia 來新夏, *Chung-kuo ti-fang-chih tsung-lan 1949-1987* 中國地方志綜覽 (Hefei, 1988).

This is a comprehensive guide to all PRC based local history activities, since 1949. Discusses both newly-compiled gazetteers, and reprints of 1949 editions. There are detailed descriptions of new gazetteers, a number of table of contents, a chronology of post-1949 gazetteer developments, information on editorial committees and conferences, and bibliographies of: specialized journals, monographs, and catalogues, and collected source materials. Also presents information on gazetteer related activities in Taiwan and Hong Kong.

Huang Wei 黃葦, comp., *Chung-kuo ti-fang-chih tz'u-tien* 中國地方志詞典 (Hefei, 1986).

This work is an 800 page encyclopedia of information, discussing both old and new gazetteers. There are nearly 2,000 entries, distributed over ten sections, including celebrated gazetteers, celebrated authors or *fang-chih* theoreticians, gazetteer terminology, catalogues, books, articles, prefaces and *fan-li*, compiling units, and so on. There is a list of contents at the beginning. Some experts consider this the richest repository of gazetteer science in compact form.

Wang Chao-ming 王兆明 and Fu Lang-yün 傅朗雲, eds. *Chung-hua ku-wen-hsien ta tz'u-tien, ti-li chüan* 中華古文獻大辭典，地理卷 (Changchun, 1991).

Arranged according to number of strokes of the first character in the title of a particular work, and then sub-divided by stroke order, with 'table of contents' in the beginning of the volume. Gives brief descriptions of existing *ti-fang-chih* and other geographical treatises. Entries generally include the history of each work, and its contents. There is also a reference in which reprint series a particular may be found (including those published in Taiwan). At the end, there is a complete stroke index for persons, places, and titles. Also a separate list for all works discussed, arranged chronologically, and sub-divided by location.

Timothy Brook, *Geographical Sources of Ming-Qing History* (Ann Arbor, 1988).

This work introduces two genres of local-level sources for the study of China's social, economic, and cultural history in the Ming-Ch'ing period (1368-1911): route books, which were practical handbooks for travellers in China; and topographical and institutional gazetteers, which were records of places such as mountains and monasteries. All works listed are extant, except a few, and the complete list was compiled from bibliographies to libraries in Canada, England, Japan, and the United States. The route books are grouped according to historical time, and from simple to complex; the gazetteers are listed on the basis of geographical location. The information on records of monasteries will be of interest to students of religion. There are separate indices for authors, titles, and for geographical names (either prefecture, sub-prefecture, or county).

Li T'ai-fen 李泰棻, *Fang-chih hsüeh* 方志學 (Taipei, 1968; original edition 1935).

Fu Chen-lun 傅振倫, *Chung-kuo fang-chih-hsüeh t'ung-lun* 中國方志學通論 (Taipei, 1966; original 1935).

The two "classic" guides to the study of local gazetteers.

Chang Kuo-kan 張國淦, *Chung-kuo ku fang-chih k'ao* 中國古方志考 (Shanghai, 1962).

The classic study on pre-Ming gazetteers. Some 2,000 works are discussed, of which only a tiny percentage is still extant.

Wang Hsiao-yen 王曉岩, *Fen-lei hsüan-chu li-tai ming-jen lun fang-chih* 分類選注歷代名人論方志 (Shenyang, 1986).

An anthology of 106 essays on local history by 86 authors, ranging from Cheng Hsüan to Liang Ch'i-ch'ao. The essays are organized into broad categories and are provided with introductions and notes.

CHAPTER SIX

DICTIONARIES

Introduction

Lexicography in the Chinese tradition is classified as a part of *hsiao-hsüeh* 小學 or "minor studies", presumably because the study of characters was considered elementary. From the Han dynasty onward the term *hsiao-hsüeh* was narrowed to refer exclusively to matters concerning the script. Over time, dictionaries came to be compiled with definite objectives and for use by persons with a certain background, education, and outlook. Thus, one should not expect to find in dictionaries composed during the imperial era the Chinese equivalent of terms related to personal hygiene, for example.

In the premodern era there were compiled three basic types of dictionaries: semantic, graphic, and phonetic. The Chinese term for semasiology, the study of the meaning of words, is *hsün-ku-hsüeh* 訓詁學. The oldest, and probably the most famous dictionary that falls under this category, is the *Erh-ya* 爾雅. Its origin is not clear, but it is certain to be of high antiquity. Since it has always been associated with the interpretation of terms in the Classics, it was elevated to the status of a Classic when the *Shih-san-ching* edition of the Classics was compiled during the T'ang dynasty. The present text of the *Erh-ya* reads like an inventory of words which occurred in writings until the late Chou.[1] Words are classified under nineteen abstract and concrete headings, such as (1) definitions; (2) concepts; (3) explanation of words; (4) family relations; (5) dwellings, etc. Pronunciation was not indicated in the original work.

Another well-known semantic lexicon is *Fang-yen* 方言 by Yang Hsiung 揚雄 (53 B.C. - 18 A.D.), which may be considered the first dictionary of dialects.[2] However, since no pronunciation is indi-

---

[1] The Harvard-Yenching Sinological Index series, Supplement no.18 is an index to the *Erh-ya*. For further up-to-date information on this important work, see references in Michael Loewe, ed., *Early Chinese Texts*, pp.94-99.

[2] There is also an index to this work, *Fang-yen chiao-chien* 方言校箋 (Centre franco-chinois d'études sinologiques; Taiwan reprint, 1968). See also Paul L. Serruys, *The Chinese Dialects of the Han Time according to the Fang-yen* (Berkeley, 1959).

cated, the nature of the dialect differences is sometimes obscure.

Works on etymology, in Chinese *wen-tzu-hsüeh* 文字學, which form the basis of graphic dictionaries, are bountiful, probably because the Chinese have always been interested in the historical development of their writing system. The first work that may be considered an etymological dictionary is the *Shuo-wen chieh-tzu* 說文解字 (Explaining single graphs and analyzing composite graphs), compiled by Hsü Shen 許慎, who lived around 100 A.D.. The *Shuo-wen* is both a dictionary and an historical explanation of the Chinese writing system. In the foreword to the *Shuo-wen*, Hsü Shen enumerates six principles, the *liu shu* 六書, that are said to have governed the development of the Chinese characters.[3] These include, with examples:

(1) *hsiang-hsing* 象形   imitation
(2) *chih-shih* 指事   indication
(3) *hui-i* 會意   suggestion (or combination)
(4) *hsing-sheng* 形聲   phonetic compound
(5) *chuan-chu* 轉注   transmission (or deflection)
(6) *chia-chieh* 假借   adoption (or loan)

The number of characters in *Shuo-wen*, per principle, respectively, are: (1) 34; (2) 125; (3) 1167; (4) 7697; (5) 7; (6) 115. Characters of the category *hsing-sheng* were divided by Hsü into classifier and phonetic, indicating the classifier with *ts'ung* 從 and phonetic by *sheng* 聲 . For *hui-i* characters, Hsü utilized the formula *ts'ung* A *ts'ung* B. So, for example, the character *nan* 男, one who puts his efforts into farming, is derived from "fields" (*t'ien* 田), and from "strength" (*li* 力) to form "male".

But Hsü's analysis of characters was not always correct. He was writing about 1000 years after the first stylistic reform that put an end to whatever may have remained of earlier archaic writing forms, and that was about 2000 to 3000 years removed from the birth of the Chinese writing system of its basis, neo-lithic picture-writing. Moreover, Hsü did not have knowledge of Shang-Yin 商殷 script forms that we have at our disposal, thanks to the discovery of inscribed oracle bones.

The oldest surviving Chinese script consists of the inscriptions on tortoise shells and ox bones of the Shang dynasty, which are

---

[3] For a modern study on these forms, see David Kuo-wu Wang, *Definitions and Classification of the Six Scripts according to Hsü Shen (A.D. 58-147)* (Ann Arbor, 1979).

called *chia-ku-wen* 甲骨文. The different styles of Chinese script, and their approximate origin are, as follows:

(1) *chia-ku-wen* 甲骨文   oracle bone and shell inscriptions, ca. B.C. 1500

(2) *ta-chuan* 大篆   great seal script by Shih Chou, ca. B.C. 900

(3) *hsiao-chuan* 小篆   small seal script by the Ch'in prime minister Li Ssu

(4) *li-shu* 隸書   "clerical script" of the Han dynasty

(5) *k'ai-shu* 楷書   "model writing"

(6) *hsing-shu* 行書   "running style"

(7) *ts'ao-shu* 草書   "cursive writing" or "grass script"

Also, one might include in this list *chin-wen* 金文 "metal inscriptions", i.e. inscriptions on metals, mostly on bronzes, during the Chou.

Until Li Ssu established *hsiao-chuan* and standardised the script throughout China, characters written for the same word differed by locality, and in the same locality, they differed according to period. There has been much less change in the main structure of the majority of characters from that time to the present day. However, as a result of the change in writing instruments from the early stylus to the brush, at about the beginning of the Han dynasty, the shape of the strokes did change considerably. Styles (4), (5), (6), and (7) were created out of the use of writing brushes. Writing styles have still continued to change, even recently. Simplified characters *chien-t'i* 簡體, found in most People's Republic of China publications, mark the difference between works published there, and those in Taiwan and Hong Kong, where *fan-t'i* 繁體 is the norm.

The other important achievement of the *Shuo-wen chieh-tzu* was to establish a system of radicals for grouping characters together. It is a system employed up to the present day. Although other graphic dictionaries were composed during the imperial era, most of which followed the *Shuo-wen*'s arrangement of more than 500 classifiers; the most recent of these works is the *K'ang-hsi tzu-tien* 康熙字典 (1710). The latter work utilized a system of 214 radicals, a system which has been accepted in most modern Chinese dictionaries, including Chinese/foreign language. For further information on the historical background and use of the *K'ang-hsi tzu-tien*, it is advised to read the section on 'Dictionaries' in TB.

The third type of lexicon, rhyming dictionaries, developed

from the fifth century onward, as phonetic awareness of the language became more important. The earliest of these dictionaries were the *Ch'ieh-yün* 切韻, published 601 A.D. by Lu Fa-yen 陸法言, and others, and a later edition, the *T'ang-yün* 唐韻, published 715 A.D.. Except for some fragments, both these works are lost. However, a third recension, the *Kuang-yün* 廣韻, published 1007 A.D., based on the material in the *Ch'ieh-yün* and *T'ang-yün*, is available, and is considered the a reliable source for phonological research into ancient Chinese pronunciations.

Since Westerners first started coming to China in the 17th century, they attempted to transcribe the sounds of the Chinese language. Each nationality seemed to invent his own alphabetization system, but with the growing dominance of British influence in the 19th century, the Wade-Giles system became the most widely used. Sir Thomas Francis Wade (1818-1895) devised a system for his elementary handbook of Chinese, and Herbert A. Giles (1845-1935) revised and popularized the system in his *Chinese-English Dictionary* (1892).

In 1918, Chinese philologists evolved their own system of phonetic writing, inspired by the Japanese syllabary system of *kana.* This Chinese syllabary was called *chu-yin tzu-mu* 注音字母 or *chu-yin fu-hao* 注音符號, but is popularly referred to as *po-p'o-mo-fo* 伯潑莫佛, from the first four sounds represented in the system. About ten years later, Chinese linguistic scholars also devised a new system of latinization or romanization, i.e. a Western alphabetic transcription of the sounds of the Chinese language. This became known as the *gwoyeu romatzh* system, and was utilized in the phonetic dictionary *Kuo-yü tzu-tien* 國語辭典, first published in 1937. A revised version of this transcription, based partially on Russian drafts, evolved into what has become known as *pinyin* 拼音, and which has gained international acceptance in recent years.

In studying contemporary Chinese development, it is essential to utilize all available lexical tools. The particularistic terminology the Communists have employed to describe their history and their policies makes close reading fundamental for this aspect of Chinese studies.[4] For example, during the period of the communes and the Great Leap Forward, a large number of military terms were employed to describe activities. A fighter (*chan-shih*

---

[4] See the important essay by Jean Chesnaux, "Lexicology as a Primary Source Material for the History of Modern China," in Leslie, Mackerras, and Wang, eds., *Essays on the Sources for Chinese History* (Canberra, 1973), pp.278-286.

戰士) became a worker in the field of production, and the battle front (*chan-hsien* 戰線) became an area where it was vital to concentrate on the effort of the masses. Certainly the implication of the old Confucian expression *cheng-ming*[5] 正名 is still relevant in the PRC today, i.e. there is a deep correspondence between words and their object.

How to Use and Find Chinese Dictionaries

Chinese characters consist of three elements: *hsing* 形 "form", *fa-yin* 發音 "pronunciation", *i* 義 "meaning". A Chinese dictionary may have the characters arranged in groups throughout the dictionary according to one of these three elements and may or may not have the other one or two elements for arranging the characters in some type of cross reference list.

There are two types of dictionaries whereby characters are arranged by form, either: (1) according to radicals (*pu-shou* 部首); or (2) according to number of strokes (*pi-hua* 筆畫). For dictionaries of the first type here, one must be familiar with the fact that radicals can have different positions in characters, and that characters change form when they are used as radicals. Moreover, in post-1949 PRC dictionary publications where simplified characters are the norm, the radicals themselves have also been simplified, the order in which they have been presented also changed, and the number of radicals diminished.

In dictionaries where characters are arranged according to strokes, characters are grouped first according to the number of strokes, and second, according to the shape of the first stroke. Thus, in order to use this kind of dictionary, one must determine correctly the number of strokes, the order of strokes, and the shape of the first stroke. For example, in the group *san-hua* 三畫 (three strokes): 一, as in *ta* 大; or | as in *k'ou* 口;), as in *ch'uan* 川; `, as in *chih* 之; ㄱ, as in *nü* 女.

There are also stroke dictionaries arranged according to "The four corner system" (*ssu-chiao hao-ma* 四角號碼), whereby numerals from 0 to 9 are used to indicate the different shapes of the four corners of each character. Thus, each character is classified according to a four digit number. Dictionaries utilizing this sys-

---

[5] Some Western scholars translate the concept of *cheng-ming* as 'rectification of names', although the verb *cheng* does not mean correcting a wrong but rather, simply appropriateness.

tem invariably also add a character index based on radicals or pronunciation or number of strokes. The four-corner system is still used in both the PRC and Taiwan.[6]

If the pronunciation (*fa-yin*) of a character is known, it may be more convenient to use a dictionary of this kind.[7] However, if the purpose is to determine the prounciation of a character, or if the pronunciation of a character is not known, then a dictionary of this type cannot be used, unless there is some kind of index which gives a certain way other than pronunciation for arranging characters (such as characters arranged by radicals or strokes). Dictionaries with characters arranged by pronunciation may follow an alphabetic transcription system or the Chinese phonetic alphabet.

There are several useful guides that provide lists of dictionaries:
For works in Chinese, one should turn first to: Ts'ao Hsien-cho 曹先擢 and Ch'en Ping-ts'ai 陳秉才, *Pa-ch'ien chung Chung-wen tz'u-shu lei-pien t'i-yao* 八千種中文辭書類編 提要 (Beijing, 1992).

This is the major guide to dictionaries in Chinese. This important listing is arranged according to subject into six main categories including: historical subjects, modern language dictionaries (since 1911), linguistic dictionaries, dictionaries for philosophy and social science subjects, natural sciences, and encyclopedic dictionaries. There are useful indices at the end of this volume: one based on number of strokes, and the other alphabetical for the *pinyin* pronunciation of the first word of each entry.

Also useful is: Huang Wen-hsing 黃文興, ed., *Tz'u-shu lei-tien* 辭書類典 (Beijing, 1993).

A 'dictionary of dictionaries': over 4,000 dictionaries, published in China, including Taiwan, Hong Kong and Macao between December 1978 and December 1990. Has extensive finding indices.

---

[6] For further information on this system, see Walter Simon, *A Beginner's Chinese-English Dictionary of the National Language (Gwoyeu)* (London, 1947).

[7] There are also pronunciation dictionaries arranged according to rhyme *yün* 韻; here words are categorized according to a number of fixed rhyme categories.

For other works, including those in English, see:
Chinese-English Translation Assistance Group, *Chinese Dictionaries in Chinese and Other Languages* (Westport, 1982).

> This is a computerized list, according to subject, of 2739 dictionaries in 30 languages (Chinese to Chinese, Chinese to non-Chinese, and non-Chinese to Chinese). Covers a wide range of subjects: from Buddhism to highway engineering. Contains both an index of dictionaries by title and an index of dictionaries by language.

Paul Fu-mien Yang, *Chinese Lexicology and Lexicography* (Hong Kong, 1985).

> A listing of all important dictionaries, including pre-modern standard Chinese-Chinese dictionaries, and secondary studies thereof until 1982. This work is indispensable for finding classical dictionaries (and all their editions). For further info, see entry p. 75.

David Chien, *Lexicography in China: A Bibliography of Dictionaries and Related Literature* (Exeter, 1986).

Of course, since the publication of these works the numbers of dictionaries continue to expand. The most common general dictionaries are listed below; to find specialist dictionaries in a library that subscribes to the Harvard-Yenching classification system, one must first determine the main classification number and sub-classification numbers for a specific subject. So, for example, if one wishes to find a dictionary that concerns the terminology of modern Chinese business organization, the first step is to determine the correct classification number according to the K.M. Ch'iu classification system. One looks for the main head number '4000-4999' (social sciences), and the sub-classification number (in this case, '4550-4559' business methods).

References—Dictionaries

Modern Chinese Dictionaries 209
    Chinese-Chinese 209
    Chinese-Foreign Language 211
Classical Chinese Dictionaries 214
    Chinese-Chinese 214
    Chinese-Foreign Language 216
Specialist Dictionaries for Modern Chinese 220
    Linguistic Dictionaries 220
    Proverbs and Sayings 221
    Dictionaries for Politics, Economics, Law, and Agriculture .. 224
    Science and Technology 228
    Dialects 229
    Specialist Dictionaries for Aspects of Premodern/Modern
       China 232
    Literary Dictionaries 232
    Religion (including Mythology) and Philosophy 235
    Administrative Terminology 238
    History 240
    Japanese Names 241

MODERN CHINESE DICTIONARIES

Unless otherwise noted, the majority of the following dictionaries are published in the PRC, and therefore employ *chien-t'i*. Also, most of these dictionaries are directed toward the modern written language, and not day-to-day ordinary conversation.

Chinese-Chinese

Hsien-tai Han-yü tz'u-tien 現代漢語詞典 (Beijing, 1977/1985; revised 1992).

This is the standard dictionary of modern Chinese in the PRC today. Entries are listed in *pinyin* alphabetical order with both radical and four-corner indexes following. Index contains both listings of simplified and *fan-t'i* forms. The revised version also includes alphabetical list of compounds based on the *pinyin* spelling of the first character. For the earlier editions, there was issued *Hsien-tai Han-yü tz'u-tien pu-pien* 補編 (Beijing, 1992).

Hsin-hua tzu-tien 新華字典 (Beijing, revised 1980).

Arranged according to *pinyin* alphabetical order. For each character, the principal meanings, with important word combinations and usages are given. There is an index arranged according to radicals. Appendices for national minorities, foreign countries and their capitals, weights and measures.

Tz'u-hai 辭海 (Shanghai: Shang-hai tz'u-shu ch'u-pan she, 1979/1982/1989), three volumes.

The original *Tz'u-hai* was put together as a combination dictionary and compact encyclopedia and meant for the study of both classical and modern terminology. These more recent editions, which should be used in conjunction with the classical dictionary *Tz'u-yüan* (see below), are directed more towards modern terminology. The 1979/82 edition of *Tz'u-hai* is arranged according to 250 radical sequence. After each main character, the arrangement is according to number of strokes. For the principal entries, the older, full characters are given and the pronunciation in *pinyin*. The definitions are written in colloquial Chinese and there are scientific and technological terms with illustrations, book titles, and Western names. Some classical phrases and famous Chinese place names are included. At the beginning of the first volume there is an index by pronunciation. Appendices include: tables of dynastic chronology according to cycles, the reign period of states and dynasties, from 841 B.C. to 1949, lists of national minorities, names of countries, units of weights and measures, currencies of the world, astronomical measurements, table of the elements, foreign names with Chinese transcriptions, Russian names with Chinese transcriptions. On the inside of the back cover of volume one is a map of China with the route of the Long March; of volume two is a table of elements; and of volume three, the International Phonetic Alphabet and the National Alphabet. Besides these three volumes of *Tz'u-hai*, there are also separate specialist volumes (*fen-ts'e* 分冊) which have been published for particular topics such as linguistics, history, economics, historical geography and so on. See the *Tz'u-hai pai-k'o tz'u-mu fen-lei so-yin* 辭海百科詞目分類索引 (Shanghai, 1986).

Tz'u-hai 辭海 (Taipei, 1980), three volumes.
This work is not to compare with the pre-war or the PRC editions. Arranged according to radical, and thereafter by number of strokes of principal characters. Pronunciation is given in *chu-yin fu-hao*. This dictionary is best used for modern written Chinese. There are appendices for chronology, administrative geography, difficult characters, and Western terms.

Kuo-yü tz'u-tien 國語辭典 (*Kuoyeu Tsyrdean*) (Shanghai, 1937; reprinted Taipei, 1966, four volumes; reprinted, Taipei, 1982, six volumes).
This is the collective work of a group of modern Chinese scholars of linguistics. Characters are arranged in the order of the Chinese phonetic syllabary (*po-p'o-mo-fo*) and pronunciation is given in the national phonetic alphabet as well as in *gwoyeu romtzh*. Each pronunciation of a character is entered separately with cross-references to the others. This dictionary is especially useful for colloquial expressions found in novels.

Shih-yung Han-yü t'u-chieh tz'u-tien 實用漢語圖解詞典 (Beijing, 1982).
Ordered according to subject, but without an explanation in Chinese (or any other language); rather, a detailed drawing is

given with all important related words. There is a character index, arranged according to radical and *pinyin* spelling. Compare with *Ying-Han t'u-wen tui-chao tz'u-tien* 英漢圖文對照詞典 (Shanghai, 1984), discussed below.

Chinese-Foreign Language

A Chinese-English Dictionary: Han-Ying tz'u-tien 漢英詞典 (Beijing, 1988).

Since its first appearance in 1978, this dictionary has become the 'standard' dictionary for the translation of written modern Chinese into English. Based on the *Hsien-tai Han-yü tz'u-tien*, this work is arranged alphabetically by *pinyin* with an index of radicals. One must be careful in using this dictionary, since so many of the expressions are outdated due to reforms and political developments. There are appendices for names of foreign countries and their capitals, weights and measures, and Wade-Giles conversion.

Liang Shih-ch'iu 梁實秋 et.al. *Tsui-hsin shih-yung Han-Ying tz'u-tien* 最新實用漢英辭典 (A New Practical Chinese-English Dictionary; Taipei, 1972).

Arranged by radical, this dictionary lists definitions for 7,331 characters and some 80,000 compounds and phrases, written out in *chu-yin fu-hao.* Coverage is not restricted to classical or vernacular Chinese nor are sources indicated, so users have no way of distinguishing between current and historical usages. There are indexes based on radical, number of strokes, *chu-yin fu-hao* pronuciation, and Wade-Giles transcription.

Lin Yutang 林語堂, *Tang-tai Han-Ying tz'u-tien* 當代英漢詞典 (Lin Yutang's Chinese-English Dictionary of Modern Usage; Hong Kong, 1972).

Contains about 8000 characters and about 100,000 entries in a somewhat unconventional arrangement, a kind of "two-corner" system, but remarkable for the excellent modern English equivalent for characters and multi-character compounds. Contents include not only modern Chinese but also classic Chinese and old *pai-hua.* For each character there is an explanation of its grammatical function, then information about pronunciation, and finally examples of word usuages. The overall arrangement of this dictionary is based on a variation of the Four Corner System; the pronunciation is given in simplified *gwoyeu romatzh*. But there are indexes in Romatzh and in English translation so that this work in effect becomes an English-Chinese dictionary.

Han-Ying ni-yin tz'u-tien 漢英逆引詞典 (A Reverse Chinese-English Dictionary; Beijing, 1985).

With about 7,000 head characters and 60,000 entries, this convenient "reverse" dictionary is helpful for the most common words in modern Chinese, as well as a number of frequently used classical Chinese terms. This dictionary collects together compound words having the same end-position in Chinese characters, and takes the end-position Chinese character as the reverse head character. The head characters and entries are arranged in *pinyin* alphabetical order and the entries having the same pronunciation and tone in the order of the number of strokes. There is also a stroke order index, and appendices for the conversion of simplified characters into their original complex form, commonly used measure words, and a separate list for active reverse head characters.

A.P.Crowe and A.Evison, *Concise English/Chinese - Chinese/English Dictionary* (Hong Kong, 1985).

Pocket-sized, this is useful for a quick reference. The Chinese/English section is arranged alphabetically according to *pinyin*, preceded by an index of radicals, based on the same order as in the *Hsien-tai Han-yü tz'u-tien*.

Han-Ying fen-lei ch'a-t'u tz'u-tien 漢英分類插圖詞典 (A Classified and Illustrated Chinese-English Dictionary; Hong Kong, 1981).

This is not a dictionary for translation, but for word usage. Characters (without pronunciation) are listed according to subject, and thereafter sub-classified. There are many illustrations. The main divisions of character classification include science and technology; education, culture, and health; economy and trade; industry, transport, and communication; and agriculture.

Ying-hua ta tz'u-tien 英華大詞典 (A New English Chinese Dictionary; Beijing, revised 1985).

A very detailed dictionary that explains all the uses of a some 120,000 English expressions and how they should be translated into Chinese (without pronunciation).

Ying-Han t'u-wen tui-chao tz'u-tien 英漢圖文對照詞典(Shanghai, 1984).

The English equivalent of the *Shih-yung Han-yü t'u-chieh tz'u-tien* in which detailed drawings are given with English words. Both volumes should be used with each other.

Chû-Nichi daijiten 中日大辞典 (Tokyo, 1968; revised and expanded 1986).

This is the most complete general-purpose bilingual dictionary for Chinese. The entries are arranged by pronunciation and tone in alphabetical sequence by *pinyin*. The main entry is given in both simplified and traditional form; different pronunciations for the same character are given, with cross-references at the appropriate places. Multiple meanings of the character follow, then compounds are listed below with romanization for the whole compound. The coverage is especially good for modern colloquial, with many sentences to illustrate usage, and for late imperial institutions and documentary style. At the front is a list of abbreviations, a table of radicals (243), and an index by radical and number of strokes. At the rear is a Japanese index, terms used to refer to radicals, a comparative list of Japanese-Chinese written forms, a survey of simplified forms, a list of "measure words" or "numerary adjuncts," tables of the governmental organization of the PRC, a calendar of important dates during the year, tables of kinship terms, a plan of a traditional Peking house, table of measurements, table of the elements, and a map of China. Inside the back cover is a table of contents, with romanization in *pinyin*, Wade-Giles, and *chu-yin fu-hao*. This dictionary is often called "Aichi", because it was composed at Aichi 愛知 University.

CLASSICAL CHINESE DICTIONARIES

Although a number of works mentioned in the section on Modern Chinese dictionaries may be useful for the study of classical terminology, e.g. *A New Practical Chinese-English Dictionary* or the *Chûnichi daijiten*, the following publications are specifically for the classical Chinese language.

Chinese-Chinese

Han-yü ta-tzu-tien 漢語大字典 [(Chengtu: Ssu-ch'uan tz'u-shu ch'u-pan-she; Wuhan: Hu-pei tz'u-shu ch'u-pan-she, 1986-1990, 8 vols.); the Taiwan version is entitled: *Yüan-tung Han-yü ta-tzu-tien: Fan-t'i-tzu-pen* 遠東漢語大字典：繁體字本(Taipei: Yüan-tung t'u-shu, 1991)].

This multi-volumed work is arranged according to radical and then stroke order (in *un*abbreviated form, with references to shortened or alternative forms) and is in effect a character dictionary. It gives the archaic form from the *Shuo-wen* and other archaic dictionaries, prounciation in *pinyin*, the history of meanings of individual characters, with detailed examples. There is an index arranged by radical, and sub-arranged by number of strokes.

Lu Erh-k'uei 陸爾奎, *Tz'u-yüan* 辭源 (original Shanghai, 1915; revised Taiwan, 1965, and Beijing, 1983 in four volumes).

With the appearance of this work in 1915, the first modern dictionary for both the contemporary and the classic language was published. The original version provided not only explanation of the characters, but also gave word combinations, names, and examples. The revised version is meant simply as a dictionary of classical Chinese. The typeface is *fan-t'i*, and the arrangement of entries is by the 216 radical system. The definitions retain a literary style and the emphasis is on literary terms. There are very few illustrations and no Western names. Entries are arranged by radical with a radical index for each volume in the front of each volume, and a four-corner index in the back of each volume. The last volume has an index by *pinyin* pronunciation to the main entries.

Shu Hsin-ch'eng 舒新城 et.al., compiler *Tz'u-hai* 辭海 (Shanghai, 1936-7; revised, 1947)[8].

This is a dictionary with a very encyclopedic character (like its modern successor). It was meant to be a dictionary of contemporary written Chinese and an aid for determining the origins of citations, as well as Western scientific terms and proper names (in Chinese translation or transcription). The arrangement is by the 216 radical sequence. Written in simple classical Chinese, it attempted to improve the references in the original *Tz'u-yüan*. There is an index based on the *gwoyeu romatzh* pronunciation of the main characters.

Han-yü ta tz'u-tien 漢語大詞典 (Shanghai: Shang-hai tz'u-shu ch'u-pan-she, 1986-1992), 12 volumes.

This recent publication is in effect the standard dictionary for classical Chinese and old *pai-hua*. Its most outstanding characteristic is its focus on examples from a wide-ranging number of periods of Chinese history. For some expressions, definitions from both the late imperial period and the PRC may be found. In each volume, there is a table of characters, in both shortened and complex form, and an index of those characters studied in that volume. The text is in *chien-t'i*, except in those cases where confusion might arise. The citations from classical Chinese and *pai-hua* are in *fan-t'i*. Sometimes this mixture of *chien-t'i* and *fan-t'i* may leave one with an impression of confusion. Also, in some places the typography is not always clear nor aesthetic. For each main character there is an extensive discussion with many examples and all possible pronunciations. The definitions also include a great number of compounds, names, places, proverbs, and bureaucratic titles. Pronunciation of compound words is not given.

Chung-wen ta tz'u-tien 中文大辭典 (Taipei, 1962-1968) 38 volumes with 2 volumes indexes.

Until the appearance of the *Han-yü ta tz'u-tien*, this dictionary was considered the most complete reference work in existence. Containing 49,905 individual characters, this work relies heavily on Ch'ing dynasty exact scholarship. Arranged by the radical system, each volume carries a stroke and a four-corner in-

---

[8] There is a useful guide for this edition. See George Kennedy, *ZH Guide, an Introduction to Sinology* (New Haven, 1953).

dex. Each character is accompanied by detailed explanations as to its etymology, morphological structure and pronunciation as well as those of its compounds. The source of all citations is noted. This work is also rich in illustrations. Volume 39 is a general index for words arranged by radicals and volume 40 is an index based on number of strokes.

Classical Chinese-Foreign Language

Tôtô Akiyasu 藤堂明保 ed., (*Gakken*) *Kanwa daijiten* (学研) 漢和大辞典 (Tokyo, 1977).

This must be the best classical Chinese dictionary in any language. Arranged according to radical with indexes for the *on* 音 (Sino-Japanese pronunciation) and *kun* 訓 (native Japanese pronunciation) and for the number of strokes. It is based in part on 'Morohashi' [see below]. This dictionary may also be used for classical Japanese. For each character there is a reconstructed form of its pronunciation, and its current pronunciation written in *pinyin,* and also an historical overview of its development, and the meaning of the main characters and compounds thereof. For most of the compounds, there is also noted an example of the way the word is used, and in many cases, references to the way in which compound characters were formed. Appendices include a reconstruction of pronunciation in written Chinese, a bibliography of important books from classical literature and old *pai-hua,* historical maps, and a chronological overview of Chinese history.

Morohashi Tetsuji 諸橋轍次, *Daikanwa jiten* 大漢和辞典 [(Tokyo, 1955-1960; reprinted 1969-71 in a reduced format, Taiwan) 12 volumes plus one volume index; one volume vocabulary index *go-i sakuin* 語彙索引 (Tokyo, 1990)].

Known in the West as 'Morohashi', this massive work contains a total of 49,964 individual entries. It gives the full range of meanings distinguished in the classical commentaries, cites numerous text passages, and includes a large number of compounds and phrases. In the index to each volume, each character is numbered in sequence and the entries under each character are also numbered, arranged by number of characters in the expression and in order of Japanese pronunciation.

Compounds are listed according to the Japanese pronunciation of the second character. The thirteenth volume is an index to the characters in the first twelve volumes, with separate listings for the total number of strokes, *on* reading, *kun* reading, and four-corner system. In general, its strong points are bureaucratic terminology and book titles, and its weak points personal names, and philosophical and religious terminology. The recent index is arranged in *kana* order, and is difficult to use without knowledge of Japanese.

R.H. Mathews, *Mathews' Chinese-English Dictionary* (Shanghai, 1931; revised edition Cambridge, Mass., 1943).

Originally intended as a revision of F.W. Baller's *Analytical Chinese-English Dictionary* (Shanghai, 1900) compiled for the China Inland Mission, Mathews realized a new work was needed. It contains 7,785 characters and over 104,000 combinations, and is arranged according to Wade-Giles pronunciation, but it is full of mistakes so that only its character index based on radicals is reliable. Word combinations for particular characters are arranged according to the radical of the second character. This dictionary should only be used for the study of classical Chinese, and with the understanding that it is heavily biased toward a Confucian interpretation of the characters and their word combinations. There are no examples of word usage.

Edwin G. Pulleyblank, *Lexicon of Reconstructed Pronunciation in Early Middle Chinese, Late Middle Chinese, and Early Mandarin* (Vancouver, 1991).

This work consists of an introduction of approximately 20 pages, followed by the lexicon itself, comprising 404 pages. There is a stroke order index at the end; and the actual entries, amounting to approximately 8,000 are arranged alphabetically according to the *pinyin* system of romanization. In order to use the present work satisfactorily, one will have to take into account the same author's book *Middle Chinese* (1984), which laid down the theoretical basis for his reconstruction of various forms of medieval Chinese pronunciation. Pulleyblank recognizes three linguistic stages: "Early Middle Chinese" (EMC), "Late Middle Chinese" (LMC), and "Early Mandarin" (EM). Access to the expressions is provided in two ways, either through the alphabetical ordering of the entries themselves, or through the stroke order index at the end. There is copious cross referencing of modern readings at the individual entries, to take account of variant pronunciations. An entry begins with the modern *pinyin* reading, accompanied by the Chinese graph. This is followed by the number of the pertinent K'ang-hsi system radical and the stroke count for the graph. Next comes a complete entry reference for Morohashi's *Daikanwa jiten* and beneath this is, where applicable, a complete reference to Karlgren's *Grammata Serica Rencensa* [see below]. Next, on the main line of the entry are in order, the EM form, marked Y (Yüan 元), the LMC form, marked L, and the EMC form, marked E. Finally, on the second line come one or more of the most important semantic glosses to the early graph. In addition, there are sometimes special comments regarding usage in early texts. After each Morohashi entry there is an apparatus of capital and lower-case letters, used to indicate the existence of early and/or modern variant readings of each entry. This is a useful sinological tool.

Bernhard Karlgren, *Grammata Serica Recensa* (Stockholm, 1957).
Until the appearance of Pulleyblank's recent volume this was the most useful Chinese-English dictionary for Chinese of the "classical" period (pre-Ch'in). It is more than a dictionary, however, since it shows the historical development of each character treated from its earliest form (usually shell and bone writing or bronze inscriptions) to its modern form. For each entry, there is: the modern form of the character, earlier and related (i.e. loan characters) forms, reconstructed pronunciation in Archaic Chinese (ca. 500 B.C.), reconstructed pronunciation in Ancient Chinese (ca. 600 A.D.), modern pronunciation, meaning, and source (for each separate meaning). There is an index arranged by radical at the back of the work for the basic or core characters, but not for every character contained in the volume.

F.S. Couvreur, s.j., *Dictionnaire classique de la langue chinoise* (Ho Kien Fou, 1890; reprint Taipei, 1966).
This dictionary has the advantage of containing a large number of characters (with some 21,400) citations arranged by radical and stroke and then by French romanization. The usages cited are confined to classical and literary texts and the source of

each is clearly indicated. This makes the work quite helpful in translation projects, but the number of characters is still too limited to meet the requirements of every occasion. There is a list in the front of the works cited.

SPECIALIST DICTIONARIES FOR MODERN CHINESE

In the last fifteen years or so there has been a great number of new specialist dictionaries published in the PRC. This trend is due to the modernization of Chinese society. The list of specialist dictionaries varies considerably from those focusing on nautical technology to those for ancient Chinese music, chess, or contemporary sociology. The following list is by no means complete, but wherever a particular well-known reference is relevant, this is noted. Most of the following works are Chinese-Chinese, but in some cases a particular bilingual dictionary may be useful, this is also noted.

Linguistic Dictionaries

These include specialist dictionaries for expanding one's knowledge of the language. For example, dictionaries of synonyms are given here.

Chung-kuo yü-yen-hsüeh ta tz'u-tien 中國語言學大辭典 (Nanchang, 1991).
     As the title says, 'an encyclopedic dictionary of Chinese linguistics'; this work is arranged according to subject, and covers many aspects of language study, including among others, *hsün-ku-hsüeh, wen-tzu-hsüeh*, and *fang-yen-hsüeh* 方言學. Entries include a brief explanation and, where applicable, examples. This work also contains a biographical index of famous scholars involved in linguistic studies, and therefore forms a good reference for the further understanding of the development of *k'ao-cheng hsüeh*.

T'ung-i-tz'u tz'u-lin 同義詞詞林 (Hong Kong, 1984).
     A rather detailed reference work, in which words are organized in groups, with all synonyms and related words grouped together. There are no translations or examples of word-usage, and in this way this dictionary may be considered a "Chinese *Roget's Thesaurus*". It covers both abstract and concrete categories, including persons, objects, time and space, and physical and psychological actions. For this group of words there is an index in *pinyin* for all obvious combinations, with reference to

all categories in which a specific compound may be used. This 'dictionary' is thus useful for writing texts in Chinese.

Tuan Te-sen 段德森, *Shih-yung ku Han-yü hsü-tz'u* 實用古漢語虛詞 (second edition, Taiyuan, 1990-1).
    Dictionary of grammar particles *yu* 又 or *yü* 與, etc.. Arranged according to number of strokes. Each entry lists uses, and gives examples from specific texts to illustrate that usage.

Hsien-tai Han-yü ch'ang-yung hsü-tz'u tz'u-tien 現代漢語常用虛詞詞典 (Zhejiang, 1992)
    Another dictionary of grammar particles, but arranged by the alphabetical order of *pinyin* romanization. Contains a stroke index at the beginning. Each entry has brief explanation, and is followed by many examples illustrating usage.

Lü Shu-hsiang 呂叔相, ed. *Hsien-tai Han-yü pa-pai-tz'u* 現代漢語八百詞 (Beijing, 1981).
    An alphabetically ordered Chinese-Chinese dictionary, in which 800 words are explained in detail what they mean and how they should be used. There is much attention paid to 'particles', known as *hsü-tzu* 虛字 in Chinese. There is a separate appendix for names.

Proverbs and Sayings

Ch'eng-yü 成語 and *Hsieh-hou-yü* 歇後語.
    Ch'eng-yü are expressions in classical Chinese, in the main composed out of four characters, what in modern Chinese may be called proverbs. They originate in the main from famous classical texts, such as the *Chan kuo ts'e* 戰國策. Texts from which proverbs and sayings originate are known as *tien-ku* 典故. *Ch'eng-yü* are often used in formal speech, both in written and spoken form. The bibliography of Paul Fu-mien Yang, *Chinese Lexicology and Lexicography* provides an extended list of dictionaries for proverbs and sayings.

Ch'en Yung-chen 陳永禎 and Ch'en Shan-tz'u 陳善慈, *Han-Ying tui-chao ch'eng-yü tz'u-tien* 漢英對照成語詞典 (Hong Kong, 1983).
    This is the standard translation dictionary for *ch'eng-yü*. Ar-

ranged according to *pinyin*, with indexes for Chinese characters and the equivalent English idiomatic expressions. This
work gives the idiomatic translation of more than 4,000 *ch'eng-
yü*, including synonyms and antonyms. The full pronunciation
of the expressions are also noted, and where possible the original source of the *ch'eng-yü*.

Hsiang Kuang-chung　向光忠, *Chung-hua ch'eng-yü ta tz'u-tien*
中華成語大辭典 (Changchun: Chi-lin wen-shih, 1986).
　　Arranged according to *pinyin*. Gives the pronunciation of some
　　12,000 expressions and included an extended investigation of
　　the sources with good examples as used in modern Chinese.
　　There is a stroke count index at the end.

Chang Tzu-ch'en　張子臣 and Chang Hsi-chih　張錫智, *Hsieh-tso
ch'eng-yü tz'u-tien* 寫作成語詞典 (Henan, 1989).
　　More than 11,000 *ch'eng-yü* arranged according to subject: *jen*
　　人, *ching* 景, *shih* 事, *li* 理, and *wu-t'ai* 物態. There are indices ac-
　　cording to the above categories, to the *pinyin* transcription,
　　and to the number of strokes of the first character. The dic-
　　tionary gives for each expression, an explanation of the source,
　　the way it should be used, and examples.

Hsieh-hou-yü (or *ch'iao-p'i-hua* 俏皮話).
　　Hsieh-hou-yü is a mixture of proverb, witticism, and joke, and
　　thereby not merely a play on words as the Western pun. It is a
　　saying in two parts, the first part giving the listener the Chinese
　　as to what the second part should be. The second part is left
　　unsaid, assuming that the listener knows it or can puzzle it out.
　　For example, *mao k'u lao-shu* 貓哭老鼠 is in fact, *chia tz'u-pei*
　　假慈悲 ('The cat sheds false tears for the mouse' is 'false com-
　　miseration, hypocrisy').

John S. Rohsenow, *A Chinese-English Dictionary of Enigmatic Folk
Similes (Xiehouyu)* (Tucson, 1991).
　　This is the first and only massive *hsieh-hou-yü* collection with
　　English glosses. It lists some 4000 entries in alphabetical *pinyin*
　　order, accompanied by boldface, simplified characters and
　　glosses for both the literal and 'idiomatic readings'. Idiomatic
　　readings are also annotated, either as figurative, punning, or
　　both. Some expressions are given further explanatory remarks
　　on their linguistic characteristics.

Li Meng-pei 李孟北, *Yen-yü hsieh-hou-yü ch'ien-chu* 諺語歇後語淺注 (Kunming, 1980).

This work consists of a dictionary of *hsieh-hou-yü* and *yen-yü* 諺語 (common sayings) arranged according to *pinyin* transcription but which is not printed in the text. It is a very extensive explanation of how these expressions are used. Index according to subject, and separate sections for *hsieh-hou-yü* about the subjects of exploitation and peasants.

Chung-hua yen-yü chih 中華諺語語志 (Taipei, 1989) eleven volumes.

An extensive dictionary of more than 52,000 *yen-yü*. Also local and rare *yen-yü* are included. For each term there is a detailed explanation including the sources of the term. Arranged according to radical, with a separate radical index.

Han-yü yen-yü tz'u-tien 漢語諺語詞典 (Beijing, 1990).

Dictionary of proverbs arranged alphabetically according to the *pinyin* transcription of the first word. There are both alphabetical and stoke count indices at the beginning of the volume. For each expression, an explanation with further examples of its usage is given. This dictionary is suitable for both colloquial and written Chinese.

Hsieh-hou-yü liang-wan t'iao 歇後語20,000條 (Beijing, 1991).

As the title suggests, a quick reference for common *hsieh-hou-yü*, arranged alphabetically according to *pinyin*, without explanation.

Chung-hua yen-yü ta tz'u-tien 中華諺語大辭典 (Shenyang, 1991).

Informative, handy dictionary of common sayings, arranged alphabetically according to *pinyin* transcriptions. There is a 'table of contents' listing all entries and a stroke count index at the end for the first character of each expression. For each expression there is an explanation and references to literary texts where the expression may be found.

Ch'eng Chih-wei 成志偉 and Hsin I 辛夷, *Chung-kuo tien-ku ta tz'u-tien* 中國典故大辭典 (Beijing, 1991).

Arranged by alphabetical *pinyin* order. Each entry notes a particular work or dynastic period from when the expression originated, with quotations from the work. This is a useful reference for denoting differences in one word expressions.

Dictionaries for Politics, Economics, Law, Agriculture

General dictionaries for modern Chinese published in the PRC are very helpful for subjects related to politics and law. Nevertheless, a satisfactory general up-to-date dictionary incorporating the many changes in Chinese political, social, and economic developments during the last 15 years has not yet been published. Thus, one must consult the most current specialist dictionaries in these fields.

Politics

D.R. Bilancia, *Dictionary of Chinese Law and Government* (Stanford, 1981).
> This Chinese-English dictionary has a very encyclopedic character, with extra-lengthy explanations of political, legal, and economic terminology used between 1939-1977. The introduction gives a detailed discussion of the author's sources. This book is arranged according to *pinyin* transcription, and contains an index of terms, arranged by radical. It gives all possible word combinations with their pronunciation and references to synonyms.

Cheng-chih-hsüeh tz'u-tien 政治學詞典 (Hangzhou, 1989).
> "A Dictionary of Political Science" which incorporates many of the expressions that became common in the media after 1978, e.g. 'Kangaroo Court'. This work is arranged according to number of strokes. For each expression in Chinese there is an English equivalent given, with various meanings where appropriate. The expressions listed are both historical and modern, ranging from the Confucian 'Ten Items of Unpardonable Sin' to the more recent 'Ten Years of Chaos'. There is also a table of contents based on subject. This work also contains an English language appendix for quick reference, including a list of Western expressions and personages, arranged alphabetically.

Hsiao Ch'ao-jan 蕭超然, *Chung-kuo tang-shih chien-ming tz'u-tien* 中國黨史簡明詞典 (Beijing, 1987), 2 volumes.
> This is a dictionary for the history of the Chinese Communist Party. It is divided into various sections, including: party organization, historical events, important meetings, historical

sources, newspapers and journals, communist terminology, international relations, and important persons (about 400 names are included). Arranged by number of strokes; each section has its own individual index based on number of strokes.

The following works are now "outdated", but may be useful for those studying the period 1949-1977, or earlier.

Warren Kuo, ed., *A Comprehensive Glossary of Chinese Communist Terminology* (Taipei, 1978).

Arranged according to Wade-Giles romanization. Gives the pronunciation of all combinations and vocabulary for the period 1921-1977. Detailed, without being "propagandistic". The author gives references to the most important Communist literature where the terms may be found. There is also an index to characters and English translations; and a section with charts of the structure of both the Communist Party and the government.

H. Martin and T. Martin-Liao, *Chinesisch-Deutsches Wortschatz: Politik und Wirtschaft der VR China* (Berlin, 1977).

Arranged according to *pinyin*. Gives the pronunciation of all main entries and word combinations. Especially good on Communist "jargon" for the period 1949-1955, with extensive explanation of the meanings and their signification. References are given to the contextual origin of the terms. There is an index based on number of strokes, and appendices for place names, capitals, and public holidays.

D.J. Dooling and C.P.Ridley, *Chinese-English Dictionary of Chinese Communist Terminology* (Stanford, 1973).

Arranged according to radical. Pronunciation is given in Wade-Giles, for vocabulary for the period ±1920-±1973. This work seems "outdated" in comparison to the three above dictionaries.

Chi Wen-shu, *Dictionary of Contemporary Usage* (Berkeley, 1977).

Over 20,000 terms arranged according to *pinyin*. Gives the translation and pronunciation of all word combinations. The English equivalents are precise and idiomatic. Offers an especially extensive word list.

Economics

Ching-chi ta tz'u-tien 經濟大詞典
(Shanghai, 1983–).
A series of specialist volumes:
Kung-yeh ching-chi chüan 工業經濟卷	(1983)
Nung-yeh ching-chi chüan 農業經濟卷	(1983)
Shih-chieh ching-chi chüan 世界經濟卷	(1985)
Shang-yeh ching-chi chüan 商業經濟卷	(1986)
Chin-jung ching-chi chüan 金融經濟卷	(1987)
Ts'ai-cheng ching-chi chüan 財政經濟卷	(1987)
Tui-wai ching-chih mao-i chüan 對外經濟貿易卷	(1990)
Shu-liang ching-chi chüan 數量經濟卷	(1990)
Chi-hua chüan 計劃卷	(1990)
Chung-kuo ching-chi shih chüan 中國經濟史卷	(1993)

A series of handy Chinese dictionaries about all aspects of the economy. Except for the volume on the agricultural economy which is arranged according to subject, the entries in all the volumes are arranged according to number of strokes. Appendices for relevant laws and regulations, weights and measures, statistics, and pronunciation.

Han-Ying ching-chi tz'u-tien 漢英經濟詞典 (A Chinese English Dictionary of Economics; Beijing, 1990).
Gives about 70,000 terms in *pinyin* without the pronunciation. Appendices with lists of the most important central and commercial banks in the world and approximate rates of exchange.

Ying-Han ching-chi yü kuan-li ta tz'u-tien 英漢經濟與管理大詞典 (An English-Chinese Dictionary on Economy and Management; Beijing, 1990).
In this dictionary some 100,000 expressions from management are examined. Terms in English for which there is no Chinese equivalent are noted as well. Appendices for the names of large companies located world-wide and a list of approximate exchange rates are included.

Shih-yung ching-mao ta tz'u-tien 實用經貿大詞典 (A Practical Dictionary of Economics and Business; Beijing, 1991).
An English-Chinese, Chinese-English dictionary with more than 60,000 key words. The Chinese-English portion is ar-

ranged according to *pinyin* without the written pronunciation. At the end of this dictionary are lists of Chinese banks, commercial organizations, and the most important government agencies dealing with foreign trade.

Ying-Han ching-chi tz'u-hui 英漢經濟詞滙 (Chongqing, 1983).
Arranged according to *pinyin*. Appendices with many common abbreviations, rates of exchange, and comparisons of American and English terminology.

Law

Chung-kuo fa-hsüeh chu-tso ta tz'u-tien 中國法學著作大詞典 (Beijing, 1992).
Bibliographical dictionary about Chinese law. Covers the period from before the Ch'in until nowadays. The book is divided into ten chapters: theory, constitutional law, administrative law, penal law, civil law, economic law, lawsuits, international law, legal history, and law in the ancient period. For each keyword, there are references to other dictionaries and relevant secondary studies. At the end there is an index of books, arranged according to number of strokes.

Chung-kuo ssu-fa ta tz'u-tien 中國司法大詞典 (Jilin, 1991).
Dictionary about ancient and modern judiciary. Divided into seven chapters: *tsung-lei* 總類 (general aspects), *hsing-shih* 刑事 (penal law), *min-shih* 民事 (civil law), *ching-chi* 經濟 (economic law), *hsing-cheng* 行政 (administrative law), *she-wai* 涉外 (international law), and *ku-tai* 古代 (ancient law). At the end there is a stroke count index.

Chien-ming fa-hsüeh ta tz'u-tien 簡明法學大詞典 (Jilin, 1991).
Dictionary with emphasis on present day law. Focuses also on foreign law and the history of Chinese law. Arranged according to number of strokes. No index.

Fa-hsüeh ta tz'u-tien 法學大詞典 (Beijing, 1991).
An extensive dictionary for both Chinese and foreign law. More than 13,000 word combinations are examined. Arranged according to the number of strokes of the first character.

Fa-hsüeh tz'u-tien (tseng-ting-pen) 法學詞典（增訂本）(Shanghai, 1984).
Detailed Chinese-Chinese dictionary about Chinese and foreign law. Arranged according to number of strokes, There are
indices based on stroke cout, *pinyin* transcription, and the
first character of all word combinations.

Agriculture

Nung-yeh tz'u-tien 農業詞典 (Jiangsu, 1979).
Systematically arranged according to number of strokes.
Treats not only all facets of agriculture, but also biology, and
forestry. Detailed explanation of all terms in Chinese, with
many illustrations.

K. Broadbent, *A Chinese English Dictionary of China's Rural Economy*
(Farnham, 1978).
The principal characters are arranged in alphabetical order
according to Wade-Giles transcription (includes a separate
pinyin list). Although "out of date" this work may be useful for
studying agricultural history, and Communist reforms before
1980. For each character, pronunciation, word combinations,
and definitions are given, accompanied where relevant, with
bibliographical references to further information. Concludes
with a bibliography, key character index, English index, and
index of scientific terms.

Science and Technology

This category of dictionary concerns the exact sciences such as
medicine, physics, chemistry, mathematics as well as mechanical
engineering. Dictionaries in this field are usually very specialized.
The following works are more general dictionaries on science and
technology, encompassing many of these specialities into one or
two volumes.

Wang T'ung-i 王同億, *Hsien-tai k'o-hsüeh chi-shu tz'u-tien* 現代科學技
術詞典 (Shanghai, 1980)
The 'standard' dictionary for scientific and engineering terms.
Arranged according to number of strokes, with indices based
on number of strokes, and *pinyin*. Contains some 16,000 ex-

pressions with an equivalent in scientific English, a Chinese explanation, and many illustrations. No Chinese pronunciation given. Appendices for weights, measures, mathematical symbols, and the periodic system.Has an English index: *Ying-Han hsien-tai k'o-hsüeh chi-shu ta tz'u-tien* 英漢現代科學技術大詞典 (Shanghai, 1982). Contains 12,000 English terms..

Han-Ying k'o-chi tz'u-tien 漢英科技詞典 (Nanchang, 1988).
Examines more than 3000 scientific and technological terms. Arranged according to number of strokes. For many terms, there are illustrations. Includes an index based on number of strokes of the first character.

Shih-yung k'o-hsüeh ming-tz'u shu-yü tz'u-tien 實用科學名詞術語詞典 (Beijing, 1990).
More than 10,000 scientific terms are examined here. Includes social science terminology as well. Arranged according to number of strokes.

Ying-Han shu-li-hua tz'u-tien 英漢數理化詞典 (Beijing, 1991).
Approximately 80,000 terms from mathematics, physics, and chemistry are examined. Appendices include mathematical symbols, and the periodic system.

K'o-hsüeh chi-shu she-hui tz'u-tien 科學技術社會詞典 (Shanghai, 1991-92) four volumes.
In four parts, *sheng-wu* 生物, *ti-li* 地理, *wu-li* 物理, *hua-hsüeh* 化學. Arranged according to *pinyin* transcription, with English terminology often added. Many illustrations.

Han-Ying k'o-chi ta tz'u-tien 漢英科技大詞典 (Harbin, 1985) two volumes.
Discusses some 30,000 terms, arranged in *pinyin* order. Pronunciation of word combinations not given.

Dialects

Before embarking on any study of Chinese dialects, one might turn to Jerry Norman, *Chinese* (Cambridge, 1988), chapters 8 and 9 which give a clear and precise historical analysis of local Chinese dialects. Another good reference work for understanding the problems involved in dialects is Paul Fu-mien Yang, *Chinese Dialectology* (Hong Kong, 1981). This volume gives a list of dialect dictionaries and a bibliography for further study of dialectology. Of the major dialects, Cantonese is most common; it is spoken not only in Kuang-tung, but also among overseas Chinese, and of course, in Hong Kong. Except for the major dialects of Cantonese, Min-nan hua, Wu, Hakka, and Pekinese, there are no real dictionaries. Much modern research on local dialects results in word lists but no real dictionaries.

Cantonese

Roy T. Cowles, *The Cantonese Speaker's Dictionary*
(Hong Kong, 1965).
> The standard Cantonese-English dictionary, arranged according to Cantonese pronunciation. An enormous number of words are listed without any information about the way in which they should be used. The standard Chinese equivalents are given only in characters, without further explication.

Kuang-chou-hua fang-yen tz'u-tien 廣州話方言詞典 (Hong Kong, 1981).
> Arranged according to Cantonese pronunciation. This dictionary may be considered the most useful Cantonese-standard Chinese dictionary available. The characters and pronunciation of all word combinations and examples of word use are also supplied. There is an introduction about the Cantonese sound system and the characteristics of Cantonese vocabulary. Also includes a table with *pinyin* and Cantonese, and a character list.

Min-nan-hua

This is the dialect of Southern Fukien, a region which attracted many missionaries, and later, Dutch colonial officials because of their involvement in the export of local labor to the East Indies under their direction. Min-nan-hua was also spoken in Taiwan before the Japanese occupation 1895-1945. Many overseas Chinese, especially those living in Southeast Asia, speak Min-nan-hua.

P'u-t'ung-hua Min-nan fang-yen tz'u-tien 普通話閩南方言詞典 (Fuzhou, 1982).
> This work is a dictionary of standard Chinese-Min-nan-hua. Ar-

ranged according to the *pinyin* pronunciation of standard Chinese, and next to it the Fukienese pronunciation. Both the classical and modern pronunciations of Min-nan-hua are given. There is extensive information by character, so that the specific questions concerning dialect use of word-combinations are addressed. There are indices for dialects and radicals, and a table for difficult characters.

Wu dialect

Chien-ming Wu fang-yen tz'u-tien 簡明吳方言詞典 (Shanghai, 1986).
A dictionary of Wu dialect-standard Chinese. Arranged according to the number of strokes of the characters, with indices based on the dialect pronunciation and number of strokes. There is also a table with local variations in the dialect for kinship terminology and personal names. What is particularly useful about this dictionary is that it gives examples from literature written in old *pai-hua*, so that the user may refer to this work as a reference for literary texts. There is also a bibliography.

Peking dialect

Pei-ching t'u-yü tz'u-tien 北京土語辭典 (Beijing, 1990).
Most of the words examined here concern the Beijing decade since 1949, with some attention paid to terms from the late Ch'ing to 1949. Arranged according to *pinyin* transcription with a stroke-count index. For some expressions, *yen-yü* and *ch'iao-p'i-hua* are also given.

Literary Dictionaries

In its long history, Chinese literature has developed various genres, usually associated with a specific period during which the genre evolved or flourished, as for instance, the *fu* 賦 in the Han dynasty, the *lü-shih* 律詩 in the T'ang dynasty, the *tz'u* 詞 in the Sung dynasty, and the *ch'ü* 曲 in the Yüan dynasty. Each genre has its own peculiar prosody and terminology.[9]

Chung-kuo wen-hsüeh ta tz'u-tien 中國文學大辭典 (Tianjin, 1991) eight volumes.

> Encyclopedic dictionary about all of Chinese literature. Arranged according to the number of strokes of the first character. In the first volume there is a table of contents and indices for *pinyin* and for the individual expressions which are categorized into one of seven major categories. This dictionary divides the study of modern literature into three categories (*chin-tai* 近代, *hsien-tai* 現代, and *tang-tai* 當代). The literature of Taiwan and Hong Kong, as well as those of minorities and folk literature are also included.

Wang Kuei-yüan 王貴元 and Yeh Kuei-kang 葉桂剛, *Shih tz'u ch'ü hsiao-shuo yü-tz'u ta tien* 詩詞曲小說語辭大典 (Beijing, 1993).

> This is an excellent work for quick reference. Arranged according to number of strokes (in simplified characters). There is a table of contents at the beginning of this work. For each expression, there is reference to the title (and location) where it may be found.

Chou Chin 周錦, ed. *Chung-kuo hsien-tai wen-hsüeh shih-liao shu-yü ta tz'u-tien* 中國現代文學史料術語大辭典 (Taipei, 1988) five volumes.

> More an encyclopedia than a dictionary, this work examines expressions from literature (including 'manifestoes'), literary movements and organzations, and journals in *pai-hua* of the 1911-1949 period. Entries are arranged according to number of strokes of the first word. Each expression is written in bold,

---

[9] For further discussion on these forms, and others, see Nienhauser, *The Indiana Companion to Traditional Chinese Literature.*

and thereafter follows an explanation, sometimes with historical references included. Also contains indices: subject index (based on keywords and listed by number of strokes), and an index of personages. Finally, there is an appendix which gives a chronological survey of the literature.

Han Wei Chin Nan-Pei ch'ao Sui shih chien-shang tz'u-tien 漢魏今南北朝隋詩鑒賞詞典 (Shanxi, 1989).

An extensive anthology of more than 1000 *shih* 詩 poems from the time of the Han, Wei, Chin, Northern and Southern dynasties, and the Sui, supplemented by 300 *yüeh-fu* 樂府 poems whose authors are unknown. Each poem receives an extensive explanation. Arranged in chronological order. Indices for well-known first lines of the poems, names of the poets, and stroke counts.

Ch'üan T'ang shih so-yin 全唐詩索引 (Beijing, since 1991), multi-volumed.

Most of these volumes (as of 1994, some 10 are in print) focus on the work of one poet. Arranged by 4-corner system, with a finding index an the end. Cites lines of poems (volume, page, *chüan*) according to the 1982 edition of the *Ch'üan T'ang shih.*

Chao Huan-kuang 趙宦光, Huang Hsi-yüan 黃習遠, Liu Cho-ying 劉卓英, *Wan shou T'ang-jen chüeh-chü* 萬首唐人絕句 (Beijing, 1983).

Help-finding index for anthologies of T'ang poetry.

Chou Hsün-ch'u 周勳初, et. al., ed. *T'ang shih ta tz'u-tien* 唐詩大辭典 (Nanjing, 1990).

This is a very comprehensive dictionary for the study of T'ang poetry. There are altogether 6,000 entries in the dictionary, divided into eight categories: (1) *shih-jen* 詩人 [poets]; (2) *t'i-lei* 體類 [styles]; (3) *chu-tso* 著作 [works]; (4) *ming-p'ien* 名篇 [famous works]; (5) *ko-lü* 格律 [poetical rules and forms]; (6) *tien-ku* 典故 [allusions]; (7) *ch'eng-yü* 成語 [idioms]; (8) *sheng-chi* 膡跡 [scenic spots and historical sites]. There is a table of contents, listed according to the above categories, and arranged by stroke number. In addition, there are a four corner general index, and a conversion table for strokes and four corner number. Two useful appendices also complete this work. The first is a general introduction to the documents of T'ang poetry; it gives a brief documentary record of T'ang poetry from the Sung through the Ch'ing dynasties (including some modern works). The second is a chronological table of important events related to T'ang poetry; this appendix registers the events to both the poems and the poets.

T'ang shih pai-k'o ta tz'u-tien 唐詩百科大辭典 (Beijing, 1990).
Encyclopedic dictionary about T'ang poetry. Divided into 13 categories, for which there are lists of the most common words found in T'ang poetry, T'ang poets, and those scholars presently studying T'ang poetry, both inside and outside China. At the end there is a stroke count index.

T'ang Sung tz'u pai-k'o ta tz'u-tien 唐宋詞百科大辭典 (Beijing, 1990).
Arranged in the same way as the work above on T'ang poetry, except this dictionary is concerned only with *tz'u* poems from the T'ang and the Sung.

Lung Ch'ien-an 龍潛庵, *Sung Yüan yü-yen tz'u-tien* 宋元語言詞典 (Shanghai, 1985).
This is not only a dictionary of literary terms, it also a reference work for studying the use of written Chinese of the Sung and Yüan periods. It examines the literature of theatre, novellas, poetry, *pi-chi* 筆記 (short notes), and dialects. There are extensive explanations and examples of word usage given. It is written in shortened characters and arranged according to number of strokes. There are indices for stroke count of characters, and *pinyin.*

Ku Hsüeh-chieh 顧學頡 and Wang Hsüeh-ch'i 王學奇, *Yüan-ch'ü shih-tz'u* 元曲釋辭 (Beijing, 1983).
This is a dictionary for Yüan dynasty drama, arranged according to *pinyin* transcription. For each expression, there is a very extensive explanation, and many examples.

Lu Tan-an 陸澹安, *Hsi-ch'ü tz'u-yü hui-shih* 戲曲詞語滙釋 (Shanghai, 1981).
Dictionary for terms concerning the traditional Chinese theatre. Arranged according to number of strokes with stroke index at end. Gives examples from specific plays.

Chung-kuo hua-pen hsiao-shuo su-yü tz'u-tien 中國話本小說俗語辭典 (Taipei, 1985).

This work is a revision of T'ien Tsung-yao's *A Glossary of Colloquial Expressions in Chinese Vernacular Fiction* (East Lansing, 1983). It is the first Chinese-English dictionary for old *pai-hua* ever published. It examines some 32,000 word combinations and gives an English translation, sometimes with a short explanation. There are references noted to examples in literature, but no citations. There is an index arranged according to the radical of the first character. There is also a *pinyin* list at the end.

Chung-kuo ku-tien hsiao-shuo yung-yü tz'u-tien 中國古典小說用語辭典 (Taipei, 1985).

This is now the "standard" dictionary for novels and short stories written in old *pai-hua.* Arranged according to the number of strokes, with an index for all terms based on number of strokes. It is considered a revision of the classic work *Hsiao-shuo tz'u-yü hui-shih* 小說詞語滙釋 (Shanghai, 1964) by the literary critic Lü Tan-an.

Religion (including mythology)[10] *and Philosophy*

The study of Chinese religion and philosophy before 1949 was a subject of great interest to academia, as well as missionaries. After that year the only research that could be done was confined to Taiwan and Hong Kong, but in the last ten years once again there has been a growing interest both within China and outside for the study of these subjects. Because of this tremendous time gap between periods of study, "old" research works may still be of use for those looking at religion from a historical and literary context.

Tsung-chiao tz'u-tien 宗教辭典 (Shanghai, 1981; revised, 1985).

This is a dictionary of vocabulary for both Chinese and non-Chinese religions, but more than two-thirds of the entries are about Chinese religion. It gives reliable, quick references to basic Chinese terms in Buddhism, Taoism, and other religions, such as Islam and Manichaeism, not admitted in other, sectarian works.

---

[10] For general and bibliographical surveys of works on Chinese myths, see Anne M. Birrell, "Review Article: Studies on Chinese Myth since 1970: An Appraisal," *History of Religions*, 39.4 (1994): 380–393; 34.1 (1994): 70–94; and W.L. Lai, "Recent Scholarship on Chinese Myths," *Asian Folklore Studies*, 53.1 (1994).

Chung-kuo ko-min-tsu tsung-chiao yü shen-hua ta tz'u-tien 中國各民族宗教與神話大詞典 (Beijing, 1990).
　　Dictionary of religion and mythology of all Chinese nationalities, including the Han. Arranged according to the *pinyin* pronunciation of the names of different nationalities. At the end indices for *pinyin*, stroke counts, and bibliographical references. Appendices for population, residential area, and languages of the various nationalities.

Mochizuki Shinkô　望月信享, *Bukkyô daijiten* 仏教大辞典 (Tokyo, 1933-1963; three revised editions) ten volumes plus index volume.
　　This is the standard dictionary for Buddhist terminology. It includes names, terms, books, events, religious terms, temples, offices, and so on, all arranged according to Japanese pronunciation. It is illustrated and contains indices for Chinese, Japanese, and Tibetan terms, as well as those in Sanskrit and Pali.

Ting Fu-pao 丁福保, *Fo-hsüeh ta tz'u-tien* 佛學大辭典 (1922; revised Beijing, 1984).
　　This is the most extensive dictionary in Chinese for the study of Buddhism, largely based on a Japanese work of the same title compiled by Oda Tokuno 織田得能, which in turn was probably based upon the *I-ch'ieh-ching yin-i*一切經音義 and the *Fan-i ming-i chu*翻譯名義集 both Buddhist dictionaries dating from the T'ang and Sung dynasties, respectively. Arranged according to the number of strokes, and written in classical Chinese. There is a stroke-count index. Includes the study of Buddhist terminology, personal names, and names of books.

Tz'u I 慈怡, *Fo-kuang ta tz'u-tien* 佛光大辭典 (Taipei, fifth edition, 1989) 7 vols. and 1 vol. index.

Fo-chiao wen-hua tz'u-tien 佛教文化辭典 (Hangzhou, 1991).
　　More like an encylopedia than a dictionary, this handy work is arranged according to subject and covers all important facets of Buddhism in its past until 1949. Includes discussions on schools, personages, customs, literature, and so on. Concludes with a chronological table, and a stroke-count index to all entries in the dictionary.

W.E. Soothill and L. Hodous, *A Dictionary of Chinese Buddhist Terms* (London, 1937; reprinted, Taiwan, 1961).
　　Because of the lack of better references, this work may still be

useful for general translations. Arranged according to number
of strokes. There is an index for Sanskrit and Pali words. Location of a term may be difficult since one cannot determine
whether it appears as an independent entry or within the definition of another term.

Yves Raguin, *Terminologie raisonée du bouddhisme chinois* (Taipei,
1985).
Brief dictionary for the most important Chinese Buddhist terminology, translated and explained in French. Based upon the
words given in *Tz'u-hai, Tz'u-yüan,* and other dictionaries. Arranged in alphabetical order of the Wade-Giles transcription.
Index to Sanskrit and French translations.

Li Shu-huan 李叔還, *Tao-chiao ta tz'u-tien* 道教大辭典 (Taipei, 1979;
reprint 1983).
Arranged by number of strokes.

Hsien-hsüeh tz'u-tien 仙學辭典 (Taipei, 1962).
A dictionary for Taoist terms, arranged by number of strokes of
the first character. Explanations are simple, with examples,
and citations (but no exact references).

E.T. C. Werner, *A Dictionary of Chinese Mythology* (Boston, 1932).
Arranged according to Wade-Giles transcription, this work is
still the only "handy" reference about the most important figures of Chinese mythology, including those from Buddhhism,
Taoism, and folk religion.

Wolfram Eberhard, *A Dictionary of Chinese Symbols: Hidden Symbols
in Chinese Life and Thought* [(London, 1986); original edition, published as *Lexikon chinesischer Symbole: geheime Sinnbilder in Kunst und
Literatur, Leben und Denken der Chinesen* (Köln, 1983)].
This is a richly illustrated summary of some 400 Chinese symbols, many of which are still in common use. Chinese characters are given only for keywords, and not in the entire explanatory text. Although there is no index, there is an extensive
bibliography. This work is somewhat difficult to use since many
terms turn up only in the explanation (without characters),
and therefore cannot be easily determined.

Yüan K'o 袁珂, *Chung-kuo shen-hua ch'uan-shuo tz'u-tien* 中國神話傳說
詞典 (Shanghai, 1985).
> For a quick handy reference to mythological stories, arranged
> according to number of strokes. Each entry contains reference
> for further investigation.

Chung-kuo che-hsüeh tz'u-tien ta-ch'üan 中國哲學詞典大全 (Beijing,
1989).
> A dictionary for Chinese philosophy, arranged according to
> number of strokes. Covers the period from before the Ch'in to
> and including the Ch'ing dynasty. There is a definite emphasis
> on Sung and Ming philosophy, with further bibliographical
> references (sometimes to Japanese and English works, as well).
> This work contains three indices: one for all terms arranged
> according to *chu-yin fu-hao* spelling, another for personal
> names (arranged according to number of strokes), and a gen-
> eral stroke-number index.

Chung-kuo ssu-hsiang ta tz'u-tien 中國思想大辭典 (Jilin, 1991).
> Dictionary about traditional Chinese thought. Covers the pe-
> riod from before the Ch'in to the May Fourth Movement. Ar-
> ranged in three parts: *jen-wu* 人物 (persons), *tien-chi* 典籍 (old
> books and commentaries), and *ssu-hsiang* 思想 (thought).
> Within the three sections, words are arranged according to
> number of strokes.

Hsin-pien che-hsüeh ta tz'u-tien 新編哲學大辭典 (Beijing, 1991).
> Dictionary for both Western and Chinese philosophical terms.
> The accent is on Marxist thinking. Arranged according to
> number of strokes, with a stroke index at the end.

Chung-kuo ju-hsüeh tz'u-tien 中國儒學辭典 (Liaoning, 1988).
> A dictionary about Confucianism, for the period from before
> the Ch'in to 1986. The more than 2200 terms are arranged in
> four sections. Those in the sections for *jen-wu* 人物, *tien-chi* 典籍,
> and *hsüeh-p'ai shu-yüan* 學派書院 are arranged chronologically,
> and those in the last section, *kai-nien tz'u-yü* 概念詞語 are or-
> dered by number of strokes. There is a general index, ar-
> ranged according to number of strokes at the end.

Administrative Terminology

Charles Hucker, *A Dictionary of Official Titles in Imperial China* (Stanford, 1985).

Listing some 8,291 significant titles found in the period from the Chou to the Ch'ing period by Wade-Giles romanization, this work has now become the 'standard reference' for translating governmental titles. Each entry notes the period during which the title was used and gives a translation and an explanation of its function. If the title occurred in more than one period with differences in function, this is clearly indicated. Alternate translations in other works are also listed. There are two indices, one for the English translation, and the other for Chinese characters, arranged by radical and stroke. The useful introduction describes in detail, with accompanying charts, the official ranking and governmental system, dynasty by dynasty.

An Tso-chang 安作璋, et.al., *Chien-ming Chung-kuo li-tai kuan-chih tz'u-tien* 簡明中國歷代官制詞典 (Jinan, 1990).

Arranged according to number of strokes. Each short entry gives a brief explanation, and a reference to the original source where the term first appeared. Good for quick reference.

David M. Farquhar, *The Government of China under Mongolian Rule: A Reference Guide* (Stuttgart, 1990).

This work is both a dictionary of administrative terminology specific to the Yüan dynasty and an historical analysis of political institutions of that period. The introductory chapter and the first chapter are historical essays giving information on the passage of the Mongols to the rulership of China and the evolution of their political positions within the Chinese system of rulership. The rest of the volume is a dictionary spread into the following subjects: (1) service agencies of the Imperial Court; (2) advisory, ideological, and religious agencies of the Emperor; (3) civil administration and its service agencies; (4) agencies for control and security; (5) agencies for the administration of fiefs and special populations; (6) governments of provinces other than the Metropolitan; (7) units of local government. Appendices include a chronology of the Yüan; weights and measures; and an essay on the Yüan currency system. There is an extensive bibliography, a general index, and one for Chinese (in Wade-Giles romanization) and Mongolian. Indispensable for scholars of the Yüan and Central Asian steppe societies.

E-tu Zen Sun, *Ch'ing Administrative Terms* (Cambridge, Mass., 1961).
This work is a translation from the Japanese edition of the Ch'ing handbook for clerks, *Liu-pu ch'eng-yü chu-chieh* 六部成語注解 (The Six Boards with Explanatory Works), an anonymous work of 1742. This work is divided into sections, according to the Six Ministries, and handles some 2500 terms. It includes a Chinese index in Wade-Giles romanization, and an extensive English index as well as bibliography.

Yamakoshi Toshihiro 山腰敏寛, *Shinmatsu Minsho bunsho dokukai jiten* 清末民初文書読解辞典 (Tokyo, 1989).
Contains definitions of some 4900 terms, all of which may be found in documents of the late Ch'ing and early Republic. Arranged by Japanese syllabary. Cites a source for each definition. Appendices include a summary of the dress code for Ch'ing officials, by rank; a stylistic guide for official correspondence; and a table of Ch'ing official ranks. No index.

History

Hoshi Ayao 星斌夫, *Chûgoku shakai keizai shi goi (zokuhen)* 中国社会経済史語彙(読編) (Yamagata-shi, 1975).
Supplements the 1966 original (*seihen* 正編), in which terms found in major Japanese studies and translations of monographs on financial administration from the dynastic histories as well as 18 other Japanese works on Chinese socio-economic history are defined. This edition contains definitions of specialized terms found in 27 Japanese sinological monographs published from 1965-72. Gives page citations to the monographic source. Arranged by Japanese syllabary. Has stroke-count and romanized indices.

Hoshi Ayao et.al., *Chûgoku shakai keizai shi goi (sanhen)* 中国社会経済史語彙三編) (Yamagata-shi, 1988).
The third edition of the above work. Covers 24 more mono-graphs, published from 1973-1983.

Shang Hai 尚海 et al., *Min-kuo shih ta tz'u-tien* 民國史大辭典(Beijing, 1991).
Useful dictionary arranged chronologically, 1894-1911, 1912-1927, 1927-1937, 1937-1945, and 1945-1949, and then sub-divided by subject (e.g. culture and education). Has finding index by stroke, and separate index for famous people. Good for quick reference.

Pak-wah Leung, ed., *Historical Dictionary of Revolutionary China, 1839-1976* (New York, 1992).
This is a short-entry reference guide to both important names and terms, and thus it may be considered a supplement to either the *Biographical Dictionary of Republican China,* or the *Biographical Dictionary of Chinese Communism.* Place names and events have entries, all of which are in Wade-Giles alphabetical order. Each entry is followed by a detailed list of readings. There is also a *pinyin* index.

Chang Tso-yao 張作耀, *Chung-kuo li-shih tz'u-tien* 中國歷史辭典 (Beijing, 1991).
Comprehensive dictionary about Chinese history, which covers entire period from the beginnings of Chinese civilization to the foundation of the PRC. Includes some 10,000 terms which are arranged according to number of strokes. Appendices for the names of dynasties, with official population totals, and their chronology.

JAPANESE NAMES

P.G. O'Neill, *Japanese Names: A Comprehensive Index by Characters and Readings* (New York, 1972).
This has become the 'standard dictionary' for Japanese names, both family and given names, arranged by pronunciation-characters and then characters-pronunciations. Contains separate character index.

Jih-pen hsing-ming tz'u-tien 日本姓名詞典 (Beijing, 1979).

In three parts: *chia-ming hsü* 假名序〔仮名〕 (according to *kana* syllabary); *La-ting hsü* 拉丁序 (according to Western romanization); *Han-tzu hsü* 漢字序 (according to Chinese characters). This work is more extensive than O'Neill.

CHAPTER SEVEN

ENCYCLOPEDIAS, YEARBOOKS, AND STATISTICAL REFERENCES

Introduction

The traditional Chinese term for encyclopedia is *lei-shu* 類書 .[1] *Lei-shu* are compendia in which materials of some length are quoted from written sources and arranged according to a systematic rubric of semantic categories. One may say that the traditional encyclopedia was usually compiled by the "scissor and paste" method and not really written. The author, or editor, expressed himself, at most, in the text which connected the individual quotations or in a short introductory chapter. The great value which was ascribed to encyclopedic writing in China may be ascertained not only from the mass distribution of this type of work, but also from the fact that they were, as a rule, assembled by highly respected scholars. Many encyclopedias were produced directly under imperial auspices and were intended to provide officialdom with an easily available means of information.

In encyclopedic works, the goal is elucidation of the topic rather than examples of usage of words, although the distinction is sometimes difficult to make. Anyone acquainted with the *Chung-wen ta tz'u-tien* knows that a good Chinese classical dictionary offers far more than the definition of words. Nevertheless, there is a difference between dictionaries and encyclopedias. A dictionary gives the definition, the significance, and the use of specific words and phrases while an encyclopedia is concerned with the entire historical and linguistic background of the same word or phrase. The *Chung-wen ta tz'u-tien* performs both functions, but many of the works discussed below will only serve as an encyclopedia.

Some scholars consider the earliest Chinese encyclopedia to be the *Huang-lan* 皇覽 [Mirror (for) the Emperor], supposedly prepared for Emperor Wu Ti of the Wei dynasty (i.e. Ts'ao Ts'ao,

---

[1] For an informative introduction to traditional Chinese encyclopedias, see Wolfgang Bauer, "The Encyclopedia in China," *Cahiers d'histoire mondiale* 9 (1966):665-691.

155-220) for the purpose of presenting a survey of all knowledge. Although no longer extant, it would seem from later surviving encyclopedia that this work set the pattern for this sort of project in the coming centuries. Classics and their commentaries were put together and classified according to one topic after another, totalling some 1000 sections. Later T'ang and Sung *lei-shu* were compiled for the purpose of providing material which would be useful in the writing of poems and essays. By that time, when writing had become highly sophisticated, encyclopedias functioned as writers' aids, particularly to provide quotations, allusions and other flowery adornments, culled not only from the Classics but also more contemporary writings. The ordering of the material had to take place twice, first in the arrangement of the headings, second in the arrangement of the material to be furnished under the headings.

The basic characteristic of the encyclopedia often proved of inestimable value to Chinese literary science; many works were only preserved because they had been included in encyclopedias. In some cases only a few fragments were remaining, but they provided, at least, a general impression of the complete text, and once in a while it was also possible to reconstruct a whole text. The *Ssu-k'u ch'üan-shu tsung-mu* listed both general encyclopedias and literary encyclopedias under the category *lei-shu*, in the main sub-division 'Philosophy'. However, encyclopedias, which are arranged phonetically, are grouped in the section dictionaries, under the sub-division 'Classics'.

The *T'ai-p'ing yü-lan* 太平御覽 is the first of the works that should have the classification 'encyclopedia', as it deals with the whole range of knowledge. It quotes on every imaginable subject from 1,690 works of which it gives a list. It was compiled by Li Fang 李昉, on the order of Sung T'ai-tsung and was completed in six years (A.D. 983). Originally, it had been called the *T'ai-p'ing pien-lei* 太平編類, but after the Emperor had read the whole of it in one year, the title was changed to *T'ai-p'ing yü-lan* (Imperially reviewed encyclopedia of the T'ai-p'ing era). It is an important source of information for both the T'ang and Five Dynasties periods.

Wilkinson, pp. 164-166, gives a selected list of ten of the most important literati *lei-shu*.[2] The last work on his list, the *Ku-chin t'u-*

---

[2] For a complete list of existing literati encyclopedia, with specific references to where they may be found in Taiwan libraries and publications, see Austin C.W. Shu, *Lei Shu: Old Chinese Reference Works* (Taipei, 1973). This work includes an au-

shu chi-ch'eng 古今圖書集成 (Synthesis of books and illustrations past and present; also called the Imperial Encyclopedia) is by far the largest of the traditional *lei-shu*. It is divided into six main categories, 32 sections, and 6,109 sub-sections, and a testament to the monumental nature of High Ch'ing literary enterprises. The encyclopedia running in its first edition to 852,408 pages, is up-to-date the most extensive work which was ever printed in China, if not the whole world. Fortunately, as Wilkinson notes, there is an excellent index to the translated titles of the sub-sections: L. Giles, *Index to the Chinese Encyclopedia* (London, 1911; Taipei reprint, 1966).

There is another kind of encyclopedia which should be mentioned, that is the sort of encyclopedia that deals especially with government matters. Although Wilkinson considers these works 'Encyclopedic Histories of Institutions', which "cover much the same subjects as the Monographs in the Standard Histories," Teng and Biggerstaff classify them as encyclopedias, and divide them into three categories: (1) the *t'ung* 通, which deal primarily with the political system in its various aspects over a long period of time; (2) the *hui-yao* 會要, which are somewhat broader in scope but are limited to single dynasties; and (3) the *hui-pien* 彙編, "statutes" concerning political, legal, and economic matters.

One should not underestimate the importance of these works. The *Shih-t'ung* 十通 (Wilkinson, p.127), which were issued by the Commercial Press in 20 volumes (Shanghai, 1936; Taipei, 1965) with its index to the 20,000 pages is a breathtaking overview of a wide range of subjects, from land taxes to music to "freaks of nature". In short, everything one would like to know about Chinese civilization. The *hui-yao* may be considered compilations of important documents. Teng and Biggerstaff list seven of these works, and Wilkinson, p.141, notes the significance of the *Sung hui-yao*, because it was the only such compilation made by a special bureau throughout its own dynastic reign.

Lastly, we should mention another late imperial work, that may or may not be considered an encyclopedia (some scholars would classify it as a dictionary), the *P'ei-wen yün-fu* 佩文韻府 issued in 1711 with supplement in 1720 (printed Shanghai, 1937; reprint

---

thor index, arranged alphabetically in Wade-Giles transcription, and also gives the authors' approximate dates.

Taipei, 1970). The name *P'ei-wen yün-fu* derives from a hall in the imperial palace, the P'ei-wen chai 佩文齋, a pavilion in honour of lettres. This work is a compendium of literary phrases arranged according to the rhyme category of the last word of the phrase quoted. There are 10,257 guide words under 106 rhyme categories. Citations under the binoms are listed in *ching, shih, tzu, chi* order and within each section in chronological order. This work is another product of the 18th century craze for philology, and textual criticism – and served as both a literary dictionary and an aid for literary composition. Further information on how to use the *P'ei-wen yün-fu* may found in the *Reference* section of this chapter.

From the Sung, and increasingly from the Yüan and Ming onward, encyclopedias were compiled for a wider audience than officialdom and literati. The so-called *jih-yung lei-shu* 日用類書 (encyclopedias for daily use) followed the arrangement of the literati *lei-shu* by categorizing citations from a variety of works, but the contents of these *lei-shu* were oriented toward practical matters (e.g. merchant routes, the weather, magic techniques) rather than on historical models from the past. For the most part, these *jih-yung lei-shu* were written in classical Chinese, but there is at least one exception, the *Chia-pao ch'üan-shu* 家寶全書 (1707), which was composed, in part, in classical Chinese, and in part, in *pai-hua.*

The popular *jih-yung lei-shu* were a product of an expanding "pulp publishing" industry, centred in Fukien and Chiangnan, and an indication of a growing literate populace that valued the advice these works had to give. Their popularity among the "semiliterate" strata reflects the interests and needs of a wider spectrum of Chinese society than the literati. The *jih-yung lei-shu* contain important materials on culture and attitudes of strata below the Confucian elite, and should provide the modern researcher with further evidence that there existed another world outside the "Confucian idealized" view of life.

This contrast becomes all the more clearer when one examines the encyclopedia Westerners were compiling about China in the 19th century. J. Dyer Ball's *Things Chinese: being Notes on various Subjects connected with China,* first published in 1892, although somewhat idiosyncratic, is an impressive compilation of how a 19th century Westerner viewed that civilization. Starting with 'Abacus', working through the alphabet via such diverse topics as 'Cormorant Fishing', 'Demoniacal Possession', 'Lighthouses', 'Poetry', 'Slavery', and 'Topsy-turvydom', and finishing on p.419, with

'Zoology', Dyer Ball's work reveals the diversity within China civilization.

Nineteenth century Chinese encyclopedia, as the comprehensive discussion in Teng and Biggerstaff indicates, were still being produced in large numbers, according to the traditional format. But none of these works attained the breath and sheer volume of the earlier Ch'ing publications; they were in the main combinations of earlier compilations of literary allusions or phrases, used as aids in preparation for the examination system. Even in the Republican period encyclopedia of literary allusions were compiled for modern students to use when writing dictionaries.

The last encyclopedia to be published according to a system of traditional categories was the *Jih-yung pai-k'o ch'üan-shu* 日用百科全書 (Collected work of 100 sciences intended for daily use), which appeared in 1919 for the first time. The revised edition, published in 1934, was divided according to thirty sections, among which modern natural sciences were given an important place. The revised edition closely followed the style of Western encyclopedias and was based upon a wide selection of books, magazines, and newspapers, both Chinese and foreign, but sources were seldom cited in the text. As a rule each entry gave the historical background of a particular subject under discussion and traced its evolution to the end of 1933.

The Republican period saw further continuation of the writing of what Teng and Biggerstaff consider encyclopedias, those works dealing with political, economic, and legal matters. For example, a work entitled *Huang-ch'ao* 皇朝 (or *Ch'ing-ch'ao* 清朝) *Hsü Wen-hsien t'ung-k'ao* 續文獻通考, compiled by Liu Chin-tsao 劉錦藻, preface dated 1921, presents a supplement to the continuations of the Ch'ien-lung period, and deals with the years 1786-1911.

The Republican period also witnessed a new genre of compilation, that in the broadest terms can also be considered 'encyclopedic', i.e. yearbooks (*nien-chien* 年鑒). Yearbooks in China were first published by Westerners to provide background data on the political and economic conditions of the country, mainly for the benefit of the trading community in the pre-World War II treaty ports. For example, the *North China Daily News* printed the *China Year Book*, edited by H.C.W. Woodhead from 1912 through 1939. It was published annually with few interruptions, and featured excellent editorial collaboration, including Owen Lattimore on the border regions, E. Kann on currency and banking, and J.C.

Ferguson on art. In the 1930s, the Chinese started their own publications of yearbooks (in Chinese). Along with handbooks (*shou-ts'e* 手冊), yearbooks were compiled by various government agencies, and reached a high point during the Nanking decade. Ministries, provinces, cities, and other government agencies published their own yearbooks, sometimes in several revised editions. The most important of these institutions issuing statistics were the National Agricultural Research Bureau, the Ministry of Railways, the National Resources Commission, the Bank of China, and the Central Bank. Invariably, these works contained about a thousand pages (or more) of laws, statistics, lists of enterprises and individuals, organizational charts, etc.. They form a wealth of data about China in the first half of the 20th century, and have yet to be exploited to their best scientific advantage.[3]

With the founding of the PRC, government reports, in the form of yearbooks, and handbooks, once again have formed a source of information, especially for statistical data. However, in its earliest history, the PRC was not as forthcoming with statistical information, as it is nowadays. The only general yearbook it published during the first decades, the *Jen-min shou-ts'e* 人民手冊 (Tianjin; 1949-1953, 1955-1965) was essentially a compilation of government policy documents and important editorials, speeches, proclamations, and communiques, and lacked the statistical and organizational data given in the Nanking decade works.[4] In 1959, in celebration of its tenth anniversary, the PRC had the State Statistical Bureau publish a statistical handbook, entitled *Ten Great Years*, which summarized the fruits of their efforts in compiling and organizing a single set of official economic data for the Chinese economy.[5] In the meantime, Taiwan intelligence sources started to publish in 1967 *Chung-kung nien-pao* 中共年報, which reported information about the PRC during the Cultural Revolution years.[6]

---

[3] According to Li Choh-ming, *The Statistical System of Communist China* (Berkeley, 1962), pp.3-4, despite the fact that a Directorate General of Budgets, Accounts, and Statistics was established by the president of the republic in 1931, it was not until 1948 that a general statistical yearbook was first issued by the government.

[4] For other early PRC compilations, see Berton and Wu, pp.106-128.

[5] The data published in *Ten Great Years* and much additional official data released by the Chinese government during the 1950s, as well as the coverage and definitions used by the Chinese, can be found in Nai-ruenn Chen, *Chinese Economic Statistics* (Chicago, 1967). See the section 'Further Sources for Statistics of China, Past and Present', in this chapter.

[6] Published in Taipei since 1967, and formerly known as *Fei-ch'ing nien-pao*

In general, for the period 1959-1978 there were next to no reliable statistics published by the PRC Government. One may at-
tribute this phenomenon to a general reluctance to disclose the
extent of the failures of the Great Leap Forward, an intense concern with national security, the destruction of the statistical network during the Cultural Revolution, and a deeply rooted cultural preference for secrecy. Thus, production statistics, population figures, government revenue and expenditure figures, data
on personal income and consumption, information on foreign
trade, employment statistics, records of major Party and government meetings, legal compendia, notices of official appointments
and dismissals, and biographical information on political and
military officials were unavailable.[7]

The PRC's post-Cultural Revolution modernization program
has facilitated the regular issue of statistics, often in the form of
yearbooks. These reference works, helpful as they can be, may
also lead to problems if one does not recognize the major division
between a "Yearbook of Unit Q" and a "Statistical Yearbook of
Unit Q"; the first lists documents and events, the second statistics.
The first is completely different from year to year, the second normally incorporates earlier data. We should not fail to mention
that nowadays almost every regional and institutional body in
China regularly reports its statistics. This has resulted in a wealth
of information presented in the form of yearbooks, some of which
are translated into English. In the section 'Further Sources for
Statistics of China, Past and Present', we list some of the most important of these yearbooks.[8]

The modernization program has also encouraged the publication of comprehensive encyclopedias, in the form of *pai-k'o
ch'üan-shu* 百科全書. The voluminous *Chung-kuo ta pai-k'o ch'üan-*

匪情年報, this yearbook collected all possible information about China from the
beginning of the Cultural Revolution. Each yearbook gave a chronological commentary of that year's events, and statistical information. What is most interesting
about this series, is that it contains many documents that are not to be found in
the PRC, such as party statements and speeches that were never published officially. Most years also feature an introduction in English.

[7] For an analytical review of what statistical material was available on the
economy until 1975, see Alexander Eckstein, ed., *Quantitative Measures of China's
Economic Output* (Ann Arbor, 1980).

[8] Although not complete, *Current Yearbooks Published in the PRC* (Berkeley,
1991) gives an overview of yearbook holdings in 11 major Asian language libraries. The listing, in Chinese, with romanized transliterations of the titles, begins
with those works published in 1988 and later. There is a preface in English.

shu 中國大百科全書 series (Beijing, Shanghai, since 1980) is a richly illustrated universal encyclopedia. There is usually one or two volumes for each subject [for further information, see below].

References—Encyclopedias, Yearbooks, and Statistical References

Early Western Language Works of an Encyclopedic Nature
  on China 252
Current Western Language Encyclopedias and 'Yearbooks'   253
Chinese Encyclopedias and 'Yearbooks' 256
  Encyclopedias 256
    Ch'ing 256
    Contemporary 257
  Yearbooks 259
Further Sources for Statistics of China, Past and Present 262
  Late Imperial and Republican China 262
  PRC 264

EARLY WESTERN LANGUAGE WORKS OF AN ENCYCLOPEDIC
NATURE ON CHINA

W.F. Mayers, *The Chinese reader's manual: a handbook of bibliographical, historical, mythological, and general literary reference* (Shanghai, 1874; reprinted Peiping, 1924)

Intended to assist users of Chinese literature to decipher personal and historical allusions encountered in Chinese texts, this work is divided into three parts: Part I is an index to 974 proper names, including mythical and historical personages and other animate and inanimate objects, with descriptive data based upon both sound secondary Chinese scholarship and original sources. Part II contains 317 entries being a list (in numerical order) of numerical terms, such as the Five Punishments and the Eight Diagrams, with explanations. Part III is "Chronological Tables of the Chinese Dynasties". Character index by radical.

Samuel Couling, *The Encyclopedia Sinica* (Shanghai, 1917).

This encyclopedia is mainly the work of Couling, although a number of articles were contributed by others. Arranged alphabetically, information is presented on Chinese history (human and natural), literature, social and political institutions, religion, Chinese personalities, flora and fauna, myths and legends, foreigners in China, Christian missionary work. Exhaustive and informative.

J. Dyer Ball, *Things Chinese or Notes connected with China* (first published Hong Kong, 1892; reissued Shanghai, 1925, 1926).

This is a wonderful compendium of material arranged by a former Hong Kong government official. Starting at 'Abacus', Ball worked his way through the alphabet via such diverse topics as 'Cormorant Fishing', 'Demoniacal Possession', 'Lighthouses', 'Poetry', 'Slavery' and 'Topsy-turvydom', and finished with 'Zoology'. To many of the entries he appended a short list of recommended reading for those who wished to delve deeper into the subject. This work gives a breath-taking sweep of Chinese culture, as seen from the eyes of a foreigner in 19th century China.

CURRENT WESTERN LANGUAGE ENCYCLOPEDIAS AND 'YEARBOOKS'

Brian Hook, ed., *The Cambridge Encyclopedia of China* (Cambridge, 1991).

A new, revised, and enlarged edition of a work originally published in 1982 under the same title. The entries, some of which read like essays, are by leading specialists in each field. The arrangement of topics is: Land and Resources (geography and the economy), Peoples, Society (including law, education, health and medicine, and sports), and The Continuity of China (justifiably the longest section, for it is a detailed history by specialists in each period); followed by Philosophy and Religion, Literature, Art and Architecture, Food and Cooking, and Science and Technology. Appendices include: guides for visitors, lists of organizations (also those within the PRC Government), transliteration tables, simplified characters, and suggestions for further reading on each section. A glossary provides the characters for most entries. Includes a detailed table of contents and index.

Colin Mackerras and Amanda Yorke, *The Cambridge Handbook of Contemporary China* (Cambridge, 1991).

This short "handbook" does not pretend to be an encyclopedia of contemporary China, but it does aim to present encyclopedia information, i.e. dates and statistics concerning China in a manageable and accessible form. In 11 chapters, this work presents information on key aspects of China, including political institutions, foreign relations, geography (in a chapter entitled "Gazetteer") population, minority nationalities, and education. There is a chronology extending from 1900 to April, 1990, a section on "eminent contemporary figures", and a bibliography of English books on post-Mao China.

China Review (Hong Kong, since 1991).

An annual collection of essays which summarize and analyze particular topics. Thus, this is not a reference work with statistical data and documents. As each essay is authored by an expert, one cannot find a better review by subject for a particular subject. For example, the 1992 edition featured a number of penetrating essays on the economy: "The Economy at the Crossroads: Growth Rates versus Deepening Reforms"; "The

Economy Impact of the Summer Floods"; "The State-owned Enterprises after the Tiananmen Incident"; "Trade across the Straits".

Asia 19– Yearbook (Hong Kong, since 1965).
This is a yearly report from the important journal, the *Far Eastern Economic Review*. Although this yearbook contains information on other regions of Asia (e.g. Japan, Korea), it gives a systematic analysis of all up-to-date information on China, for that year, under sub-sections, such as 'trade and aid', 'energy', 'population', etc.

Chinese Academy of Social Sciences, comp.; C.V. James, editor.
Information China: The Comprehensive and Authorative Reference Source of New China (New York, 1989), 3 vols.
A comprehensive reference work that gives most info on the post-Mao reforms, according to the "official Chinese view". A great deal of the information here is from selections of other reference works: almanacs, yearbooks, and statistical compilations already available. Each volume is aimed at a different audience: the first volume is for the first-time reader looking for general information, the second at the business community, and the third at scholars. The entire work is divided into twenty major subject areas, and includes extensive appendices on a variety of subjects, such as the traditional calendar, traditional festivals, and Chinese cuisine, teas, and drinks. There are seemingly worthwhile sections on enterprises and regulations for foreign investors, but these may no longer be valid for the late 1990s. Detailed tables of contents make cross-references relatively easy. There are also three cumulative indices: by subject, name, and place name.

Encyclopedia of New China (Beijing, 1987).
A five part encyclopedia that conveys basic information about the 'Land and the People', History, Politics (including the legal system), Economy, and Culture. Appendices include chronology and government offices. Brief, and compact.

Western language encyclopedias on China, published before 1980

Wu Yuan-li, ed. *China: A Handbook* (New York, 1973)

W. Franke and B. Staiger. *China Handbuch* (Düsseldorf, 1974)

H.C. Hinton, ed. *The People's Republic of China: A Handbook* (Boulder/Folkestone, 1979)

F.M. Kaplan, J.M. Sobin, and S. Andors, comp. *Encyclopedia of China Today* (New York, 1979)

Encyclopedias

Ch'ing

Chang Yü-shu 張玉書 et.al., comp.,
P'ei-wen yün-fu 佩文韻府, 106 *chüan*. Separate index volume prepared for *Wan-yu wen-k'u* 萬有文庫 (1937) edition.

This work, first printed in 1712, consists of an enormous number of phrases, usually of two characters, arranged according to the traditional rhyme of the last character of the phrase, and followed by one or more passages, culled from a wide range of literature, in which the phrase occurs. The literature that was put under scrutiny here include the Classics and the Dynastic Histories, but the majority of entries are from belles-lettres and poetry. There is seemingly no order except that those phrases from older sources such as the Classics tend to be placed earlier in this work, and those with three or more character phrases are found at the end. There are no definitions in this work (except for some references to commentaries about the Classics); what is given are the passages in which the phrase appears. The entries to the index are arranged according to the four-corner system (there is a finding table for four-corner numbers at the end of the index volume which arranges each character by stroke and radical). For each two-word phrase, first, the page number is given where that character may be found according to the traditional rhyme, as the second character of the phrase. Then one finds listed the phrases in which that character occurs in the first position. These phrases are listed in sequence according to the first two digits of the four-corner number of the second character of the phrase. Under each entry is the page and register number where the phrase may be located in the 1937 edition of the *P'ei-wen yün-fu.*

Kao Yü 高興 (d.1717) et.al., comp.,
P'ien-tzu lei-pien 駢字類編 (printed in 1726; modern Taiwan reproduction, Taipei: Hsüeh-sheng shu-chü 學生書局, 1963).

This work groups binoms under 13 main sections: Heaven and Earth, precious objects, utensils, animals, time and calendar, mountains and rivers, etc., arranged according to the rhyme of the first of the two characters, with the second characters arranged topically, in the same order as the main groupings. Under each binom the quotations are arranged in the *ching, shih, tzu, chi* order. There are some 40,000 entries. There is an index to the edition of this particular work: Wallace Johnson (Chuang Wei-ssu 莊爲斯), compiler, *P'ien-tzu lei-pien yin-te* 駢字類編引得 (Taipei, 1966). The arrangement is by stroke and radical, and greatly facilitates the use of this reference.

Contemporary

Chung-kuo ta pai-k'o ch'üan-shu 中國大百科全書 (Beijing and Shanghai, since 1980–), not yet complete.

This work, issued in a series of volumes, is truly a universal encyclopedia. Each volume, or set of volumes, concentrates on one subject and presents information for that subject, on a grand scale, not only for China but also for other countries as well. Each volume has an index of encyclopedia entries arranged by stroke order and a detailed index of contents (including personal names, books titles, and place names), arranged in alphabetical order according to the *pinyin* romanization of the index item's characters. For most volumes there is also an index for relevant terms in English. To date, there have appeared volumes for:

electronics and computers (two volumes), law, textiles, geology and topography, air science, environmental science, communications, education, archaeology, physics (two volumes), ethnography, astronomy, sport, religion, engineering, foreign literature (two volumes), drama and opera, Chinese literature (two volumes), philosophy (two volumes), religion, architecture-gardens-city planning, economics (three volumes), spoken and written language, music and dance, military affairs (two volumes), Chinese history (separate volumes for Ch'in-Han, Sui-T'ang-Wu-tai, Liao-Sung-Hsi Hsia-Chin, Yüan), mechanics, mathematics, optics, biology, chemistry (two volumes), chemical engineering, mining, physical engineering.

Chang Ch'i-yün 張其昀, *Chung-hua pai-k'o ch'üan-shu* 中華百科全書 (Taipei, 1981), 10 vols.

A general encyclopedia, arranged by number of strokes. Each volume has its own index; the tenth volume contains a cumulative index arranged by stroke order and an index of entries by

38 general headings (history, economics, etc.). This work is highly relevant for understanding the Taiwan version of China, before the reforms were instituted.

Chung-hua wen-hua pai-k'o ch'üan-shu 中華文化百科全書 (Taipei, 1982), 15 vols.
Unlike the work directly above, this encyclopedia is oriented toward Taiwan.

Ch'en Tai-sun 陳岱孫, principal editor, *Chung-kuo ching-chi pai-k'o ch'üan-shu* 中國經濟百科全書 (Beijing, 1991), two volumes.
Comprehensive encyclopedia about every aspect of China's economy, written by a variety of experts. Includes table of contents, and index by stroke count.

Chung-kuo ch'i-yeh kuan-li pai-k'o ch'üan-shu 中國企業管理百科全書 (Beijing, 1984), two volumes.
A systematically ordered encyclopedia on business management in and outside China. Gives much information about all aspects of business management until the mid-1980s. It is arranged according to subject, such as 'technology and business management', accounting, the history of business management. A review of laws and regulations is also supplied. A stroke-count index, and an index for English terminology are included.

Chung-kuo nung-yeh pai-k'o ch'üan-shu 中國農業百科全書 (Beijing, since 1987), 10 parts in 13 volumes.
Encyclopedia about Chinese agriculture, arranged according to *pinyin*. Volumes concern a diverse number of subjects from vegetable farming to water control. Full of diagrams, charts, and bibliographical references. There are also a list of all entries according to number of strokes, and an index for English terms, and one for key words.

Chung-kuo shui-li pai-k'o ch'üan-shu 中國水利百科全書 (Beijing, 1991), four volumes.
Specialist encyclopedia for water control.

Yearbooks

The following list of yearbooks are only the most general ones, many of which are translated into English. It should be noted that all provinces and other regional bodies, such as metropolitan areas, issue yearbooks. Again, one should pay attention to the distinction between a "Yearbook of Unit Q" and a "Statistical Yearbook of Unit Q": the first lists documents and events, the second statistics. The fact that specialized groups publish yearbooks, e.g. those for medicine, light industry, printing, textiles, etc., means that in doing research on a particular industry, one should establish if a yearbook exists before commencing to use other statistical sources. Lastly, one should note that there are frequent name changes for one and the same series.

Chung-kuo nien-chien 中國年鑒 (Hong Kong, since 1981).
China's official annual report, issued in Chinese and English at the same time. Full of statistics and chronology for that year.

Chung-kuo pai-k'o nien-chien 中國百科年鑒 (Beijing and Shanghai, since 1980–).
Richly illustrated encyclopedic yearbook, arranged by themes. Each volume offers a general discussion of Chinese and foreign countries' political organization. There is much up-to-date statistical info, as well as, general discussion on political and ideological changes. Contains an extensive alphabetical index.

Chung-kuo t'ung-chi nien-chien 中國統計年鑒 (Hong Kong, since 1981–).
Issued in Chinese, from the PRC, and in English from Hong Kong, at the same time. Both versions are identical. Contains statistical information on every aspect of Chinese life.

Chung-kuo ching-chi nien-chien 中國經濟年鑒 (Beijing and Hong Kong, since 1981–).
Gives both descriptive and statistical information. Also contains details about important regulations and laws. There is a table of contents, but no index. Appendices include statistics and addresses of relevant organizations.

Chung-kuo nung-yeh nien-chien 中國農業年鑒 (Beijing, since 1980–).
Arranged thematically. There is a table of contents, but no index. Explains in detail agricultural improvements, on both a practical and theoretical basis.

Chung-kuo ch'eng-shih t'ung-chi nien-chien 中國城市統計年鑒 (Beijing, since 1985–; *China: Urban Statistics*, London/Beijing, since 1985–).
Chinese and English version are identical. Both provided general and detailed information about cities, including special locations, like those urban areas located in 'Special Economic Zones'.

Jen-k'ou nien-chien (1985) 人口年鑒 (1985) (Beijing, 1986).
A demographic reference with more than 1200 pages about the Chinese population. Contains the following sections: (1) documents about family planning, marriage, population registration and the preparations for census registration; (2) analyses and summaries of the 1982 census findings about marriage, birth, and death rates, also according to geographical region; (3) complete statistics of the 1982 census, with comparative figures from the 1953 and 1964 census reports; (4) comparison of population figures from 1949 to 1984; (5) population planning; (6) specific demographic analyses; (7) comparative population figures from other countries; (8) addresses of demographic research organizations; (9) brief bibliography. There are tables of contents in both Chinese and English. One should note that the figures from 1953, 1964, and 1982 are based on census documentation, but the figures from other years are taken from local population registers, and thus should be used with caution.

Chung-kuo jen-k'ou t'ung-chi nien-chien 中國人口統計年鑒 (Beijing, since 1988).

Chung-hua jen-min kung-ho-kuo: Ch'üan-kuo fen hsien shih jen-k'ou t'ung-chi tzu-liao 中華人民共和國全國分縣市人口統計資料 (Beijing, yearly, since 1986).
Both these works supply population figures for the year before issue.

Chung-kuo ch'i-yeh kuan-li nien-chien 中國企業管理年鑒 (Beijing, since 1990).
   Yearbook on business management.

Chung-kuo ch'i-yeh teng-chi nien-chien 中國企業登記年鑒 (Beijing, since 1984).
   Annals of Chinese enterprise.

Chung-kuo tui-wai ching-chi mao-i nien-chien 中國對外經濟貿易年鑒 (Beijing, since 1985).
   Almanac of China's foreign relations and trade.

FURTHER SOURCES FOR STATISTICS OF CHINA, PAST AND PRESENT

Late Imperial and Republican China

Note: The following information should add to what is given in Nathan, pp.50-54; TB, Chapter VII 'Yearbooks'; and Fairbank and Liu, sections 1.4, 4.11, 4.12, 6.1, 6.4, 6.7, 6.8., 7.5, and 7.6.

Liang Fang-chung 梁方仲, *Chung-kuo li-tai hu-k'ou t'ien-ti t'ien-fu t'ung-chi*中國歷代戶口田地田賦統計 (Shanghai, 1980).
    A collection of population and land tax data for the period from the Han through the Ch'ing. Contains 241 detailed, annotated statistical tables, charts, and graphs. There is a 19 page appendix where changes in Chinese weights and measures, plus 8 pages of tables comparing weights and measures in different dynasties is given.

Yen Chung-p'ing 嚴中平, et.al. *Chung-kuo chin-tai ching-chi shih t'ung-chi tzu-liao hsüan-chi* 中國近代經濟史統計資料選輯 (Beijing, 1955).
    Information comprehensive for the period 1840-1948. Contains 179 detailed, annotated statistical tables.

Hsü I-sheng 徐義生, *Chung-kuo chin-tai wai-chai shih t'ung-chi tzu-liao (1853-1927)*中國近代外債史統計資料 (Hong Kong, 1978).
    Reprints the Beijing, 1962 original.

Hsiao Liang-lin, *China's Foreign Trade Statistics 1864-1949* (Cambridge, Mass., 1974).

For government statistics:

Ministry of Agriculture and Commerce, *Nung-shang t'ung-chi piao* 農商統計表 (Shanghai, 1914-1919; Peking, 1920-1924).

Ministry of Communications (Ministry of Railways, Bureau of Railway Statistics from 1925 issue), *Statistics of Government Railways, 1915-1936* (Peking, 1916-28; Nanking, 1931-36).

Ministry of Finance, *Annual Reports for the 17th, 18th, 19th, 21st, 22nd, and 23rd Fiscal Years* (Nanking, 1930-36).

National Government, Directorate of Statistics, *Chung-hua min-kuo t'ung-chi t'i-yao 1935* 中華民國統計提要 (Nanking, 1936).

For private statistics:

Nan-k'ai ta-hsüeh ching-chi yen-chiu-so 南開大學經濟研究所, *1913-nien – 1952-nien Nan-k'ai chih-shu tzu-liao hui-pien* 1913年1952年南開指數資料彙編 (Beijing, 1958).
  Nankai price indices for 1913-1952.

China Institute of Economic and Statistical Research, *Ching-chi t'ung-chi yüeh-chih* 經濟統計月志 (Shanghai, 1934-41).
  Bilingual monthly journal of statistics.

Chung-kuo k'o-hsüeh-yüan Shanghai ching-chi yen-chiu-so 中國科學院上海經濟研究所, *Shang-hai chieh-fang ch'ien-hou wu-chia tzu-liao hui-pien (1921-1957)* 上海解放前後物價資料滙編 (Shanghai, 1958).
  Collected materials on Shanghai prices, before and after liberation, for the period 1921-1958.

J.L. Buck, *Land Utilization in China: A Study of 16,786 Farms in 168 Localities, and 38,256 Farm Families in 22 Provinces in China, 1929-1933*, 3 vols. (Nanking, 1937; reprinted, New York, 1964).

Juan Hsiang 阮湘, et. al., comp. *Ti-i-hui Chung-kuo nien-chien* 第一回中國年鑑 (Shanghai, 1924; reprint, 1927).
  A very excellent yearbook. Although published by the Commercial Press, it contains much information on governmental organization. It has also has sections on population, and industry.

J. Arnold, *China: A Commercial and Industrial Handbook* (Washington, 1926).
  Compiled by the U.S. commercial attaché in Peking for the purpose of supplying comprehensive, current data for manufacturers and merchants. General data in narrative and tabular form is provided in Part I on geography, import and export trade by product, marketing currency, industry, mining, communications, and taxation. American firms in China are given special attention. Part II is a lengthy report by consular districts on topics similar to those noted above. Extensive subject index.

China Industrial Handbook: Chekiang (Shanghai, 1935).

Compiled on the basis of firsthand investigation and supplementary documentary material by the National Industrial Investigation, Bureau of Foreign Trade, Ministry of Industry, for the industrialization of the Yangtze Valley. This is a compendium of statistical data on population, economic conditions, cities, agriculture and forest stations, fishery and stock raising, mining, manufacturing industries, financial institutions, and communication and transportation in Chekiang Province.

China Industrial Handbook: Kiangsu (Shanghai, 1935).

A similar handbook as the work directly above, made by the same organization. Contains much information on both Nanking and Shanghai. With an index.

PRC

Note: For references to statistical information for the period prior to 1967, see Berton and Wu, pp.129-132.[9]

Kuo-chia t'ung-chi-chü tsung-ho-ssu 國家統計局綜合司 ed.,
(Ch'üan-kuo ko sheng, tzu-chih-ch'ü, chih-hsia-shih) Li-shih t'ung-chi tzu-liao hui pien (1949-1989) （全國各省，自治區，直轄市）歷史統計資料滙編 (1949–1989)(Beijing: Chung-kuo t'ung-chi ch'u-pan-she, 1990).

An important source for official government statistics for this period.

China: Facts and Figures Annual (USA, since 1978).

Yearly review of PRC events and organizations, based on various US government sources. Wide-ranging facts from government to health and leisure organizations.

China: A Statistical Survey in 1986 (Beijing, since 1986).

Synopsis of Chinese statistics from other sources from various organizations, that cover the economy, agriculture, population, finance, and education and science. Appears annually.

---

[9] For an excellent summary of the issues facing those who wish to find statistics on the present day PRC economy, see Eduard Vermeer, "Chinese Economic Data − How Much and How Good?", *China Information* 1.2 (1986):49-54.

Chung-kuo nung-ts'un ching-chi t'ung-chi ta-ch'üan (1949-1986)
中國農村經濟統計大全 (*Statistical Book of the Chinese Rural Economy*;
Beijing, 1989).
> General statistics of China's rural economy, 1949-1986. English
> and Chinese versions published at the same time.

William T. Liu, *China Rural Statistics* (New York, 1989).
William T. Liu, *China Urban Statistics* (New York, 1990).
> Valuable analyses of China's statistics, as issued by the State Sta-
> tistical Bureau.

World Bank: Catalogue of Staff Working Papers (Washington, since
1985).
> To find the many separate research papers written on China's
> economy and its statistical references, use the annual catalogue
> of this institution.

Newspapers and Journals for up-to-date statistical information:

Ching-chi jih-pao 經濟日報
Nung-min jih-pao 農民日報
China Statistics Monthly (since, 1988)
> Privately issued from Chicago by the China Statistics Archives,
> with excellent graphic analyses.
T'ung-chi 統計
> Monthly, since 1992, appears in English translation, as well.

Chung-kuo t'ung-chi yüeh-pao 中國統計月報
Ching-chi yen-chiu 經濟研究
Ching-chi ti-li 經濟地理
Ching-chi kai-ko 經濟改革
Nung-yeh chi-shu tzu-liao 農業技術資料
Nung-yeh ching-chi wen-t'i 農業經濟問題
Kung-yeh ching-chi wen-t'i 工業經濟問題
Chung-kuo nung-ts'un ching-chi 中國農村經濟
T'e-ch'ü yü k'ai-fang ch'eng-shih ching-chi 特區與開放城市經濟

CHAPTER EIGHT

TS'UNG-SHU AND MISCELLANEOUS COLLECTANEA

Introduction

Ts'ung-shu 叢書 ('collectanea') is a compendium of two to thousands of independent works which are published together under one title, "in order that they may not be lost, or in order to give wider circulation to the writings of a particular locality, of one person, or of one family." [TB (1969 ed.) p.83]. There are perhaps 3000 *ts'ung-shu* in existence, the contents of some of which have never been catalogued. *Ts'ung-shu* occupies a special place for research and study because this type of collection brings together carefully edited ancient texts, often considered lost, incomplete or rare before their publication in that form.

The term *ts'ung-shu* appeared for the first time in a poem by Han Yü 韓愈 (768-824). Han Yü used the expression to designate the notion of placing several works between wooden bookends. By that he meant simply that he possessed a library containing many books. The first occasion when *ts'ung-shu* appears in a title of a work was a collection of miscellaneous essays, the *Li-tse ts'ung-shu* 笠澤叢書 , compiled by Lu Kuei-meng 陸龜蒙 (died circa 878 A.D.). Here, too, it does not yet have the meaning we give to *ts'ung-shu* nowadays, for it then meant something like "selected passages" or "brief quotes". It was only in the Sung dynasty, with the spread of book production, that *ts'ung-shu* came to mean "compendium of works by different authors". The Sung collection *Ju-hsüeh ching-wu* 儒學警悟, a collection of seven works, published by Yü Ting-sun 俞鼎孫 in 1202, is generally recognized as the first real *ts'ung-shu.*

In a sense, *ts'ung-shu* served the same purpose as our modern periodical press does nowadays—*ts'ung-shu* became a medium in which the 'miscellaneous writings', short articles, poetry, or monographs of an author, or a group of authors, could be printed. *Ts'ung-shu* also offered a medium in which collectors and owners of great private libraries could get their rare works published. It was convenient to give designations to such *ts'ung-shu* by prefacing the title with the name of the library where deposited (e.g. *Chih-pu-tsu-chai ts'ung-shu* 知不足齋叢書 [Collectanea of the Can't Know Enough Studio]), or with the owner's studio or fancy name. In the 18th and early 19th centuries, the great historical critics led the way in printing newly recovered fragments of ancient writings in *ts'ung-shu*; examples of this phenomenon include: Sun Hsing-yen's (1753-1818) 孫星衍, *P'ing-chin kuan ts'ung-shu* 平津館叢書, and Ma Kuo-han's (1794-1857) 馬國翰, *Yü-han shan-fang chi-i-shu* 玉函山房輯佚書. In this century with even more economical means to reproduce books, large sets of *ts'ung-shu* began to appear in the 1920s. *Ts'ung-shu* are still printed nowadays, in Hong Kong, Taiwan, and the PRC. In the case of many modern *ts'ung-shu*, the motivation for publication is clearly more commercial than the traditional collectanea compiled out of scholarly interest. Modern *ts'ung-shu* resemble a 'miniature library', a group of well-selected works, like the British Penquin 'classic series', to guide one toward a particular genre of literature.

One may well ask what is the difference between encyclopedias (*lei-shu*) and *ts'ung-shu*. In general, encyclopedias may include no more than citations from earlier writings, whereas *ts'ung-shu* will reproduce the complete text of literary works. Also, *ts'ung-shu* may be more "scholarly" than encyclopedias. Although the text of an early piece of writing, which may have originated in the fourth century B.C. or so, may appear in a number of different *ts'ung-shu*, the text may not always be identical; as the compilers of *ts'ung-shu* did not necessarily draw on one and the same exemplar to copy. Moreover, encyclopedia editors did not search for so many editions as *ts'ung-shu* compilers did. Thus, *ts'ung-shu* editions tend to be more exact, and complete. Some of the largest and most comprehensive *ts'ung-shu* are those that have been produced in this century with the help of lithography or other modern methods, and are listed in a separate section in this chapter.

In general, scholars divide traditional *ts'ung-shu* into several classes: works arranged according to authorship (including the collected writings of one family or lineage); to contents (such as the Classics or dynastic histories); locality (like the *Chi fu ts'ung-shu* 畿輔叢書, that contains works written by natives of Chihli province from ancient to modern times); to chronology (such as those incorporating the rare works of particular dynasties); to those issued by schools or societies. However, for the purpose of library classification, works of these classes are not always considered *ts'ung-shu*. For example, the collected works of one author, even though they may be about many different subjects, cannot properly be called *ts'ung-shu*. Thus, the writings of individual authors may not be classified under '9100' (*ts'ung-shu*), but under another number more relevant to that person's life history, or the subject about which he/she was writing, e.g. Chang P'u (1602-1641)'s 張溥 *Han Wei liu-ch'ao pai san chia chi* 漢魏六朝百三家集 (Collection of literary works by 103 authors of the Han, Wei, and Six Dynasties) is listed as part of Harvard-Yenching classification number '5235'.

Collected works of individual authors (*wen-chi* 文集 or *ch'üan-chi* 全集) are important sources of information for both historical and literary purposes. They usually include the author's poetry, letters, prefaces, memorials and other official writings, commemorative works. These more 'formal' writings should be distinguished from a particular writer's 'miscellaneous notes', *pi-chi* 筆記 or *sui-pi* 隨筆, that usually embrace a great quantity of very uneven jottings on a wide range of subjects. Sometimes they were based on a writer's direct observations, or they reported gossip and rumor. And more often than not, these jottings were considered "unfit" for inclusion in *wen-chi*. For further explanation, with important references to this genre of writing, see Wilkinson, pp. 173-175.

Since the beginning of this century, it has been customary to assign the expression *tzu-liao ts'ung-k'an* 資料叢刊 or simply *tzu-liao* to the title of the large published collections of documents (some of which may already have been published), manuscripts, contracts, etc. Most of these collections are literally just that, collections, and contain no form of critical annotation. For examples, see the list at the end of this chapter 'Important Collections of Published Archival Documents'.

Ts'ung-shu serve a useful purpose because they preserve individual works that might not survive over time. But as one approaches the present, another type of bibliographic problem arises: not whether a particular text has survived, but rather, in what form it has survived. One would like to know what editions are available, and for that reason, one must turn to catalogues of rare books and guides to editions [see below 'Catalogues of Rare Books and Guides to Editions'].

Traditional and Modern Ts'ung-shu

Traditional ts'ung-shu

Ssu-k'u ch'üan-shu 四庫全書 (SKCS), completed in 1782, under imperial auspices. Recent edition: Taipei, 1983 which is a facsmile reproduction of the Ta-tung shu-chü 大東書局 edition.

For general information concerning this work, see chapter I 'Introduction—Classification Systems and the Chinese Library'. For a convenient English language index to the shorter bibliography of the SKCS, see William Y. Chen, *A Guide to the Ssu-k'u ch'üan-shu chien-ming mu-lu* (Taipei, 1985). This guide consists of three indexes: author, title, and subject, in alphabetical order, based on Wade-Giles romanization. The *(Ying-yin) Wen-yüan-ko Ssu-k'u ch'üan-shu shu-ming chi chu-che hsing-ming so-yin* （景印）文淵閣四庫全書書名及著者姓名索引 (Taipei, 1986) is an index to the recent reproduction of the SKCS. One finds here seperate indices for titles and authors, arranged by the four-corner system (there is a separate finding list for the four-corner numbers). The first number next to either the title or author refers to the volume, and the second to the exact page. There are also separate indices for both title and author based on number of strokes in the first word of the title or the author's surname. A separate table of contents which lists all the titles in order of their appearance may also be found in the volume. The *wen-chi* in the SKCS also have a separate five volume index entitled, *Ssu-k'u ch'üan-shu wen-chi p'ien-mu fen-lei so-yin* 四庫全書文集篇目分類索引 (Taipei, 1989). The indices are divided as *hsüeh-shu* 學術, *tsa-wen* 雜文, and *chuan-chi* 傳記.

For further information on some of the most important *ts'ung-shu* printed during the Ming and Ch'ing, see Liu Shang-heng 劉尙恒, *Ku-chi ts'ung-shu kai-shuo* 古籍叢書概說 (Shanghai, 1989).[1]

Modern ts'ung-shu

Ssu-pu ts'ung-k'an 四部叢刊 (SPTK) (Shanghai, 1920-1936). 468 titles in 3,100 *ts'e*, excluding 24 dynastic histories, issued separately.
This work by the Commercial Press contains photographic reprints of rare Sung, Yüan, and Ming editions. The SPTK consists of three series: *ch'u-pien* 初編 (first series), *hsü-pien* 續編 (second series), and *san-pien* 三編 (third series), each of which is divided into four classes [*ching-pu* 經部 (classics), *shih-pu*

---

[1] For information in English on *ts'ung-shu*, one may turn to Alexander Wylie, *Notes on Chinese Literature* (Shanghai, 1867), pp. 255-271. Note this work was reprinted in a second edition (Shanghai, 1922), that was further reprinted (New York, 1964). Wylie's *Notes...* follows the arrangement of the four divisions of classics, history, philosophers, and belles-lettres of the SKCS.

史部 (history), *tzu-pu* 子部(miscellaneous), and *chi-pu* 集部 (collected works)]. The titles of the first series include a fairly large
proportion of works in the SKCS, whereas those works in the
second and third series, are not represented in the imperial
collection. The subject range of the collection is very broad,
including medicine, poetry, botany, the arts, and even a Yüan
dynasty cookbook. Karl Lo, *A Guide to the Ssu-pu ts'ung-k'an*
(Lawrence, Kansas, 1965) is an index to authors, titles, and subjects, arranged alphabetically according to Wade-Giles
romanization. Also helpful is Lani Brook, *The Ssu-pu ts'ung-
k'an: A Guide to the First Series* (Taipei, 1980).

Ssu-pu pei-yao 四部備要 (SPPY) (Shanghai, 1927-1937; Taiwan reprint, 1966). 351 titles in 2,500 *ts'e*.
   Works in this collectionea are all selected from the SKCS. This
ts'ung-shu is specialized in the reproduction of important Classics, and their commentaries, and in particular, the Four
Books. The Taiwan reproduction consists of 610 hardback volumes in western-style format. William C.Ju, *A Guide to the Ssu-pu
pei-yao* (Taipei, 1971) serves as an index to the Taiwan reprint
editon, arranged according to author, title, and subject.

Ts'ung-shu chi-ch'eng 叢書集成 (TSCC) (Shanghai, 1935-1937).
4,100 titles in 4,100 *ts'e*.
   This is a compilation based on the contents of some 100 other
ts'ung-shu. There is a catalogue available: Wang Yün-wu 王雲五 ,
Ts'ung-shu chi-ch'eng ch'u-pien mu-lu 叢書集成初編目錄 (Shanghai,
1935) that lists the contents according to modern categories.
There is also an index for the continuation of this work, see
Ts'ung-shu chi-ch'eng hsü-pien mu-lu so-yin 叢書集成續編目錄索引
(Taipei, 1971). See also the *Ts'ung-shu chi-ch'eng hsin-pien*
叢書集成新編 (Taipei, 1986), which indexes more than 120
ts'ung-shu, dating from the Ch'in period through the Ch'ing.
This work has a finding list at the end and is arranged by
number of strokes for the titles and authors.

Ssu-k'u ch'üan-shu chen-pen 四庫全書珍本 (SKCSCP) (Taipei, 1971-).
Reproductions of books from the imperial collection at the
Wen-yüan-ko palace, colorfully bound in western-style format.

Kuo-hsüeh chi-pen ts'ung-shu 國學基本叢書 (Shanghai, 1932-?)
 Contains a variety of collections, from the personal writings of
 T'ang Chien 唐鑑 (1778-1861) to Liang Ch'i-ch'ao.

Pi-chi hsiao-shuo ta-kuan 筆記小說大觀 (Shanghai, 1936?; Taipei reprint, 1973; revised Yangzhou, 1983, in 17 vols.).
 This work encompasses ten parts and is formed out of a collection of other *ts'ung-shu.* The works included are historical, literary, and for a large part from the *pi-chi* of particular authors.
 The Taiwan reprint has an index, *Pi-chi hsiao-shuo ta-kuan
 ts'ung-k'an so-yin* 筆記小說大觀叢刊索引 (Taipei, 1981) divided
 into two parts, one for authors, and the other for titles.

Pai-pu ts'ung-shu chi-ch'eng 百部叢書集成 (Taipei, 1967-).
 A collection of a large number of *ts'ung-shu* found on Taiwan.

*Documentary Compilations, Archives, and Buddhist/Taoist
 Collectanea*

Documentary Collections

A documentary compilation is a collection of related primary
sources that has not been printed before. The documents may
vary from the private letters of an individual to imperial court dia-
ries, to collections of government papers, which are usually arranged either by subject and time and place. The Chinese, being
strong believers in historical and cultural continuity attached
great importance to the preservation of historical or literary works
for posterity. Interestingly, once printing became common during
the Sung dynasty, the preservation of the original manuscripts
from which a collectanea was reproduced seemed unnecessary. As
Lo Hui-min pointed out:

> Throughout China's long history, there have been numerous pri-
> vate and public libraries famous for their collections of printed
> works, but we hear little of any possessing manuscript sources that
> might be described as archives, as distinct from collections of hand-
> copied books. Practically every man of note in late Ch'ing China
> had a collection of his papers printed, but nothing was heard of the
> original files of the papers themselves.[2]

---

[2] Lo Hui-min, "Some Notes on Archives on Modern China," in Leslie,
Mackerras, and Wang, *Essays on the Sources for Chinese History* (Canberra, 1973),
p.204.

The printing of large collections of government documents is, in fact, a 19th century phenomenon, made popular through philological study in the West. The 20th century printing of Chinese documents, hitherto hidden in imperial archives, may be compared to the publication of such 19th century works as *Die Grosse Politik der Europäischen Kabinette.* In any event, once the reproduction of these Chinese documents became relatively more routine during the 1930s, it was clear that scholars and publishers had two purposes in mind. The first was to make such materials available to the public at large, and second, to preserve texts so that they would not get lost or destroyed. Given the large number of government documents (*tang-an* 檔案) that both the Ming and Ch'ing dynasties issued, it is essential that historical research include recognition of what materials are available (see below the section 'Important Collections of Published Archival Materials').[3]

Nevertheless, the process by which the printing of documents became common was anything but routine. While a number of collections like the *Ch'ou-pan i-wu shih-mo* 籌辦夷務始末 (The Beginning and End of the Management of Barbarian Affairs, 1836-1874), completed in 1931 in 130 volumes, was initiated by government commission through the Palace Museum, others were published by private individuals, e.g. *Ch'ing-chi wai-chiao shih-liao* 清季外交史料 (Documents on Foreign Relations of the Last Two Reigns of the Ch'ing Dynasty, 1875-1911), printed in 1932. This series was first compiled by Wang T'ao-fu 王韜夫, who as a member of the Secretariat of the old Privy Council, began to make copies of all documents relating to foreign affairs in 1875. His record covered the period 1875-1904, with a few minor gaps. His son Wang Hsi-yin 王希隱 continued the work, covering the years 1905-1911, making it complete for the two reigns of Emperor Kuang-hsü and Emperor Hsüan-t'ung. The whole set has a subject index.

Not all documentary collections were so fortunate. It is a well-known phenomenon that immediately after the foundation of the Republic, there seems to have been little importance attached to

---

[3] In order to use archival material in unpublished or published form, it is necessary to understand the communication system that produced the two basic types of documents, i.e. edicts from the emperor, and memorials from officials. See Wilkinson, pp. 142-145, and 150-156. Two important studies that explicate the workings of that system are: Silas Wu, *Communication and Imperial Control in China, 1693-1735* (Cambridge, Mass., 1970); and Beatrice Bartlett, *Monarchs and Ministers: The Grand Council in mid-Ch'ing China, 1723-1820* (Berkeley, 1991). See also Pei Huang, "The Confidential Memorial System of the Ch'ing Dynasty Reconsidered," *Bulletin of the School of Oriental and African Studies,* 57.2 (1994):329-338.

"old and useless" archival material, much of which dating from the Ming and Ch'ing periods was sold as 'old paper'. For example, the majority of the documents kept in the Ch'ing Nei-ko 清內閣 (Imperial Cabinet) were preserved thanks to the efforts of the scholar Lo Chen-yü [see chapter I 'A Brief History of Chinese Studies...'] who twice saved them, the second time by purchase from a Peking paper merchant of large lot in some 7,000 bags weighing 150,000 catties (nearly 10 tons) destined for the pulp mill. While the documents were in his possession, Lo published some of them in a collection known as *Shih-liao ts'ung-k'an ch'u-pien* 史料叢刊初編. Even after the value of such collections was recognized by the general public, their protection was not necessarily insured: the many violent political upheavals of the 1920s, 30s, and 40s, and the political campaigns of the PRC government against "rightist elements" contributed to their devastation. Those manuscript materials such as personal histories, familial land-holding deeds, lineage genealogies, and temple inscriptions were particularly vulnerable to confiscation, and eventually, destruction during the Cultural Revolution.

A good example of a collection of documentary materials, both in the hands of public institutions and private individuals, which has experienced a 'topsy-turvy' history is that originating from the region of Hui-chou 徽州 in southern Anhwei province.[4] In 1956 the late Fu I-ling 傅衣凌, a well-known professor of Ming-Ch'ing social and economic history at Hsia-men University discovered in a storage cabinet at the Peking branch of the Academy of Sciences a collection of tenant contracts (*tien-pu* 佃簿), dating from the Ming and Ch'ing, from Hui-chou. Two years later Fu published these documents in a well-known local journal *An-hui shih-hsüeh t'ung-hsün* 安徽史學通訊. Fu had already done an investigation of the famous merchants of this region, known as Hsin-an merchants, and published a study about them in *Fu-chien sheng yen-chiu-yüan yen-chiu hui-pao* 福建省研究院研究滙報 in 1947.[5] In the sec-

---

[4] For an introductory history of this region and to some of the Hui-chou documentary materials such as government contracts (*ch'ih-ch'i* 赤契), fish-scale registers (*yü-lin ts'e* 魚鱗册), registers of estates (*chih-ch'an pu* 置產部), rent books (*tsu-pu* 租 or *ch'i-pu* 契簿), and family account books (*chiu-shu* 闈書 or *fen-chia-shu* 分家書), see Harriet T. Zurndorfer, *Change and Continuity in Chinese Local History: The Development of Hui-chou Prefecture* (Leiden, 1989).

[5] Fu had maintained good contacts with Japanese scholars both before and during the war (for which he later suffered political recrimination) and no doubt his friendship with the famous historian of Chinese agriculture Amano Moto-

ond half of the 1950s, Fu's own research into Hui-chou was pulled
into two directions; he wrote about Hui-chou's "slave-like tenancy" and the region's rich merchants who participated in Ming
China's burgeoning "sprouts of capitalism" empire-wide enterprises. From his publications, and those from a few other scholars
working on similar problems, it became clear that there was no
one central location where these Hui-chou documents were located. Meanwhile another group of researchers originating from
the University of Tun-hsi in Hui-chou set out to study the architecture, and in particular, the elaborate hand-carved frontal doors of
the Hui-chou merchants' homes.[6] At no point, as this research
and publication activity was going on during the late 50s, did anyone make a precise account of what materials, either relating to
the local families or to local government activities, were available,
and more importantly, where they were to be found.

It would take some 20 years before another PRC scholar Yeh
Hsien-en 葉顯恩 was to write a definitive history of the region and
its people, *Ming Ch'ing Hui-chou nung-ts'un she-hui yü tien-p'u chih*
明清徽州農村社會與佃僕制 (Hefei, 1983). Yeh's work was a landmark
in Chinese historiography for he systematically cited his sources,
and in the case of archival materials, their holding location, and
when possible, their classification number. Writing in the spirit of
the 'Annales school',[7] he was able to utilize all sorts of documents,
stored in a variety of libraries and institutes all over the PRC.[8] The
success and acclaim for Yeh's work, also outside China, has led to
a whole series of documentary collections that reprint the Hui-
chou materials held by research institutes, museums, and universities. The most important Hui-chou collection that has appeared
is: *Hui-chou ch'ien-nien ch'i-yüeh wen-shu* 徽州千年契約文書 (Shijiazhuang, 1991-93; 40 vols.). One might even say that the importance of Hui-chou may be compared to that assigned to Tun-
huang.[9]

---

nosuke 天野元之助 was the link between him and another famous Japanese scholar
Fujii Hiroshi 藤井宏, who published a classic study of "Hsin-an merchants" in *Tôyô
gakuhô* 東洋学報 1953-54.

[6] Published in Chang Chung-i 張仲- and Ts'ao Chien-pin 曹見賓, eds., *Hui-chou
Ming-tai chu-chai* 徽州明代住宅 (Peking, 1957).

[7] See comments by Michel Cartier, "Naissance de la Huizhoulogie," *Revue
bibliographique de Sinologie 1990* (Paris, 1991), p.96.

[8] I have discussed most of these locations in my article "Doing Library and Archival Research on Local History: A Study of Huizhou Prefecture during the Ming
and Ch'ing Periods," *China Exchange News*, 12.3 (1984), 5-8.

[9] Cartier, "Naissance de la Huizhoulogie", p.98 makes this conclusion. There

Archives

The Hui-chou documents represent materials from what scholars conventionally consider regional or local archives, in contrast to central archives. As we have noted, China does not have a long tradition of public archives, i.e. depositories for documents concerning political, judicial, commercial, or industrial administration open to the general public. In 1925, the entire northern section of the Forbidden City in Peiping was turned into a museum and established there were a section for antiquities and another for a library, which contained both books and documents.[10] It was this Palace Museum Collection which became the basis for the two primary late 20th century archives for the study of China, those in present-day Beijing and Taipei. The most important of these major archival collections include: the 'Number One Historical Archive' in Beijing for documents from the Ming and Ch'ing periods;[11] the 'Number Two Historical Archive' in Nanjing for documents from the Republican Period; the National Palace Museum of Taipei for the Ming and Ch'ing periods.[12] The Academica Sinica in Taipei also has two institutes which contain important materials. The Institute of Modern History holds documents relevant to late Ch'ing and Republican history, while the Institute of

---

are many works that reproduce Hui-chou documents, see for example *Ming Ch'ing Hui-chou she-hui ching-chi tzu-liao ts'ung-pien* 明清徽州社會經濟資料叢編 series (Beijing, since 1988).

[10] For a brief history of the Palace Museum and a list of its contents in the 1930s, see Hermann Koester, "The Palace Museum of Peiping," *Monumenta Serica* 2 (1936-37):167-130. For further information concerning the history of Chinese archives, past and present, see Tsou Chia-wei 鄒家煒 , et.al., *Chung-kuo tang-an shih-yeh chien-shih* 中國檔案事業簡史 (Beijing, 1990).

[11] A useful introduction to this collection, which includes a list of what collections of archival documents were published between 1949-1985 (only PRC collections considered after 1949), is to be found in Ni Tao-shan 倪道善, *Ming Ch'ing tang-an kai-lun* 明清檔案概論 (Chengdu, 1990), pp.267-269. There is now a 'Historical Archive Number Three', located in Shenyang, which, according to Beatrice Bartlett, comprises the largest number of items of any local archive in China. For a recent "update" on various archives in the PRC, see *China Exchange News* 19.3-4 (1991).

[12] For the Ch'ing materials, see the catalogue *Ch'ing-tai wen-hsien tang-an tsung-mu* 清代文獻檔案總目 (Taipei, 1982). Also most recently, thanks to the efforts of Chang Wei-jen, a substantial portion of the Ming-Ch'ing archive in Taipei has been made available in reprint form. See *Ming-Ch'ing tang-an* 明清檔案 (Taipei, since 1986), more than 166 volumes in large format. This work supersedes Li Kuang-t'ao 李光濤 and Li Hsüeh-chih 李學智, *Ming Ch'ing tang-an ts'un-chen hsüan-chi* 明清檔案存眞選輯 (Taipei, since 1959).

History and Philology possesses a major collection of Grand Secretariat materials. The Number One Archive in Beijing houses approximately 90% of the Grand Council and Grand Secretariat archives, while 10% of the same collection is in Taipei.

In addition, there are local and regional archives: the Liaoning
Provincial Archive, the Baxian (district) Archive in Sichuan, and
the Archive of the Descendants of Confucius in Qufu. Not all regions are so lucky as to have a particular archive, and until now,
only the particular archival records of certain regions, such as
those from Ssu-ch'uan or Hui-chou, have been reprinted [see below, 'Important Collections of Published Archival Documents'].
One can also say that both the governments of the PRC and Taiwan have improved the facilities for utilizing documentary study,
not only by providing good facilities for their storage, but also by
promoting the cooperation between institutions of different interests and regions to utilize these materials.[13] However, because
catalogues in Taiwan are technically more advanced, access easier,
and working conditions more pleasant, it is advisable for researchers to begin their work in Taipei before moving to Beijing.

There are also other archives for the study of China, among
which those in Japan form central places of research. As
Wilkinson, pp. 19-22, writes, there are a number of libraries in Japan that hold large numbers of rare books and archival collections. The Tôyô Bunko and Tokyo University's Tôyô bunka
kenkyûjo in Tokyo contain extensive materials as does the Jimbun
kagaku kenkyûjo in Kyoto.[14]

In conclusion, it should be stressed that whatever the improved
availability of archival collections in the world, the documentary
materials themselves should not give one a (false) sense of security. With few exceptions, archives are primarily and predomi-
nantly the records of the ruling classes. The official documents of
imperial China, written at a time when literacy was the privilege of
the few, could not but be one-sided documents. Archival material,
by its very nature, is "purged material". As Lo Hui-min wrote:

---

[13] There are a number of journals that periodically "update" matters pertaining to Chinese historical archives and archival documents. These include: *Li-shih
tang-an* 歷史檔案 , *Min-kuo tang-an* 民國檔案 , *Tang-an-hsüeh t'ung-hsün* 檔案學通訊,
Tang-an kung-tso 檔案工作, *Tang-an yen-chiu* 檔案研究, *Tang-an yü li-shih* 檔案與歷史.
[14] For updates on the library catalogues of these collections, see Cole, pp. 46-
48. One important work that has appeared since publication of Cole's list is:
Tôyô bunko shozô Kindai Chûgoku kankei zusho bunrui mokuroku: Chûgokubun
東洋文庫所藏近代中国関係図書分類目録 : 中国文 volume II (Tokyo, 1992).

"Chinese government archives are not strictly speaking archives of original records but of copied documents, each carefully phrased, endeavouring to hide as much as to expound, and completely lacking in 'spontaneity'.[15]

Buddhist/Taoist Collectanea

Nowhere may the limitations of archives be more evident than when we consider the lack of attention in "official documents" to the Buddhist and Taoist traditions in Chinese historical development (except on the occasion of these two religions becoming agents of heterodox protest movements). The pervasive influence these traditions exerted is not easily found among the millions of pieces that constitute official archives. Although the present study will not go into any historiographical discussion of the role of these two religions, suffice it to say that both the Buddhist and Taoist canons are important sources for the study of Chinese society at any given time.

The body of the Buddhist canon and Buddhist writings is called the *Ta-tsang-ching* 大藏經. This expression represents the Sanskrit word Tripitaka, or "three baskets", and means "great collection of writing". The "three baskets" are: (1) *sutra*, the words of Buddha; (2) *vinaya*, the ruler; and (3) *sastra* (*abhidharma*), the discussion of metaphysics and doctrines. The Buddhist Canon has seen a great number of versions, but the "standard version" was compiled in Japan at the beginning of this century. It is called *Taishô shinshû Daizôkyô* 大正新修大蔵経, compiled between 1924-1932, and published in 85 volumes [Tokyo, 1960; indexed in *Taishô shinshû Daizokyô sakuin* 大正新修大蔵経索引 (Tokyo, 1975-88), 44 volumes, and commonly known as 'Sakuin'].[16]

The Taoist canon, *Tao-tsang* 道藏, was brought together during the Northern Sung, collated during the Yung-lo period of the Ming (1403-1424), and printed in the ninth year of Cheng-t'ung 正統 (1444). It is known as the *Cheng-t'ung tao-tsang* or simply *Tao-*

---

[15] Lo Hui-min, "Archives in Modern China", p.217.

[16] See also P. Demiéville et al., *Répertoire du Canon Bouddhique Sino-Japanais* (Paris, 1978). This work lists all texts in order of their Taishô number with pronunciation given in Japanese. There are indices in the back of the volume to author and title by Japanese pronunciation, and Sanskrit or pali for texts originally in those languages. Titles and author/translators are also listed according to stroke number. There is a table that converts from Wade-Giles pronunciation of titles and authors to Japanese pronunciation.

tsang. In 1607, the Cheng-t'ung edition was supplemented with an additional 430 *chüan.* The edition of the Canon used by scholars today is a reprint of the Cheng-t'ung edition with the 1607 supplement published in 1925-27 in Shanghai, and reprinted in Taipei in 1962.[17] The original printing blocks of the Ming edition were stored in Peking, and what was left of them was destroyed during the Boxer uprising in 1900. The Shanghai printed edition originated from a complete set that had been kept in the White Cloud Monastery in Peking.[18]

Both the Buddhist and Taoist canons may be considered *ts'ung-shu;* they are compendia of sutras, rituals, incantations, biographical collections, records of conversations, all arranged under one title. The individual titles in both canons are not included in the standard *ts'ung-shu* catalogue *Chung-kuo ts'ung-shu tsung-lu,* and thus one must turn to the indices mentioned in the footnotes here.

---

[17] The history of the consecutive Taoist Canons has been described by Liu Ts'un-yan, "The Compilation and Historical Value of the Tao-tsang," in Leslie, Mackerras, and Wang, *Essays on the Sources for Chinese History,* pp.104-119, and in great detail, by Piet van der Loon, *Taoist Books in the Libraries of the Sung Period* (London, 1984).

[18] Indices to the Taoist Canon include *Tao-tsang tzu-mu yin-te* 道藏子目引得 in the Harvard Yenching Sinological Index series number 25, and K.M. Schipper, *Concordance du Tao-tsang: titres des ouvrages* (Paris, 1975).

References—Ts'ung-shu and Miscellaneous Collectanea

Indexes to the Contents of *Ts'ung-shu* 280
Guides to the Collected Works of Individual Authors 282
Important Collections of Published Archival Documents..... 284
Catalogues of Rare Books and Guides to Editions 287

The value of *ts'ung-shu* is that they reproduce works that may have been otherwise unpublished, unavailable, or lost. The huge volume of such works makes it impossible to list each book title separately in library catalogues. Thus, over time many attempts have been made to provide listings, in a sense indices to the titles of works within a particular *ts'ung-shu*. In addition, to the indexes specific to the works mentioned in the section 'Some Traditional and Modern *Ts'ung-shu*', the following publications will prove useful for finding *ts'ung-shu* titles.[19]

Shang-hai t'u-shu-kuan 上海圖書館 ed., *Chung-kuo ts'ung-shu tsung-lu* 中國叢書總錄 (Shanghai, 1959-62), 3 vols.

> An inventory of the collections of 41 public libraries in the PRC, representing 2,797 traditional *ts'ung-shu* and 38,891 ancient books. Volume 1 arranges the collectanea in the four SKCS bibliographic categories with the individual works contained in each collectanea listed. Volume 2 is arranged by the 70,000 individual works in each collectanea, arranged by the four categories, and further subdivided into sub-categories. Volume 3 is an author-title index to volume 2. The main classes of *ts'ung-shu* (subject, period, region, etc.) are given in the table of contents. This monumental work was immediately recognized by scholars all over the world as an indispensable tool for research. In Taiwan, a group of researchers reproduced the first volume of this work under another title, *Ts'ung-shu ta tz'u-tien* 叢書大辭典 (1971), and the second volume, under the title *Ts'ung-shu tzu-mu lei-pien* 叢書子目類編 (1974). In 1984, the *Chung-kuo ts'ung-shu tsung-lu* was "corrected"—see Yang Hai-ch'ing 陽海清 and Chiang Hsiao-ta 蔣孝達, *Chung-kuo ts'ung-shu tsung-lu pu-cheng* 中國叢書綜錄補正 (Yangzhou, 1984). This work contains a four-corner index of alternate titles of *ts'ung-shu*, giving one the opportunity to verify whether a *ts'ung-shu* in the original edition is listed under another title.

---

[19] No attempt has been made here to survey what *ts'ung-shu* collections are held outside East Asia. A recent outstanding catalogue for those *ts'ung-shu* collections in Europe is: Françoise Wang, *Catalogue des congshu de la Bibliothèque de l'Institut des Hautes Études chinoises* (Paris, 1991). This work reviews 1267 *ts'ung-shu*, arranged in the same order as the Shanghai tu-shu-kuan catalogue, and contains numerous indices (number of strokes, *pinyin*, and *ts'ung-shu* editors). It may be considered a supplement to the Shanghai catalogue.

Tôyô Bunko 東洋文庫, *Kanseki sôsho shozai mokuroku* 漢籍叢書所在目録 (Tokyo, 1965).

Lists the contents of Chinese *ts'ung-shu* in seven leading Japanese libraries. Catalogues 1,990 *ts'ung-shu*.

Wang Pao-hsien 王寶先, *T'ai-wan ko t'u-shu-kuan hsien-ts'un ts'ung-shu tzu-mu so-yin* 台灣各圖書館現存叢書子目索引 (San Francisco, 1975), 3 vols.

Catalogues the collections of ten Taiwan libraries, covering a total of 1500 *ts'ung-shu*. Volumes 1 and 2 (Part I) is a title index, including a stroke-count index, and library holding information. Volume 3 (Part II) is an author index, by stroke-count.

Brian McKnight, comp. *Ts'ung-shu so-yin Sung wen tzu-mu* 叢書索引宋文子目 (San Francisco, 1977).

As the title indicates, an index to Sung dynasty titles extant in *ts'ung-shu*. Lists 4500 titles, including variant titles, by 1664 authors.

Chung-kuo ts'ung-shu mu-lu chi tzu-mu so-yin hui-pien 中國叢書目錄及子目索引滙編 (Nanjing, 1982).

Lists the contents of 977 traditional *ts'ung-shu*, omitted from the 1959-62 *Chung-kuo ts'ung-shu tsung-lu*. Contains indices for the titles of the *ts'ung-shu* and for the titles of the individual works contained in each *ts'ung-shu*, but has no table of contents.

Chung-kuo chin-tai hsien-tai ts'ung-shu mu-lu 中國近代現代叢書目錄 (Shanghai, 1979; reprinted Hong Kong, 1980).

Lists the contents of 5549 *ts'ung-shu* (including 31,000 titles therein), published between 1902 and 1949, but not included in the 1959-62 *Chung-kuo ts'ung-shu tsung-lu*. Arranged by stroke-count of *ts'ung-shu* title. There is a separate appendix which lists *ts'ung-shu* by publication date. In 1982, a separate two volume index to this work appeared, *Chung-kuo chin-tai hsien-tai ts'ung-shu mu-lu so-yin* 中國近代現代叢書目錄索引 (Shanghai, 1982). Volume 1, arranged by stroke count, is an index to the titles of the items contained in the various *ts'ung-shu*. Volume 2, also arranged by stroke-count, contains: (1) an index to the authors of the titles in the various *ts'ung-shu*; and (2) an index to the editors of the *ts'ung-shu*.

GUIDES TO COLLECTED WORKS OF INDIVIDUAL AUTHORS

In addition to the listing of reference works to locate an author's collected works in Wilkinson, pp.171-172, there have appeared other important guides for this subject.[20]

Hsien-ts'un Sung-jen chu-shu mu-lüeh 現存宋人著述目略 (Chung-hua ts'ung-shu kuo-li chung-yang t'u-shu-kuan mu-lu ts'ung-k'an 7 中華叢書國立中央圖書館目錄叢刊第 7 輯 (Taipei, 1971).

Lists primarily those collections in premodern editions, held in Taiwan libraries. The table of contents arranges the included titles by categories (e.g. ritual, classics, literature, etc.) Writers are given chronologically according to category. No index. This work should be used in conjunction with the following bibliography.

Hsien-ts'un Sung-jen pieh-chi pan-pen mu-lu 現存宋人別集版本目錄 (Chengdu, 1989).

Arranged chronologically according to writer. Each entry includes title of extant work(s), edition(s) available (with details of *ts'ung-shu* editions) and holding location (includes those in Japan). There are separate indices for *ts'ung-shu* collections based on the four-corner system, a list of holding libraries arranged by location, and authors' finding list by four-corner number.

Lu Chün-ling 陸峻嶺, *Yüan-jen wen-chi p'ien-mu fen-lei so-yin* 元人文集篇目分類索引 (Beijing, 1979).

Contains three major sections: (1) biographical (pp.1-311); (2) historical (pp.312-421); (3) literary (pp.422-538). The first section is sub-divided into men, women, Buddhists, and Taoists. The second contains some subdivisions, such as those on examinations or on temples. The third is a rich literary source. Under *shan-shui* 山水 (pp.452-454), for example, a good portion of the landscape literature of the Yüan can be found. Information on ritual, customs, and religion are bountiful.

---

[20] For T'ang poets whose work appears in the *Ch'üan T'ang-shih*, see chapter VI References 'Literary Dictionaries'.

Yamane Yukio, 山根幸夫, *Zôtei Nihon genson Minjin bunshû mokuroku* 増訂日本現存明人文集目録 (Tokyo, 1978).

Revised and expanded edition of the 1966 original, originally discussed in Wilkinson, p. 172.

Chang Shun-hui 張舜徽, *Ch'ing-jen wen-chi pieh-lu* 清人文集別錄 (Beijing, 1963; reprinted, 1980) 2 vols.

Contains entries on 599 collections of writings by Ch'ing authors, each with detailed annotations (in classical Chinese), but in no apparent order. With author index.

IMPORTANT COLLECTIONS OF PUBLISHED ARCHIVAL DOCUMENTS

This list updates that compiled in Ni Tao-shan, *Ming Ch'ing tang-an kai-lun*, pp.267-268 and that in *Chung-kuo ti-i li-shih tang-an kuan kuan-ts'ang tang-an kai-shu* 中國第一歷史檔案館館藏檔案概述 (Beijing, 1985), pp.11-12, 23.[21]

Tao Hsien T'ung Kuang ssu-ch'ao tsou-i 道咸同光四朝奏議 (Memorials of the four reign-periods Tao-kuang, Hsien-t'ung, T'ung-chih, and Kuang-hsü; Taipei, 1970), 12 volumes.

Hai-fang tang 海防檔 (Archive of maritime defense; Taipei, 1957), 9 volumes.

K'uang-wu tang 礦物檔 (Archive of mining affairs; Taipei, 1960), 8 volumes.

Nien Keng-yao tsou-che chuan-chi 年羹堯奏摺專集 (Special collection of palace memorials of Nien Keng-yao; Taipei, 1971), 3 volumes.

Kung-chung-tang Kuang-hsü-ch'ao tsou-che 宮中檔光緒朝奏摺 (Secret palace memorials of the Kuang-hsü reign period at the National Palace Museum; Taipei, 1973), 25 volumes.

Kung-chung-tang K'ang-hsi-ch'ao tsou-che 宮中檔康熙朝奏摺 (Secret palace memorials of the K'ang-hsi reign period at the National Palace Museum; Taipei, 1976), 7 volumes.

Kung-chung-tang Yung-cheng-ch'ao tsou-che 宮中檔雍正朝奏摺 (Secret palace memorials of the Yung-cheng reign period at the National Palace Museum; Taipei, 1977), 28 volumes.

Chiao-wu chiao-an tang 教物教案檔 (Archive of religious affairs and religious incidents; Taipei, 1981), 21 volumes.

Ssu-ch'uan Hsin-hai ko-ming shih-liao 四川辛亥革命史料 (Historical material on the 1911 revolution in Ssu-ch'uan; Chengdu, 1981), 2 volumes.

---

[21] In preparing this list, I benefitted from the excellent advice of Professor Hans Ulrich Vogel, Tübingen University.

Kung-chung-tang Ch'ien-lung-ch'ao tsou-che 宮中檔乾隆朝奏摺 (Secret palace memorials of the Ch'ien-lung reign period at the National Palace Museum; Taipei, 1970), 70 volumes (and more to follow)

Ch'ing-tai ti k'uang-yeh 清代的礦業 (The Mining industry of the Ch'ing period; Beijing, 1983), 2 volumes.

Ch'ing-tai ti-ch'i tang-an shih-liao (Chia-ching chih Hsüan-t'ung) 清代地契檔案史料（嘉慶至宣統） (Archival material concerning land deeds of the Ch'ing period [from the Chia-ching to the Hsüan-t'ung periods 1796-1911]; Xindu, 1985).

Min-kuo ti-ch'i tang-an shih-liao (Min-kuo yüan-nien chih Min-kuo erh-shih-ch'i nien) 民國地契檔案史料（民國元年至民國二十七年） (Archival material concerning land deeds of the Republican period [from Min-kuo 1 to Min-kuo 27 1912-1938]; Xindu, 1985).

Tzu-kung yen-yeh ch'i-yüeh tang-an hsüan-chi 自貢鹽業契約檔案選集 (Selections from the archives of salt industry contacts of Tzu-kung; Beijing, 1985).

Chung-kuo chin-tai yen-wu-shih tzu-liao hsüan-chi 中國近代鹽物史資料選集(Selected material on the history of salt affairs in modern China; Tianjin, 1985ff), 4 volumes to date.

Tzu-kung yen-yeh kung-jen tou-cheng-shih tang-an tzu-liao hsüan-pien (1915-1949) 自貢鹽業工人鬥爭史檔案資料選編（1915－1949） (Selected material on the history of the struggles of the salt industry workers of Tzu-kung [1915-1949]; Chengdu, 1986).

Ch'ing-mo T'ien-chin hai-kuan yu-cheng tang-an hsüan-pien 清末天津海關郵政檔案選編 (Selected postal archives of the T'ien-chin Maritime Customs of the late Ch'ing; Beijing, 1988).

Ch'ung-te san-nien Man-wen tang-an i-pien (Selected translations from the Manchu archives of the third year of the Ch'ung-te reign period [1638]; Shenyang, 1988).

Man-wen T'u-erh-hu-t'e tang-an i-pien 滿文土爾扈特檔案譯編 (Selected translations from the Manchu archives of T'u-erh-hu-t'e; Beijing, 1988).

Ssu-ch'uan kung-jen yün-tung shih-liao hsüan-pien 四川工人運動史料選編 (Selected historical material on the workers' movements in Ssu-ch'uan; Chengdu, 1988).

Ch'ing-tai Ch'ien Chia Tao Pa-hsien tang-an hsüan-pien 清代乾嘉道巴縣檔案選編 (Selections from the archives of Pa-hsien from the Ch'ien-lung, Chia-ch'ing and Tao-kuang periods [1736-1850] of the Ch'ing; Chengdu, 1989).

Ch'ing-mo Ch'uan Tien pien-wu tang-an shih-liao 清末川滇邊物檔案史料 (Historical material from the archive on Ssu-ch'uan-Yunnan border affairs during the late Ch'ing; Beijing, 1989), 3 volumes.

Ch'ing-tai ti ch'i-ti 清代的旗地 (Banner land of the Ch'ing period; Beijing, 1989), 3 volumes.

Chin-tai K'ang-ch'ü tang-an tzu-liao hsüan-pien 近代康區檔案資料選編 (Selections of archival material on the [Hsi] K'ang region of the modern period; Chengdu, 1990).

Chung-kuo hai-kuan mi-tang—Ho-te, Chin-teng-kan han-tien hui-pien 1874-1907 中國海關密檔——赫德金登幹函電滙編1874 - 1907 (The secret archives of the China Imperial Customs: Collections of letters and telegrams of Hart and Campbell; Beijing, 1990). 2 volumes.

Yung-cheng-ch'ao Han-wen chu-p'i tsou-che hui-pien 雍正朝漢文硃批奏摺彙編 (Collection of Chinese palace memorials with vermillion endorsements from the Yung-cheng reign period; Shanghai, 1991), 40 volumes.

Hui-chou ch'ien-nien ch'i-yüeh wen-shu (40 volumes) See above in the Introduction to this chapter.

CATALOGUES OF RARE BOOKS AND GUIDES TO EDITIONS

Kuo-li chung-yang t'u-shu-kuan shan-pen shu-mu 國立中央圖書館善本書目 (Taipei, 1957-58, 3 volumes; revised edition, 1967, 4 volumes).

This catalogue lists some 143,000 volumes (*ts'e* 冊) of rare materials brought to Taiwan and housed in the National Central Library. It is divided into two sections: 1) Ming and earlier, rare Ch'ing manuscripts, drafts and items with the notes or other writings of particular persons; 2) all other material. Arranged in SKCS order, but there is a fifth category for *ts'ung-shu* of miscellaneous content. The usual entry includes title, number of *chüan* and volumes, dynasty, author and brief description of the edition. The listings include 200 Sung editions, 5 Chin, 230 Yüan, 6219 Ming, as well as Ch'ing works, Tun-huang manuscripts, and items in Korean, Japanese, and Annamese.

This following works bring up to date those titles listed by Cole, pp. 21, 24, and 57-60.

Chung-kuo ku-chi shan-pen shu-mu 中國古籍善本書目 (Shanghai, since 1986) 20 *ts'e* to date.

This beautifully string-bound set of volumes lists rare books found in libraries all over the PRC. It is arranged according to SKCS classification. For each title, the number of *chüan*, the name and dynastic origin of each author or compiler, and the location of the extant edition(s) available are given.

Hu Tao-ching 胡道靜, *Chien-ming ku-chi tz'u-tien* 簡明古籍辭典 (Jinan, 1989).

Although compact, this reference is truly a "connoisseur's guide" to everything one might want to know about the basics of Chinese collectanea. This volume gives definitions of words concerning bibliography, short biographical sketches of leading figures in Chinese history since the Ch'in who were involved either in bibliography, collectanea, or printing. There are also entries about the most important relevant works in the history of printing, publishing, bibliography (arranged in SKCS order). Another section includes the leading Chinese collections, arranged chronologically, from earliest times through the Ch'ing. Numerous appendices concerning a variety of related topics complete this useful work.

Wang Chung-min 王重民, *Chung-kuo shan-pen shu t'i-yao pu-pien* 中國善本書提要補編 (Beijing, 1991).
> Updates the same author's *Chung-kuo shan-pen shu t'i-yao* (Shanghai, 1983). See Cole, p.57.

Ku-chi cheng-li t'u-shu mu-lu 1949-1991 古籍整理圖書目錄1949 - 1991 (Beijing, 1992).
> Arranged according to year, and then sub-divided by subject (literature, linguistics, history, etc.). Each entry includes title of work, author and his dynastic origin, name of publisher, and date of publication. There is a separate title index arranged according to four-corner system (with separate finding list according to number of strokes of the first character of the title).

Lo Wei-kuo 羅偉國 and Hu P'ing 胡平, *Ku-chi pan-pen t'i-chi so-yin* 古籍版本題記索引 (Shanghai, 1991).
> Begins with a table of contents which lists title of work, author and dynastic origin, specifics of edition under investigation, and other editions available. The main portion of the index gives the title of the work, the number of its *chüan*, the author and his era, the name of the *ts'ung-shu* or other set of collected works in which an edition of the title may appear, and whether the work has been included in the SKCS. There is also an author index followed by the titles of his work(s). A separate index for works authored anonymously may be found in the appendix.

Sören Edgren, *Chinese Rare Books in American Libraries* (New York, 1984).

CHAPTER NINE

INDEXES AND CONCORDANCES

Introduction

Indexes are among the most important tools for research in Chinese studies. In general, they can be distinguished by any of the following terms in the title: *so-yin* 索引 (in Japanese, *sakuin*), or *t'ung-chien* 通檢. Indexes identify 'key words' in a text, whether they be literary terms, the names of persons or places, or book titles. Usually, at the beginning of an index, it is made known which editions of a particular text were utilized for examination, and how the index was constructed. In contrast to an index which generally concentrates on certain kinds of key words, i.e. names of persons, or place names, a concordance identifies all words from a text, and includes the cited portions of that text. Concordances may be identified by the expression *yin-te* 引得 in the title. They are usually based on a critical edition of a certain text; sinologists commonly use concordances to look up citations in the Classics. Thus, concordances may be considered an important tool for those studying texts from a literary or linguistic perspective.

Until this century, there were no indexes for Chinese books, because the 'ideal' Chinese scholar was supposed to know books by heart, and he should have had a sort of index in his head. Even nowadays, it is unusual for Chinese books (in contrast to Japanese books) to have indexes. The idea of making indexes for important works was first suggested in 1930 by William Hung, who worked in the Harvard-Yenching Institute, and at Yenching University.[1] He asked the Institute to finance a Sinological Index Series (SIS) to compile systematic indices to all the Chinese Classics

---

[1] The first modern concordance to a classical text was made by Ts'ai T'ing-kan 蔡廷幹 (1861-1935), a Chinese admiral. He compiled: *Lao-tzu Tao-te-ching* 老子道德經 (Shanghai, 1922). The cover title of this work is preceded by the words "Lao chieh Lao" 老解老 (Lao-tzu explained in Lao-tzu's terms). A full text of the work precedes the concordance which has characters arranged in order of their appearance in the text, with a stroke-count index at the end. For Hung's activities, see Chapter I 'A Brief History of Chinese Studies and Sinology'.

and make them accessible to modern scholars. Prior to the SIS, only a few ancient Chinese texts had been indexed by European, Japanese, and Chinese scholars, but not on a systematic basis.

The Harvard-Yenching Institute Sinological Index Series (HYISIS) which Hung developed and supervised, has been regarded by most scholars as the most important reference series produced in the first half of the 20th century for the study of traditional Chinese civilization. In this series, Hung and his small staff set themselves the task to evaluate systematically the most important books ever written in China, establish any textual variants of these books, and provide them with indexes or concordances.[2]

The Series eventually encompassed 64 titles.[3] In 23 cases, not only the index but also an authorative text of the actual work was published; these 23 were numbered separately and called 'Supplements'. Only one title is concerned with belles-lettres, i.e. the *Concordance to the Poems of Tu Fu*, with a preface by Hung. Indices or concordances were completed for all but one of the traditional 'Thirteen Classics'. The first four of the 24 Standard Histories was each indexed. HYISIS 17 is an index for the sixth century *Water Classic and Commentary*, one of the oldest Chinese books on geography, which traces the courses of 137 rivers and their tributaries as well as locating lakes, ponds, and canals. Fifteen titles are indices of personal names in works on Chinese history, arts, and literature. Other volumes indexed 10,000 titles in the SKCS (HYISIS 7),[4] historical bibliographies found in 14 official and dynastic bibliographies (HYISIS 10); a number of volumes in the series were published indices to Buddhist and Taoist texts, and two bibliographies of 20th century Japanese Sinological studies. Volume 4 of the supplemental series gives a historical overview and explanation of the indexing method.

Hung was assisted in the Index production during the 1930s by Nieh Ch'ung-ch'i 聶崇岐, a great Confucian scholar. After the

---

[2] For the details on how this was done, see William Hung, "Indexing Chinese Books," *Chinese Social and Political Science Review*, 15.1 (1931):48-61. Further information about the life of William Hung may be found in his charming autobiography, as told to Susan Chan Egan, *A Latterday Confucian:* See infra, Chapter I.

[3] All the titles, with their translation, are listed in the Appendix.

[4] For further information on the creation of this particular volume, see William Hung, "Preface to an Index to *Ssû-k'u ch'üan-shu tsung-mu* and *Wei-shou shu-mu*," HJAS 4 (1939): 47-58.

Harvard-Yenching Institute was forced to close during the Japanese occupation of the Yenching campus, Nieh continued the index work under the auspices of the Centre Franco-chinois at the Sino-French University. The series upon which he work was entitled *Centre Franco-chinois d'Études sinologiques*. Since 1949, indexes have been compiled in Taiwan, Hong Kong, Japan, and on a lesser scale in the West. Both the HYISIS and the Centre Franco-chinois d'Études sinologiques were reissued in Taiwan.[5]

The most complete listing of indexes and concordances up to 1975 is:

D.L. McMullen, *Concordances and Indexes to Chinese Texts* (San Francisco, 1975).[6]

McMullen's work examines 282 indexes and concordances of books that were published before 1900. For each entry, he reports the way in which the index is arranged, and what its particular advantages (or disadvantages) are. Since the appearance of McMullen's book, there have been published in Western languages a number of indexes and concordances for Neo-Confucianist, Taoist, and literary works.[7] They have not yet been systematically catalogued and can only be found by using a catalogue of a library that holds them. For indexes of works dealing with modern China, there are only those for bibliographical and biographical materials, as discussed in Chapters II and IV of this present work.[8]

Nowadays it seems common in the PRC, Hong Kong, and Taiwan to make available computerized concordances to all sorts of traditional Chinese literary and historical works. Already a data base and indexing system has been completed by the Academia Sinica in Taiwan for the twenty-five Dynastic Histories. This full-text database, consisting of some sixty million Chinese characters, which make up the entire text of all the Dynastic Histories, can be searched for personal names, place names, phrases, and so on.

Another major computer concordance project, under the directorship of Professor D.C. Lau and Dr. F. Chen, at the Institute

---

[5] See the Appendix for further details concerning reprints.

[6] This work includes all the indexes mentioned in TB.

[7] One of the most important series is: *The Stanford Chinese Concordance Series*, edited by P.J. Ivanhoe, under the supervison of David Nivison, and published by the Chinese Materials Center (San Francisco, 1979), 4 volumes. This series indexes six texts to works by Chu Hsi, Wang Yang-ming, and Tai Chen.

[8] One notable exception seems to be the index to the collected works of Hu Shih. See T'ung Shih-kang 童世綱 , *Hu Shih wen-ts'un so-yin* 胡適文存索引 (Taipei, 1969).

of Chinese Studies (ICS, hereafter), the Chinese University of
Hong Kong, is a database of concordances.[9] In 1992, the first of
93 planned volumes, covering all 103 extant Chinese writings
from antiquity to the end of the Eastern Han in A.D. 220, appeared. The ICS Series commemorates the twenty-fifth anniversary of the Institute and the ninety-fifth anniversary of the publisher, the Commercial Press.[10] ICS group view their project as a
continuation of the indexing concordance work begun by Hung
and his Harvard-Yenching Institute colleagues.

No doubt with improved facilities for easy access to computer
technology, conventional indexes and concordances may soon become cultural relics, and the electronic age may eliminate their
use altogether. However, until that time, students and researchers
may continue to profit from knowing their use.

How to Use the Harvard-Yenching Index System

The indexes and concordances in the HYISIS both utilize a
unique indexing system. To illustrate how to use one of the Harvard-Yenching series concordances, we have chosen to examine
Number 9 of the Supplement series, entitled *Mao-shih yin-te*
毛詩引得 (A Concordance to the *Shih-ching*), first published in
Peiping, 1934, and reprinted Tokyo, 1962. This concordance consists of the following parts:
  (1) An explanation in Chinese, pp.iii-vi; a character index arranged by strokes, pp. vii-xvii; a character index arranged by
  Wade-Giles transcription, pp. xix-xxx; an explanation in Chinese of the Harvard-Yenching number system, pp.xxxi-xxxii.
  (2) The Chinese text (in the Mao version) of the *Shih-ching*,
  pp.1-83.
  (3) The concordance, pp.1-243; for each character listed there
  is a "Harvard-Yenching number" (consisting of a Roman nu-
  meral from I to V, a slash /, and then a five digit Arabic
  number, under which are the fragments of the text where the
  character(s) may be found).

---

[9] The information and that what follows is from Russell McLeod, "Sinological
Indexes in the Computer Age: The ICS Ancient Chinese Text Concordance
Series," *China Review International*, 1.1 (1994):48-53.
[10] The first volume was the concordance to the *Chan kuo ts'e* 戰國策 [see
Loewe, *Early Chinese Texts*, p.11].
For a complete list of published and planned volumes (valid until March,
1994), see McLeod, *ibid.*, pp.51-53.

When one looks up a citation, it is best to choose a less common character within that citation (otherwise there might be too great a choice of references where the character might be mentioned). So, for example, if one looks up the character *t'i* 題 in the expression *t'i pi chi ling* 題彼脊令 , one finds in the list of characters at the beginning of the concordance [part (1)] that *t'i* is classified under II/89795. Then one turns to the concordance [part (3)], and finding that number, sees a list of all fragments in which the character *t'i* is present. It turns out that in this case, *t'i* is only found in the fragment *t'i pi ch'i ling*. There is a cross reference number *46/196/4*, next to the expression. *46* refers to the page of the citation in the text [part (2)] of the concordance. 196 is the number of the poem, and 4 is the number of the couplet.

The indexes in the HYISIS system work somewhat differently. At the very beginning of the index, there is a list of which sources have been indexed; the listing of the sources includes the author/editor(s), edition, and the total number of *chüan*. For example, Harvard-Yenching Index No. 9, *Index to Thirty-three Collections of Ch'ing Dynasty Biographies*, specifies 33 different works that contain the biographies of individuals who lived during the Ch'ing period. The first column of that list is a set of bold-faced numbers. When one looks up a character, say a personal name, one first determines the Harvard-Yenching number (a Roman numeral/5 digit Arabic number) of the surname. Finding that number in the index and the person's full name, one sees another number, e.g. *33/7/2a*. In this case, *33* refers to the 33rd title listed at the beginning of the Index, *Kuo-shih lieh-chuan* 國史列傳, 7 refers to which *chüan* of the *Kuo-shih...*, and 2a the page of that *chüan*.

Information on the ICS Concordance Series

Each ICS concordance includes the complete text of the original work, with added punctuation and footnotes on textual variants and editorial emendations. The concordance itself indexes only single characters, romanized in *pinyin* and arranged in alphabetical order. Variant readings are also cross-referenced. Characters may be located either by romanization (there is a Wade-Giles–*pinyin* conversion table) or by character stroke count. The number of occurrences of a given character is indicated at the first entry and then followed by a listing, in order of their appearance in the text, of all phrases and sentences where the character occurs. Characters are located in the text by section, page, and line number. A table at the back provides a total character count for a given work and the single character ("vocabulary") count, and lists each character in the order of frequency from highest to lowest.[11]

According to McLeod, it may still be more convenient to use the Harvard-Yenching series in some cases. Since the Harvard-Yenching *Index* entries include words and names of more than one syllable, and also phrases, one may locate more easily a given word or phrase there than in the ICS *Concordance* which gives lists of single characters only.

---

[11] McLeod, *ibid.*, 49.

References—Indexes and Concordances

Guides to Indexes.. 296

GUIDES TO INDEXES

P'an Shu-kuang 潘樹廣, *Ku-chi so-yin kai-lun* 古籍索引概論 (Beijing, 1984).

> Gives a full account of the history, types, editing and organization of indexes and concordances to premodern Chinese writings. Pages 169-229 consist of a classified listing of indexes to all sorts of old Chinese texts compiled in China, Taiwan, Japan, and the West, stating the title, author, and publication date, together with very brief notes on content, where this is not evident from the title. There is an index to the whole volume (text and bibliography). The best book on the subject.

Chang Chin-lang 張錦郎, *Ch'üan-kuo so-yin pien-chi yen-t'ao-hui ts'an-k'ao tzu-liao* 全國索引編輯研討會參考資料 (Taipei, 1977).

> Divided into five sections. These include: (1) a chronological listing of indexes published in Taiwan, since 1948; (2) a subject index [cross-referenced to section (1)]; (3) title index based on number of strokes of first word in title [cross-referenced to section (2)]; (4) guides to indexes of leading Taiwan periodicals for all subjects, including the hard sciences; (5) listing of important journals published in Taiwan, Japan, and the United States that include indexes. The last section is presented by a reproduction of a page of a particular journal's index. The American references include *The New York Times Index*.

Cheng Heng-hsiung 鄭恆雄, *Han-hsüeh so-yin tsung-mu* 漢學索引總目 (Taipei, 1975).

> Arranged by category. Contains citations to 790 entries, but no annotations. Includes indexes published as journal articles. With author index.

William Nienhauser, "A Note on Some Recent Lexica and Indexes on Traditional Chinese Literature," *CLEAR* 10 (1988):153-165.

> A very thorough listing of indexes and concordances for literary works, including indexes published in Japan through 1989. Encompasses personal name indexes as well as those to Buddhist and Taoist works. This article is useful for those scholars working with specialized texts who might suspect that an index may be available for their particular project.

Ch'üan T'ang shih so-yin 全唐詩索引 (Beijing, since 1991) multi-volumed.

> See chapter VI Dictionaries under 'Literary Dictionaries'.

CHAPTER TEN

THE CHINESE CALENDAR

Introduction

The Chinese calendar, like its Western counterpart, is an arbitrary attempt to combine the solar-year (the time during which the earth completes a total revolution around the sun, i.e. 365.24219 days) with the lunar-month (the period during which the moon makes a circle around the earth, i.e. 29.5365879 days). The solar or tropical year contains a slight gap, requiring an additional day to be added every four years, known as 'leap year'. Otherwise, the solar year would be out of step with the seasons. Twelve lunar or synodic months (based on one month accounting for 29.53 days) may be reckoned 354 days. The lunar year corresponds even less to the seasonal year, so that even greater adjustments are necessary. Thus, there are serious discrepancies between the two calculatory periods, and, within the two types of year. This accounts for the seemingly insatiable demand on the part of Chinese rulers for precision in calendrical calculation that far exceeded normal agricultural, bureaucratic, and economic requirements. As is well known, every official dynastic history included a substantial section on the calendar, since one of the most important acts of any new regime was to fix the time (*shou-shih* 授時) or (*shih-ling* 時令) and to regulate the calendar (*chih-li* 治曆).

It should be clear that a calendar is not the same as an almanac. Generally speaking, "the term 'calendar' refers exclusively to an annual publication authorized and usually issued directly by the Chinese central government, while the word 'almanac' denotes an unofficial calendrical work which may be informally sanctioned, merely tolerated, or in fact expressly forbidden, by the State."[1] Part of the confusion that persists concerning these devices stems from the close historic relationship between the two that has existed throughout the imperial era. Both kinds of works took into account solar days and lunar years, with an intercalary month in-

---

[1] From Richard J. Smith, *Chinese Almanacs* (Hong Kong, 1992), p.1.

serted periodically to agree with the revolution of the earth around the sun.[2]

Although successive Chinese rulers not only monopolized the production of the annual calendar, and maintained the supervision of astrological divination, the identification of lucky and unlucky days, and the records of auspicious omens and portents, local almanac makers undertook similar responsibilities. Over time, as the facilities for printing and the popularity of literacy extended, popular almanacs became even more common. Affluent families sponsored many compilations, while a high number of forgers made copies for sale of the official State calendar. By the time of the Yüan dynasty, officials recognized that popular almanacs could no longer be controlled, and even more significantly, authorized that the day-selection tables of popular almanacs become a regular and integral part of official calendars – a tradition that continued until 1911. These day selection tables were at the core of all state calendars and almanacs. They are a month-by-month, day-by-day breakdown of the entire year, obviously designed to coordinate and control all aspects of Chinese political, social, ritual, and economic life. In this chapter, we shall outline the structure of the traditional calendar, and, explain, how to calculate and convert "Chinese time" and "Western time".

The Structure of the Traditional Chinese Calendar

The determination of Chinese historical dates is a complicated process. In China's earliest history, dates were reckoned in terms of the number of years, according to a lunar reckoning, from the beginning of the reign of a particular ruler. What evolved was a complex sexagenary cycle, based on a combination of two series, that of twelve earthly branches *ti-chih* 地支 and ten celestial stems *t'ien-kan* 天干.[3] The twelve branches were applied to the twelve

---

[2] The official calendar was known as the *Shou-shih li* 授時曆 in the Yüan dynasty, the *Ta-t'ung li* 大統曆 in the Ming dynasty, and either the *Shih-hsien li* 時憲曆 or *Shih-hsien shu* 時憲書 after 1736 in the Ch'ing. Almanacs were termed simply *li-shu* 曆書 or *t'ung-shu* 通書.

[3] Here again we see how both State calendars and popular almanacs share important features. In both works, correlative cosmology occupies a central position. The fundamental premise of this cosmology was an ordered universe in which the unseen forces of *yin* 陰 and *yang* 陽, the so-called five 'phases' or 'activities' (*wu-hsing* 五行), identified with the 'elements' earth, wood, fire, water, and metal), the eight trigrams of the *I-ching* 易經 (Classic of Changes), the ten 'heav-

months of the year. Conversion of these sexagenary date-codes into the corresponding years of the Western calendar system is usually done by means of tables, which is explained below.

Table 1: Earthly Branches (*ti-chih*)

Earthly Branches		Corresponding Animals		
1. *tzu*	子	*shu*	鼠	rat
2. *ch'ou*	丑	*niu*	牛	ox
3. *yin*	寅	*hu*	虎	tiger
4. *mao*	卯	*t'u*	兔	rabbit
5. *ch'en*	辰	*lung*	龍	dragon
6. *ssu*	巳	*she*	蛇	snake
7. *wu*	午	*ma*	馬	horse
8. *wei*	未	*yang*	羊	sheep
9. *shen*	申	*hou*	猴	monkey
10. *yu*	酉	*chi*	雞	chicken
11. *hsü*	戌	*ch'üan*	犬	dog
12. *hai*	亥	*chu*	豬	pig

The cycle of twelve animals was correlated with the twelve branches fairly early on. One can find similar cycles in other geographical regions. For example, in India there is an analogous animal cycle, except for a crocodile in place of the dragon.

The ten celestial stems were probably associated specifically with the traditional ten day cycle.

Table 2: Celestial Stems (*t'ien-kan*)

A. *chia* 甲
B. *i* 乙
C. *ping* 丙
D. *ting* 丁
E. *wu* 戊
F. *chi* 己
G. *keng* 庚
H. *hsin* 辛
I. *jen* 壬
J. *kuei* 癸

The branches and stems are combined by matching the two, thus

enly stems' (*t'ien-kan*) and twelve 'earthly branches' (*ti-chih*), and a host of other cosmic variables – including both 'real' stars and 'star-spirits' – interacted with each other and resonated with 'like things' (*t'ung-lei* 同類).

A1 is 甲子, B2 is 乙丑, C3 is 丙寅, up to J10; then the stems begin again with *chia* so that one continues: A11, B12, C1, D2, and so on. In this way there will be 60 pairs before one again reaches A1 or *chia-tzu*. It is this series of 60, the sexagesimal cycle, which was used on the oracle bones to indicate the sequence of days. Because each year contained roughly five cycles, it was necessary to mark which month in order to make clear what date was meant. This system was used in the *Spring and Autumn Annals,* and was carried down through the *pen-chi* 本紀 or annals of all the Histories.

Table 3: The Cyclical Characters

1 甲子	11 甲戌	21 甲申	31 甲午	41 甲辰	51 甲寅
2 乙丑	12 乙亥	22 乙酉	32 乙未	42 乙巳	52 乙卯
3 丙寅	13 丙子	23 丙戌	33 丙申	43 丙午	53 丙辰
4 丁卯	14 丁丑	24 丁亥	34 丁酉	44 丁未	54 丁巳
5 戊辰	15 戊寅	25 戊子	35 戊戌	45 戊申	55 戊午
6 己巳	16 己卯	26 己丑	36 己亥	46 己寅	56 己未
7 庚午	17 庚辰	27 庚寅	37 庚子	47 庚戌	57 庚申
8 辛未	18 辛巳	28 辛卯	38 辛丑	48 辛亥	58 辛酉
9 壬申	19 壬午	29 壬辰	39 壬寅	49 壬子	59 壬戌
10 癸酉	20 癸未	30 癸巳	40 癸卯	50 癸丑	60 癸亥

From the Han dynasty onward reign period titles (*nien-hao* 年號) were employed to indicate years. These were auspicious names for the whole, or part of the reign of the emperor, and were chosen either to commemorate lucky events and perpetuate their good influence, or to counteract the effects of unlucky events. Examples of common *nien-hao* are 'T'ien-an' 天安 (Heavenly Peace) or 'T'ai-ho' 太和 (Great Harmony). Most *nien-hao* consist of two characters, but some were four characters. The first year of the reign period was known as *yüan-nien* 元年; the second year was *erh-nien* 二年, and so on. If in a given year the emperor died, his death brought to a close the *nien-hao,* but the *nien-hao* of the new emperor did not begin until the following calendar year. Thus, if an emperor died in the eighth month, events occurring after his death would still be reported in terms of the *nien-hao,* the ninth month, or tenth month, and so on.

The *nien-hao* could be changed as often as rulers wished.[4] The

---

[4] The most extreme example is T'ang Empress Wu, who reigned from 685 to 704, and in those 20 years changed the *nien-hao* 11 times.

Chinese expression *kai-yüan* 改元 (to change the first year) refers
to the process whereby a reigning monarch altered the *nien-hao*
during his/her rule. Acceptance of an era name signified alle-
giance, and rebels were quick to proclaim their own.

During the Ming and Ch'ing dynasties, it became customary to
assign only one reign period title to each reign and the emperors
became known in history by their reign period title, e.g. the
Ch'ien-lung 乾隆 Emperor, rather than by the posthumous title by
which earlier emperors were usually designated. These posthumous titles usually ended in the expression *ti* 帝 (emperor) or
tsung 宗 (ancestor). Often the same posthumous terms were assigned so that the first emperor of a particular dynasty might be
known as Kao-tsu 高祖, and his successor T'ai-tsung 太宗. Thus, it
became common to refer to the name of the dynasty and the individual monarch, e.g. T'ang Kao-tsu, for the first T'ang emperor.

In 1912 the Republic of China adopted a system of referring to
years, as so many years after the official founding of the Republic
at the beginning of 1912, e.g. Min-kuo 民國 4, that is the fourth
year of the Republic (or in Western reckoning 1915). Since 1949,
the PRC has used the Western calendar, while the Government of
Taiwan continues to employ the Republican reckoning system.

In traditional China the age of a person was not counted in
nien, but in *sui* 歲. Birthdays, except those of members of the imperial family, were not an occasion for celebration as they are in
the West. There may have been some festivity at the beginning of
a new decennium, e.g. the 21st birthday. One was considered one
year old, on the day of his/her birth, and reached the age of two
by the time of the beginning of the new year. Thus, in reading a
person's age in traditional literature, one should reckon to sub-
tract at least one year to determine the real age. Nowadays, there
is still not much uniformity about the matter of age. In theory,
one reckons age in the Western sense in *chou-sui* 周歲 (entire year)
or in *tsu-sui* 足歲 (full year); or age in the Chinese sense in *sui* 歲
or *hsü-sui* 虛歲 (nominal age), reckoned by the traditional method,
so that a person is one year at birth, and two at the time of the lunar new year.

The calendar in imperial China was a lunar one, so that the first
day of the month was always a new moon, and the basic year was
determined by counting off a number of the moons or months.
There were twelve moon months ranging from 29 (*hsiao-yüeh* 小月)
to 30 (*ta-yüeh* 大月) days per month. In some years a thirteenth
month known as *jun-yüeh* 閏月 was added in spring, summer, or

autumn. This extra month inserted seven times in 19 years made
up the discrepancy between the solar and lunar years. The year itself was divided into four seasons, spring, summer, autumn, and
winter, but there was a much more precise division also.

The solar year was divided into twelve periods, known as *chieh-
ch'i* 節氣, each of which was intersected by a *chung-ch'i* 中氣.[5] The
time periods were established by marking the solstices and equi-
noxes, each of which was marked by a *chung-ch'i*. The resulting 24
time periods, each roughly two weeks in length, had names which
were related to the weather and agriculture. [See the Chart 'The
Twenty-four Festivals and their Concordances with the Seasons' in
the Appendix]. The medial points denote the mid-point between
the divisions, generally speaking 14 days after the beginning of
each division. These periods realistically reflected the actual tem-
perature changes and so were important for farmers. The terms
appear usually in almanacs, sometimes in the closing of letters, or
in the colophons of paintings, but generally not in official documents. It is by these periods however that the seasons were
signaled and they also played a part in making up the calendar.

Traditional China had a twelve hour day, in which each hour
was the equivalent of two hours by our reckoning. The names of
12 cyclical animals were used for the hours, as follows:

shu	鼠	(rat)	11.p.m.- 1.a.m.
niu	牛	(ox)	1 .a.m.- 3.a.m.
hu	虎	(tiger)	3 .a.m.- 5.a.m.
t'u	兔	(rabbit)	5 .a.m.- 7.a.m.
lung	龍	(dragon)	7 .a.m.- 9.a.m.
she	蛇	(snake)	9 .a.m.- 11.a.m.
ma	馬	(horse)	11.a.m.- 1. p.m.

In traditional Chinese literature, one may come across the expression "the hour of...", e.g. the rat, meaning the period of the middle of the night. Chinese horoscopes utilize the hour of one's
birth so that one must know four relevant periods before application, i.e. the year, month, day, and hour (usually expressed in
dual cyclical characters) of one's birth.

A typical Chinese date found in any literary or history work
would resemble the following: 大宋元嘉五年冬閏月癸未

---

[5] The word *ch'i* here may be translated as 'vapours', or in other words, the
weather.

This may be read as the *kuei-wei* 癸未 day of the intercalary month (*jun-yüeh* 閏月), winter (*tung* 冬), of the fifth year of the Yüan-chia era (Yüan-chia *wu-nien* 元嘉五年), of the Great Sung dynasty (Ta Sung 大宋; in this case the Sung of the Six Dynasties period). Thus, in imperial China, time was formally designated by an expression containing the name of the dynasty, the year of a reign title, a season (not essential), the designation of a month, and one of a sexagismal cyclic system used to specify a date.

Historical events were also specified in terms of the cyclical compilation of the year in which they occurred, e.g. *wu-hsü pien-fa* 戊戌變法 (Reform of 1898), or the *hsin-hai ko-ming* 辛亥革命 (Revolution of 1911). In religious terminology, there were many combinations of the cycle that had significance, such as *chia-tzu* 甲子 , the first year of the 60 year cycle when a Chinese messiah such as Maitreya might visit this earth.

The first month was always expressed as *cheng-yüeh* 正月 (not *i-yüeh* 一月!). For the last month of the year, there was also an alternative name, *la yüeh* 臘月. Ten days composed a unit known as *hsün* 旬. The first ten days of a month were designated as *ch'u* 初, and the first day in the series was *ch'u-i* 初一. Other specific calendric expressions include *shuo-yüeh* 朔月, the first day of the lunar month (or new moon), and *wang-yüeh* 望月, the full moon, on the 15th day of the month.

In imperial China there never was a system of weeks, culminating in a seventh day of rest or sabbath. When holidays and festivals did occur, they were regulated according to the moon calendar, with the exception of the *ch'ing-ming* 清明 celebration, one of the 24 *ch'i* of the solar year, which happened on April 5, every year. The first day of the Chinese new year in Taiwan, Hong Kong, and overseas Chinese communities continues to be reckoned by the moon calendar. Although the PRC formally is regulated by the Western calendar (and thus New Year's day is January 1), many traditional festivals are now being again celebrated. The date of their occurrence is also determined by the lunar calendar. In regions where local religious cults flourish, traditional festivals have become a fundament of daily life and thus knowledge of the lunar year is once again deemed important.

The PRC does subscribe to a work week of seven days, (*li-pai* 禮拜 or *hsing-ch'i* 星期). *Li-pai-jih* 禮拜日 is Sunday, but it is not a country-wide day of rest, except for educational and governmental bureaucratic institutions. Factories and shops are not shut on *li-pai-jih* so that recreational facilities and public transport will not be overburdened by an excess number of people using them. For the same reason, work schedules do not begin and end at the same time for everyone and thus, traffic may be staggered.

Converting Chinese and Western Time

To convert a Chinese date to the Western calendar, one should begin with the year. First, it is necessary to identify the *nien-hao*. There are a number of chronologies which specialize in identifying *nien-hao*, but the quickest way is simply to consult *Tz'u-hai*, *Tz'u-yüan*, or the back of *Mathews' Chinese-English Dictionary*. One may use the tables in *Mathews'*, which are convenient, but one should recognise that they also contain errors. One needs to remember that in converting to a Western date, one does not add the year of the reign to the Western year in which it began, that is to say, the second year of a reign which began in 712 is not 714, but 713. Therefore, one subtracts one year before adding.

For the conversion of months and days, one needs to know that the Gregorian calendar replaced the Julian calendar in 1582. The Julian calendar, named for Julius Caesar, covers the period B.C.1 through October 4, 1582 A.D.. The Gregorian calendar, named for Pope Gregory XIII who initiated the new calendar, began on October 15, 1582. For these more exact conversions, one employs a concordance.[6] A concordance is a manual which allows one to convert not only the year, but the specific day from one dating system to another. Since days in the Chinese calendar are noted in terms of cyclical characters, one must consult the concordance to determine the exact day of a particular month (also determined by the cyclical system).

To explain this process, we shall begin by giving a particular Chinese date, and demonstrating how different concordances may aid one in the conversion. The date is the 29th day of the third month of the 24th year of Emperor Kuang-hsü (in Chinese, given as 光緒戊戌年丙辰月壬子日). From looking at three concordances [see *References* in this chapter], those of the Tung, Hoang, and Hsüeh, we may immediately see what notations are given.

---

[6] Although the name is identical, a concordance for converting time is not the same type of reference work as that used for the identification of terms in a text. See Chapter IX for further explanation.

Table 4: Information from Three Concordances

	(4)	(5)	(6)	(7)	(8)
戊戌 1898	甲 寅	正	乙 酉	1	22
(1) wu-hsü	乙 卯	二	庚 辰	2	21
清	丙 辰	三	甲 申	3	22
Ts'ing	閏	三	甲 寅	4	21
	丁 巳	四	癸 未	5	20
德宗	戊 午	五	癸 丑	6	19
(2) Tè Tsung	戊 申	六	癸 未	7	19
(愛新覺羅載湉)	庚 酉	七	壬 子	8	17
	辛 戌	八	壬 午	9	16
光緒	壬 亥	九	辛 亥	10	15
(3) Kuang-hsü	癸 子	十	庚 巳	11	14
二十四	甲	十一	己 戌	12	13
24		20	己 巳	1	1
14 6611	乙 丑	十二	庚 辰	1	12
(1316.)		(四3)		384	

Tung

N.d'or 13. 1898 AP-I.-C.
Ep.gr.:. 大清 L-d.gr.b.
Ta Ts'ing
德宗
(2) *Tè Tsung*
光緒
(3) *Kuang-hsü*
24
III. 戊戌 35.
(1) *Meou-sin*

Cycle du la lune	Lune, 1er jour	Mois polaire	Jour du mois	Cycle du jour
51	1	1	22	22
52	2	2	21	52
53	3	3	22	21
.	3	4	21	51
54	4	5	20	20
55	5	6	19	50
56	6	7	19	20
57	7	8	17	49
58	8	9	16	19
59	9	10	15	48
60	10	11	14	18
1	11	12	13	47
	j.20	1	1	6
2	12	1	12	17
(4)	(5)	(7)	(8)	

Hoang

陰曆日序
Order of days (Lunar)

年序 月序 → 陰曆 (8)
Year Moon

星期 干支
Week Cycle

Year	Moon	1	2	3	4	5	6	7	8	9	10	11	12	13	14	15	16	17	18	19	20	21	22	23	24	25	26	27	28	29	30	Week	Cycle
50	1	22	23	24	25	26	27	28	29	30	31	21	2	3	4	5	6	7	8	9	10	11	12	13	14	15	16	17	18	19	20	5	21
	2	21	22	23	24	25	26	27	28	31	2	3	4	5	6	7	8	9	10	11	12	13	14	15	16	17	18	19	20	21	—	0	51
(5)	3	㉒	23	24	25	26	27	28	29	30	31	41	2	3	4	5	6	7	8	9	10	11	12	13	14	15	16	17	18	19	20	1	20
	3	21	22	23	24	25	26	27	28	29	30	51	2	3	4	5	6	7	8	9	10	11	12	13	14	15	16	17	18	19	—	3	50
	4	20	21	22	23	24	25	26	27	28	29	30	31	61	2	3	4	5	6	7	8	9	10	11	12	13	14	15	16	17	18	4	19
(7)	5	19	20	21	22	23	24	25	26	27	28	29	30	71	2	3	4	5	6	7	8	9	10	11	12	13	14	15	16	17	18	6	49 (6)
	6	19	20	21	22	23	24	25	26	27	28	29	30	31	81	2	3	4	5	6	7	8	9	10	11	12	13	14	15	16	—	1	19
	7	17	18	19	20	21	22	23	24	25	26	27	28	29	30	31	91	2	3	4	5	6	7	8	9	10	11	12	13	14	15	2	48
	8	16	17	18	19	20	21	22	23	24	25	26	27	28	29	30	01	2	3	4	5	6	7	8	9	10	11	12	13	14	—	4	18
	9	15	16	17	18	19	20	21	22	23	24	25	26	27	28	29	30	31	11	2	3	4	5	6	7	8	9	10	11	12	13	5	47
	10	14	15	16	17	18	19	20	21	22	23	24	25	26	27	28	29	30	21	2	3	4	5	6	7	8	9	10	11	12	—	0	17
	11	13	14	15	16	17	18	19	20	21	22	23	24	25	26	27	28	29	30	31	11	2	3	4	5	6	7	8	9	10	11	1	46
	12	12	13	14	15	16	17	18	19	20	21	22	23	24	25	26	27	28	29	30	31	21	2	3	4	5	6	7	8	9	—	3	16

(3) (1) 光緒 2 4 戊戌 1898-99

Hsüeh

Key: (1) Cyclical characters for the year (*wu-hsü*); (2) Posthumous title for Emperor Kuang-hsü (Te-tsung); (3) Title of the reign; (4) Cyclical characters for the month; (5) Number of the Chinese month (the "3rd month" is a *jun-yüeh*; (6) Cyclical characters for the first day of the Chinese month; (7) Western month; (8) The day of the Western month which corresponds with the first day of the Chinese month.

First, we find that the *nien-hao* of the reign Kuang-hsü refers to Emperor Te-tsung of the Ch'ing dynasty; he reigned from 1875 through 1908.[7] The 24th year of his reign is 1898.

Next we proceed to determine the month in the Western calendar. The third month is *ping-ch'en* 丙辰 or #53 of the cyclical characters.[8] According to all three concordances, the third month of that Chinese year began March 22 and lasted until April 20 of the Western calendar. It should also be noted from these three tables that in 1898 there were two "3rd" months, the second of which was a *jun-yüeh*.

The conversion of days is the most difficult task. There are two ways to do this. First, one may simply count the number of days from the first day of the "first 3rd month", i.e. March 22. One finds that the 29th day becomes April 19, by calculating 28 days (29-1 = 28), and then counting 28 days from March 22. Second, one can look at the cyclical characters and see that the combination *jen-tzu* 壬子 was #49 of the cyclical characters, and that the first day of the "first 3rd month", according to the tables, was *chia-shen* 甲申, #21 of the cyclical characters. By subtracting 49—21, we find a difference of 28, or 28 days from the first day of the "first 3rd month".

The tables for the conversion of days in the Hsüeh volume works somewhat differently. One turns to the column "cycle". Each number represents the cyclic designation of the first day of the lunar month in that row, minus one. For the day we are investigating, we see that its number in the cycle column is 50. On the table on p.438 of the Hsüeh volume, we note that the *jen-tzu* day is #49. Therefore 50–49 = 1. Then looking at the columns once more, we see that the *jen-tzu* day was the first day of that month, or March 22, and the 29th day was April 19.

---

[7] To determine this date, we use either a chronology [see list in the Reference section of this chapter] or Mathews.

[8] Note that the Tung concordance lists *ping-ch'en* under the column marked 4, and the Hoang concordance lists "53" under the title 'Cycle de la lune'.

References—The Chinese Calendar

Chronologies 309
Concordances 310

CHRONOLOGIES

The following works are useful for converting *nien-hao* to Western reckoning:

Chung-kuo li-shih chi-nien piao 中國歷史紀年表 (Beijing, 1986).
Each year of every reign period is listed along with the ruler of the reign period. There is an index by number of strokes to both ruler and *nien-hao* at the end of the book.

Chung-kuo li-tai nien-hao k'ao 中國歷代年號考 (Beijing, 1981).
Arranged chronologically from B.C.140 to 1945 A.D.. Has stroke-order name index of reign periods. Includes non-Chinese dynasties and rebel pretenders. Detailed annotations give quotations from primary sources, providing information on obscure reign periods and rebel leaders. Sometimes indicates exact month of a reign period's beginning and end.

M. Tchang, *Synchronismes chinois, chronologie complete et concordance l'ère chrétienne de toutes les dates concernant l'histoire de l'Extrême-Orient (Chine, Japon, Corée, Annam, Mongolie, etc.) (2345 avant J.C. à 1904 après J.C.)* [Variétés sinologiques no.24] (Shanghai, 1905; Taipei, 1967 reprint)
As the title indicates, this work encompasses all *nien-hao* up to 1904, including those tributary states. Cyclical character combinations are also included.

CONCORDANCES

Tung Tso-pin 董作賓 comp. *Chung-kuo nien-li tsung-p'u* 中國年曆總譜 also called, *Chronological Tables of Chinese History* (Hong Kong, 1960), two volumes.

Here one may find both Western and Moslem dates. This work also contains much astronomical and calendrical information. The first volume has tables for the years 2674—1 B.C. and seven appendices; volume 2 has tables for 1-2000 A.D. and 12 appendices, mostly for non-regular dynasties, including the Taiping. There are indices to *nien-hao* both by stroke and by romanization.

P. Hoang, *Concordance des chronologies neomaniques chinoise et Euro-péene* [Variétés sinologiques no.29] (Shanghai, 1910; T'ai-chung, 1968 facsimile reproduction).

This concordance begins with the year B.C. 841. There is much information contained in the entry for each year, including such items as the Western year, name of the dynasty, the emperor, the *nien-hao* and year, the cyclical designation of the year and its number in the sexagenary cycle. The bottom half of each panel for each year contains the material correlating the two calendars. The first column, giving the cyclical designation of the month is called "cycle de la lune". One should note that intercalculary months, marked by an asterisk, are not included in this cycle. The next column, "lune 1er jour" represents the first day of each lunar month. The next two columns give the Western date of that first day and the last column gives the cyclical designation of that day. The boldface type indicates months of 30 days, light-faced numbers indicate months of 29 days. The number below each annual entry is the number of days in that year. The Western New Year's Day is indicated for each year, with the lunar column giving the day (= j.) of that lunar month. In this concordance, the cyclical designation is exact, and not reduced by one for convenience in calculation. The chart of the sexagnary cycle is on page X. There are appendices for the non-regular dynasties, one for temple names of emperors, *nien-hao* and dynastic names, by classifier and stroke, as well as one by number of strokes for first characters, keyed to the previous one, and one by romanization.

Hsüeh Chung-shan 薛仲山 et. al., comp. *Liang-ch'ien nien Chung-hsi li tui-chao piao* 兩千年中西曆對照表 also known, as *A Sino-Western Calendar for Two Thousand Years, 1-2000 A.D.* (Changsha, 1940; second edition, Beijing, 1956).

This is a bilingual concordance, with instructions in both Chinese and English. The first column gives the *nien-hao*, year, its cyclical designation and the Western year. Since the Chinese year usually ran over into the next solar year, the Western date usually indicates both solar years. The days are enumerated in order. The first day of each month in the Western calendar is in boldface type giving that month's number from 1 to 9. For October through December, the letters O, N, or D are used. The date of the first day of any lunar month is the first day appearing in column 1 (of "Order of Days") next to the number of that lunar month. The date of the second day is in column 2 and so on. The identification of days in a cyclical designation employs a method different from the other concordances. The last two columns on each page are labeled "week" and "cycle". The first helps identify the day of the week. Each number in the column "cycle" represents the cyclic designation of the first day of the lunar month in that row, minus one. One must utilize the table on p.438 to make a calculation.

Cheng Ho-sheng 鄭鶴聲, *Chin-shih Chung-hsi shih-jih tui-chao piao* 近世中西史日對照表 (Nanking, 1936; Taipei, 1966 reprint; Beijing, 1985)

This work gives the cycles of all years and days from 1516, the arrival of Rafael Perestello in China, to 1941, for easy conversion to Western dates and the reverse. There is a special calendar for the Taiping kingdom (1851-1865).

Fang Shih-ming 方侍名 and Fang Hsiao-fen 方小芬, comp. *Chung-kuo shih li-jih ho Chung-hsi li jih tui-chao piao* 中國史曆日和中西曆日對照表 (Shanghai, 1987)

This work handles four years per page. It is divided into two major calculating tables, one for the period B.C. 841—B.C. 1 and another for 1 A.D.—1949. It also contains appendices for the calendars of the Shang (Yin) and Chou dynasties, a conversion table for the period 1949-2000, and an index of year titles.

K. Hazelton, *A Synochronic Chinese-Western Daily Calendar 1341—1661 A.D.* (Minneapolis, 1984; revised, 1985).

Provides the equivalent Chinese and Western designation of every day from 1341 to 1661 A.D. Uses *pinyin* system for the romanization of Chinese terms. Information identifying the year is found along the top line of each page. The top line gives, from left to right, the pair of Western years spanned by the Chinese year, the sexagenary year designation, the page number, the alternate *nien-hao* and year, if any, in parentheses, and the standard *nien-hao* and year abutting the right margin. As a convenience, the sequence of stems and branches are tabulated in the right margin in their Chinese character form, in *pinyin* and in Wade-Giles.

CHAPTER ELEVEN

TRANSLATIONS

Introduction

In the course of time, there have been thousands of works either in classical or modern Chinese translated into Western languages. These works include many genres, from classical poetry and novels written in old *pai-hua* to modern day newspaper articles and radio broadcast transcriptions. These translations serve a useful purpose: they allow China scholars a quick "update" about what is happening in China at any given moment. For example, the student of classical literature may just want to know what was the "official party line" toward a particular classical writer during one of the major political campaigns. By consulting the translation series in the periodical *China Quarterly,* "Quarterly Chronicle and Documentation," s/he may find a translation of a speech, editorial, or communique where the writer's name may have been referred to.

When making a translation of a famous classical text, it is always practical to have at hand a good rendition by someone else to compare one's own work with that of another. Nowadays, it is widely recognized that the translations of such well-respected authorities as James Legge for the Classics, and Arthur Waley for Chinese literature, are not always the most correct rendering.[1] There are better translations to many of the works which these two authors made, and one may easily improve own's own rendition by consulting other translations.

Students of modern Chinese political culture regularly consult a variety of translated sources which bring rapidly changing trends and events into clearer focus.[2] According to one account, the

---

[1] No doubt the most prolific translator of Chinese in this century is the American scholar Burton Watson—the list of his published volumes is long, and it includes renderings of philosophical, historical, and poetic texts spanning nearly 2 millennia of Chinese literary history.

[2] It has only been since the decade of the 1980s that the Chinese press, both in its translated and untranslated forms, has been a good source of information. Until then a great number of subjects had been excluded from extensive treatment. These include such matters as natural disasters and the extent of starvation and malnutrition during 1960-62; or the extent of terror and death during the Cultural Revolution.

percentage of Chinese-language publications available in English translation probably was at a low ebb during two particular periods: first, from 1949 to 1954 when Western translation services were first being formed, and second, from 1978 to the present during which time the number of newspapers, journals, and books published in China has risen so dramatically that translation services were unable to keep up with the proliferating amount of information.[3]

Thus, one may find that not only is coverage in the original sources to be uneven, but also that other sources of information, such as provincial newspapers, ministerial journals, and book-length monographs are not extensively translated. Moreover, the sponsors of these translation services, the governments of China, America, or Great Britain finance these projects for their own immediate interests, which do not necessarily agree with the objectives of historians, and other China experts. The following guide is a brief presentation of some of the most obvious translations for the study of China.

---

[3] *Cambridge History of China* volume XIV (Cambridge, 1987), p.559.

References—Guide to Translations

Guide to Translations 316
  Chinese Literature 316
  Scientific Publications 317
  Current Affairs in the PRC 318
  Official Documents 320

GUIDE TO TRANSLATIONS

This guide should direct one to the most obvious sources for translations from either classic and/or modern Chinese into Western languages. This list is by no means comprehensive, but provides what is easily available for literature, "scientific publications" in history, philosophy, and the social sciences, current affairs in the PRC, and official documents.

There are also noteworthy Japanese sinological publications that are translated into English. For periodicals, one thinks of *Acta Asiatica*, which concentrates on history, but sometimes also carries translations of leading Japanese literary experts, and *Memoirs of the Research Department of the Tôyô Bunko (Tokyo)*, now in its fifty-second year of issue. Reference has already been made to the excellent translations by Joshua Fogel in chapter II 'Chinese Bibliography— 'Periodical Bibliographies for Chinese History'. Several years ago, Linda Grove and Christian Daniels edited a collection *State and Society in China: Japanese Perspectives on Ming-Qing Social and Economic History* (Tokyo, 1984), which is a translation of journal articles by leading "Tokyo school" historians.

Literature

To find what is available in translation up to 1986 for traditional literature, one should first turn to the indexes in Nienhauser, *The Indiana Companion to Traditional Chinese Literature*, and "update" information here, with the listing in Robert Hegel, "Traditional Chinese Fiction: The State of the Field", *Journal of Asian Studies* 53 (1994): 394-426, pp.423-25 'Translations'.

For translations of contemporary literature, including anthologies of translations and those of individual authors, one should refer to the list in Louie and Edwards, *Bibliography of English Translations...Contemporary Chinese Fiction* [listed in chapter II 'Bibliographies in Western Languages—Literature']; or Helmut Martin and Jeffrey Kinkley, eds., *Modern Chinese Writers: Self Portrayals* (Armonk, New York, 1992), pp. 347-370. Compare Leo Ou-fan Lee, "Contemporary Chinese Literature in Translation: A Review Article," *Journal of Asian Studies* 44 (1985):561-567. Leading journals on Chinese literature such as CLEAR or *Modern Chinese Literature* also list the publication information of new translations for premodern and modern literature, respectively.

Chinese Literature (Beijing, 1951 to present).
   Quarterly. Formerly, monthly journal of translations of 'acceptable' Chinese literature. Indexed annually in the winter issue. There are two cumulative indexes. See Donald Gibbs, *Subject and Author Index to Chinese Literature Monthly (1951-1976)* (New Haven, 1978); Hans J. Hinrup, *An Index to 'Chinese Literature' 1951-1976* (London, 1978).

Renditions (Hong Kong, 1973 to present).
   Bi-yearly journal with translations from both classical and modern Chinese. This journal is more scholarly than *Chinese Literature*. Often one issue is devoted to a single theme, such as "historiography and Chinese literature". There is an index for issues 1 through 16.

Wen Yuan: Studies in Language, Literature, and Culture (Beijing, since 1988)
   Bi-yearly journal with both analyses and translations of both Chinese and Western language. Gives scholarly insight into current translation trends in the PRC.

Scientific Publications

Social Sciences in China (Beijing, quarterly, since 1980).
   Despite the title, this journal publishes translations of history, literary, philosophical works, as well as general policy statements. The quality of the translations varies, with earlier issues not as good as later ones.

History and Philosophy
Chinese Studies in History (Seattle, 1978 to present).
Chinese Studies in Philosophy (Seattle, 1977 to present).
   Before these dates, these two translation journals appeared as one journal, entitled *Chinese Studies in History and Philosophy* (1967-1977).

Social Sciences
Chinese Studies in Sociology and Anthropology (Seattle, 1968 to present).
Chinese Economic Studies (Seattle, 1978 to present).

Chinese Education (Seattle, 1978 to present).
Chinese Law and Government (Seattle, 1968 to present).
 The translations in all the above named journals come from Chinese newspapers, radio broadcasts, and journals, and are published quarterly by M.E. Sharpe, Inc.. They are usually not 'extensive', and are useful for 'basic' information, reference to a particular document, or a particular party congress. Since none of the translations in these series give characters, it is necessary to have the original Chinese document in order to make a 'serious' translation. In some instances, the English translations themselves are not of the highest quality. But in general, these series are useful for those students who wish to take a 'quick look' at what is available about a particular theme. Sometimes, a whole issue in any of the series is devoted to special topics. For example, *Chinese Law and Government* has focused separate issues on the Lin Piao affair, the Party constitution, personnel management, and so on.

Current Affairs in the PRC

Much of what appears in the 'official' Chinese press is translated into a number of series, and offers the 'China watcher' a certain amount of 'basic facts' about current happenings. These include the following series:

Survey of the China Mainland Press [since 1973, also known as *Survey of People's Republic China Press*, 1950-1979].
Current Background (1950-1977).
Extracts of China Mainland Magazines (1953-1977).
 [From 1961-1972, known as *Selection of China Mainland Magazines*, and since 1973, known as *Selection of People's Republic of China Magazines*].
 Together these three series provide a complete background history of China's development from 1949-1979. There are indices to each of these journals, which were issued four times a year (hence, each series is indexed every three months). The indices here do not refer to a 'supplementary' series, which carried a low-level security classification and was released to the general public only later.

Since 1977, these three series have been superseded by:

Daily Report (since 1977; first issued in 1970).
Selections are based on newspapers, radio broadcasts, and journals. It is heavily orientated toward foreign news. There are indexes for printed and microfiche versions.

China Report (since 1980; appeared several times a week)
This translation series issued by the Joint Publication Research Service (JPRS) appeared in six parts, until 1987: (1) *Agriculture*; (2) *Economic Affairs*; (3) *Political, Sociological, and Military Affairs* (especially good on matters relating to education and youth); (4) *Science and Technology*; (5) *Plant and Installation Data*; (6) *Red Flag*. Since 1987, the series became divided into three parts: (1) *Report China*; (2) *China/Red Flag*; (3) *China/State Council Bulletin*. The translations here are from national, provincial, and local newspapers, from 'scientific' as well as 'ordinary' journals, and radio broadcasts. The PRC Government bulletin *Ch'iu shih* (Seeking Truth) [see chapter III Journals and Newspapers—'A Partial Listing of Important Current Chinese Journals' has also been translated into the *China Report* series. There are special issues with entire translations from important documents, such as economic reports. Unfortunately, there is no convenient and continuous index for the entire series, but only indices for specific periods.[4]

Summary of World Broadcasts Part III: Far East Daily, Far East Weekly (British Broadcasting Company, since 1949).
The *Daily* and the *Weekly* are both translations and summaries of news from newspapers, journals, and radio broadcasts.

The Weekly Economic Report (British Broadcasting Company, since 1949)
Many important economic reports are summarized. These translations form the background to the yearly publication in the *China Quarterly*, called "Quarterly Chronicle and Documentation" which contains a systematic index of everything in the *Weekly Economic Report* of that year.

---

[4] See Richard Sorich, ed., *Contemporary China: A Bibliography of Reports on China Published by the Joint Publications Research Service* (New York, 1961); Theodore Kyriak, ed., *Bibliography-index to US JPRS research translations*, vols.1-8 (Annapolis, Md., 1962). These have been updated by *Bibliography and Index to the United States Joint Publication (JPRS translations)* (New York, 1974).

Xinhua News Agency (since 1949).
   Also known as *New China News Agency* or the *Hsin Hua News Agency*. China's "official" selection of news by the "official" news agency, Hsin-hua. Issues daily English language compilation of dispatches.

Official Documents

W.T. DeBary, et.al., eds., *Sources of Chinese Tradition*
(New York, 1960), 2 vols. [updated version expected in 1995]
   This work contains translations for all types of genres, from classical literature to 20th century political pronouncements. Thus, one will find here translations of government pronouncements from early on until the 20th mid-century.

Ssu-yü Teng and John King Fairbank, eds., *China's Response to the West* (Cambridge, Mass., 1954).
   A classic collection of documents that form the basis for Fairbank's once highly influential thesis that "China failed to respond to the encroachments of the West, thereby insuring the destruction of its own 'old-style' society."

Milton J.T. Shieh, *The Kuomintang: Selected Historical Documents, 1894-1949* (Collegeville, Minn., 1970).

Hyobom Pak, *Documents of the Chinese Communist Party, 1927-1930* (Hong Kong, 1971).

C. Martin Wilbur and Julie Lien-ying How, eds., *Documents on Communism, Nationalism, and Soviet Advisers in China, 1918-1927: Papers seized in the 1927 Peking raid* (New York, 1956).

For the PRC, a number of special compilations on limited topics provided translations on special topics.

Education:
Stewart Fraser, *Chinese Communist Education: Records of the First Decade* (Nashville, Tenn., 1965).

Stewart Fraser, ed., *Education and Communism in China: An Anthology of Commentary* (Hong Kong, 1969).

Peter J. Seybolt, *Revolutionary Education in China: Documents and Commentary* (White Plains, New York, 1973).

Agricultural Policy:
Chao Kuo-chün, *Agrarian Policies of Mainland China: A Documentary Study, 1949-1956* (Cambridge, Mass., 1957).

Economic Organization:
Chao Kuo-chün, *Economic Planning and Organization in Mainland China: A Documentary Study, 1949-1957* (Cambridge, Mass., 1959), 2 vols.

Military Directives:
Ying-mao Kau, ed., *The People's Liberation Army and China's Nationbuilding* (White Plains, New York, 1973).

Ying-mao Kau, ed., *The Political Work System of the Chinese Communist Military* (Providence, Rhode Island, 1971).

Sino-American Relations:
Roderick MacFarquhar, *Sino-American Relations, 1949-1971* (New York, 1972).

Gene Hsiao and Michael Witunski, *Sino-American Normalization and its Policy Implications* (New York, 1983).

Sino-Soviet Dispute:
G.F. Hudson, Richard Lowenthal, and Roderick MacFarquhar, *The Sino-Soviet Dispute* (New York, 1961).

David Floyd, ed., *Mao against Khrushchev* (New York, 1963).

Alexander Dallin, ed., *Diversity in International Communism: A Documentary Record 1961-1965* (New York, 1962).

John Gittings, ed., *Survey of the Sino-Soviet Dispute: A Commentary and Extracts from the Recent Polemics 1963-1967* (London, 1968).

William Griffith, *Albania and the Sino-Soviet Rift* (Cambridge, Mass., 1963).

William Griffith, *The Sino-Soviet Rift* (Cambridge, Mass., 1964).

William Griffith, *Sino-Soviet Relations, 1964-1965* (Cambridge, Mass., 1967).

Major Policy Pronouncements:
Robert R. Bowie and John K. Fairbank, eds., *Communist China, 1955-1959: Policy documents with analysis* (Cambridge, Mass., 1962).

Union Research Institute (URI), *CCP Documents of the Great Proletarian Cultural Revolution, 1966-1967* (Hong Kong, 1968).

URI, *Documents of the Chinese Communist Party Central Committee* (Hong Kong, 1971).

Leadership Doctrine:
John W. Lewis, *Major Doctrines of Communist China* (New York, 1974).

Some 800 important documents, published since 1949, may be found in the following two collections:
H.C. Hinton, ed., *The People's Republic of China, 1949-1979: A Documentary Survey* (Wilmington, 1980), five parts.

H.C. Hinton, ed., *The People's Republic of China, 1979-1984: A Documentary Survey* (Wilmington, 1986), two parts.

APPENDICES

Ch'iu's Classification System for the East Asian Library
  Table of Main Classes 324
Works in the Harvard-Yenching Index Series and Centre-
  Franco-chinois d'Études sinologiques 327
The Twenty-four Festivals and their Concordances with the
  Seasons 336

CH'IU'S CLASSIFICATION SCHEME FOR THE EAST ASIAN LIBRARY

TABLE OF MAIN CLASSES

100– 999	CHINESE CLASSICS
1000–1999	PHILOSOPHY AND RELIGION
2000–3999	HISTORICAL SCIENCES
4000–4999	SOCIAL SCIENCES
5000–5999	LANGUAGE AND LITERATURE
6000–6999	FINE AND RECREATIVE ARTS
7000–7999	NATURAL SCIENCES
8000–8999	AGRICULTURE AND TECHNOLOGY
9000–9999	GENERALIA AND BIBLIOGRAPHY

SUMMARY TABLE OF MAIN CLASSES

100– 999	**CHINESE CLASSICS**
200– 299	I CHING (BOOK OF CHANGES)
300– 399	SHU CHING (BOOK OF DOCUMENTS)
400– 499	SHIH CHING (BOOK OF POETRY)
500– 599	SAN LI (RITUALS)
680– 799	CH'UN CH'IU (SPRING AND AUTUMN ANNALS)
800– 849	HSIAO CHING (BOOK OF FILIAL PIETY)
850– 999	SSU CHING (THE FOUR BOOKS)
1000–1999	**PHILOSOPHY AND RELIGION**
1000–1008	PHILOSOPHY IN GENERAL
1009–1499	ORIENTAL PHILOSOPHY
1010–1429	CHINESE PHILOSOPHY
1430–1469	JAPANESE PHILOSOPHY
1470–1499	HINDU PHILOSOPHY
1500–1539	OCCIDENTAL PHILOSOPHY
1540–1569	PHILOSOPHICAL PROBLEMS AND SYSTEMS
1570–1609	LOGIC
1610–1649	METAPHYSICS
1650–1699	ETHICS
1700–1729	RELIGION IN GENERAL
1730–1738	MYTHOLOGY
1739–1749	OCCULTISM, NUMEROLOGY
1750–1779	HISTORY OF RELIGONS
1780–1799	CHINESE STATE CULTS
1800–1919	BUDDHISM
1920–1939	TAOISM
1940–1974	SHINTOISM
1974–1987	CHRISTIANITY

1988–1999	OTHER RELIGIONS
2000–3999	**HISTORICAL SCIENCES**
2000–2199	ARCHAEOLOGY
2000–2049	GENERAL ARCHAEOLOGY OF VARIOUS COUNTRIES
2050–2194	ASIA
2060–2159	CHINA
2160–2184	JAPAN
2185–2187	KOREA
2200–2249	ETHNOLOGY, ETHNOGRAPHY
2250–2256	GENEALOGY AND HERALDRY
2257–2299	BIOGRAPHY
2300–3999	HISTORY AND GEOGRAPHY
2450–3299	CHINA
3300–3469	JAPAN
3470–3479	TAIWAN
3480–3499	KOREA
4000–4999	**SOCIAL SCIENCES**
4000–4019	GENERAL
4020–4099	STATISTICS
4100–4299	Sociology
4300–4599	ECONOMICS
4600–4899	POLITICS AND LAW
4900–4999	EDUCATION
5000–5999	**LANGUAGE AND LITERATURE**
5000–5039	LINGUISTICS IN GENERAL, COMPARATIV PHILOLOGY
5040–5059	LITERATURE IN GENERAL, COMPARATIVE LITERATURE
5060–5199	CHINESE LANGUAGES
5200–5799	CHINESE LITERATURE
5800–5809	MINOR LANGUAGES IN CHINA
5810–5859	JAPANESE LANGUAGE
5860–5969	JAPANESE LITERATURE
5970–5972	MINOR LANGUAGES IN JAPAN
5973	KOREAN LANGUAGE AND LITERATURE
6000–6999	**FINE AND RECREATIVE ARTS**
6070–6139	CHINESE CALLIGRAPHY AND PAINTING
6140–6289	Japanese CALLIGRAPHY AND PAINTING
6290–6299	MATERIALS AND INSTRUMENTS
6300–6349	WESTERN PAINTING
6350–6399	ENGRAVINGS, PRINTS, PHOTOGRAPHY
6400–6599	SCULPTURE, ARCHITECTURE

6600–6799   INDUSTRIAL ARTS, MUSIC
6800–6999   AMUSEMENTS AND GAMES, PHYSICAL TRAINING AND
             SPORTS
7000–7999   NATURAL SCIENCES
8000–8999   AGRICULTURE AND TECHNOLOGY
9000–9999   GENERALIA AND BIBLIOGRAPHY
  9100–9163   CHINESE GENERAL SERIES (TS'UNG-SHU), CHINESE
               INDIVIDUAL POLYGRAPHIC BOOKS
  9164–9189   JAPANESE GENERAL SERIES (SOSHO), JAPANESE
               INDIVIDUAL POLYGRAPHIC BOOKS
  9400–9699   BIBLIOGRAPHY
  9520–9639   CHINESE BIBLIOGRAPHIES
  9640–9684   JAPANESE BIBLIOGRAPHIES
  9685–9694   KOREAN BIBLIOGRAPHIES
  9700–9929   LIBRARIANSHIP (LIBRARY SCIENCE)
  9930–9999   JOURNALISM, NEWSPAPERS

INDEXES

Note: The original Harvard-Yenching Institute Sinological Index Series has been reprinted several times. The series was first reprinted by the Chinese Materials and Research Aids, Inc. for the Association for Asian Studies, in Taipei, 1965-1969. Indexes 9, 34, and 35 and Supplements 9 and 21 were reprinted by the Japan Council for East Asian Studies, Toyo Bunko; Index 40 and Supplement 20 were reprinted by the Harvard University Press.

1. *Shuo-yüan yin-te* 說苑引得
(Index to the *Shuo-yüan*)

2. *Po-hu t'ung yin-te* 白虎通引得
(Index to the *Po-hu t'ung*)

3. *K'ao-ku chih-i yin-te* 考古質疑引得
(Index to the *K'ao-ku chih-i*)

4. *Li-tai t'ung hsing-ming lu yin-te* 歷代同姓名錄引得
(Index to the *Li-tai t'ung hsing-ming lu*)

5. *Ts'ui Tung-pi i-shu yin-te* 崔東壁遺書引得
(Index to the *Ts'ui Tung-pi i-shu*)

6. *I-li yin-te fu Cheng chu chi Chia shu yin-shu yin-te* 儀禮引得附鄭注及賈疏引書引得 (Index to the *I-li* and the titles quoted in the commentaries by Cheng [Hsüan] and Chia [Kung-yen])

7. *Ssu-k'u ch'üan-shu tsung-mu chi Wei-shou shu-mu yin-te* 四庫全書總目集未收書目引得 (Index to the *Ssu-k'u ch'üan-shu tsung-mu* and the *Wei-shou shu-mu*)

8. *Ch'üan Shang-ku San-tai Ch'in Han San-kuo Liu-ch'ao wen tso-che yin-te* 全上古三代秦漢三國六朝文作者引得
(Index to the Authors in the *Ch'üan Shang-ku San-tai Ch'in Han San-kuo Liu-ch'ao wen*)

9 *San-shih-san chung Ch'ing-tai chuan-chi tsung-ho yin-te* 三十三種清代傳記綜合引得
(Combined Indices to the Thirty-three Collections of Ch'ing dynasty Biographies)

10. *I-wen chih erh-shih chung tsung-ho yin-te* 藝文志二十種綜合引得
(Combined Indices to the Twenty Collections of *I-wen chih*) 4 Vols.

11. *Fo-tsang tzu-mu yin-te* 佛藏子目引得
(Combined Indices to the Authors and Titles of Books and Chapters in Four Collections of Buddhist Literature) 3 Vols.

12. *Shih-shuo hsin-yü yin-te fu Liu chu yin-shu yin-te* 世說新語引得附劉注引書引得 (Index to the *Shih-shuo hsin-yü* and the Titles Quoted in the Commentary by Liu [Hsiao-piao])

13. *Jung-chai sui-pi wu-chi tsung-ho yin-te* 容齋隨筆五集綜合引得
(Combined Indices to the Five Collections of Miscellaneous Notes by Hung Mai)

14. *Su shih yen-i yin-te* 蘇氏演義引得
(Index to the *Su Shih yen-i*)

15. *T'ai-p'ing kuang-chi p'ien-mu chi yin-shu yin-te* 太平廣記篇目及引書引得
(Index to the *T'ai-p'ing kuang-chi* Catalogue and to the Titles quoted therein)

16. *Hsin T'ang shu tsai-hsiang shih-hsi piao yin-te* 新唐書宰相世系表引得
(Index to the Genealogical Tables of the Families of Chief Ministers in the *Hsin T'ang shu*)

17. *Shui-ching chu yin-te* 水經注引得
(Index to the *Shui-ching* and Commentary) 2 vols.

18. *T'ang shih chi-shih chu-che yin-te* 唐詩紀事著者引得
(Index to the Authors in the *T'ang shih chi-shih*)

19. *Sung shih chi-shih chu-che yin-te* 宋詩紀事著者引得
(Index to the Authors in the *Sung shih chi-shih*)

20. *Yüan shih chi-shih chu-che yin-te* 元詩紀事著者引得
(Index to the Authors in the *Yüan shih chi-shih*)

21. *Ch'ing-tai shu-hua-chia tzu-hao yin-te* 清代書畫家字號引得
(Index to the Fancy Names of Calligraphers and Painters of the Ch'ing Dynasty)

22. *K'an-wu yin-te* 刊誤引得
(Index to the *K'an-wu* [the Rectification of Errors of Li Fou])

23. *T'ai-p'ing yü-lan yin-te* 太平御覽引得
(Index to the *T'ai-p'ing yü-lan*)

24. *Pa-shih-chiu chung Ming-tai chuan-chi tsung-ho yin-te* 八十九種明代
傳記綜合引得 (Combined Indices to Eighty-nine Collections of
Ming Dynasty Biographies)

25. *Tao-tsang tzu-mu yin-te* 道藏子目引得
(Combined Indices to the Authors and Titles of Books in Two
Collections of Taoist Literature)

26. *Wen Hsüan chu yin-shu yin-te* 文選注引書引得
(Index to the Titles Quoted in the Commentary to *Wen Hsüan*)

27. *Li-chi yin-te* 禮記引得
(Index to the *Li-chi*)

28. *Ts'ang shu chi-shih shih yin-te* 藏書記事詩引得
(Index to the Poetical History of Book Collecting)

29. *Ch'un-ch'iu ching chuan chu-shu yin-shu yin-te* 春秋經傳注疏引書引
得 (Combined Indices to the Titles Quoted in the Commentaries
on Ch'un-ch'iu, Kung-yang, Ku-liang, and Tso-chuan)

30. *Li-chi chu-shu yin-shu yin-te* 禮記注疏引書引得
(Index to the Titles Quoted in the Commentaries on the *Li Chi*)

31. *Mao shih chu-shu yin-shu yin-te* 毛詩注疏引書引得
(Index to the Titles Quoted in the Commentaries on the *Shih
ching*)

32. *Shih-huo chih shih-wu chung tsung-ho yin-te* 食貨志十五種綜合引得
(Combined Indices to the Economic Sections of the Fifteen
Standard Histories)

33. *San-kuo chih chi P'ei chu tsung-ho yin-te* 三國志及裴注綜合引得
(Combined Indices to the *San-kuo chih* and the Commentary by
P'ei [Sung-chih])

34. *Ssu-shih-ch'i chung Sung-tai chuan-chi tsung-ho yin-te* 四十七種宋代傳記綜合引得 (Combined Indices to Forty-seven Collections of Sung Dynasty Biographies)

35. *Liao Chin Yüan chuan-chi san-shih chung tsung-ho yin-te* 遼金元傳記三十種總和引得 (Combined Indices to Thirty Collections of Liao, Chin, and Yüan Dynasty Biographies)

36. *Han shu chi pu-chu tsung-ho yin-te* 漢書及補助綜合引得 (Combined Indices to the *Han Shu* and the Notes of Yen Shih-ku and Wang Hsien-ch'ien)

37. *Chou li yin-te fu chu-shu yin-shu yin-te* 周禮引得附注疏引書引得 (Index to the *Chou Li* and to the Titles Quoted in the Commentaries)

38. *Erh ya chu-shu yin-shu yin-te* 爾雅注疏引書引得 (Index to the Titles Quoted in the Commentaries on the *Erh Ya*)

39. *Ch'üan Han San-kuo Chin Nan-pei ch'ao shih tso-che yin-te* 全漢三國晉南北朝詩作者引得 (Index to the Authors in the *Ch'üan Han San-kuo Chin Nan-pei-ch'ao shih*)

40. *Shih-chi chi chu-shih tsung-ho yin-te* 史記及注釋綜合引得 (Combined Indices to the *Shih chi* and the Notes of P'ei Yin, Ssu-ma Cheng, Chang Shou-chieh, and Takigawa Kametaro)

41. *Hou Han-shu chi chu-shih tsung-ho yin-te* 後漢書及注釋綜合引得 (Combined Indices to the *Hou Han-shu* and the Notes of Liu Chao and Li Hsien)

SUPPLEMENTS

1. *Tu shih nien-piao fu yin-te* 讀史年表附引得
(Chinese Chronological Charts with Index)

2. *Chu-shih jan-i chiao-ting fu yin-te* 諸史然疑校訂附引得
(*Chu-shih jan-i* re-edited and indexed)

3. *Ming-tai ch'ih chuan shu k'ao fu yin-te* 明代敕撰書考附引得
(*Ming-tai ch'ih chuan shu k'ao* with Index)

4. *Yin-te shuo* 引得說
(On Indexing)

5. *Shao-yüan t'u-lu k'ao* 勺園圖錄考
(A Study of the Mi Garden)

6. *Jih-pen ch'i-k'an san-shih-pa chung chung-tung-fang-hsüeh lun-wen p'ien-mu fu yin-te* 日本期刊三十八種中東方學論文篇目附引得
(Index to the Bibliography of Orientological Contributions in Thirty-Eight Japanese Periodicals)

7. *Feng shih wen-chien chi chiao-cheng fu yin-te* 封氏聞見記校證附引得
(Miscellaneous Notes of Feng Yen, and Re-edited and Indexed by Chao Chen-hsin) 2 Vols.

8. *Ch'ing hua-chuan chi-i san-chung fu yin-te* 清畫傳輯佚三種附引得
(Index to Biographies of Ch'ing Dynasty Painters in Three Collections)

9. *Mao shih yin-te* 毛詩引得
(A Concordance to the *Shih ching*)

10. *Chou i yin-te* 周易引得
(A Concordance to the *I Ching*)

11. *Ch'un-ch'iu ching chuan yin-te* 春秋經傳引得（附標校經文全文）
(Combined Concordances to the *Ch'un-ch'iu, Kung-yang, Ku-liang, and Tso-chuan*) 4 Vols.

12. *Wan Yen chi shan-ts'un fu yin-te* 琬琰集珊存附引得
(Index to the abridged *Wan Yen chi*)

13. *I-pai ch'i-shih-wu chung Jih-pen ch'i-k'an chung-tung-fang-hsüeh lun-wen p'ien-mu fu yin-te* 一百七十五種日本期刊中東方學論文篇目附引得
(Index to a Bibliography of Orientological Contributions in One Hundred and Seventy-five Japanese Periodicals)

14. *Tu shih yin-te* 杜詩引得
(A Concordance to the Poems of Tu Fu) 3 Vols.

15. *Liu i chih i lu mu-lu fu yin-te* 六藝之一錄目錄附引得
(An Index to the Table of Contents in the *Liu i chih i lu*)

16. *Lun-yü yin-te* 論語引得（附標校經文）
(A Concordance to *Lun-yü*)

17. *Meng-tzu yin-te* 孟子引得（附標校經文）
(A Concordance to *Meng-tzu*)

18. *Erh-ya yin-te* 爾雅引得
(A Concordance to *Erh-ya*)

19. *Tseng chiao Ch'ing-ch'ao chin-shih t'i-ming pei-lu fu yin-te* 增校清朝進士題名碑錄附引得 (Index to the Revised Listing of Steles of Ch'ing dynasty *chin-shih* Candidates)

20. *Chuang-tzu yin-te* 莊子引得
(A Concordance to *Chuang-tzu*)

21. *Mo-tzu yin-te* 墨子引得
(A Concordance to *Mo-tzu*)

22. *Hsün-tzu yin-te* 荀子引得
(A Concordance to *Hsün-tzu*)

23. *Hsiao-ching yin-te* 孝經引得
(A Concordance to the *Hsiao-ching*)

CENTRE FRANCO-CHINOIS D'ETUDES
SINOLOGIQUES

1. *Lun heng t'ung-chien* 論衡通檢
(Index to the *Lun heng*)

2. *Lü-shih ch'un-ch'iu t'ung-chien* 呂氏春秋通檢
(Index to the *Lü-shih ch'un-ch'iu*)

3. *Feng-su t'ung-i fu t'ung-chien* 風俗通義附通檢
(Appendix and Index to the *Feng-su t'ung-i*)

4. *Ch'un-ch'iu fan-lu t'ung-chien* 春秋繁露通檢
(Index to the *Ch'un-ch'iu fan-lu*)

5. *Huai-nan-tzu t'ung-chien* 淮南子通檢
(Index to the *Huai-nan-tzu*)

6. *Ch'ien-fu lun t'ung-chien* 潛夫論通檢
(Index to the *Ch'ien-fu lun*)

7. *Hsin hsü t'ung-chien* 新序通檢
(Index to the *Hsin hsü*)

8. *Shen chien t'ung-chien* 申鑒通檢
(Index to the *Shen chien*)

9. *Shan-hai-ching t'ung-chien* 山海經通檢
(Index to the *Shan-hai-ching*)

10. *Chan kuo ts'e t'ung-chien* 戰國策通檢
(Index to the *Chan-kuo ts'e*)

11. *Ta Chin kuo chih t'ung-chien* 大金國志通檢
(Index to the *Ta Chin kuo chih*)

12. *Ch'i tan kuo chih t'ung-chien* 契丹國志通檢
(Index to the *Ch'i tan kuo chih*)

13. *Ch'o-keng lu t'ung-chien* 輟耕錄通檢
(Index to the *Ch'o-keng lu*)

14. *Fang-yen chiao-chien fu t'ung-chien* 方言校箋附通檢
(Appendix and Index to the *Fang-yen*)

15. *Wen-hsin tiao-lung hsin-shu t'ung-chien* 文心雕龍新書通檢
(The *Wen hsin tiao-lung hsin shu* with Index)

The Twenty-four Festivals and their Concordances with the Seasons

ASTRONOMICAL MONTHS	子 tzu	丑 ch'ou	寅 yin	卯 mao	辰 ch'en	巳 ssu	午 wu	未 wei	申 shen	酉 yu	戌 hsü	亥 hai
Seasons	mid-winter	late winter	early spring	mid-spring	late spring	early summer	mid-summer	late summer	early autumn	mid-autumn	late autumn	early winter
THE FESTIVALS: 'Divisional' Chieh	Dec.7 Heavy snow	Jan.6 Little cold	Feb.5 Spring begins	Mar.5 Excited insects	Apr.5 Clear and bright	May 5 Summer begins	June 6 Grain in ear	July 7 Slight heat	Aug.7 Autumn begins	Sept.8 White dew	Oct.8 Cold dew	Nov.7 Winter begins
'Medial' Chung	Dec. 22 Winter Solstice	Jan. 21 Severe cold	Feb. 19 Rain water	Mar. 20 Vernal Equinox	Apr. 20 Grain rains	May 21 Grain fills	June 21 Summer Solstice	July 23 Great heat	Aug. 23 Limit of heat	Sept. 23 Autumnal Equinox	Oct. 23 Frost descends	Nov. 22 Little snow

INDEX OF PERSONS

[Note: Those names in **bold** refer to names with characters in the text]

Aarsleff, H.   6
Abel-Rémusat, J.P.   12, 13, 14, 32
Allen, Y. J.   107
Almond, P.   13
Amano Motonosuke   273
Amiot, J.   11
An Tso-chang   239
Anaximander   170
Andersen, P.   xiii
Andors, S.   255
Aoyama Sadao   155, 176
Arkush, D.   29
Arnold, J.   263
Aubin, F.   69
Ayers, W.   138
Aymer, C.   51

Balazs, E.   15, 40, 69
Baller, F.W.   217
Banno, M.   16, 92
Barrett, T.   11
Bartke, W.   151
Bartlett, B.   272, 275
Bauer, W.   71, 244
Beasley, W.   6, 137
Bennett, A.   107
Bernal, M.   7
Berry, M.   78
Berton, P.   2, 66, 127, 248, 264
Biggerstaff, K.   2, 30, 54, 58, 84, 245, 247, 266
Birrell, A.M.   235
Bismarck, O.   140
Bliancia, D.R.   224
Biot, E.   15
Boas, F.   29
Bøckman, H.   xiv
Bol, P.   69
Bold, J.   8
Boltz, J.   74
Bonner, J.   19
Boorman, H.   150
Bowie, R.R.   322
Boxer, C.   6
Boym, M.   7
Bridgman, E. C.   101
Britton, R.S.   106
Broadbent, K.   228

Brook, L.   270
Brook, T.   47, 191, 200
Brown, Y.Y.   54
Buck, J.L.   263

Cahill, J.   80, 162
Cannon, G.   6
Cartier, M.   xiii, 274
Carus, P.   31
Chan, Hok-lam   149
Chan, M.K.   71
Chan, Wing-tsit   72
Chang Ch'en-shih   152, 154, 155
Chang Ch'i-yün   257
Chang Chih-che   164, 176
Chang Chih-i   28
Chang Chih-tung   49, 50
Chang Chin-lang   296
Chang Chu-hung   93
Chang Chü-cheng   140, 141
Chung Chung-i   274
Chang Chung-shu   66
Chang Erh-t'ien   29
Chang Hai-p'eng   182
Chang Heng   171
Chang Hsi-chih   222
Chang Hsiao-chung   143
Chang Hsien-chung   137
Chang Hsüeh-ch'eng   58
Chang Kuo-kan   200
Chang Kwang-chih   81
Chang Lien-fang   142
Chang Ping-lin   22, 23, 24, 109, 126
Chang P'u   268
Chang Shou-chieh   331
Chang Shun-hui   283
Chang Tsai-p'u   174
Chang Tso-yao   241
Chang Tz'u-ch'en   222
Chang Wan-ch'i   155
Chang Wei-jen   100, 275
Chang Yü-shu   256
Ch'ang Pi-te   155, 157
Chao Chen-chi   168
Chao Chen-hsin   332
Chao Huan-kuang   233
Chao Kuo-chün   321
Chao Yuen-ren   27, 75

Chavannes, E. 14
Chen Cheng-hsiang 177
Chen, F. 291
Chen, Nai-ruenn 248
Chen Ta 29
Chen, William Y. 269
Ch'en Ch'ing-hao 90
Ch'en Chung-an 154
Ch'en I-lin 141
Ch'en Mei-kui 168
Ch'en Nai-ch'ien 145, 159
Ch'en Ping-ts'ai 206
Ch'en Shan-tz'u 221
Ch'en Sheng-hsi 92
Ch'en Shih-hsiang 140
Ch'en Shou-yi 8, 9
Ch'en Tai-sun 258
Ch'en Te-yün 145
Ch'en Yung-chen 221
Ch'en Yüan 29
Cheng Heng-hsiung 296
Cheng Ho-sheng 311
Cheng Hsüan 200, 328
Cheng, Lucie 79
Cheng, S. 71
Cheng Te-k'un 29
Ch'eng Chih-wei 223
Ch'eng Han-ch'ang 93
Chesnaux, J. 204
Chi Wen-shu 225
Chi Yün 48, 49
Chia Kung-yen 328
Chia Tan 171, 177
Chiang Hsiao-ta 280
Chiang Liang-fu 147
Chien, David 207
Ch'ien-lung Emperor 46, 178, 301
Ch'ien Mu 29
Ch'ien Nan-yang 28
Ch'ih Hsiu-yün 168
Chin Sheng-ho 174
Ch'in Shih Huang-ti 45
Ch'iu, Alfred K.M. 21, 31, 50
Ch'iu Shu-sen 165
Cho Ch'eng-yüan 164
Chou Chen-liang 58
Chou Chin 97, 232
Chou Chün-fu 160
Chou Hsün-ch'u 233
Chou Min-chih 24
Chou Tso-jen 29
Chou Yung-nien 52
Chou Yü-t'ung 20
Chow Tse-tung 71, 108
Christiansen, F. 51

Chu Hsi 7, 291
Chu I-hsüan 97
Chu I-tsun 57
Chu Pao-chiung 167
Chu Pao-liang 145
Chu Shih-chia 156, 197
Chu Ssu-pen 177
Chu Tung-jun 140, 141
Chung Hua 152
Ch'ü T'ung-tsu 29
Ch'üan Han-sheng 28
Clark, A. P. 150
Clark, P. 105
Clausen, S. 190
Cleyer, A. 7
Cohen, A. 73
Cohen, P. 35, 38, 39
Cole, J. 2, 59, 67, 197, 276, 287, 288
Coleman, P. 103
Conze, E. 74
Cordier, H. 11, 56, 61, 62, 101
Couling, S. 252
Couvreur, F.S. 218
Cowles, R.T. 230
Craig, A. 17
Crouch, A. 106
Crowe, A.P. 212

Dallin, A. 321
Daniels, C. 316
Davidson, J. 197
Dawson, R. 57
DeBary, W. Th. 72, 320
DeFrancis, J. 135
Demiéville, P. 14, 277
Dien, A. xiii
Digby, S. 101
Dirlik, A. 27, 28
Dolezélova-Velingerova, M. 76
Dooling, D.J. 225
Dudink, A. 80
Duiker, W. 26
Duus, P. 16
Duyvendak, J.J.L. 8
Dyer Ball, J. 246, 247, 252

Eberhard, W. v, 237
Eberstein, B. 76
Ebrey, P. xiii
Eckstein, A. 249
Edgren, S. 31, 58, 288
Edwards, L. 78, 316
Egan, S. 30, 56, 290
Egerod, S. xiii
Eichhorn, W. 61

Elisséeff, D. 8
Elisséeff, S. 31, 58
Elman, B. 5, 23, 49, 52, 58
Embree, A. 72
Enwall, J. 58
Eratosthenes 170
Evans, P. 32, 34, 35, 36
Evison, A. 212

Fairbank, J.K. 2, 16, 17, 25, 32, 33, 34, 35, 36, 37, 38, 39, 44, 66, 67, 92, 93, 105, 108, 126, 262, 320, 322
Fan Ch'eng-ta 190
Fang, A. 53
Fang Chao-ying 29, 149
Fang Hsiao-fen 311
Fang I 147
Fang K'o-li 98
Fang Shih-ming 311
Farquhar, D. 239
Fei Hsiao-t'ung 28, 29
Feifel, E. 77
Feng Erh-k'ang 89
Feng Hui-min 91
Feng Yu-lan 28
Feng Yüan-chün 28
Ferguson, J.C. 80, 248
Feuerwerker, A. 71
Floyd, D. 321
Fogel, J. 17, 22, 25, 42, 95, 316
Ford, H. 140
Foss, T. 178
Foster, R. 69
Fourmont, E. 8, 9, 12
François Premier 13
Franke, H. 15, 149
Franke, W. 69, 255
Frankel, H. 68
Fraser, S. 320
Frèches, J. 5
Freedman, M. 33, 36
Fryer, J. 31
Fu Chen-lun 200
Fu Ssu-nien 27
Fu, C. W. 72
Fu Hsüan-ts'ung 154
Fu I-ling 273
Fu Lang-yün 199
Fujii Hiroshi 274
Fujita Toyohachi 21
Furth, C. 22, 28

Gallagher, L. 6
Gandhi, M. 140
Garon, S. 40

Geelen, P.J.M. 184
Gernet, J. 17
Gibbs, D. 77, 127, 317
Giles, H. 147, 204
Giles, L. 19, 245
Gittings, J. 321
de Glemona, B.B. 12
Goehlert, R. 81
Golas, P. 81
Goldman, M. 35
Golius, I. 8, 23
Goodman, D. 113
Goodman, H. 7
Goodrich, L.C. 26, 149
Grafton, A. 7
Granet, M. 32, 33
Graves, M. 33, 34
Grieder, J. 24
Grier, P. 149
Griffith, W. 321, 322
de Groot, J.J.M. 15
Grove, L. 316
de Guignes, Fils 12, 29
de Guignes, J. 7, 12
Gulden, G.E. 26, 27
v. Gulik, R. H. 15
Gützlaff, K. 106
Guy, R. K. 46

Haft, L. 76, 77
Hahn, T. 69
du Halde, J.B. 10, 178
Hamaguchi Shigekuni 22
Han Yü 266
Hanayama, S. 14
Harbsmeier, C. xiii
Harding, H. 37
Hardy, G. 138
Hartwell, R. 79
Haswegawa, Y. 69
Hawkes, D. 9
Hazleton, K. 312
Hegel, G.F. 27
Hegel, R. 82, 316
Hervouet, Y. 68, 69
Heurnius, J. 8
Hightower, J. R. 76
Hinrup, H. 317
Hinton, H.C. 255, 322
Hiraoka Takeo 154, 173, 186
Hirth, F. 31
Hitler, A. 140
Ho Tung 160
Hoang, P. 305, 307, 310
Hodous, L. 236

Holt, J.   73
Hook, B.   253
Hoshi Ayao   240, 241
Hourani, A.   39
Hovell, Lin-cheung   80
How, J.L.Y.   320
Howard, R.   135, 138, 150
Hsia, C.T.   36
Hsiang Kuang-chung   222
Hsiao Ch'ao-jan   224
Hsiao Ch'i-ch'ing   149
Hsiao Chien-chung   185
Hsiao, G.   321
Hsiao Liang-lin   262
Hsieh P'ei-lin   167
Hsieh, W.   71
Hsieh Wei   167
Hsin I   223
Hsu Cho-yin   81
Hsu, David   131, 132
Hsu, Mei-ling   177
Hsü Hsia-k'o   171
Hsü, I.   24
Hsü I-sheng   262
Hsü Shen   202
Hsüeh Chung-shan   306, 311
Hsün Hsü   46, 50
Hu Hua   160
Hu K'o-hsien   163
Hu P'ing   288
Hu Shih   22, 23, 24, 25
Hu Tao-ching   287
Hu Wen-k'ai   164
Huang, A. [also known as Hoang, A.]   8
Huang Fu-ch'ing   20
Huang Han-chu   131, 132
Huang Hsi-yüan   233
Huang Jungui   51
Huang, Pei   272
Huang, Ray   141
Huang Wei   199
Huang Wen-hsing   206
Hucker, C.   66, 174, 239
Hudson, G.F.   321
Hummel, A.   19, 23, 24, 33, 34, 139, 150
Hung Chang-tai   23
Hung Hsiu-ch'üan   140
Hung Mai   328
Hung Yeh (Hung, William)   25, 30, 32, 289, 290
Hwang, S.C.   71

Ichiko, C.   93

Idema, W.L.   77
Intorcetta, P.   7
Israeli, R.   74
Ivanhoe, P.J.   291
Iwasaki Yanosuke   53
Iwasaki Yatarô   53

Jacobs, J. B.   81
James, C.V.   254
Jansen, M.   35
Jartoux, P.   10
Jen I-min   169
Jensen, L.   7
Johnson, M.   79
Johnson, W.   257
de Josselin de Jonge, P.E.   16
Ju, William C.   270
Juan Hsiang   263
Juan Yüan   19
Julien, S.   13, 14
Jung Keng   29
Jung T'ien-lin   93

Kamachi, N.   93
Kaneda Hiromitsu   165
K'ang-hsi Emperor   8, 47
K'ang Yu-wei   20, 25, 140
Kann, E.   247
Kao Hsiu-fang   169
Kao Ming-shih   40, 87
Kao Ying-mao   321
Kao Yü   256
Kaplan, F.M.   255
Karlgren, B.   218
Kennedy, G.   215
King, A.   28
King, F. H. H.   105
Kinkley, J.   316
Kinugawa Tsuyoshi   157
Kirchner, A.   7
Klein, D.   150
Koester, H.   275
Ku Chieh-kang   23, 25, 29, 140
Ku Hsüeh-chieh   234
Ku Tsu-yü   176
Ku Yen-wu   21, 171, 190
Kuang-hsü Emperor   304
Kuhn, D.   69
Kuhn, P.   47
Kuo Ch'ün-i   53
Kuo Mo-jo   27, 182
Kuo Tai-chün   38
Kuo, Warren   225
Kwee Swan-liat   73
Kyriak, T.   319

Lai Hsin-hsia 199
Lai, W.T. 235
Lancaster, L. 74
Lao-tzu 163, 289
Lattimore, O. 103, 247
Lau, D.C. 291
Laufer, B. 31
Lavely, W. 82
Lawrence, A. 72
Lee, James 82
Lee, Leo Ou-fan 316
Lee, S. 16
Lee, Wei-chin 81
Legge, J. 14, 106, 313
Lenin, V. 140
Leslie, D. 67, 167, 197, 204, 271, 278
Leung, Pak-wah 241
Levenson, J. 35, 36, 38
Lewis, J.W. 322
Li, Alice 80
Li Chao-lo 178
Li Chi 26
Li Chih-ting 58
Li Choh-ming 246
Li Fang 244
Li Fang-kuei 27
Li Han-chieh 185
Li Hsiao-lin 91
Li Hsien 331
Li Hsüeh-chih 275
Li Hung-chang 140
Li Jianjun 10
Li Kuang-ming 28
Li Kuang-t'ao 275
Li Kuo-hsiang 159
Li Meng-pei 223
Li Pao-yin 147
Li P'ao-kuang 51
Li, Peter 76
Li Sheng-wen 91
Li Shu-chi 162
Li Shu-huan 237
Li Ssu 203
Li T'ai-fen 200
Li Tien-yi 77
Li Tzu-ch'eng 137
Li Wan-chien 91
Li Wen-fang 186
Li Yen-p'ei 148
Li Yun-chen 77
Li Yung-p'u 94
Li Yü-min 152, 157
Liang Chan 53
Liang Ch'i-ch'ao 20, 24, 25, 48, 58, 108, 125, 140, 200, 271

Liang Fang-chung 262
Liang Kuei-chih 165
Liang Shih-ch'iu 211
Lieberman, F. 79
Lin Mei-jung 99
Lin Shu 108
Lin T'ieh-sen 87
Lin Yutang 106, 107, 211
Lindbeck, J. 36, 37
Littrup, L. xiv
Liu Chao 331
Liu Chien-tai 97
Liu Chin-tsao 247
Liu Cho-ying 233
Liu Chun-jo 136
Liu Hsiang 25, 45
Liu Hsin 25, 45, 46
Liu, K.C. 2, 66, 108, 262
Liu O 19
Liu Shang-heng 269
Liu Shih-p'ei 109
Liu Ts'un-yan 278
Liu Tzu-chien (James T.C. Liu) 29
Liu, William T. 265
Liu Wu-chi 9
Liu Yao-hua 145
Lo Chao-p'ing 198
Lo Chen-yü 18, 19, 21, 22, 26, 273
Lo Hui-min 271, 276, 277
Lo Hung-hsien 177
Lo, Karl 270
Lo Wei-kuo 288
Loewe, M. xiii, 2, 68, 201, 292
van der Loon, P. 278
Lopez, M. D. 78
Louie, K. 78, 316
Lowenthal, Richard 321
Löwenthal, Rudolph 101, 106
Lu Chün-ling 282
Lu Erh-k'uei 214
Lu Fa-yen 204
Lu Hsün 23, 24, 58
Lu Hsin-yüan 53
Lu Kuei-meng 266
Lu Tan-an 234, 235
Lü Shu-hsiang 221
Lucas, A. 75
Lung Ch'ien-an 234
Lundbaeck, K. 9
Lust, J. 61, 62

Ma Kuo-han 267
Ma, Lawrence J.C. 80, 172
Ma Wei-yi 94
Macartney, G. 11

MacFarquhar, R.   102, 321
Mackerras, C.   67, 204, 253, 271, 278
Mansvelt-Beck, B.J.   175
Mao, Nathan K.   76
Martin, H.   225, 316
Martin-Liao, T.   225
Martini, M.   7, 8
Marx, K.   16, 27, 140
Masao, M.   69
Mason, E.   35
Maspero, H.   14, 32, 33
Masson, M.   28
Masuda Kenji   165
Matheson, J.   104
Mathews, R.H.   217, 307
Mayers, W.F.   252
McCaughey, R.A.   31, 34
McDermott, J.P.   42
McGough, J.   29
McGrath, M.   69
McKnight, B.   281
McLeod, R.   292, 294
McMullen, D.   291
Metzger, T.   39
de Mendoza, G.   6
Miao Chuang   163
Miao Ch'üan-sun   49, 50
Mihashi Masanobu   164
Mill, J.S.   17
Milne, W.C.   106
Min Ku-ti   47
Minford, J.   9
Mirsky, J.   19
Miyakawa, H.   18
Miyamoto Katsu   164
Miyazaki Ichisada   41, 42
Mochizuki Shinkô   236
Mohr, W.   112
Moloughney, B.   137, 138, 140
Morohashi Tetsuji   54, 216, 218
Morrison, R.   104, 106
Mote, F.   36
Müller, F.M.   14
Mungello, D.   8
Murphey, R.   35, 36
Myers, R.   16, 38, 39

Naitô Konan   17, 18, 21, 22, 41
Naka Michiyo   17, 20
Nakano, M.   157
Napoleon (B.)   12, 140
Naquin, S.   xiii
Narramore, T.   113
Nathan, A.   2, 66, 262
Nee, V.   38

Needham, J.   78, 171, 177
Neu, S.   79
Nevadonsky, J.   80
Ni Tao-shan   275, 284
Nickum, J.   120
Nieh Ch'ung-ch'i   290, 291
Nien Keng-yao   284
Nienhauser, W.   36, 76, 77, 163, 232,
   296, 316
Niida Noboru   22, 41, 42
Nivison, D.   35, 58, 137
Norman, J.   229

Oda Tokuno   236
O'Neill, P.G.   241, 242
Oh, B.   178
Oksenberg, M.   68
Olbricht, P.   137
Otsuka Hidetaka   97
Ou-yang Chien   96

Pak Chi-won   47
Pak, Hyobom   320
Pan Ku   45, 46, 57, 138
P'an Kuang-tan   29
P'an Ming-shen   168
P'an Shu-kuang   296
Pannell, C. W.   172
Parker, B.   80
Parker, F.   80
Parsons, T.   35
Pas, J.   74
Peatty, M.   35
P'ei Hsiu   177
P'ei Yin   331
Péllisier, R.   54
Pelliot, P.   16, 31, 32
Perestello, Rafael   311
Perkins, D.   81
Pfister, L.F.   14
Phillippe d'Orléans   8
Polo, M.   57
de Premare, J.H.M.   9, 10
Pritchard, E.H.   62
Ptolemy   171
Pulleyblank, E.   xiii, 6, 137, 217

de Rachewitz, I.   149, 157
de Rada, M.   6
Radcliffe-Brown, A.R.   29
Raguin, Y.   237
Ranke, L.   16, 17
Rawski, E.   82
Reischauer, E.   17, 31, 40
Reiss, L.   17

Reynolds, D.   20, 21
Reynolds, F.   73
Ricci, M.   6, 22, 178
Richter, U.   23
Ridley, C.P.   225
Rohsenow, J.   222
Ronan, C.   178
Rowe, W.   25, 70
Roy, David   27
Rule, P.   7, 10
Ryckmans, P.   138

Saeki Tomi   41
Said, E.   11, 39
Sanae Yoshio   89
Scalipino, R.   35
Schafer, E.H. v, 6
Schipper, K.M.   278
Schmidt, M.   81
Schmutz, G.M.   25, 29
Schneider, L.   23
Schwab, R.   11
Schwartz, B.   35, 36, 39
Seidel, A.   74
Selya, R. M.   172
Semedo, A.   6
Serruys, P.   201
Seybolt, P.J.   321
Seymour, N. N.   162
Shambaugh, D.   37, 51
Shang Hai   241
Shearman, H.   105
Shen Kua   171
Shieh, M.   320
Shih Chou   203
Shimada Kenji   22, 24
Shiratori Kurakichi   17, 18, 40
Shirokogoroff, S.M.   26, 27
Shu, Austin C.W.   145, 244
Shu Chao-hu   34
Shu Hsin-ch'eng   215
Shue, V.   38
Shulman, F.   2
Silbergeld, J.   81
Silvestre de Sacy, A.I.   11, 28, 29
Simmonds, S.   101
Simon, W.   206
Sivin, N.   79, 81, 184
Skinner, G.W.   36, 71, 91
Slupski, Z.   76
Smith, R.J.   297
Sobin, J.M.   255
Soong, James C. Y.   136
Soothill, W.E.   236
Sorich, R.   319

Spence, J.   7
van der Sprenkel, O.B.   167
Ssu-ma Cheng   331
Ssu-ma Ch'ien   25, 138
Stackmann, U.   52
Stahl, H.   69
Staiger, B.   255
Standaert, N.   80
Stark, D.   38
Stein, A.   19
Stifler, S. R.   11
Strabo   170
Strachey, L.   141
Strong, J.   73
Sun, E.T. Zen   25, 135, 240
Sun Hsing-yen   267
Sun I-jang   19
Sun T'a   162
Sun Ts'ung-t'ien   53
Sun Yat-sen   126, 139
Sung Hsi   90
Sung T'ai-tsung   244
Sutô Yoshiyuki   41, 42
Suzuki Shun   22
Swann, N.L.   52, 175

Taga Akigorô   165
Tai Chen   21, 23, 291
Takigawa Kametaro   331
Tamai Zehaku   22
T'an Cheng-pi   163
T'an Ch'i-hsiang   181
Tanaguchi Fusao   122
Tanaka, S.   17, 40
T'ang Chien   271
T'ang Kao-tsu   301
T'ang T'ai-tsung   301
T'ang Yüan   135
Tanigawa Micho   42
T'ao Hsi-sheng   28
Tchang, M.   309
Telford, T. A.   168
Teng Ching-yüan   154
Teng Kuang-ming   28
Teng, S.Y.   2, 30, 54, 58, 70, 84, 165,
      245, 247, 266, 320
Thogersen, S.   190
Thompson, L.   31, 73
T'ien Tsung-yao   235
Ting Fu-pao   236
Ting, Lee-hsia Hsu   113
Ting Ning   144
Tôtô Akiyasu   216
Totok, W.   72
Trigault, N.   6

Tsai, Meishi 78
Ts'ai Kuan-lo 159
Ts'ai T'ing-kan 289
Ts'ai Yüan-pei 50
Tsang Li-ho 186
Ts'ao Chien-pin 274
Ts'ao Ch'ou-sheng 162
Ts'ao Hsien-cho 206
Ts'ao Ts'ao 243
Ts'ao Wan-ju 181
Tseng Chien-jung 145
Tseng I-fen 156
Tsien Tsuen-hsuin 45, 61
Tsou Chia-wei 275
Tsuboi Kumazô 20
Tsuda Sôkichi 40
Ts'ui Shu 25
Ts'ui Wen-yin 156
Tu Fu 290
Tu Lien-che 24
Tuan Te-sen 221
Tung Tse-yün 97
Tung Tso-pin 26, 30, 305, 307, 310
T'ung Shih-kang 291
Twitchett, D. 19, 22, 36, 67, 137, 184
Tz'u I 236

Umehara Kaoru 157

Vandermeersch, L. xiii
Vanderstappen, H.A. 79
Varo, F. 8, 9
Vermeer, E. 190, 264
Vogel, H.U. 80, 284

Wade, T.F. 204
Wagner, D. xiv
Wakeman, F. 81, 140
Walder, A. 38
Waley, A. 15, 313
Walf, K. 74
Walker, R. 101
Wang An-shih 140
Wang Chao-ming 199
Wang Chi-hsiang 161
Wang Chung-min 288
Wang Ch'ung-wu 28
Wang, David Kuo-wu 202
Wang Fen-sen 23
Wang Feng 82
Wang, Françoise 280
Wang Gungwu 67, 137, 139, 140, 141, 204, 271, 278
Wang Hsi-yin 272
Wang Hsiao-yen 200

Wang Hsien-ch'ien 331
Wang Hsüeh-ch'i 234
Wang I-jung 19
Wang, James C.F. 80
Wang Kuei-yüan 232
Wang Kuo-wei 18, 19, 21, 22, 26, 28
Wang Mang 25
Wang, May 157
Wang Nien-sun 24
Wang Pao-hsien 167, 281
Wang, Phyllis 127
Wang, Richard 91
Wang T'ao-fu 272
Wang Te-i 145, 156, 157, 158, 167, 197
Wang Tse-sang 28
Wang T'ung-i 228
Wang Yang-ming 291
Wang Yin-chih 24
Wang Yün-wu 270
Washington, G. 140
Watson, B. 313
Webb, J. 7, 8
Weber, M. 16, 32
Wei, Karen T. 79
Wei Lien-k'o 152
Wei Sung-shan 186
Wen I-to 29
Werner, E.T.C. 237
West, P. 29, 30
Whitaker, K.P.K. 20
White, T. 32
Wilbur, C.M. 320
Wilkinson, E. 2, 67, 175, 187, 188, 245, 268, 272, 282
Will, P.E. xiii, 187, 190
Williams, J. 179
Wilson, W. 140
Witunski, M. 321
Wixted, J.T. 17, 165
Wong Fook-luen 153
Wong Siu-kit 9
Wong Siulun 28
Wood, W. 104
Woodhead, H.C.W. 247
Wright, A. 10, 17, 137
Wright, H.M. 175
Wright, M. 36
Wong, Siu-kit 25
Wu Chih-ho 91
Wu, E. 2, 51, 66, 124, 248, 264
Wu Hai-lin 148
Wu Han 28
Wu Ju-yü 163
Wu Jung-kuang 19

Wu Pei-yi   140
Wu, Silas   272
Wu Ta-ch'eng   19
Wu T'ing-fang   112
Wu Wen-tsao   28
Wu Yuan-li   255
Wylie, A.   106, 269

Yamakoshi Toshihiro   240
Yamamoto, S.   16, 92
Yamane Yukio   87, 91, 93, 158, 283
Yang Chih-chiu   90
Yang Hai-ch'ing   280
Yang Hsiu-chün   98
Yang Hsiung   201
Yang Kui-chen   164
Yang Lien-sheng   28
Yang, Paul Fu-mien   75, 207, 221, 230
Yang Shou-ching   182
Yang, Teresa S.   75
Yang Tien-hsün   167
Yang T'ing-fu   145
Yang T'ung-fu   145
Yang, Winston L.Y.   75, 76
Yao Ching-an   156
Yao Ming-ta   58
Yee, E.   78
Yeh Hsien-en   274

Yeh Kuei-kang   232
Yeh Wen-hsin   25, 29, 58
Yen Ch'ung-nien   185
Yen Ch'ung-p'ing   262
Yen Shao-tang   166
Yen Shih-ku   331
Yoo, Y.   74
Yorke, A.   253
Young, J.   16
Yu, David C.   73
Yu, P.K.   109
Yuan, Florence C.   81
Yü Chien-hua   162
Yü Ju-yün   156
Yü Ping-ch'üan   134
Yü Tan-ch'u   20
Yü Ting-sun   266
Yü Ying-shih   30
Yü Yüeh   23
Yüan Hsüeh-liang   96
Yüan K'o   238
Yüan Shao-ying   164
Yüan Tung-li   61, 62

Zunz, O.   70
Zürcher, E.   80
Zurndorfer, H.   14, 39, 70, 273, 274

INDEX OF TITLES

[Note: The titles listed here refer only to books or journals, not journal articles. For those titles in **bold**, one may find the characters in the text. Journal and newspaper titles listed in Chapter III are not included. However, those titles, which are mentioned either in the narrative sections or in footnotes wherever in the volume, are cited.]

A Abelha da China   104
Acta Asiatica   69, 316
Acta Orientalia   31
Agrarian Policies of Mainland China: A Documentary Study, 1949-1956   321
Ajia shi kenkyû   41
Albania and the Sino-Soviet Rift   321
The Alienated Academy: Culture and Politics in Republican China, 1919-1937   25, 29, 58
American Studies of Contemporary China   37, 51
Analytical Chinese-English Dictionary   217
An-hui shih-hsüeh t'ung-hsün   273
Annals of the Association of American Geographers   177
Année littéraire   101
An Annotated Bibliography of Chinese Painting: Catalogues and Related Texts   80
An Annotated Bibliography of Selected Reference Works [also known as TB in the text]   2, 30, 54, 58, 84, 134, 147, 203, 245, 247, 262, 266
Annotated Bibliography to the Shike shiliao xinbian [New Edition of Historical Materials Carved on Stone]   69
Annual Reports for the 17th, 18th, 19th, 21st, 22nd, and 23rd Fiscal Years   262
The Antiquity of China, or an Historical Essay, Endeavouring a Probability That the Language of the Empire of China...   7-8
Arte de la lengua mandarina   8
Asia Major   7
Asia 19- Yearbook   254
Asian Folklore Studies   235
Association de la Propagation de la Foi, Annales...Collection faisant suite à toutes les éditions des Lettres édifantes   101
Atlas of the People's Republic of China   179
Australian Journal of Chinese Affairs   39, 190
Author Index to the Bibliotheca Sinica   61
The Autobiography of a Chinese Historian Being the Preface to a Symposium on Ancient Chinese History   23
A Beginner's Chinese-English Dictionary of the National Language   206

Beijing Review   104
De bello Tartarico historia   7
Bibliographic and Administrative Problems Arising from the Incorporation of Chinese Books in American Libraries   53
Bibliographie zur Geschichte der chinesischen Literatur   77
Bibliographie des travaux en langues occidentales sur les Song parus de 1946 à 1965   68
Bibliography of Asian Studies   62, 63
Bibliography on Buddhism   14
Bibliography of the Chinese Language   75
A Bibliography of Chinese-language Materials on the People's Communes   94

A Bibliography of Chinese Newspapers and Periodicals in European Libraries 132
Bibliography of Chinese Social History: A Selected and Critical List of Chinese Periodical Sources 135
Bibliography of Chinese Studies 64, 103
Bibliography of English Translations and Critiques of Contemporary Chinese Fiction (1945-1992) 78, 316
Bibliography-index to US JPRS research translations 319
Bibliography and Index to the United States Joint Publication (JPRS translations) 319
Bibliography of the Jesuit Mission in China ca. 1580-ca. 1680 80
Bibliography of Selected Western Works on T'ang Dynasty Literature 77
A Bibliography of Studies and Translations of Modern Chinese Literature, 1918-1942 77
Bibliotheca sinica: dictionnaire bibliographique des ouvrages relatifs à l'empire chinoise 56, 61, 62, 101
Les Bibliothèques en Chine première moitié du xx siècle 54
Biographical Dictionary and Analysis of China's Party Leadership 1922-1988 151
Biographical Dictionary of Chinese Communism (1921-65) 139, 150, 241
Biographical Dictionary of Republican China 139, 150, 241
Black Athena: The Afroasiatic Roots of Classical Civilization 7
Books and Articles on Oriental Subjects, Published in Japan 64
The British Discovery of Buddhism 13
Buddhism: A Subject Index to Periodical Articles in English 74
Buddhist Scriptures: A Bibliography 74
Bukkyô daijiten 236
Bulletin de l'École française d'Extrême-Orient 102
Bulletin of the European Association of Sinological Librarians 51
Bulletin of Far Eastern Bibliography 62
Bulletin of the School of Oriental and African Studies 272
Bulletin of Sung and Yüan Studies 69

Cahiers d'Extrême-Asie 74
Cahiers d'histoire mondiale 243
The Cambridge Encyclopedia of China 253
The Cambridge Handbook of Contemporary China 253
The Cambridge History of China 25, 67, 68, 105, 314
Canton Register 104
The Cantonese Speaker's Dictionary 230
Catalogue des congshu de la Bibliothèque de l'Institut des Hautes Études chinoises 280
Catalogue of Translations from the Chinese Dynastic Histories for the Period 220-960 68
Catalogues of Chinese Local Gazetteers 197
CCP Documents of the Great Proletarian Revolution, 1966-1967 322
CCP Research Newsletter 51
Centre Franco-chinois d'Études sinologiques 291, 334-335
Ch'a shih-su mei-yüeh t'ung-chi chuan 106
Chan-hou Jih-pen ti Chung-kuo shih yen-chiu 40
Chan-kuo Ch'in Han shih lun-wen so-yin 89
Chan kuo ts'e 221, 292
Chan kuo ts'e t'ung-chien 334
Chang Chü-cheng ta-chuan 140
Change and Continuity in Chinese Local History: The Development of Hui-chou Prefecture 273
Che-chiang ta-hsüeh hsüeh-pao (she-k'o); (tzu-jan) 111
Cheng-chih-hsüeh tz'u-tien 224
Chi-fu ts'ung-shu 267
Ch'i tan kuo chih t'ung-chien 334
Chia-pao ch'üan-shu 246

Chiao-ch'ou t'ung-i   58
Chiao-wu chiao-an tang   284
Chiao-yü shih-chieh   21
Chieh-fang-ch'ü ken-chü-ti t'u-shu mu-lu   94
Ch'ieh-yün   204
Chien-kuo i-lai Chung-kuo shih-hsüeh lun-wen-chi p'ien-mu so-yin   89
Chien-ming Chung-kuo li-tai kuan-chih tz'u-tien   239
Chien-ming fa-hsüeh ta tz'u-tien   227
Chien-ming ku-chi tz'u-tien   287
Chien-ming Wu fang-yen tz'u-tien   231
Ch'ien-fu lun t'ung-chien   334
Chih-pu-tsu-chai ts'ung-shu   266
Chin Chung-ching   46
Chin-shih Chung-hsi shih-jih tui-chao piao   311
Chin-shih jen-ming so-yin   156
Chin-shu jen-ming so-yin   154
Chin-tai K'ang-ch'ü tang-an tzu-liao hsüan-pien   286
Chin Yüan jen wen-chi chuan-chi tzu-liao so-yin   157
China aktuell   64, 103, 169
China: An Annotated Bibliography of Bibliographies   61
China: A Commercial and Industrial Handbook   263
China: A Critical Bibliography   66
China Directory   169
China, 1898-1912: The Xinzheng Revolution and Japan   20
China Exchange News   274, 275
China: Facts and Figures Annual   264
China: The Geography of Development and Modernization   172
China: A Handbook   255
China Handbuch   255
China Industrial Handbook: Chekiang   264
China Industrial Handbook: Kiangsu   264
China Informatie   73
China Information   264
China in Maps, 1890-1960: A Selective and Annotated Cartobibliography   179
China News Analysis   103
The China Quarterly   36, 102, 106, 169, 313, 319
China Reconstructs   104
China Report   319
China Review   253
China Review International   103, 292
China Rural Statistics   265
China in the Sixteenth Century: The Journals of Matteo Ricci, 1583-1610   6
China: A Statistical Survey in 1986   264
China: Tradition and Transformation   17
China Urban Statistics   265
China: Urban Statistics   260
China in Western Literature: A Continuation of Cordier's Bibliotheca Sinica   61, 62
China Year Book   247
Chinabound: A Fifty-Year Memoir   34
China's Foreign Trade Statistics 1864-1949   262
China's New Party Leadership: Biographies of Members and Analysis of the Twelfth Central committee of the Chinese Communist Party   151
China's Response to the West   38, 320
La Chine antique   33
Chinese   229

Chinese Almanacs 297

A Chinese Biographical Dictionary 147

The Chinese Chameleon 57

The Chinese Classic Novels: An Annotated Bibliography of Chiefly English-language Studies 78

Chinese Communist Education: Records of the First Decade 320

Chinese Communist Studies of Modern Chinese History 71

Chinese Communist Who's Who 151

Chinese Culture 91

Chinese Dialectology: A Selected and Classified Bibliography 75, 230

The Chinese Dialects of the Han Time according to the Fang-yen 201

Chinese Dictionaries in Chinese and Other Languages 207

Chinese Drama: An Annotated Bibliography of Commentary, Criticism, and Plays in English Translation 78

Chinese Economic Statistics 248

Chinese Economic Studies 317

Chinese Education 318

Chinese-English Dictionary 204

A Chinese-English Dictionary of China's Rural Economy 228

Chinese-English Dictionary of Chinese Communist Terminology 225

A Chinese-English Dictionary of Enigmatic Folk Similes (Xiehouyu) 222

A Chinese-English Dictionary: Han-Ying tz'u-tien 211

Chinese Genealogies at the Genealogical Society of Utah: An Annotated Bibliography 168

Chinese Historiography on the Revolution of 1911: A Critical Survey and a Selected Bibliography 71

Chinese Law and Government 318

Chinese letterkunde: Inleiding, historisch overzicht en bibliographieën 77

Chinese Lexicology and Lexicography: A Selected and Classified Bibliography 75, 207, 221

Chinese Linguistics: A Selected and Classified Bibliography 75

Chinese Literature 104, 317

Chinese Local Gazetteers: An Historical and Practical Introduction 187

Chinese Music: An Annotated Bibliography 79

Chinese Newspapers in the Library of Congress: A Bibliography 132

Chinese Periodical Literature on CD-ROM 110

The Chinese Periodical Press, 1800-1912 106

Chinese Periodicals in the Library of Congress: A Bibliography 131

Chinese Rare Books in American Libraries 288

The Chinese reader's manual: a handbook of bibliographical, historical, mythological, and general literary reference 252

Chinese Recorder 101

Chinese Religion: Publications in Western Languages 1981-1990 73

Chinese Religion in Western Languages: A Comprehensive and Classified Bibliography of Publications in English, French and German through 1980 73

Chinese Repository 101

Chinese Science 103

Chinese Social and Political Science Review 8, 102, 290

The Chinese in Southeast Asia: A Selected and Annotated Bibliography of Publications in Western Languages, 1960-1970 80

Chinese Students in Japan in the Late Ch'ing Period 20

Chinese Studies in History 93, 95, 317

Chinese Studies in History and Philosophy 317

Chinese Studies in Philosophy 317

Chinese Studies in Sociology and Anthropology 93

The Chineseness of China: Selected Essays 137

Chinesisch-Deutsches Wortschatz: Politik und Wirtschaft der VR China   225
Ching-chi ta tz'u-tien   226
Ching-chi t'ung-chi yüeh-chih   263
Ching-hsüeh yen-chiu lun chu mu-lu 1912-1987   98
Ching-i-k'ao   57
Ch'ing Administrative Terms   240
Ch'ing-chi wai-chiao shih-liao   272
Ch'ing Documents: An Introductory Syllabus   35
Ch'ing hua-chuan chi-i san chung-fu yin-te   332
Ch'ing-i pao   108
Ch'ing-jen pieh-ming tzu-hao so-yin (fu i-ming piao)   145
Ch'ing-jen shih-ming pieh-ch'eng tzu-hao so-yin   145
Ch'ing-jen wen-chi pieh-lu   283
Ch'ing-mo Ch'uan Tien pien-wu tang-an shih-liao   286
Ch'ing-mo T'ien-chin hai-kuan yu-cheng tang-an hsüan-pien   285
Ch'ing-shih lun-wen so-yin   91
Ch'ing-shih yen-chiu kai-shuo   92
Ch'ing-tai ch'i-pai ming-jen chuan   159
Ch'ing-tai Ch'ien Chia Tao Pa-hsien tang-an hsüan-pien   286
Ch'ing-tai chuan-chi ts'ung-kan so-yin   160
Ch'ing-tai hsüeh-shu kai-lun   24
Ch'ing-tai jen-wu chuan kao   160
Ch'ing-tai pei-chuan-wen t'ung-chien   159
Ch'ing-tai pien-chiang shih ti lun-chu so-yin   92
Ch'ing-tai shu-hua-chia tzu-hao yin-te   329
Ch'ing-tai ti-ch'i tang-an shih-liao (Chia-ching chih Hsüan-t'ung)   285
Ch'ing-tai ti ch'i-ti   286
Ch'ing-tai ti k'uang-yeh   285
Ch'ing-tai wen-hsien chuan-pao, chuan-kao jen-ming so-yin   160
Ch'ing-tai wen-hsien tang-an tsung-mu   275
Ch'iu shih   109
Ch'o-keng lu t'ung-chien   334
Chou i yin-te   332
Chou li yin-te fu chu-shu yin-shu yin-te   331
Ch'ou-pan i-wu shih-mo   272
De christiana expeditione apud Sinas suscepta a Societate Jesu, ex. P. Matth. Riccii ejusdem Societatis commentariis libri V   6
Christianity in China: A Scholar's Guide to Resources in the Libraries and Archives of the United States   106
Chû-Nichi daijiten   213, 214
Chu-shih jan-i chiao-ting fu yin-te   332
Chuang-tzu yin-te   333
Chûgoku hôseishi kenkyû: dorei nôdo hô kazoku sonaraku hô   41
Chûgoku kankei ronsetsu shiryô   128
Chûgoku shakai keizai shi goi (sanhen)   241
Chûgoku shakai keizai shi goi (zokuhen)   240
Chûgoku shi kenkyû nyûmon   87
Chûgoku sôfu no kenkyû   167
Chûgoku tochi seidoshi kenkyû   41
Ch'un-ch'iu ching chuan chu-shu yin-shu yin-te   330
Ch'un-ch'iu ching chuan yin-te   332
Ch'un-ch'iu fan-lu t'ung-chien   334
Chung-hang yüeh-k'an   108
Chung-hua ch'eng-yü ta tz'u-tien   222
Chung-hua fo-chiao jen-wu ta tz'u-tien   164

Chung-hua jen-min kung-ho-kuo: Ch'üan-kuo fen hsien shih jen-k'ou t'ung-chi tzu-liao 260
Chung-hua jen-min kung-ho-kuo fen-sheng ti-t'u chi 179, 183
Chung-hua jen-min kung-ho-kuo ti-ming tz'u-tien 187
Chung-hua ku-wen-hsien ta tz'u-tien, ti-li chüan 199
Chung-hua min-kuo ch'i-k'an lun-wen so-yin hui-pien 86
Chung-hua min-kuo hsin ti-t'u 179
Chung-hua min-kuo T'ai-wan ti-ch'ü kung-ts'ang fang-chih mu-lu 197
Chung-hua min-kuo tang-tai ming-jen lu 161
Chung-hua min-kuo t'u-shu tsung mu 85
Chung-hua min-kuo t'ung-chi t'i-yao 1935 263
Chung-hua pai-k'o ch'üan-shu 257
Chung-hua wen-hua pai-k'o ch'üan-shu 258
Chung-hua yen-yü chih 223
Chung-hua yen-yü ta tz'u-tien 223
Chung-kung jen-ming lu 151
Chung-kung nien-pao 248
Chung-kung tang-shih jen-wu chuan 160
Chung-kung ti-hsia tang-shih ch'i-pao-k'an tiao-ch'a yen-chiu 1919-1949 133
Chung-kuo che-hsüeh nien-chien 98
Chung-kuo che-hsüeh-shih lun-wen so-yin 98
Chung-kuo che-hsüeh tz'u-tien ta-ch'üan 238
Chung-kuo cheng-chih 111
Chung-kuo ch'eng-shih t'ung-chi nien-chien 260
Chung-kuo Chi-tu-chiao-shih yen-chiu shu-mu 99
Chung-kuo ch'i-yeh kuan-li nien-chien 261
Chung-kuo ch'i-yeh kuan-li pai-k'o ch'üan-shu 258
Chung-kuo ch'i-yeh teng-chi nien-chien 261
Chung-kuo chin erh-shih nien wen-shih-che lun-wen fen-lei so-yin 134
Chung-kuo chin-hsien-tai cheng-ch'ü yen-ko piao 174
Chung-kuo chin-hsien-tai jen-wu chuan-chi tzu-liao so-yin 161
Chung-kuo chin pa-shih nien Ming-shih lun-chu mu-lu 91
Chung-kuo chin-tai ching-chi shih lun-chu mu-lu t'i-yao 94
Chung-kuo chin-tai ching-chi shih t'ung-chi tzu-liao hsüan-chi 262
Chung-kuo chin-tai hsien-tai ts'ung-shu mu-lu 281
Chung-kuo chin-tai hsien-tai ts'ung-shu mu-lu so-yin 281
Chung-kuo chin-tai shih-kao ti-t'u chi 182
Chung-kuo chin-tai shih lun-chu mu-lu (1949-1979) 92
Chung-kuo chin-tai shih lun-wen tzu-liao so-yin (1949-1979) 92
Chung-kuo chin-tai wai-chai shih t'ung-chi tzu-liao (1853-1927) 262
Chung-kuo chin-tai yen-wu-shih tzu-liao hsüan-chi 285
Chung-kuo chin wu-pai nien han-lao fen-pu t'u-chi 182
Chung-kuo ching-chi nien-chien 259
Chung-kuo ching-chi pai-k'o ch'üan-shu 258
Chung-kuo ch'u-pan nien-chien (Beijing) 85
Chung-kuo ch'u-pan nien-chien (Taipei) 86
Chung-kuo hsien shih kai-lan 185
Chung-kuo fa-chih shih shu-mu 100
Chung-kuo fa-hsüeh chu-tso ta tz'u-tien 227
Chung-kuo fa-lü t'u-shu tsung-mu (1911-1990) 99
Chung-kuo fang-chih ts'ung-shu 198
Chung-kuo fang-chih-hsüeh t'ung-lun 200
Chung-kuo fen sheng-shih-hsien ta tz'u-tien 185
Chung-kuo fu-nü 109
Chung-kuo fu-nü ming-jen tz'u-tien (Changchun) 164

Chung-kuo fu-nü ming-jen tz'u-tien (Hebei)   164
Chung-kuo hai-kuan mi-tang: Ho-te, Chin-ten-kan han-tien hui-pien 1874-1907   286
Chung-kuo hsien-tai ko-ming-shih shih-liao hsüeh   93
Chung-kuo hsien-tai-shih lun-wen chu-tso mu-lu so-yin 1949-1981   93
Chung-kuo hsien-tai-shih lun-wen chu-tso mu-lu so-yin 1982-1987   93
Chung-kuo hsien-tai-shih lun-wen shu-mu so-yin   94
Chung-kuo hsien-tai tang-tai wen-hsüeh yen-chiu   98, 111
Chung-kuo hsien-tai wen-hsüeh ch'i-k'an mu-lu ch'u-kao   135
Chung-kuo hsien-tai wen-hsüeh ch'i-k'an mu-lu hui-pien   135
Chung-kuo hsien-tai wen-hsüeh shih-liao shu-yü ta tz'u-tien   232
Chung-kuo hsien-tai wen-hsüeh tso-p'in shu-ming ta-tz'u-tien   97
Chung-kuo hsien-tai wen-t'an pi-ming-lu   145
Chung-kuo hua-chia jen-ming ta tz'u-tien   162
Chung-kuo hua-pen hsiao-shuo su-yü tz'u-tien   235
Chung-kuo i-shu chia tz'u-tien: hsien-tai pu-fen   162
Chung-kuo jen-k'ou ti-t'u chi   183
Chung-kuo jen-k'ou t'ung-chi nien-chien   260
Chung-kuo jen-ming ta tz'u-tien (Shanghai, 1921)   147
Chung-kuo jen-ming ta tz'u-tien (Shanghai, 1989)   148
Chung-kuo jen ti hsing-ming   142
Chung-kuo ju-hsüeh tz'u-tien   238
Chung-kuo ke-ming shih jen-wu tz'u-tien   160
Chung-kuo ko-min-tsu tsung-chiao yü shen-hua ta tz'u-tien   236
Chung-kuo k'o-hsüeh shih t'ung-hsin   111
Chung-kuo ku-chi shan-pen shu-mu   287
Chung-kuo ku-chin ti-ming ta tz'u-tien   186
Chung-kuo ku fang-chih k'ao   200
Chung-kuo ku-tai hsiao-shuo jen-wu tz'u-tien   163
Chung-kuo ku-tai she-hui yen-chiu   27
Chung-kuo ku-tai-shih lun-wen tzu-liao so-yin   88
Chung-kuo ku-tai ti-t'u-chi   181
Chung-kuo ku-tien hsi-ch'ü yen-chiu tzu-liao so-yin   97
Chung-kuo ku-tien hsiao-shuo yung-yü tz'u-tien   235
Chung-kuo ku-tien wen-hsüeh li-lun p'i-p'ing shih tzu-liao so-yin 1949-1979   97
Chung-kuo ku-tien wen-hsüeh wen-hsien chien-so yü li-yung   96
Chung-kuo ku-tien wen-hsüeh yen-chiu lun-wen so-yin (Hong Kong)   96
Chung-kuo ku-tien wen-hsüeh yen-chiu lun-wen so-yin (Beijing)   96
Chung-kuo ku-tien wen-hsüeh yen-chiu lun-wen so-yin (1949-1980)   96
Chung-kuo ku-tien wen-hsüeh yen-chiu nien-chien   97
Chung-kuo kung-i mei-shu ta tz'u-tien   100
Chung-kuo li-shih chi-nien piao   309
Chung-kuo li-shih-hsüeh nien-chien   89, 95, 110
Chung-kuo li-shih jen-wu sheng-tsu nien-piao   148
Chung-kuo li-shih jen-wu tz'u-tien   148
Chung-kuo li-shih kung-chü-shu chih-nan   87
Chung-kuo li-shih ti-li hsüeh lun-chu so-yin   88
Chung-kuo li-shih ti-li wen-hsien kai-lun   176
Chung-kuo li-shih ti-ming tz'u-tien   186
Chung-kuo li-shih ti-t'u chi   181
Chung-kuo li-shih tz'u-tien   241
Chung-kuo li-tai hu-k'ou t'ien-ti t'ien-fu t'ung-chi   262
Chung-kuo li-tai jen-wu nien-p'u k'ao-lu
Chung-kuo li-tai ming-jen nien-p'u tsung-mu   167
Chung-kuo li-tai nien-hao k'ao   309
Chung-kuo li-tai nien-p'u tsung-lu   167

Chung-kuo mei-shu-chia jen-ming tz'u-tien   162

Chung-kuo ming-sheng so-yin   186

Chung-kuo mu-lu-hsüeh nien-piao   58

Chung-kuo mu-lu-hsüeh shih   58

Chung-kuo nien-chien   259

Chung-kuo nien-li tsung-p'u [also known as   *Chronological Tables of Chinese History*]   307, 310

Chung-kuo nung-ts'un ching-chi t'ung-chi ta-ch'üan (1949-1986)   265

Chung-kuo nung-yeh nien-chien   260

Chung-kuo nung-yeh pai-k'o ch'üan-shu   258

Chung-kuo pai-k'o nien-chien   259

Chung-kuo pao-k'an mu-lu   132

Chung-kuo pao-k'an ta-ch'üan   131

Chung-kuo po-shih jen-ming tz'u-tien   165

Chung-kuo shan-pen shu t'i-yao   288

Chung-kuo shan-pen shu t'i-yao pu-pien   288

Chung-kuo she-hui ching-chi shih lun-chu mu-lu, 1900-1984   88

Chung-kuo she-hui k'o-hsüeh wen-hsien t'i-lu   100

Chung-kuo she-hui shih yen-chiu kai-shu   89

Chung-kuo shen-hua ch'uan-shuo tz'u-tien   238

Chung-kuo shih-chi kai-lun   176

Chung-kuo shih-hsien ta tz'u-tien   185

Chung-kuo shih-hsüeh-chia tz'u-tien   165

Chung-kuo shih-hsüeh lun-wen so-yin   134

Chung-kuo shih-hsüeh lun-wen yin-te   134

Chung-kuo shih-kao ti-t'u chi   182

Chung-kuo shih li-jih ho Chung-hsi li-jih tui-chao piao   311

Chung-kuo shih yen-chiu chih-nan   87

Chung-kuo shui-li pai-k'o ch'üan-shu   258

Chung-kuo ssu-fa ta tz'u-tien   227

Chung-kuo ssu-hsiang ta tz'u-tien   238

Chung-kuo ssu-hsiang, tsung-chiao, wen-hua kuan-hsi lun-wen mu-lu   99

Chung-kuo ta pai-k'o ch'üan-shu   249-250, 257

Chung-kuo tang-an shih-yeh chien-shih   275

Chung-kuo tang-shih chien-ming tz'u-tien   224

Chung-kuo tang-tai ming-jen lu   161

Chung-kuo ti-fang-chih chi-ch'eng   198

Chung-kuo ti-fang-chih lien-ho mu-lu   197

Chung-kuo ti-fang-chih tsung-lan 1949-1987   199

Chung-kuo ti-fang-chih tz'u-tien   199

Chung-kuo ti-i li-shih tang-an kuan kuan-ts'ang tang-an kai-shu   284

Chung-kuo ti-li chu-tso yao-lan   176

Chung-kuo ti-ming tz'u-tien   185

Chung-kuo tien-ku ta tz'u-tien   223

Chung-kuo ts'ung-shu mu-lu chi tzu-mu so-yin hui-pien   281

Chung-kuo ts'ung-shu tsung-lu   280, 281

Chung-kuo ts'ung-shu tsung-lu pu-cheng   280

Chung-kuo tui-wai ching-chi mao-i nien-chien   261

Chung-kuo t'ung-chi nien-chien   259

Chung-kuo t'ung-su hsiao-shuo tsung-mu t'i-yao   96

Chung-kuo tzu-jan ti-li t'u-chi   184

Chung-kuo wen-hsüeh-chia ta tz'u-tien   163

Chung-kuo wen-hsüeh ta tz'u-tien   232

Chung-kuo wen-hsüeh yen-chiu nien-chien   97

Chung-kuo yin-yüeh wu-tao hsi-ch'ü jen-ming tz'u-tien   162

Chung-kuo yü-yen-hsüeh lun-wen so-yin: 1950-1980 98
Chung-kuo yü-yen-hsüeh lun-wen so-yin: 1981-1985 98
Chung-kuo yü-yen-hsüeh ta tz'u-tien 220
Chung-wai hsin-pao 112
Chung-wen ho-hsin ch'i-k'an yao-mu tsung-lan 132
Chung-wen kung-chü-shu shih-yung fa 87
Chung-wen ta tz'u-tien 215, 243
Ch'üan Han San-kuo Chin Nan-pei ch'ao shih tso-che yin-te 331
Ch'üan-kuo chu-yao pao-k'an tzu-liao so-yin 85
Ch'üan-kuo Chung-wen ch'i-k'an lien-ho mu-lu tseng-ting pen 1833-1949 131
Ch'üan-kuo hsin shu-mu 84
Ch'üan-kuo ko-chi cheng-hsieh wen-shih tzu-liao p'ien-mu so-yin 1960-1990 94
(Ch'üan-kuo ko sheng tzu-chih-ch'ü, chih-hsia-shih) Li-shih t'ung-chi tzu-liao hui pien (1949-1989) 264
Ch'üan-kuo nei-pu fa-hsing t'u-shu tsung-mu 51
Ch'üan-kuo so-yin pien-chi yen-t'ao-hui ts'an-k'ao tzu-liao 296
Ch'üan-kuo tsung shu-mu 84
Ch'üan Shang-ku San-tai Ch'in Han San-kuo Liu-ch'ao wen tso-che yin-te 328
Ch'üan T'ang shih jen-ming k'ao 163
Ch'üan T'ang shih so-yin 233, 296
Cities and City Planning in the People's Republic of China: An Annotated Bibliography 80
Classical Chinese Fiction: A Guide to its Study and Appreciation, Essays, and Bibliographies 76
Classicism, Politics, and Kinship: The Ch'ang-chou School of New Text Confucianism in Late Imperial China 23, 26
A Classification Scheme for Chinese and Japanese Books 50
Clavis medica ad Chinarum doctrinam de pulsibus 7
CLEAR 296, 316
Communication and Imperial Control in China, 1693-1735 272
Communist China, 1955-1959: Policy documents with analysis 322
Communist Neo-Traditionalism: Work and Authority in Chinese Industry 38
Comparative Literature 9
A Comprehensive Glossary of Chinese Communist Terminology 225
Concise English/Chinese – Chinese/English Dictionary 212
Concordance des chronologies neomaniques chinoise et Européene 307, 310
Concordance du Tao-tsang: titres des ouvrages 278
Concordances and Indexes to Chinese Texts 291
Confucian Personalities 137
The Confucian's Progress: Autobiographical Writings in Traditional China 140
Confucius Sinarum Philosophus sive Scientia Sinicia Latine exposita 7
The Contemporary Atlas of China 184
Contemporary China: A Bibliography of Reports on China Published by the Joint Publications Research Service 319
Contemporary China: A Research Guide 2, 66, 127
Contemporary Chinese Novels and Short Stories, 1949-1974: An Annotated Bibliography 78
Controversies in Modern Chinese Intellectual History: An Analytical Bibliography of Periodical Articles, Mainly of the May Fourth and Post-May Fourth Era 136
The Cultural Revolution in China: An Annotated Bibliography 80
Cumulative Bibliography of Asian Studies 62
Curious Land: Jesuit Accommodation and the Origins of Sinology 8
Current Background 318
Current Chinese Newspaper Holdings in the Asian Library Collection of the University of California System and the Hoover Institution, Stanford University 133

Current Contents of Academic Journals in Japan: The Humanities and Social Sciences 65

Current Contents of Foreign Periodicals in Chinese Studies–Wai-wen ch'i-k'an Han-hsüeh lun-p'ing hui-mu 64, 101, 128

Current Yearbooks Published in the PRC 249

Daikanwa jiten 54, 216, 218

Daily Report 319

David Hawkes: Classical, Modern, and Humane–Essays on Chinese Literature 9

Definitions and Classification of the Six Scripts according to Hsü Shen (A.D. 58-147) 202

Description géographique, historique, chronologique, politique, et physique de l'Empire de la Chine 10, 178

The Description of the World 57

The Development of the Chinese Collection in the Library of Congress 34

A Dictionary of Chinese Buddhist Terms 236

Dictionary of Chinese Law and Government 224

A Dictionary of Chinese Mythology 237

A Dictionary of Chinese Symbols: Hidden Symbols in Chinese Life and Thought 237

Dictionary of Contemporary Usage 225

Dictionary of Ming Biography 149, 150

A Dictionary of Official Titles in Imperial China 174, 239

Dictionnaire classique de la langue chinoise 218

Dictionnaire mandchou-française 11

Dictionnaire polyglotte sanskrit-tibétain-mandchou-mongol-chinois 11

Discovering History in China 38

Diversity in International Communism: A Documentary Record 1961-1965 321

Documents of the Chinese Communist Party Central Committee 322

Documents of the Chinese Communist Party, 1927-1930 320

Documents on Communism, Nationalism, and Soviet Advisers in China, 1918-1927: Papers seized in the 1927 Peking raid 320

Dream of the Red Chamber 24

Early Chinese Texts: A Bibliographical Guide 2, 68, 201, 292

Earthbound China: A Study of Rural Economy in Yunnan 28

East Asia: Tradition and Transformation 17

East Asian History 137

East Meets West: The Jesuits in China, 1582-1773 178

Economic Planning and Organization in Mainland China: A Documentary Study, 1949-1957 321

Economic Reforms in the People's Republic of China since 1979: A Bibliography of Articles and Publications in English-language Magazines and Newspapers 81

Education and Communism in China: An Anthology of Commentary 320

Education in the People's Republic of China, Past and Present: An Annotated Bibliography 80

Élements de la grammaire chinoise ou principes généraux du kou-wen ou style antique et du kouan-hou,... 12

Emigrant Communities in South China 29

Eminent Chinese of the Ch'ing Period [also known as ECCP] 19, 24, 139, 150

Encyclopedia of China Today 255

Encyclopedia of New China 254

The Encyclopedia Sinica 252

Ennin's Diary: The Record of a Pilgrimage to China in Search of the Law 32

The Emperor's Four Treasuries: Scholars and the State in the in the Late Ch'ien-lung Era 46

Erh-shih-ssu shih chi-chuan jen-ming so-yin   152
Erh-ya   201
Erh ya chu-shu yin-shu yin-te   331
Erh-ya yin-te   333
Essai sur la langue et la littérature chinoise   12
Essays on the Sources for Chinese History   67, 167, 204, 271, 278
Extracts of China Mainland Magazines   318

Fa-hsüeh ta tz'u-tien   227
Fa-hsüeh tz'u-tien (tseng-ting-pen)   228
Fa-lü   111
Fairbank Remembered   35
The Fall of Imperial China   140
Fan-i ming-i chu   236
Fang-chih hsüeh   200
Fang-yen   202
Fang-yen chiao-chien   201
Fang-yen chiao-chien fu t'ung-chien   335
Far Eastern Bibliography   63
Far Eastern Economic Review   103, 254
Far Eastern Quarterly   18, 63, 140
Fei-ch'ing nien-pao   248
Fei Hsiao-t'ung: The Dilemma of a Chinese Intellectual   29
Fei Xiaotong and Sociology in Revolutionary China   29
Fen-lei hsüan-chu li-tai ming-jen lun fang-chih   200
Feng shih wen-chien chi chiao-cheng fu yin-te   332
Feng-su t'ung-i fu t'ung-chien   334
1587, A Year of No Significance: The Ming Dynasty in Decline   141
Flora Sinensis   7
Fo-chiao wen-hua tz'u-tien   236
Fu-chien sheng yen-chiu-yüan yen-chiu hui-pao   273
Fo-hsüeh ta tz'u-tien   236
Fo-kuang ta tz'u-tien   236
Fo-kuo-chi   13
Fo-tsang tzu-mu yin-te   329
Food and Money in Ancient China   175
Four Books   7
From Locke to Saussure   6
From Philosophy to Philology: Intellectual and Social Aspects of Change in Late Imperial China   5, 52, 58
Fu-yin pao-k'an tzu-liao   98, 110, 120, 136

Gazeta de Macau   104
Geographical Names in Sung China   175
Geographical Sources of Ming-Qing History   191, 200
The Geography of China, 1975-91: An Annotated Bibliography   172
German Impact on Modern Chinese Intellectual History   71
Die Geschichte der Chinesischen Bibliothek Tian Yi Ge vom 16-Jahrhundert bis in die Gegenwart   52
A Glossary of Colloquial Expressions in Chinese Vernacular Fiction   235
Going to the People: Chinese Intellectuals and Folk Literature   23
The Government of China under Mongolian Rule: A Reference Guide   239
Government Control of the Press in Modern China   113
Grammata Serica Recensa   218
Die Grosse Politik der Europäischen Kabinette   272

Guide to Buddhist Religion 73
Guide to Chinese Philosophy 72
Guide to Chinese Religion 73
A Guide to the Oriental Classics 72
A Guide to the Sources of Chinese Economic History 79
A Guide to the Ssu-k'u ch'üan-shu chien-ming mu-lu 269
A Guide to the Ssu-pu pei-yao 270
A Guide to the Ssu-pu ts'ung-k'an 270

Hai-fang tang 284
Hai-nei hua-i t'u 177
Han-hsüeh yen-chiu 121, 187
Han-hsüeh so-yin tsung-mu 292
Han-shu 45, 46, 57, 175
Han-shu chi pu-chu tsung-ho yin-te 153, 331
Han-shu jen-ming so-yin 152
Han-shu so-yin 153
Han-tzu hsi-i 12
Han Wei Chin Nan-pei ch'ao Sui shih chien-shang tz'u-tien 233
Han Wei liu-ch'ao pai san chia chi 268
Han-Ying ching-chi tz'u-tien 226
Han-Ying fen-lei ch'a-t'u tz'u-tien 212
Han-Ying k'o-chi ta tz'u-tien 229
Han-Ying k'o-chi tz'u-tien 229
Han-Ying ni-yin tz'u-tien 212
Han-Ying tui chao ch'eng-yü tz'u-tien 221
Han-yü ta-tzu-tien 214
Han-yü ta tz'u-tien 215
Han-yü yen-yü tz'u-tien 223
Handbuch der Geschichte der Philosophy 72
Harvard Journal of Asiatic Studies 31, 50, 52, 53, 102, 290
Harvard-Yenching Sinological Index Series [HYSIS] 30, 153, 289, 290, 291, 292, 294, 328 ff
Historia de las cosas mas notables, ritos y costumbres del Gran Reyno de la China 6
Historians of China and Japan 6, 137
Historical Dictionary of Revolutionary China 241
Historiography of the Chinese Labour Movement, 1895-1949: A Critical Survey and Bibliography of Selected Source Materials at the Hoover Institution 71
Historiography of the Taiping Rebellion 70
A History of Chinese Civilisation 17
The History of Chinese Literature: A Selected Bibliography 77
The History of Imperial China: A Research Guide 2, 67
A History of Modern Chinese Fiction 36
A History of the Press and Public Opinion in China 106, 107
History of Religions 235
History and Theory 138
Hôbôgirin: dictionnaire encyclopédique du bouddhisme d'après les sources chinoises et japonaises 74
Hommage à Henri Maspero 33
Hou Han-shu chi chu-shih tsung-ho yin-te 153, 331
Hou Han-shu jen-ming so-yin 152
Hou Han-shu so-yin 153
Hsi-ch'ü tz'u-yü hui-shih 234
Hsi-shih ch'i-shih-lu: Chuan-chia t'an ju-ho hsüeh-hsi Chung-kuo chin-t'ai shih 92
Hsiao-ching yin-te 333

Hsiao-hsüeh wen-ta   24
Hsiao-shuo tz'u-yü hui-shih   235
Hsieh-hou-yü liang-wan t'iao   223
Hsieh-tso ch'eng-yü tz'u-tien   222
Hsien-hsüeh tz'u-tien   237
Hsien-tai Han-yü ch'ang-yung hsü-tz'u tz'u-tien   221
Hsien-tai Han-yü pa-pai-tz'u   221
Hsien-tai Han-yü tz'u-tien   209
Hsien-tai Han-yü tz'u-tien pu-pien   209
Hsien-tai k'o-hsüeh chi-shu tz'u-tien   228
Hsien-ts'un Sung-jen chu-shu mu-lüeh   282
Hsien-ts'un Sung-jen pieh-chi pan-pen mu-lu   282
Hsin-chiu T'ang-shu jen-ming so-yin   155
Hsin-chiu Wu-tai shih jen-ming so-yin   155
Hsin-hua tzu-tien   209
Hsin-hsiu fang-chih ts'ung-k'an   198
Hsin hsü t'ung-chien   334
Hsin-hua pan-yüeh-k'an   109
Hsin-hua wen-chai   109
Hsin-hua yüeh-pao   109
Hsin-pien che-hsüeh ta tz'u-tien   238
Hsin T'ang shu tsai-hsiang shih-hsi piao yin-te   329
Hsüeh-lin   20
Hsün-tzu yin-te   333
Hu Shih and the Chinese Renaissance: Liberalism in the Chinese Revolution   24
Hu Shih and Intellectual Choice in Modern China   24
Hu Shih wen-ts'un   24
Hu Shih wen-ts'un so-yin   291
Hua-hsia fu-nü ming-jen tz'u-tien   164
Huai-nan-tzu t'ung-chien   334
Huang-ch'ao Hsü Wen-hsien t'ung-k'ao   247
Huang-ch'ao i-t'ung yü-t'u   178
Huang-lan   243
Hui-chou ch'ien-nien ch'i-yüeh wen-shu   274, 286
Hui-chou Ming-tai chu-chai   274
Hung Ch'i   109

I-ch'ieh-ching yin-i   236
I-chih hsin-pao   107
I-ching   298
I-li yin-te fu Cheng chu chi Chia shu yin-shu yin-te   328
I-lin   108
I-pai ch'i-shih-wu chung Jih-pen ch'i-k'an chung-tung-fang-hsüeh lun-wen p'ien-mu fu yin-te   333
I-wen chih erh-shih chung tsung-ho yin-te   329
I wen lu   106
Index to the Chinese Encyclopedia   245
An Index to 'Chinese Literature' 1951-1976   317
Index Dictionary of Chinese Artists   162
An Index of Early Chinese Painters and Paintings: T'ang Sung, and Yüan   80, 162
Index to Learned Chinese Periodicals (1927-54)   135
Index sinicus: A Catalogue of Articles Relating to China in Periodicals and Other Collective Publications   61
The Indiana Companion to Traditional Chinese Literature   36, 76, 163, 232, 316
Information China: The Comprehensive and Authorative Reference Source of New China   254

Institute of Chinese Studies Concordance Series   292, 293, 294
Intellectual Trends in the Ch'ing Period   24, 58
International Review of Social History   70
International Studies and Academic Enterprise   31
Introduction to the Sources of Chinese History   69
Inventaire des périodiques chinois dans les bibliothèques françaises   131
Isis   79
Islam in China: A Critical Bibliography   74
Islam in European Thought   39

Japan's Orient: Rendering Pasts into History   17
The Japanese Informal Empire in China, 1895-1937   16
Japanese Names: A Comprehensive Index by Characters and Readings   241
Japanese Scholars of China: A Bibliographical Handbook   17, 165
Japanese Studies on Japan and the Far East: A Short Biographical and Bibliographical Introduction   165
Japanese Studies of Modern China: A Bibliographical Guide to Historical and Social Science Research on the 19th and 20th Centuries   16, 92
Japanese Studies of Modern China since 1953: A Bibliographical Guide to Historical and Social Science Research on the 19th and 20th Centuries, Supplementary Volume for 1953-1969   93
Jen-k'ou nien-chien (1985)   260
Jen-min jih-pao   109, 113
Jen-min shou-ts'e   248
Jen-wu kung-chü-shu tz'u-tien   147
Jih-pen ch'i-k'an san-shih-pa chung chung-tung-fang-hsüeh lun-wen p'ien-mu fu yin-te   332
Jih-pen hsing-ming tz'u-tien   242
Jih-pen ti Chung-kuo hsüeh-chia   166
Jih-pen ts'ang Chung-kuo han-chien ti-fang-chih ts'ung-k'an   198
Jih-yung pai-k'o ch'üan-shu   247
John Fairbank and the American Understanding of Modern China   32, 35, 36, 40
Joseph de Prémare (1666-1736), s.j.: Chinese Philology and Figurism   9
Journal of Asian Studies   26, 34, 36, 39, 40, 42, 56, 79, 81, 82, 102, 137, 138, 316
Journal of the Economic and Social History of the Orient   15, 39
Journal encyclopédique   101
Journal of Higher Education   34
Journal of the History of Ideas   10
Journal of the North China Branch of the Royal Asiatic Society   11
Journal of Oriental Studies   54
Journal des savants   101
Journal of Sung Yuan Studies   69, 95, 103
Ju-hsüeh ching-wu   266
Jung-chai sui-pi wu-chi tsung-ho yin-te   329

K'an-wu yin-te   330
Kandai kenkyû bunken mokuroku–hôbun hen   89
K'ang-hsi tzu-tien   203
Kanseki sôsho shozai mokuroku   281
Kanwa daijiten   216
K'ao-ku chih-i yin-te   328
K'o-hsüeh chi-shu she-hui tz'u-tien   229
Ku-chi cheng-li t'u-shu mu-lu 1949-1991   288
Ku-chi pan-pen t'i-chi so-yin   288
Ku-chi so-yin kai-lun   296

Ku-chi ts'ung-shu kai-shuo 269
Ku Chieh-kang and China's New History: Nationalism and the Quest for Alternative Traditions 23
Ku-chin ch'eng-wei-yü tz'u-tien 143
Ku-chin jen-wu pieh-ming so-yin 145
Ku-chin t'u-shu chi-ch'eng 47, 244-45
Ku shih pien 23
Ku-shih-pien yün-tung ti hsing-ch'i I-ko ssu-hsiang-shih ti fen-hsi 23
Ku-tien hsiao-shuo hsi-ch'ü shu-mu 1949-85 97
Kuang-chou-hua fang-yen tz'u-tien 230
Kuang-fu i-lai T'ai-wan t'i-ch'ü ch'u-pan jen-lei-hsüeh lun-chu mu-lu 100
Kuang-ming jih-pao 113
Kuang-tung ti-fang-chih chuan-chi so-yin 168
Kuang-yü t'u 178
Kuang-yün 204
K'uang-wu tang 284
Kung-chung-tang Ch'ien-lung-ch'ao tsou-che 285
Kung-chung-tang K'ang-hsi-ch'ao tsou-che 284
Kung-chung-tang Kuang-hsü-ch'ao tsou-che 284
Kung-chung-tang Yung-cheng-ch'ao tsou-che 284
K'ung-tzu or Confucius?: The Jesuit Interpretation of Confucianism 7, 10
K'ung-tzu yen-chiu lun-wen chu-tso mu-lu 1949-1986 98
Kuo Mo-jo: The Early Years 27
Kuo-hsüeh chi-k'an 30
Kuo-hsüeh chi-pen ts'ung-shu 271
Kuo-li chung-yang t'u-shu-kuan shan-pen shu-mu 287
The Kuomintang: Selected Historical Documents, 1894-1949 320
Kuo-ts'ui hsüeh-pao 108
Kuo-wen chou-pao 107
Kuo-wen chou-pao tsung-mu 107
Kuo-wen yü-yüan chieh 24
Kuo-yü tzu-tien 204, 210

Late Imperial China 95
Land Tenure and the Social Order in T'ang and Sung China 19, 22
Land Utilization in China: A Study of 16,786 Farms in 168 Localities, and 38,256 Farm Families in 22 Provinces in China, 1929-1933 263
Lao-tzu Tao-te-ching 290
A Latterday Confucian: Reminiscences of William Hung (1893-1980) 30, 32, 290
Lei Shu: Old Chinese Reference Works 244
Lettres édifiantes et curieuses écrites des missions étrangères par quelques missionaires de la Compagnie de Jésus 10, 101
Lexicography in China: A Bibliography of Dictionaries and Related Literature 207
Lexikon chinesischer Symbole: geheime Sinnbilder in Kunst und Literatur, Leben und Denken der Chinesen 237
Lexicon of Reconstructed Pronunciation in Early Middle Chinese, Late Middle Chinese, and Early Mandarin 217
Li-chi chu-shu yin-shu yin-te 330
Li-chi yin-te 330
Li-shih tang-an 276
Li-tai chu lu-hua mu 80
Li-tai fu-nü chu-tso k'ao 164
Li-tai jen-wu nien-li pei-chuan tsung-piao 147
Li-tai ming-hua chi 162
Li-tai ming-jen nien-p'u tsung-mu 167

Li-tai ts'ang-shu-chia tz'u-tien　53

Li-tai t'ung hsing-ming lu yin-te　328

Li-tai yü-ti yen-ko hsien-yao t'u　182

Li-tse ts'ung-shu　266

Liang-ch'ien nien Chung-hsi li tui-chao piao [also known as *A Sino-Western Calendar for Two Thousand Years, 1-2000 A.D.*]　311

Liao Chin Yüan chuan-chi san-shih chung tsung-ho yin-te　156, 331

Liao-shih jen-ming so-yin　156

The Liberal Conspiracy: The Congress for Cultural Freedom and the Struggle for the Mind of Postwar Europe　103

The Library Quarterly　45

Lieh-nü chuan　138

The Life and Mind of Oriental Jones: Sir William Jones, the Father of Modern Linguistics　6

The Life and Thought of Chang Hsüeh-ch'eng　58

The Limits of Change: Essays on Conservatives in Republican China　22, 28

Linguae Sinarum mandarinicae hieroglyphicae grammatica duplex　9

Linguistics in East Asia and South East Asia　75

Linguistique chinoise: bibliographie　75

Liu-ho ts'ung-t'an　106

Liu i chih i lu mu-lu fu yin-te　333

Liu-pu ch'eng-yü chu-chieh　240

Lun heng t'ung-chien　334

Lun-yü yin-te　333

Lü-shih ch'un-ch'iu t'ung-chien　334

Magasin encyclopédique　12

Major Doctrines of Communist China　322

Man-wen T'u-erh-hu-t'e tang-an i-pien　285

Mao against Khrushchev　321

Mao shih chu-shu yin-shu yin-te　330

Mao-shih yin-te　292, 332

Mao Zedong: A Bibliography　72

Mathews' Chinese-English Dictionary　217, 304, 307

Medieval Chinese Society and the 'Local Community'　42

Mémoire dans lequel on prouve, que les chinois sont une colonie égyptienne　7

Mémoires concernant l'histoire, les sciences, les arts, les moeurs, les usuages etc., des Chinois　101

Memoirs of the Research Department of the Tôyô Bunko　316

The Memory Palace of Matteo Ricci　7

Meng-tzu tzu-i shu-cheng　24

Meng-tzu yin-te　333

Middle Chinese　217

Mindai shi kenkyû bunken mokuroku　91

Mindaishi kenkyû　129, 158

Min-kuo jen-wu chuan　160

Min-kuo shih-ch'i tsung shu-mu　85

Min-kuo shih ta tz'u-tien　241

Min-kuo tang-an　276

Min-kuo ti-ch'i tang-an shih-liao (Min-kuo yüan-nien chih Min-kuo erh-shih-ch'i nien)　285

Min, Shin shûkyôshi kenkyû bunken mokuroku (kô)　99

Ming Ch'ing chin-shih t'i-ming pei-lu so-yin　167

Ming Ch'ing Hui-chou nung-ts'un she-hui yü tien-p'u chih　274

Ming Ch'ing Hui-chou she-hui ching-chi tzu-liao ts'ung-pien　275

Ming Ch'ing tang-an   275
Ming Ch'ing tang-an kai-lun   275, 284
Ming Ch'ing tang-an ts'un-chen hsüan-chi   275
Ming-jen chuan-chi tzu-liao so-yin   157
Ming-shih jen-ming so-yin   157
Ming shih-lu lei-tsuan Jen-wu chuan-chi   159
Ming-shih yen-chiu pen-lan   91
Ming Studies   69, 78
Ming Studies in Japan 1961-1981: A Classified Bibliography   91
Ming-tai ch'ih chuan shu k'ao fu yin-te   332
Ming-tai shu-mu t'i-pa ts'ung-k'an   91
Ming-tai ti-fang-chih chuan-chi so-yin (Chung Rih hsien-ts'ang san-pai chung)   158
Missionary Journalist in China: Young J. Allen and His Magazines, 1860-1883   107
Modern Asian Studies   28
Modern China   190
Modern China: A Bibliographical Guide to Chinese Works 1898-1937   2, 66, 108
Modern China, 1840-1972: An Introduction to Sources and Research Aids   2, 66
Modern Chinese Authors: a List of Pseudonyms   145
Modern Chinese Fiction: A Guide to its Study and Appreciation, Essays, and Bibliographies   76
Modern Chinese Literature   316
Modern Chinese Society 1644-1970: An Analytical Bibliography vol.I, 71; vols. II and III,   91
Modern Chinese Writers: Self Portrayals   316
Die Moderne Chinesische Tagepresse: ihre Entwicklung in Tafeln und Dokumenten   112
Moi, Arcade, interprète chinois du Roi-Soleil   8
Monarchs and Ministers: The Grand Council in mid-Ch'ing China, 1723-1820   272
Le monde chinois   17
Monumenta Serica   275
Mo-tzu yin-te   333

Nan-ch'ao wu-shih jen-ming so-yin   154
Nankai Social and Economic Quarterly   102, 106
Nan-tzu-han   109
The National Economic Atlas of China   183, 184
National Polity and Local Power: The Transformation of Late Imperial China   47
Nien Keng-yao tsou-che chuan-chi   284
Nihon genzon Mindai chihôshi denki sakuin kô   158
North China Herald and Supreme Court and Consular Gazette [also known as the *North China Herald*]   105, 112
North China News   105, 247
Notes on Chinese Literature   269
Notitia linguae sinicae   9, 12
Nouvelle atlas de la Chine   178
Nouvelles lettres édifantes des missions de la Chine et des Indes Orientales   101
Novus Atlas Sinensis   7
Nung-shang t'ung-chi piao   262
Nung-yeh tz'u-tien   228

Oediupus aegyptiacus   7
Oxford Companion to English Literature   76
The Oriental Renaissance: Europe's Discovery of India and the East 1680-1880   11
Orientalism   11, 39
L'orthographe des noms chinois écrits en caractères d'Europe   9

An Outline and Annotated Bibliography of Chinese Philosophy 72
Outstretched Leaves on his Bamboo Staff: Studies in Honour of Gören Malmquist on his 70th Birthday 58
Oxford Art Journal 8

Pa-ch'ien chung Chung-wen tz'u-shu lei-pien t'i-yao 206
Pa-shih chiu chung Ming-tai chuan-chi tsung-ho yin-te 158, 330
Pa-shih-nien lai shih-hsüeh shu-mu 88
Pacific Historical Review 21
Pai chia hsing 142
Pai-pu ts'ung-shu chi-ch'eng 271
Pao-k'an tzu-liao so-yin 136
Papers on Far Eastern History 138
Peasant Life in China 29
Pei-ch'ao ssu-shih jen-ming so-yin 154
Pei-ching T'ien-chin ti-fang-chih jen-wu chuan-chi so-yin 169
Pei-ching t'u-shu-kuan kuan-ts'ang pao-chih mu-lu 132
Pei-ching t'u-yü tz'u-tien 231
P'ei-wen yün-fu 245, 246, 256
The People's Liberation Army and China's Nation-building 321
The People's Republic of China: A Handbook 255
The People's Republic of China, 1949-1979: A Documentary Survey 322
The People's Republic of China, 1979-1984: A Documentary Survey 322
Périodiques en langue chinoise de la Bibliothèque nationale 131
Perspectives on a Changing China 25
Pi-chi hsiao-shuo ta-kuan 271
Pi-chi hsiao-shuo ta-kuan ts'ung-k'an so-yin 271
P'ien-tzu lei-pien 256
P'ien-tzu lei-pien yin-te 257
Philosophy and Tradition: The Interpretation of China's Philosophical Past: Fung Yu-lan (1939-49) 28
P'ing-chin kuan ts'ung-shu 267
Pioneer of the Chinese Revolution: Zhang Binglin and Confucianism 22
Po-hu t'ung yin-te 328
The Political Work System of the Chinese Communist Miliary 321
Politics and History: The Case of Naitô Konan 17
The Population Atlas of China 183
Positions: East Asian Cultures Critique 7
Preliminary notes on the important Chinese literary sources for the history of the Ming dynasty (1368-1644) 70
Premodern China: A Bibliographical Introduction 66
Progress in Human Geography 177
La pronunciation chinoise 9
Protest and Crime in China: A Bibliography of Secret Associations, Popular Uprisings, Peasant Rebellions 70
Publications on Religions in China, 1981-1989 73
P'u-t'ung-hua Min-nan fang-yen tz'u-tien 230

Quantitative Measures of China's Economic Output 249

Rapports à l'Empereur sur le progrès des sciences, des lettres et des arts depuis 1789 11
The Reach of the State: Sketches of the Chinese Body Politic 38
Reader's Guide to China's Literary Gazette, 1949-1966 127
Recent Japanese Studies of Modern Chinese History: A Special Issue of Chinese Studies in History 95

Recent Japanese Studies of Modern Chinese History: Translations from Shigaku Zasshi for 1983-86   95
Red Flag, 1958-1968: A Research Guide   136
'Rekishi kenkyû' sômuku, sakuin   122
Relazione della Grande Monarchia della China   6
The Religion of the Chinese People   33
Religion in Postwar China   73
The Religious Periodical Press   101
Reliving the Past: The Worlds of Social History   70
Remaking the Economic Institutions of Socialism: China and Eastern Europe   38
Renditions   317
Répertoire du Canon Bouddhique Sino-Japanais   277
Repertory of Proper Names in Yüan Literary Sources   157
The Research Activity of the South Manchurian Railway Company   16
A Research Guide to China-Coast Newspapers, 1822-1911   105
Research Guide to Chinese Provincial and Regional Newspapers   113
A Research Guide to Jingji Yanjiu (Economic Studies)   120
Research Guide to the May 4th Movement: Intellectual Revolution in Modern China, 1915-1924   71, 108
Research Materials on Twentieth-Century China: An Annotated List of CCRM Publications   109
Research Tools for the Study of Sung History   69
Research on Women in Taiwan   79
Retsujoden sakuin (fu honbun)   164
Revolution and History: Origins of Marxist Historiography in China, 1919-1937   27
Revolutionary Education in China: Documents and Commentary   321
Revue bibliographique de Sinologie   63, 274
Revue européene des sciences sociales   14
The Royal Asiatic Society: Its History and Its Treasures   101
Ryô Kin Genjin denki sakuin   157

Sacred Books of the East   14
Saeculum   137
The Saga of Anthropology in China: From Malinowski to Moscow to Mao   26, 27
San-kuo-chih chi P'ei chu tsung-ho yin-te   154, 330
San-shih-san chung Ch'ing-tai chuan-chi tsung-ho yin-te   159, 328
San-tsang fa-shih chuan   13
Science and Civilisation in China   78, 171
A Select Bibliography on Taoism   74
A Selected Bibliography on Urbanization in China   81
Selection of China Mainland Magazines   318
Selection of People's Republic of China Magazines   318
A Selective Guide to Chinese Literature, 1900-1949   76
In the Service of the Khan: Eminent Personalities of the Early Mongol-Yüan Period (1200-1300)   149
Shan-hai-ching t'ung-chien   334
Shan-hsi t'ung-chih jen-wu chuan so-yin   168
Shang-hai chieh-fang ch'ien-hou wu-chia tzu-liao hui-pien (1921-1957)   263
Shang-hai hsin-pao   112
Shang-hai tsung shang-hui yüeh-pao   108
Shang-hai t'u-shu-kuan kuan-ts'ang Chung-wen fu-k'an mu-lu (1898-1949)   133
Shang-hai t'u-shu-kuan kuan-ts'ang Chung-wen pao-chih mu-lu (1862-1949)   133
Shao-yüan t'u-lu k'ao   332
She-hui k'o-hsüeh tsa-chih   107
Shen chien t'ung-chien   334

Shen-pao 112, 113, 179
Shen-pao so-yin 112
Sheng-huo 107
Shigaku Kenkyû 20
Shigaku zasshi 95, 111
Shih-chi chi chu-shih tsung-ho yin-te 152, 331
Shih-chi jen-ming so-yin 152
Shih-chi so-yin 153
Shih-chieh ti-ming lu 186
Shih-ching 292
Shih-hsüeh ch'ing-pao 95
Shih-hsüeh lun-wen fen-lei so-yin 88
Shih-hsüeh-shih yen-chiu 20
Shih-huo 30
Shih-huo chih shih-wu chung tsung-ho yin-te 330
Shih-liao ts'ung-k'an ch'u-pien 21, 273
Shih-ming pieh-hao so-yin 145
Shih-shuo hsin-yü yin-te fu Liu chu yin-shu yin-te 329
Shih-t'ung 245
Shih tz'u ch'ü hsiao-shuo yü-tz'u ta tien 232
Shih-wu pao 108
Shih-yung ching-mao ta tz'u-tien 226
Shih-yung Han-yü t'u-chieh tz'u-tien 210
Shih-yung k'o-hsüeh ming-tz'u tz'u-tien 229
Shih-yung ku Han-yü hsü-tz'u 221
Shina tsûshi 20
Shinmatsu Minsho bunsho dokukai jiten 240
Shinpen shingai kakumei bunken mokuroku 93
Shu-ching 170
Shu-mu chü-yao 58
Shui-ching chi-shih chu-che yin-te 329
Shuo-wen chieh-tzu 202, 203, 214
Shuo-yüan yin-te 328
Singular Listlessness: A Short History of Chinese Books and British Scholars 11
Sinicae historiae decas prima 7
La sinologie 5
Sino-American Normalization and its Policy Implications 321
Sino-American Relations, 1949-1971 321
The Sino-Soviet Dispute 321
Sino-Soviet Relations, 1964-1965 322
The Sino-Soviet Rift 321
Sino-Western Cultural Relations 14
Sir Aurel Stein: Archaeological Explorer 19
Six Centuries of Tunhuang 19
Social Sciences in China 317
La sociologie de la Chine: Matériaux pour une histoire 1748-1989 25, 29
Sociology and Socialism in Contemporary China 28
Sôdai kenkyû bunken mokuroku 90
Sôdai kenkyû bunken teiyo 90
Sôfu no kenkyû: shiryô hen 168
Sôjin denki sakuin 155
Sources of Chinese Tradition 320
South China Morning Post 104
Specimen medicinae Sinicae 7
Spring and Autumn Annals 300

Ssu-ch'uan chin-hsien-tai jen-wu chuan 169
Ssu-ch'uan Hsin-hai ko-ming shih-liao 284
Ssu-ch'uan kung-jen yün-tung shih-liao hsüan-pien 286
Ssu-k'u ch'üan-shu (SKCS) 46, 268, 290
Ssu-k'u ch'üan-shu chen-pen 270
Ssu-k'u ch'üan-shu chien-ming mu-lu 49
Ssu-k'u ch'üan-shu tsung-mu 48, 244
Ssu-k'u ch'üan-shu tsung-mu chi Wei-shou shu-mu yin-te 328
Ssu-k'u ch'üan-shu wen-chi p'ien-mu fen-lei so-yin 269
Ssu-pu pei-yao 270
Ssu-pu ts'ung-k'an 269
The Ssu-pu ts'ung-k'an: A Guide to the First Series 270
Ssu-shih-ch'i Sung-tai chuan-chi tsung-ho yin-te 155, 331
The Stanford Chinese Concordance Series 291
State and Society in China: Japanese Perspectives on Ming-Qing Social and Economic History 316
The Statistical System of Communist China 248
Statistics of Government Railways, 1915-1936 262
Structural Anthropology in the Netherlands 16
Su shih yen-i yin-te 329
Subject and Author Index to Chinese Literature 317
Sui-shu ching-chi chih 46
Sui-shu jen-ming so-yin 154
Sui T'ang Wu-tai shih lun-chu mu-lu 1900-1981 89
Summary of World Broadcasts Part III: Far East Daily, Far East Weekly 319
A Sung Bibliography 69
Sung Biographies 149
Sung hui-yao 245
Sung hui-yao chi-kao jen-ming so-yin 156
Sung-jen chuan-chi tzu-liao so-yin 155
Sung Liao Chin shih shu-chi lun-wen mu-lu t'ung-chien Chung-wen pu-fen (1900-1975) 90
Sung Liao Hsia Chin shih yen-chiu lun-chi so-yin 90
Sung-shih chi-shih chu-che yin-te 329
Sung-shih jen-ming so-yin 156
Sung-shih yen-chiu lun-wen yü shu-chi mu-lu 90
Sung Studies Newsletter 69
Sung Yüan fang-chih chuan-chi so-yin 156
Sung Yüan hsi-ch'ü k'ao 21
Sung Yüan hsi-ch'ü shih 21
Sung Yüan ti-fang-chih ts'ung-shu 198
Sung Yüan yü-yen tz'u-tien 234
Survey of the Sino-Soviet Dispute: A Commentary and Extracts from the Recent Polemics 1963-1967 321
A Survey of Taoist Literature: Tenth to Seventeenth Centuries 74
Synchronismes chinois, chronologie complete et concordance l'ère chrétienne de toutes les dates concernant l'histoire de l'Extrême-Orient (Chine, Japon, Corée, Annam, Mongolie, etc.) (2345 avant J.C. à 1904 après J.C.) 309
A Synochronic Chinese-Western Daily Calendar 1341-1661 A.D. 312

Ta-chia tien-ying 109
Ta Chin kuo chih t'ung-chien 334
Ta-tsang-ching 277
Taishô shinshu Daizôkyo 277
Taishô shinshu Daizokyô sakuin 277

Taiwan 81
Taiwan: A Comprehensive Bibliography of English Language Publications 81
T'ai-p'ing kuang-chi p'ien-mu chi yin-shu yin-te 329
T'ai-p'ing pien-lei 244
T'ai-p'ing yü-lan 244
T'ai-p'ing yü-lan yin-te 330
T'ai-wan ch'ü tsu-p'u mu-lu 168
T'ai-wan ko t'u-shu-kuan hsien-ts'un ts'ung-shu tzu-mu so-yin 281
T'ai-wan min-chien hsin-yang yen-chiu shu-mu 99
T'ai-wan ti-ch'ü Han-hsüeh lun-chu hsüan-mu 86
T'ai-wan ti-ch'ü Han-hsüeh lun-chu hsüan-mu hui-pien pen 86
Tang-an-hsüeh t'ung-hsün 276
Tang-an kung-tso 276
Tang-an yen-chiu 276
Tang-an yü li-shih 276
Tang-tai Chung-kuo pao-chih ta-ch'üan 114
Tang-tai Han-Ying tz'u-tien 211
T'ang hui yao jen-ming so-yin 155
T'ang shih chi-shih chu-che yin-te 329
T'ang shih pai-k'o ta tz'u-tien 234
T'ang shih ta tz'u-tien 233
T'ang Studies 6
T'ang Sung tz'u pai-k'o ta tz'u-tien 234
T'ang-tai ti Ch'ang-an yü Lo-yang so-yin 186
T'ang Wu-tai jen-wu chuan-chi tzu-liao tsung-ho so-yin 154
T'ang-yün 204
Tao-chiao ta tz'u-tien 237
Tao Hsien T'ung Kuang ssu-ch'ao tsou-i 284
Tao-te-ching 13
Tao-tsang 277, 278 [also known as *Cheng-t'ung tao-tsang*]
Tao-tsang tzu-mu yin-te 278, 330
Taoist Books in the Libraries of the Sung Period 278
Ten Great Years 248
Terminologie raisonée du bouddhisme chinois 237
Things Chinese: being Notes on various Subjects connected with China 246, 252
Ti-i-hui Chung-kuo nien-chien 263
Ti-li hsüeh-pao 172
T'ien-hsia chün-kuo li-ping shu 190
T'ien-hsia Monthly 9, 102
T'ien-i-ko Ming-tai ti-fang-chih ts'ung-shu 198
T'ien-i-ko ts'ang Ming-tai fang-chih hsüan k'an jen-wu chuan-chi tzu-liao jen-ming so-yin 159
T'ien-i-ko ts'ang Ming-tai ti-fang-chih k'ao-lu 198
The Times Atlas of China 184
The T.L. Yuan Bibliography of Western Writings on Chinese Art and Archaeology 79
Tôdai no gyôsei chiri 175
Tôjin no denki sakuin 155
Tokushi hôyu kiyô sakuin, Shina rekidai chimei yôran 176
Topics in Chinese Literature: Outlines and Bibliographies 76
Tô Sô hôritsu bunsho no kenkyû 22
T'oung Pao 8, 11, 32, 102
Tôyô bunko shozô Kindai Chûgoku kankei zusho bunrui mokuroku: Chûgokubun 276
Tôyô gakuhô 274
Tôyôgaku Bunken Ruimoku 63
Tôyôshi Kenkyû 111

Tôyôshi Kenkyû Bunken Ruimoku   63, 86
Transactions of the International Conference of Orientalists in Japan   113
The Treatises of the Later Han   175
Ts'ai Yüan-p'ei: Educator of Modern China   26
Ts'ang shu chi-shih shih yin-te   330
Ts'ang-shu chi-yao   53
Tseng chiao Ch'ing-ch'ao chin-shih t'i-ming pei-lu fu yin-te   333
Tsing-hua Journal of Chinese Studies   31
Tsui-hsin shih-yung Han-Ying tz'u-tien   211, 214
Ts'ui Tung-pi i-shu   25
Ts'ui Tung-pi i-shu yin-te   328
Tsung-chiao tz'u-tien   235
Ts'ung-shu chi-ch'eng   270
Ts'ung-shu chi-ch'eng ch'u-pien mu-lu   270
Ts'ung-shu chi-ch'eng hsin-pien   270
Ts'ung-shu chi-ch'eng hsü-pien mu-lu so-yin   270
Ts'ung-shu so-yin Sung wen tzu-mu   281
Ts'ung-shu ta tz'u-tien   280
Tu-shih fang-yü chi-yao   176
Tu-shih nien-piao fu yin-te   332
Tu-shih yin-te   333
Tung-fang tsa-chih   107
Tung-fang tsa-chih tsung-mu   107
Tung-hsi yang k'ao mei-yüeh t'ung-chi chuan   106
T'ung-chien kang mu   7
T'ung-i-tz'u tz'u-lin   220
Twentieth Century Chinese Writers and their Pen Names   145
Tzu-kung yen-yeh ch'i-yüeh tang-an hsüan-chi   285
Tzu-kung yen-yeh kung-jen tou-cheng-shih tang-an tzu-liao hsüan-pien (1915-1949)   285
Tz'u-hai   xiii, 304
Tz'u-hai (Shanghai, 1947)   215
Tz'u-hai (Shanghai, 1989)   209
Tz'u-hai (Taipei, 1980)   210
Tz'u-hai tz'u-mu fen-lei so-yin   210
Tz'u-shu lei tien   206
Tz'u-yüan   209, 214, 304

Understanding China: An Assessment of American Scholarly Resources   37
Understanding Communist China: Communist China Studies in the United States and the Republic of China 1949-1978   38
Updating Wilkinson: An Annotated Bibliography of Reference Works on Imperial China Published since 1973   2, 59, 67, 197
Urbanism in China: A Selected Bibliography   81

Voyages à Pekin, Manille et l'Ile de France dans l'intervale des années 1784-1801   12

Wan shou T'ang-jen chüeh-chü   233
Wan Yen chi shan-ts'un fu yin-te   332
Wang Kuo-wei: An Intellectual Biography   19
The Weekly Economic Report   319
Wei Chin Nan-pei ch'ao shih yen-chiu lun-wen shu-mu yin-te   89
Weltgeschichte   17
Wen-hsin tiao-lung hsin-shu t'ung-chien   335
Wen Hsüan chu yin-shu yin-te   330
Wen-hui pao   109

Wen shih che kung-chü-shu chien-chieh 87
Wen-wu san-wu-ling ch'i tsung-mu so-yin 123
Wen-yüan-ko Ssu-k'u ch'üan-shu shu-ming chi chu-che hsing-ming so-yin 269
Wen Yuan: Studies in Language, Literature, and Culture 317
Western Books on China Published up to 1850 in the Library of the School of Oriental and African Studies, University of London: A Descriptive Catalogue 62
Western Language Periodicals on China (A Selective List) 102
Westliche Taoismus-Bibliographie (WTB): Western Bibliography of Taoism 74
What and How is Sinology 6
Who's Who in China: Current Leaders 152, 169
Who's Who in Communist China 150
Who's Who in the PRC 151
Women in China: Bibliography of Available English Materials 79
Women in China: A Selected and Annotated Bibliography 79
World Bank: Catalogue of Staff Working Papers 265
Wu-ssu shih-ch'i ch'i-k'an chieh-shao 108

Yen-yü hsieh-hou-yü ch'ien-chu 223
Yenching Journal of Chinese Studies 30
Yenching University and Sino-Western Relations, 1916-1952 29, 30
Yin-hang chou-pao 108
Yin-te shuo 332
Ying-Han ching-chi tz'u-hui 227
Ying-Han ching-chi yü kuan-li tz'u-tien 226
Ying-Han hsien-tai k'o-hsüeh chi-shu ta tz'u-tien 229
Ying-Han shu-li-hua tz'u-tien 229
Ying-Han t'u-wen tui-chao tz'u-tien 211, 213
Ying-hua ta tz'u-tien 213
Yü-han shan-fang chi-i-shu 267
Yü-ti t'u 177
Yüan-ch'ü shih-tz'u 234
Yüan-jen chuan-chi tzu-liao so-yin 157
Yüan-jen wen-chi p'ien-mu fen-lei so-yin 282
Yüan shih chi-shih chu-che yin-te 329
Yüan-shih jen-ming so-yin 156
Yüan-shih hsüeh kai-shuo 90
Yüan-tung Han-yü ta tzu-tien: Fan-t'i-tzu-pen 214
Yung-cheng-ch'ao Han-wen chu-p'i tsou-che hui-pien 286
Yung-le ta-tien 47, 49
Yung-yen 108

ZH Guide, an Introduction to Sinology 215
Zôhô Chûgoku tsûzoku shôsetsu shomoku 97
Zôtei Nihon genson Minjin bunshû mokuroku 283
Zweifel am Altertum: Gu Jiegang und die Diskussion über Chinas alte Geschichte als Konsequenz der 'Neuen Kulturbewegung' ca. 1915-1923 23

SUBJECT INDEX

[Note: For those expressions in **bold**, one may find the characters in the text.]

Academia Sinica: in Republican China 21, 26, Institute of History and Philology 26, Institute of Social Research 26, **yü-yen tsu** 26; in Taiwan 121: data base and indexing system 291; Institute of History and Philology 121, 276; Institute of Modern History 121, 275

Académie des Inscriptions et Belles-Lettres 8

academies 25, 52

administrative terminology: dictionaries for 239-240

agriculture: dictionaries for 228; encyclopedia about 258; yearbooks about 260

All Federation of Trade Unions 127

almanacs 297-298 [see also Chinese calendar]

American Council of Learned Societies (ACLS) 33, 37, 50

American Oriental Society 101

Amsterdam 178

Anhwei Province 273; documentary collections in 273-274

Annales school 274

anthropology 15, 26, 28-29, 34; bibliography for: works published in Taiwan 100

Anyang 19, 26

area studies 34, 36-37, 39

archaeology 2, 18-19, 21, 26, 33; bibliographies for 79, 81

archives 57, 275-277; Baxian Provincial Archive 276; difference between central and regional/local 275; Liaoning Provincial Archive 276; National Palace Museum (Taipei) 275-276; Number One Historical (Beijing) 275; Number Two Historical (Nanjing) 275; published collections of archival documents 284-286; Qufu Archive of the Descendants of Confucius 276

art 56, 116; bibliographies for 79-80, 81, 100

artists: biographical dictionaries for 162

Asia 6, 11, 12, 39, 102

Association for Asian Studies 36, 102

assyriology 6

astronomy 5, 106

atlases xiii, 176-179; economic 183; historical 181-182; modern 183-184; population 183 [see also maps]

auspicious omens 298

autobiographical writing 140

Babel, tower of 8

banking 108

Baxian District Archive 276

Beijing 169, 174, 185, 275; Number One Historical Archive 275-276 [see also Peking]

bibliographies xiii, 3, 5, 45, 56-100; in Chinese and Japanese: 20, 57-59; annual 85-86; on anthropology 100; on art 100; on Buddhism 98; on Ch'in dynasty 89; on Ch'ing dynasty 91-93, 95; on Christianity 99; on the Classics 98; on communist movements before 1949 93; on Confucianism 98; on contemporary China 94; cumulative 84-85; on economic history 94; on Han dynasty 89; on historical geography 89, 92; on history: 87, 88-95, in Harvard-Yenching Sinological Index Series 290; **kung-chü-shu** 86-87; on language 98; on law 99-100; on linguistics 98; on literature 96-98; on May Fourth Movement 92, 108, 136; on modern Chinese society 91; on **nei-pu** publications 51; on Northern and Southern dynasties 89; on people's communes 94; on philosophy and religion 98-99; for Republican China 94; on Revolution of 1911 93; on social sciences 100; on the Sui dynasty 89; on the Sung dynasty 90, 95; on Taiping Rebellion 92; on T'ang dynasty 89; on Wei dynasty 89; on Wu-tai period 89; on Yüan dynasty 90, 95; in Western languages: 56-57; annual 62-65; on archaeology 79, 81; on art and painting 79-80, 81; on Buddhism 73-74, 77; on Ch'in dynasty 67; on Ch'ing dynasty 67-68; on Chinese in Southeast Asia 80; on Christianity 80, 106; on cities and urbanism 80-81; on the Classics 72; on communist studies of history 71; composite 66-67; on Confucianism 73; on contemporary China 66, 68; on the Cultural Revolution 80; cumulative 61-62; on demography 82; for dictionaries 75; on economic history 70, 79; on economic reform 81; on education 80; on the Han dynasty 67; on history 67-72, 81-82; on Islam 74; Japanese studies of China 165; on Jesuits 80; on labour history 71; on language and linguistics 75; on lexicology 75; on literature (traditional and modern) 76-78, 82; on Mao Tse-tung 72; on May Fourth Movement 71; on Ming-Ch'ing history 70, 82; on modern China 66, 70-72; on modern Chinese society 71; on modern poetry 76; on music 79; on peasant rebellions 70, 81; on philosophy 72-73; on popular movements 70, 81; on premodern China 66, 67; on religion 72-74; on salt 80; on science and technology 78-79; 'state of the field' 81-82; on stone inscriptions 69; Sung dynasty 68-69, 81; Taiping Rebellion 70; on Taiwan 81; on T'ang literature 77; on Taoism 73, 74, 77, 98; on violence 70; on women 79; Yüan dynasty 67, 69 [see also under the names of individual dynasties: Chin, Ch'in, Ch'ing, Han, Ming, Sui, Sung, T'ang, Wu-tai, Yüan; see also under translations 'bibliographies']

Bibliothèque imperiale 11
Bibliothèque nationale 11, 22, 131
Bibliothèque du Roi 8
biographical dictionaries: for Buddhism 155, 157, 164; for Chin dynasty (265-419) 154; for Chin dynasty (1115-1234) 156-157; for Ch'ing dynasty 150, 159-160; communist movements before 1949 150; comprehensive 147-148; for contemporary China 94; for Han dynasty 152-153; for Japanese sinologists 165-166; in kung-chü-shu 147; for Liao dynasty 156-157; for local gazetteers 156, 168-169; for Ming 149, 157-159; for music 162-163; for newspaper publishing 105; for Northern and Southern dynasties 154; for painters 80, 155, 159, 162; for People's Republic of China 150-152, 160-161; for poets 155, 159; for Republican China 139, 150, 160;

specific by period in Chinese 152-161, in Western languages 149-152; for Sui dynasty 154; for Sung dynasty 139, 149, 155-156, 162; for Taiwan 161; for T'ang dynasty 154-155, 162; for Taoism 155, 157; Three Kingdoms 154; topical 162-166; on women 157, 164; for Wu-tai period 154-155; for Yüan dynasty 139, 149, 156-157

biographical writing 137-141; characteristics thereof 137, 141; and Dynastic Histories 137-138; and the lieh-chuan model 138; in People's Republic 138; and 'rebel-reformer' 137; and 'rebel-reformer' model 140; in Taiwan 138

bone inscriptions 19, 27, 202
book-collecting 52-53, 57
book reviews 103, 165
Boxer Indemnity 16
Boxer Rebellion 54
British Museum 22
bronze inscriptions 19, 27, 29
Buddhism 2, 13, 14, 33, 43, 52, 117; bibliographies: 73-74, 77, 98; and Tun-huang 19; biographical dictionaries for 155, 157, 164, 282; dictionaries for 236-237
Buddhist canon 277; collectanea 277
Buddhist texts: in the Harvard-Yenching Sinological Index Series 290
business management: encyclopedia about 258; yearbooks on 261

calendar [see Chinese calendar]
calligraphy 29
Cambridge 14
Canton 104, 106, 126
Cantonese: dictionaries for 230
cartography 171, 177, 179; and grid format 171, 177; history of 181
catalogues [see under libraries: classification systems]
Catayan system of cycles 8
Catholics 104, 106
censorship 113, 313
Centre Franco-chinois at the Sino-French University 291
Centre Franco-chinois d'Études sinologiques 291, 334-335
Changsha 171, 176
Ch'ang-an 186
Chekiang Province 264
ch'eng-yü 221

chi-i 58
chia-ku-wen 203
chia-pu 139
Ch'iang-hsüeh hui 125
chiao-k'an 58
ch'iao-hua 222
chien-t'i 203, 209, 215
Chin dynasty (265-419) 46, 50; bibliography for: 89; biographical dictionary for 154
Chin dynasty (1115-1234) 69, 155; biographical dictionaries for 156-157
chin-wen 203
Ch'in dynasty 47, 172; bibliographies for 67, 89
China: image of and Jesuits 10; as Confucian society 14; sinology in 22-31; study within a discipline 32, 35, 36; universities 107-108 [see also sinology]
Chinese Academy of Sciences 171, 273
Chinese calendar 297-308; chronologies 309; concordances to 304-307, 310-312; conversion of Chinese, Moslem and Western time 304-307; difference with almanac 297-298; structure of traditional 298-303; and twenty-four festivals 302, 336
Chinese Communist Party 113, 118, 124, 127, 150, 151; biographical dictionary for members 160; record of meetings 249
Chinese Communists: biographical dictionaries for 139; 150
Chinese-French/Latin dictionary 12
Chinese studies: definition of 4 [see also area studies, sinology]
Ch'ing dynasty 41, 47, 55, 104, 117, 147, 164, 168, 178, 182, 301; administrative terminology 240; bibliographies 67-68, 91-93, 95; biographical dictionaries for: 150, 159-160, 162; collected works of individual authors 282; documentary collections 272; documents 35; encyclopedias 245, 247, 256-257; local gazetteers 189; newspapers 125-126; ts'ung-shu 269
Ch'iu's Classification System for the East Asian Library 324-326
Christianity 10, 105; bibliographies for: study of Jesuits 80, period 618-1960 in Chinese 99, study of Protestant resources 106
chronologies 308
Chung-hua shu-chü 152

Chungking 171
ch'üan-chi 268 [see also ts'ung-shu]
cities in the PRC: as basic geographical unit 174; bibliographies for 80-81 [see also urbanization]
Classics (Chinese) 2, 5, 14, 23, 24, 31, 48, 201, 244, 256, 289; bibliography of Chinese references 98; and Harvard-Yenching Institute 30; indexes to 289-294; and Kyoto-based sinology 18; and the Ssu-k'u ch'üan-shu project 49; study of 21, in Republican China 23-24, 25; during the Tokugawa era 16; translations of 72, 106, and James Legge 313
collectanea 266-288 [see also ts'ung-shu]
Collège de France 13
colonialism 16
Columbia University 31, 36, 168
'commentarial tradition' 43; in Europe 15; in Japan 16, 18;
commerce 11, 13
Commercial Press 292
Committee on the Promotion of Chinese Studies 33
communist movements before 1949: bibliography 93; biographical dictionary for 150
communist studies of history: bibliography for 71
Compact Disk-Read-Only-Memory (CD-ROM) 52, 110, 152
computer technology 30; for concordances and indexes 291-292, 293-294; for libraries 51-52
concordances 289-294; computerized 291-292; and Institute of Chinese Studies, Hong Kong 291-291, 293-294; for study of Chinese calendar 304, 310-312
Confucianism 38, 43; bibliographies: of PRC publications on 98, of Western language publications 73; as 'central tradition' 43; dictionary for 238; Jesuit conception of 14
Confucius 7; Jesuit invention of 7; subject of scholarly Chinese attack 22
contemporary China (People's Republic since 1949): bibliographies 66, 68, 94; biographical writing in 138; library resources for 51; study of in United States 36-38, 44 [see also People's Republic of China]
crime: bibliography 70
Cultural Revolution 37, 44, 109,

151, 189, 248, 249, 273; bibliography for 80

demography: bibliography 82
Democracy Movement 151
Deutsche Morgenländische Gesellschaft 101
Dewey Decimal system 50
dialects: dictionaries for 229-231
disaggregation 37
dictionaries xiii, 5, 8, 11, 30, 44, 201-242; for administrative terminology 239-240; for agricultural terminology 228; appellation 143; bibliographies: for dialects 75, for lexicography 75, 207; and Chinese characters 205; Chinese-French/Latin 12; for classical Chinese 214-219; 'connoisseurs' 59; for dialects 229-231; for economics 226-227; geographical 185-187; graphic 202-203; guides for finding 206-207; for history 240-241; for Japanese names 241-242; for law 227-228; linguistic 220-221; literary 232-235; **ming-jen** 148; for modern Chinese 209-213; need for in France 10-11; phonetic 203-204; for politics 224-225; for proverbs and sayings 221-223; for religion and philosophy 235-238; for science and technology 228; semantic 201-202
documentary collections 271-274; Ch'ing dynasty 272; definition of 271; Hui-chou collection, 273-274; Ming dynasty 272; People's Republic of China 94, 273-274; and printing 271-272; Republican China 272
documents 22; Ch'ing 35; collections of published archival 284-286; for study of land tenure 22, 41-42, 273-274; translations of official 320-322
drama 9, 21, 23, 28; bibliographies for modern 76, 78; biographical dictionaries for 163; and Ku Chieh-kang 23; Yüan 9
droughts 182
Dynastic Histories 5, 256, 300; and biographical writing 137-138; 152; computerized database 291; indexes to 290 [see also Standard Histories]

l'École des langues orientales vivantes 13
economic history 28, 33; bibliographies 79, 94
economic reform in the PRC: bibliography 81
Economic and Technological Development Zones 175
economics 35, 108, 109, 118; dictionaries for 226-227
economy: encyclopedia about 258
edicts 112
education 118; bibliography 80
Egypt, ancient and link to China 7
egyptology 6
encyclopedias 5, 20, 243-247; characteristics of 243; Ch'ing dynasty 245, 247, 256-257; comprehensive 249-250; contemporary 257-258; difference with dictionary 243; **jih-yung lei-shu** 246; Ming dynasty 246; Sung dynasty 244-246; for Taiwan 258; by Westerners: current 253-255; historical 246-247, 252; Yüan dynasty 246
Encyclopedic History of Institutions 245
England 11; East Indian Company 104; sinology in 11
Enlightenment 10
epitaphs 137, 159
ethnography 33
ethnology 26
etymology 19, 24, 201, 216
Europe 111, 117, 178; sinology in 4-16; post-War sinology 40
European scholars in United States and sinology 31
examination candidates: guide to 167; in local gazetteers 193

fan-t'i 203, 215
Far Eastern Association 36
festivals [see Chinese calendar]
festschriften 165
feudal society 41
fiction [see under literature]
film 109, 123
floods 182
folk literary movement 23
Forbidden City 47, 275; Palace Museum 275
foreign relations: yearbooks on 261
Four Books 7
four-corner system 205
France 6, 11, 13; chair of Chinese at the Collège de France 13; Jesuit sinology in 8, 10; Revolution and Chinese studies 11; sinology 13, 32-33, 116; trading empire 10
French Chinese dictionary 11

French sinology, characteristics of 13; impact on Harvard University 32

functionalism 29

Genealogical Society of Utah 168
genealogical writing 139, 273; guides to 167-168

gentry 28; and local gazetteers 190-191 [see also academies]

geographical dictionaries 185-187

geographical units 172-175

geography 1, 7, 10, 106, 170-179, 187, 290; history of 170-172

Golden Decade 20

grammar 8, 9, 12

Grand Council 21, 272, 276

Grand Secretariat 276

Great Leap Forward 109, 204, 249

"great learning" 5

Great Wall 10

Gregorian Calendar 304

Guangdong Province 152

gwoyeu romatzh system 204, 210, 212

Hainan Island 174

Hai-yüan ko 53

Hamburg 14

Han Chinese 142

Han dynasty 5, 25, 42, 45, 68, 139, 164, 171, 172, 176, 201, 292, 300; bibliographies 67, 89; biographical dictionaries for 152-153; **fu** 232

Han learning 5, 23

handbooks: in Western languages 255

Hangchow 52

Hanlin Academy 47

Harvard University 30, 31, 35, 36, 40, 44, 102, 117, 168; and area studies 33, 36; and John Fairbank 32, 34, 44

Harvard University Press 31

Harvard-Yenching: Institute 29, 30, 35, 289; classification schema 50, 52, 54, 207, 268, 324-326; Library 31

Harvard-Yenching Sinological Index Series xiii, 25, 30, 153, 155, 156, 158, 159, 160, 201, 328-333; history of 289-290; how to use 292-293; and the Institute of Chinese Studies database of concordances 292

historians: Chinese, biographical dictionary for 165

historical documents 21, 271-274; for the study of land-holding 22

historical geography 175-176; bibliographies 88, 92; guides to 176

historical positivism 18

historical writing 6; annalistic and dynastic 2, 27; during the 'golden age' 28; in Japan 17, 21, 27; in scholarly journals 107; 'slave society' in 27

history 1, 2, 7, 10, 25, 34, 35, 37, 56, 109, 116, 119, 120, 132, 140, 215, 290; bibliographies: in Western languages 67-72, 81-82, in Chinese and Japanese 87, 88-95; dictionaries for 240-241; Japanese studies of 95; Marxist interpretation of 27; of science 33, 78-79; and the **Ssu-k'u ch'üan-shu** project 49

Holland: early Chinese studies in 8 [see also the Netherlands]

Hong Kong xiii, 64, 87, 96, 99, 102, 103, 104, 105, 109, 112, 113, 118, 120, 124, 125, 126, 132, 134, 158, 168, 181, 203, 230, 232, 252, 259; and local gazetteers 199; and **ts'ung-shu** 267

Hoover Institution 133

hsiao-pao 112

hsieh-hou-yü 221, 222, 223

hsien 172

hsin fang-chih 189

Hsin-hua she 113, 127

hsün-ku-hsüeh 201

Hui-chou 273, 276; architecture 274; documents 274, 286: and comparison with Tunhuang 274, as regional archives 275; merchants 274

hui-pien 245

hui-yao 245

I-ku pa'i 25

imperialism 38

indexes xiii, 25, 30, 44, 111, 289-294; difference with concordances 289; guides to 296; history of 289-290; to literary works 291; for modern China studies 291; to Neo-Confucian works 291; to periodical literature 110, 134-136; to Taoist works 291; to **ts'ung-shu** 276

Institute of Chinese Studies concordance series 291-292; 293-294

intellectual history 23, 113; German impact on Chinese 71

intellectuals: modern, biographical dictionary for 165

Islam: bibliography 74

jade 14

Japan 111
Japanese collections of Chinese books 53-54, 276; ts'ung-shu collections 281
Japanese journals 111; language 3, 63, 64; studies: of Chinese history 87, 92, 93, 95, 165, of Chinese thought and religion 99
Japanese names: dictionaries for 241-242
Japanese sinologists: biographical dictionaries for 165-166
Japanese sinological publications: translations for 316 [see also translations]
Japanese sinology 3, 16-22, 24, 40-42, 43, 44, 64-65; in Harvard-Yenching Sinological Index Series 290
Jesuits 5-10, 13, 43, 101; bibliography for study of 80; on Chinese geography, history, medicine 7; French 8-10, and map-making 178, 192; translations of 7
jih-yung lei-shu 246 [see also encyclopedias]
Joint Committee on Contemporary China 37
journalism 104-105, 113
journals 30, 31, 101-104, 106-111; in Chinese 120-124; indexes for 134-136; cultural 123; in Japanese 131-133; leisure 123-4; national in the Republican era 107; 'popular' 109; in the PRC 109-111; scholarly in the Republican era 107-108; of specialized professional communities in the Republican era 108; of specific intellectual trends in the Republican era 108; summary 124; for translations about current affairs 318-320; for translations of literature 317; university in the PRC 111; 'watchdog' 109, 124; union catalogues for 131-133; university 123; in Western languages 116-119
Julian calendar 304

kangakusha 16
k'ao-cheng scholarship [see also Han learning] 5, 21, 23, 24, 57
K'ao-ku p'ai 26
Kiangsu Province 264
Korean language 63
Kuangtung Province 168 [see also Guangdong Province]

ku-tien wen-hsüeh 9
kung-chü-shu 59; bibliographies 86-87; for biographical references 147
kyôdôtai 42
Kyoto University 17, 21, 41; Jimbun kagaku kenkyûjo 276; and Naitô Konan 17, 41; and Shinagaku 18; and Tokyo school 41-42

labour history: bibliography 71
land taxes: in local gazetteers 193; statistics for 262
landholding 64, 273-274
language 6-9, 12; bibliographies 75, 98; dictionaries: for classical 214-219, for modern 209-213; distinctions of Chinese 9; study of Chinese 7, 9, 15, 27; study of Japanese 21
law 2, 121; bibliographies 99-100; dictionaries for 227-228
learned societies 101
Leiden University 14-15, 102
lei-shu 243 [see also encyclopedias]
leisure journals 123
lettres édifantes 10, 101
lexicography 201
lexicology: bibliography 75
Liao dynasty 155; biographical dictionaries for 156-157
Liaoning Provincial Archive 276
Library of Congress 33, 34, 131, 132, 139, 168; classification schema 52, 54-55
libraries: automatization 51; catalogues 30; classification systems 1, 45, history of 45-51; Confucian 52; introduction of Western classification 50
lieh-chuan 138
linguistics 2, 6, 10, 27, 56; bibliographies 75, 98; dictionaries for 220-221
literary revolution 23, 24
literature 1, 2, 12, 25, 26, 56, 123, 290, 302; bibliographies: in Western languages 76-78, for modern 76, for T'ang 77, for traditional 76, 82, in Chinese and Japanese 96-98; biographical dictionaries for 163; 'classical' 9; dictionaries of 232-235; encyclopedia for 252; and local gazetteers 194; journals of translation 317; modern as study subject 36; 'popular' 19, 21; premodern as study subject 36; and the Ssu-k'u ch'üan-shu project 49; and translations 316-317, and Arthur Waley

and Burton Watson 313; and Tun-huang 19; vernacular 10, 43, 235 [see also under drama, novel, poetry, short story]
Liu-li-ch'ang 53
local gazetteers 170, 187-195; biographical dictionaries to 156, 168-169; and biographical writing 137-138; catalogues of 197; Ch'ing 189-190; definition of 187; Ming 157, 158, 159, 190, 198; People's Republic of China 189, 199; principal subject headings 191-195; reprint series 198; specialized 191, 200; Sung 156, 170, 190, 198; T'ang 170; Yüan 156, 157, 198
local history 92, 93 [see also local gazetteers]
London 14
Loyang 186

Macao 104, 132
Macartney Embassy 11
Major Brothers Limited 113
Malacca 106
Manchu-Chinese dictionary 11
Manchu conquest 7
Manchu Imperial Library 48
Manchu language 2, 11, 12, 178
Manchu rulers 47
Maoist thought 94, 100
maps 30, 44, 171, 177, 188; map-making 171, 178, 179
Marxism 27, 71, 98; and Japanese historiography 16, 40-42
Marxist-Leninist thought 94, 100
mathematics 10
May Fourth Movement 18, 22, 108; bibliographies for 71, 92, 108, 136
medicine 7
Middle East 39
Ming dynasty 41, 67, 117, 140, 150, 182, 188, 301; bibliographies 67, 69-70, 91, 95; biographical dictionaries for 139, 149, 157-159; collected works of individual authors 282; concordance for calendar 312; documentary collections 272; drama 78; and encyclopedias 246; and Taoist canon 277-278; **ts'ung-shu** 269
ming-jen tz'u-tien 148
Min-nan-hua: dictionary for 230
"minor learning" 5, 201
minorities 26, 142, 174
missions 101, 117
missionaries: and American sinology 31, role of in first newspaper

publications in Chinese 106-107, 113; French 178; study of 2
Mitsubishi *zaibatsu* 53
'Modern China' studies 35
modernization 40
Mongol conquests 149, 177
Moslem calendar 310
music 56; bibliography 79; biographical dictionaries for 162-163
mythology: dictionaries of 237-238

Naitô hypothesis 18
names and the naming process 141-142; guides to alternative 145-146
Nanking 26, 126, 264, 275; Number Two Historical Archive 275
National Central Library (Taipei) 197, 287
National Defense Education Act 35
National Library (Beijing) 48, 52
National Palace Museum Library (Taipei) 48, 121, 160, 275
nationalism 140
nationalistic heroes 140
Nei-ko 273
nei-pu publications 111, 114, 131: definition of 51; bibliographies of 51
Neo-Confucian scholars 5
Netherlands 14
news: translation publications for 318-320
newsletter 103, 111
newspapers 104-105, 112-114, 124, 125-127; Chinese local 113; during late Ch'ing 125-126; of the PRC 113-114; of the Republican era 113; union catalogues for 131-133
nien-chien 247 [see also yearbooks]
nien-hao 300-301; chronologies for conversion 309 [see also Chinese calendar]
nien-p'u 138, 140; guides to 167
Ningpo 52, 159
northern warlords 92, 93
Northern and Southern dynasties 182; bibliography for 89; biographical dictionaries for 154
novel 9, 23, 57; bibliographies of translations for classic 78, contemporary Chinese 78, for modern Chinese 76
Number One Historical Archive 275
Number Two Historical Archive 275

Old versus New Text Debate 25
Online Computer Library Center 51, 55
Opium War 12, 92, 182
oracle bones 19, 300
Oxford 14
Orientalism 39; definitions of 39
orientalist 11

Pa ch'ien chüan lou 53
Pacific War 34
pai-hua 9, 211, 215, 232, 235, 313
pai-k'o ch'üan-shu 249 [see also encyclopedias]
painters: biographical dictionaries for 80, 155, 159, 162
Palace Museum 272
paradigms: China-centred versus Western centric 38
'Paris-based type of sinology' 32
peasant rebellions: bibliographies 70, 81
Peking 30, 102, 105, 108, 126, 178, 278 [see also Beijing]
Peking dialect: dictionary for 231
Peking University 21, 22, 23, 26, 29
"Pelliotism" 32
people's communes: bibliography 94
People's Republic of China 111, 168; Army 127, 151; biographical dictionaries for 150-152, 160-161; calendar 301, 303-304; documentary collections 273-274; economic and political policies 2; local gazetteers 189, 199; and modernization program 249; newspapers 113; ts'ung-shu 267; writing styles 203
Ph.D. dissertations 2, 103; degree 35
philology 6, 13, 24, 29, 32, 34, 58
philosophy 10, 26, 28, 33, 43, 48, 109, 132; bibliographies: 72-73, 98-99; dictionaries for 238; and the Ssu-k'u ch'üan-shu project 49
phonetic alphabet 24
phonology 24
pi-chi 139, 268, 271; dictionary for Sung and Yüan 234 [see also ts'ung-shu]
Pi Sung lou 53
pieh-chuan 139
pinyin transcription 3, 204
pirate editions 4

poetry 9, 57; lyric 9; bibliographies: of modern 76; of translations of classic 72
poets: biographical dictionaries for 155, 159
politics 68, 109, 123, 140; dictionaries for 224-225
po-p'o-mo-fo 204, 210
popular movements: bibliography 70, 81
popular religion 33
population statistics 175, 254, 260, 262; in local gazetteers 193
primary and secondary sources 32, 59; distinction of 56-57
printing 57; of Chinese books 53; of Chinese characters in Europe 8; dictionary 11; and documentary collections 271-272; guide to 287
Privy Council 272
propaganda 119
Protestant Ethic 32
Protestants 105, 106
proverbs and sayings: dictionaries for 221-223
"pulp-publishing" industry 246

Qufu Archive of the Descendants of Confucius 276

rare books: catalogues of 287-288
'rebel-reformer' 140
reform movement 20, 104, 107, 108, 125, 303
religion 13, 33, 43, 116, 117, 200; bibliographies 73-74, 99; dictionaries of 235-237; Jesuit attitude toward Chinese 13, 43; popular 33
religious periodicals 101
"reprint organ" 109
Republican China 5, 18, 119, 179; bibliographies: 68, 94; biographical dictionaries for 139, 150, 160; calendar 301; documentary collections 272-273; higher education in 24-30; historical archives 275; index to journals published during 135; journals published during 30, 107-109; libraries during 53-54; local gazetteers 189; newspapers published during 113, 126; yearbooks 247
Research Libraries Information Network (RLIN) 51, 55
Revolution of 1911 21, 22, 56, 126, 179: bibliographies: 71, 93

Royal Asiatic Society 101, 117
rural economy: statistics 265

science and technology: bibliographies 78-79; dictionaries for 228-229
secret associations (or societies): bibliography 70
Seikadô Bunko 53, 54
self-strengthening 17, 92
sexagenary cycle 298-300 [see also Chinese calendar]
Shang dynasty 170, 202
Shanghai 102, 104, 105, 106, 107, 108, 125, 126, 174, 179, 185, 186, 264
Shang-wu yin-shu kuan 107
Shanhsi Province 168
Shenyang 48
shih poetry 233
shih-t'ung 245 [see also Encyclopedic Histories of Institutions]
Shinagaku 18
short story 123; bibliographies: for modern 76, for translation of 78
shou-ts'e 248
Sino-Japanese War 54, 107
sinology 42, 116; definition of 4, 6, 66; history of: in China 22-31, 43, 108; in Europe 4-16, 40, 43, 44, in Japan 16-22, 40-42, 43; study of in European universities 14-15; in United States 31-40, 44
sinophilia 10
slave society [see also under slavery] 27; in historical writing 27, 41
slavery 42
social history 28, 135; bibliographies 70, 89; and Tun-huang documents 22
Social Science Research Council 37
social sciences 15, 25, 28-29, 132; bibliography: 100; translation journals 317-318
Société Asiatique 101, 116
society 56; bibliography on modern Chinese 71, 91
sociology 25, 29, 34; "missionary" 28
Southeast Asia 36, 63, 230; bibliography of Chinese in 80; linguistics in 75
South Manchurian Railway Company 16
Special Economic Zones 152, 175

"sprouts of capitalism" 274
Ssu-ch'uan Province 169, 276
Ssu-k'u ch'üan-shu project 46-49
Standard Histories 175 [see also Dynastic Histories]
Stanford University 36, 168
'state-of-the-field': bibliographies 56, 81-82; information 111
statecraft 5
statistics xiii, 248-250, 253; historical 262; in journals 265; for land taxes 262; in newspapers 265; for People's Republic of China 248-250, 264-265; population 260, 262; for Republican China 248; 262-264; for rural regions 265; for urban regions 260; in yearbooks 259
stone inscriptions: bibliography 69
Sui dynasty 46, 67, 182, 188; bibliography for 89; biographical dictionary for 154
sui-pi 268
Sung dynasty 9, 17, 26, 40, 41, 42, 64, 117, 139, 154, 177, 188, 244, 271; bibliographies 68-69, 81, 90, 95; biographical dictionaries for 139, 149, 155-156, 162; collected works of individual authors 282; encyclopedias 244-246; landholding during 64; ts'ung-shu 266, 281; tz'u 232

Taipei 126
Taiping Rebellion 48, 53, 68, 105; bibliographies 70, 92
Taiwan xiii, 3, 53, 64, 79, 87, 96, 99, 108, 109, 111, 118, 120, 124, 134, 158, 168, 203, 230, 232, 291; archives in 275-276; bibliographies in general 81, 85, 86, for folk belief 99, for literature 97, for women in 79; biographical dictionary for 161; calendar 301, 303-304; encyclopedia 258; and local gazetteers 199; and statistical data 248; ts'ung-shu 267, 271, 281
tang-an 272 [see also documentary collections]
T'ang dynasty 9, 17, 22, 26, 40, 41, 42, 67, 112, 117, 162, 177, 186, 244, 301; bibliographies on history 89, literature (Western languages) 77; biographical dictionaries for 154-155, 162; lü-shih 232; poetry 233-234
Taoism 2, 13, 14, 33, 43, 52, 117; bibliographies 73, 74, 77, 98; bio-

graphical dictionaries for 155, 157, 282; dictionaries for 237; literature 76
Taoist canon 277-278
Taoist texts: in the Harvard-Yenching Sinological Index Series 290
textbooks for the study of China 17
textual criticism in Japan 18
Three Kingdoms: biographical dictionary for 154
ti-ch'ü 174
ti-pao 112
Tianjin 174, 185, 186 [see also Tientsin]
T'ieh-ch'in t'ung-chien lou 53
Tientsin 126
T'ien-an-men 119
T'ien-i-ko 52, 159
Tokyo 126
Tokyo Marxists 41
Tokyo University 16, 21, 31; and Shiratori Kurakichi 17, 40; and 'Tokyo school' of Marxist historiography 40, 316; Tôyô bunka kenkyûjo 276
totalitarianism 37
Tôyô Bunko 276
tôyôshi 17
tôyôshigaku 17
trade 118
translations 3, 7, 10, 13, 33, 57, 116, 165, 313-322; bibliographies: for period 220-960, 68, for Classics 72, for contemporary Chinese fiction 1945-1992 78, of Japanese books in early 20th century 20, for Japanese studies of Chinese history 95, 116; for current affairs in the PRC 318-320; Japanese sinological publications 316; in Latin by Jesuits 7; for literature 316-317; in Manchu 11; for modern Chinese literature 1918-1942 77; for novels 72, 78; for official documents 320-322; for poetry 72; for scientific publications 317-318
transliteration 8
Tsing Hua University 28
tsung-pu 139
ts'ung-shu 266-271, 288; Buddhist collectanea 277-278; characteristics of 266; Ch'ing dynasty 267, 269; classes of 267; difference with encyclopedias 267; history of 266-267; Ming dynasty 269; indexes to 280-282; mod-

ern 269-271; and Ssu-k'u ch'üan-shu project 268-269; Sung dynasty 266; Taiwan 271; Taoist collectanea 277-278; traditional 268-269; Tun-huang 19; and land documents 22, manuscripts 287
t'ung 245
Tung-wen hsüeh-she 21
t'ung-hsün 111
T'ung-meng hui 126
tzu-liao ts'ung-k'an 268
tz'u-tien 59

union catalogues 110; for journals 131-132; for newspapers 132-133
United States 111; sinology in 31, 33-34; study of contemporary China 36-38
University of California, Berkeley 31, 36, 168
University of Chicago 31, 168
University of Michigan 36
University of Washington 36
urban statistics 260
urbanization: bibliographies for 80-81

Vietnam War 38
village 172
violence: bibliography 70

Wade-Giles transcription 3, 147, 149, 204
Wei dynasty: bibliography for 89
wen-chi 268; guides to collections 282-283; [see also ts'ung-shu]
Wen-su-ko 48
wen-tzu-hsüeh 202
wen-yen 9, 113, 125
Wen-yüan-ko 47, 48, 270
White Cloud Monastery 278
women 56, 139, 149; bibliographies: 79, in literature 76, in Taiwan 79; biographical dictionaries for 157, 164, 282; journals for 109
World Bank 265
Wu dialect: dictionary for 231
Wu-tai period 41; bibliography 89; biographical dictionaries for 154-155

Xi'an 171

yearbooks xiii, 247-248; on business management 261; current: in Chinese 259-261, in Western languages 253-254; on foreign relations 261; for history 95, for literature 97; in People's Republic of China 248; in Republican China 247-248

Yenan 126

Yenching University 28-29, 30, 289

yen-yü 223

Yüan dynasty 188, 298; bibliographies 67, 69, 90, 95; biographical dictionaries for 139, 149, 156-157, 162; **ch'ü** 232; collected works of individual authors 282; dictionary of administrative terminology 239; drama 9, 234; and encyclopedias 246

yüeh-fu poetry 233

Zen dialogues 9

Zikawei 106